A RENAISSANCE LIKENESS

Raphael, *Portrait of Pope Julius II*, 1511–12.
London, National Gallery.

Loren Partridge
and Randolph Starn

A Renaissance Likeness

ART AND CULTURE IN
RAPHAEL'S *JULIUS II*

University of California Press
Berkeley · Los Angeles · London

LIBRARY OF CONGRESS CATALOGING IN PUBLICATION DATA

Partridge, Loren W.
    A Renaissance likeness.

    Bibliography: p.
    Includes index.
    1.   Raphael, 1483–1520.   Portrait of Pope
Julius II.   I.   Starn, Randolph, joint author.
II.   Title.
ND623.R2P26   759.5   79–63549
ISBN 0-520-03901-7

University of California Press
Berkeley and Los Angeles, California

University of California Press, Ltd.
London, England

1 2 3 4 5 6 7 8 9

For Orin,
     Drina,
     Wendy,
     and
     Amy —
     sharp seers.

Contents

Illustrations

Preface

This book is at once sharply focused and wide-angled. It is an analysis of Raphael's *Portrait of Pope Julius II* in the National Gallery at London and a case study in the content and context of High Renaissance portraiture. It is also an essay in cultural history broadly defined, for like the microcosms Renaissance writers discerned in very particular things, Raphael's *Julius* opens whole worlds worth exploring.

Raphael's portrait is full of messages from Renaissance culture in part because the circumstances in which it was made were so full. At the earliest date —27 June 1511—when the painter could have begun his work, Pope Julius had ruled eight years at his furious pace, "the eighth wonder of the world," a Renaissance pope in all his roles but always in his own way. Contemporaries had already found it easy to speak of a new Golden Age or to fear the coming of the Apocalypse. During the nine-month period in which the London panel was apparently painted, the character of the pope and the culture of Julian Rome were being tested more intensely than ever. Instead of triumphs everywhere, now there were challenges on every side. In northern Italy papal territory only recently regained by Julius himself had been lost to the French. A council of schismatic cardinals was

meeting at Pisa. The pope was struck by a nearly
fatal illness, and Rome flew into revolt. The resources of the papacy were strained to the breaking
point. By March 1512 the situation was still in some
doubt, still near the beginning of what was to seem a
miraculous series of victories before Julius's death in
February 1513.

The time had been right for taking a full measure
of the man and the pope. But the London portrait
also coincided with Raphael's arrival at new heights
of achievement in the company of an extraordinary
group of artists working in a High Renaissance style.
A brief, classical moment held visions empirical and
ideal in balance. The great Julian projects were under
way. Some commissions were complete, or nearly
so, and all were to be new classics in their own
right—Bramante's Belvedere and St. Peter's; Michelangelo's Sistine Ceiling and tomb for Julius;
Raphael's own fresco cycles for the papal apartments
in the Vatican palace, the *Stanza della Segnatura* and
the *Stanza d'Eliodoro*. The Julian additions to the
church of Santa Maria del Popolo seem relatively
minor only in comparison with the overwhelming
scale of what was happening elsewhere in Rome. By
September 1513, and probably during Julius's
lifetime, the panel now in the National Gallery had
entered the church which had long been a favorite
sanctuary and Roman showplace of the pope and his
Della Rovere relations.

No Renaissance figure had inspired (or provoked)
a more vivid response than the *papa terribile*. There
were other painted portraits of the pope besides the
London likeness, at least five of them by Raphael

himself. Medals, coins, drawings, woodcuts, and sculpture also displayed the papal image. Vignettes in words appeared in chronicles, histories, memoirs, literary works, sermons, and letters. We even have the perspective from the diaries of a papal master of ceremonies, and to counteract the flattery of court-iers and would-be clients we have the antidote of critical tracts and satire. One of a kind, Raphael's picture should be seen in light of this rich and many-sided record of the Julian Age.

This is not the usual view. The relevant volume of Ludwig von Pastor's monumental *History of the Popes* is still a valuable mine of information, but it is also fragmented in form and apologetic in tone. From more recent historians we must make do with more or less casual profiles, passing references, and a few specialized monographs. From the art historians, who could hardly be expected to slight one of the great moments in the history of art, there is no shortage of very good work on individual artists or commissions in Julian Rome. What is usually lacking is a thoroughgoing concern for the historical setting and the interrelationships of form, content, and style. The only recent writing on Raphael's *Julius,* for example, is brief and mainly devoted to the art his-torical detective work which established some ten years ago that the National Gallery panel, among several extant versions, was Raphael's original. It is as if the Julian world were too vast for the far-reaching kind of inquiry it deserves. Perhaps only the range of scholarly specialization has become too small.

It is a welcome sign, though not always a very

carefully articulated one, that some current attempts to see art in context take wide-ranging views of culture. The best of these are more likely to speak of complicated circumstances than of single causes. They have made issues of the cultural themes and cognitive skills peculiar to different times and places, the patronage and commissioning of culture, and the particular functions of art. Individual works have been reconsidered, as art certainly, but also as artifacts. In this spirit we mean to cross and combine different kinds of evidence and lines of approach, keeping Raphael's *Julius* in sight, but moving from it to the concerns of the culture around it, and back again. By varying the levels of analysis we hope to avoid the narrowness of purely formal, iconographical, or "sociological" explanations, and to confront something of the sheer complexity of whatever men have made. By concentrating on a single object we hope to respect the integrity of the work of art, to resist losing it either in the high abstraction of a prescriptive period style or in historical detail.

In the newly restored radiance of Raphael's portrait masterpiece both art and culture shine through.

However small, this book has accumulated large debts. Its origins go back at least to Harvard, to Myron Gilmore and to Sydney Freedberg, Master of Seeing. It owes much to the patience of our Berkeley undergraduates, who have often had good reason to wonder whether two heads, historian's and art historian's, were better than one. To the "Julian Institute" of our joint graduate seminar special thanks, in particular to Priscilla Albright, Carroll Brentano, Mark Fissel, Barbara Wollesen-Wisch, Brian Horrigan, Christy Junkerman, Elliott Kai-Kee, Gregory Lubkin, Frederick McGinness, Lorean De Pontee, and Keith Thoreen. Elliott Kai-Kee contributed extra time and expertise in research, and Patricia Fortini Meyer had much to show us about the church of Santa Maria del Popolo, of which she has done the drawings for this volume. Dorothy Shannon has typed it all with her generous care. The Committee on Research and the Humanities Institute at Berkeley have given their support. For the efforts of so many our sense of *magna in parvo* is complete.

1
Raphael's Julius *and Renaissance Individualism*

The earliest responses to Raphael's portrait of
Julius II took it to be natural and lifelike. Vetor
Lippomano had observed the *papa terribile* at dan-
gerously close quarters during his years as Venetian ambassador in Rome, and when the portrait was
displayed on the altar of Santa Maria del Popolo
early in September 1513, he found it "very similar to
nature." The pope had been dead since the second of
February, but, reported Lippomano, "all Rome" had
crowded to see "him" again, as if for a jubilee. We
can only guess at the reactions of the anonymous
writer of the 1540s who limited himself to mention-
ing that the *Julius* and Raphael's *Madonna of the Veil*
were hung for feast days on pillars in the church of
the Popolo (Plates 1–3). But for Giorgio Vasari in
the 1550 edition of his *Lives of the Most Eminent
Painters, Sculptors, and Architects* the portrait seemed
still "so wonderfully lifelike and true that it inspired
fear as if it were alive."

Although Vasari often saw only what he thought
fitting to see, there is, for once, no reason to doubt
him. His reaction was the conventional one, inspired
by classical writing on art; and yet it *is* the illusion of

nature, the sense of a powerful individual presence
portrayed in a moment of time, which confronts us
first and foremost in Raphael's *Julius*. The figure of
the pope appears nearly lifesize, not encased forbid-
dingly in full pontifical regalia but dressed in the less
formal *camauro* and *mozzetta*—the short, hooded
cape and the cap, red velvet and ermine-trimmed—
of his everyday appearances. Seated at an oblique
angle and projected in three-quarter length toward
the surface and edge of the panel, he seems to occupy the corner of a room. As if to make this angle
of space more approachable, Raphael, as we know
from X-ray analysis, painted out the papal tiara-
and-keys which had originally figured on the green
background cloth. There is little of the purely
emblematic, official profile here and even less of the
relentless hieratic display of the later, full-length
state portrait. The hardening of the image into the
model of a conventional portrait type was the work
of its imitators. What strikes us immediately in the
original is the animated repose of an individual, the
rich topography of the face, the believable anatomy,
the firm composition enlivened by the play of color,
texture, and detail.

The likeness is individualized from its surfaces—
literally from the tip of the beard—to the character
they seem at once to express and enclose. More than
any other feature, the beard fixed and dated the
unique physical presence of Pope Julius in the eyes of
his contemporaries. One of his favorite preachers,
the Augustinian Giles of Viterbo, exaggerated (as

usual) in claiming that Julius was the first pope "for centuries" to wear a beard. French popes at Avignon had been bearded until the mid-fourteenth century, but the spectacle of Julius's beard cut memories short. With a hint of exasperation understandable in a master of ceremonies at the Julian court, Paris de'Grassis noted in his diary that the pope had first begun to let his beard grow during his long illness at Bologna after October 1510. Early in November of the same year he was reported to have "a palm's breadth of white beard," and a little over a month later he appeared, fully bearded, in procession through the streets of Bologna. Before March 1511 the news had reached Spain, where Peter Martyr wrote about wits in the Roman court complaining that "this bearded Peter, fisher of men, had absconded from Rome with the keys to Paradise." When Julius returned to Rome on 27 June 1511 from his campaigns in northern Italy, Roman observers took in the sight for themselves—"no one remembers anything like it," exclaimed one chronicler— and they were not to see their bishop clean-shaven again until early March 1512. By that time, presumably during the intervening nearly nine months, Raphael had certainly captured and had probably completed the likenesses of the pope in the National Gallery portrait and elsewhere.

Other physical details rendered in the portrait seem to correspond to particular contemporary impressions. Raphael's *Julius* presents an awesome old man of about seventy—*il vecchione* of the diplomatic

correspondence and the chronicles. Nearly ten years
earlier Francesco Gonzaga had commented on the
"ruddy and robust" appearance of the new pontiff.
During the pope's triumphant stay at Bologna in
1507 a chronicler from Forlì had described "the
round face, all rosy," "the fine, big eyes," "the
short neck, like all his other members, well-pro-
portioned." For him the pope was "a man of average stature," who "paced with sweeping steps."
Some of the features described in those earlier and
better days are still evident in the London likeness.
But the illnesses and trials of 1510–12 have left
their mark. Raphael's subject no longer seems decid-
edly "erect in his person," as he had been at Bologna;
his age appears more invasive than "prosperous,"
and the flush hints as much at fever as high spirits.
Without violating decorum Raphael shows us the
Pope Julius whose erratic health and political mis-
fortunes during these years were being watched
with macabre fascination. The likeness is plausibly
that of a man reportedly afflicted by gout, infected
with syphilis, and prone to drunkenness; plausibly,
too, that of the pope whose earlier victories were
threatened by the loss of Bologna to the French, the
schismatic council of Pisa, and unrest in Rome itself.

But it would surely be wrong to see only the
characterization of a broken man. The driving animation of the pope and his inner reserves of resistance press into the picture as they do into the
written record. The torso may be bent in the portrait, but it is powerful; the mouth is clamped as
much in determination as dejection, and the down-

cast eyes are fiery. Through the worst of times Venetian ambassadors saw the pope as "strong," as "above all others *fortissima.*" For Machiavelli, Julius remained "violent," "audacious," "unstable," "hasty," "rash." Other contemporaries agreed that the pope was "choleric." This quality was hardly exhausted by a raging tongue. "What is more, he pushes and punches someone, cuts at someone else . . . with so much choler that *nihil supra,*" wrote one witness of the famous siege Julius led in person against Mirandola in January 1511. These violent scenes—one thinks of psychoanalytical discussions of "primitive rage"—were interrupted by periods of brooding, of half-spoken soliloquies, of plans or reasons changed without warning. "The pope has a mind all his own, and its depths cannot be fathomed."

The Venetians, a Florentine ambassador, agents of the Gonzaga of Mantua, Julius's own master of ceremonies, and, eventually, the king of France concentrated the impact of the pope and the man into a single word. For all of them Pope Julius was *terribile.* This Julian *terribilità* was understood as a function of the pope's "terrible nature." It was associated, almost clinically, with the physical centers of his being—heart, brain, and soul. It was a brute, animal force. But *terribilità* also implied in Julius, as it was beginning to do in the artists he patronized, a consummate ability to master nearly insuperable obstacles. At these outer limits in the vocabulary of his contemporaries the power of Julius (or of Michaelangelo) was *deinotic,* a power of divinity. In language used not by courtiers alone but also by tough-minded diplomats, Pope Julius, like a supreme deity, "makes all tremble," "fulminates," "without reason obtains whatever he wishes." Raphael's *Julius* might have served as an illustration. Our uncertainty over what to expect were the figure to rise connects us perhaps as closely as art can ever do with an individual presence in the past.

A portrait seemingly true to nature and to life, the sense of a powerful, unmistakably individual presence—contemporary testimony and our own first impressions converge. But this convergence brings us only to the beginning of a classic problem in Raphael's *Julius* and the culture in which it was made.

In what must be the most celebrated and the most controversial passage of *The Civilization of the Renaissance in Italy,* Jacob Burckhardt described a kind of individualism he considered Italian and Renaissance in origin. Renaissance Italians had pierced a medieval "veil . . . woven of faith, illusion and childish prepossession, through which the world and history were seen clad in strange hues." Where men had been conscious of themselves in the Middle Ages "only through some general category," in Renaissance Italy, claimed Burckhardt, "an objective treatment" of the world had merged with a subjective consciousness of self as "man became a spiritual individual, and recognized himself as such."

A whole history of subsequent views of the Renaissance might be written around reactions to these

lines by medievalists objecting to the timing, national historians (non-Italians at least) critical of
the location, and specialists who have hedged
Burckhardt in with qualifications. Medieval "veils,"
we have been reminded, were often transparent and
not easily lifted; Renaissance men had their share of
"childish prepossession" and often perceived themselves through general categories. But Burckhardt's
insight has shown little sign of going away. Even if
it did not "swarm with individuality," the culture of
the Italian Renaissance was driven by complex sets
of tensions between tradition and innovation, patterns of integration and pressures for dispersion,
conventions of thought and feeling and a fresh
openness to experience. In such a culture the resources of the individual could surface to be thrust
and measured against traditional expectations and
collective restraints. Perhaps no individual has ever
been the utterly free agent of Burckhardt's nineteenth-century imagination, but the concrete experience and the potential of the individual personality did
become one persistent dimension of a search for bearings in Renaissance Italy.

It is consistent with this outlook that portraiture
became a major genre of Italian Renaissance art. But
this does not mean that the qualities of Renaissance
individualism are easy to define in any given instance, still less that they are easy to account for. The
problem is complicated in the case of art by the
difficulty of translating visual experience into words.
The term *individualism* was coined in the nineteenth
century for nineteenth-century sensibilities. It tells us

nothing at all about formal qualities in works of art; for that matter, it may be positively misleading for directing our attention elsewhere. If individualism in art was a good child of Renaissance culture, then it really must be seen, not heard.

Contemporary reports and our own responses have already helped us see, but we can bring Raphael's *Julius* into sharper focus by examining the visual relationship of the painting to motifs and forms in portraiture which preceded it. By viewing a particular papal portrait in the context of traditions of papal portraiture, it should be possible to determine something about the extent of its particularity. Renaissance traditions of independent secular portraiture supply another context for comparison and for contrast. We can also locate the London panel in the development of Raphael's own portrait style. Where precedent proves to be lacking or where the sources in art available to Raphael and his patron were used in self-consciously inventive ways, there at least Renaissance individualism can be given quite precise visual meaning.

Two conventions of papal portraiture were especially important to the making of the London panel. For more than half a century before 1511–12 popes had been commonly represented as supplicating donors, standing or kneeling in profile in the company of saints to offer good works in pious appeal for salvation. Increases in scale and apparent verisimilitude can be traced within this portrait type through the Quattrocento: the kneeling figures of

Eugenius IV in Filarete's bronze doors for St. Peter's
(c. 1440–45); Perugino's Sixtus IV in the lost *Assumption of the Virgin* for the Sistine Chapel altar
(c. 1481–82); Pinturicchio's Alexander VI for the
Resurrection of the Borgia Apartments in the Vatican
Palace (c. 1492–94). Profile medals of fifteenth-
century popes exhibited the same direction of development in a more restrictive medium. By the
1490s Pinturicchio could suggest Alexander VI's
boundless personal ability and equally boundless
self-indulgence in the intimate and almost embar-
rassingly frank profile he painted atop a stiff, jewel-
encrusted cope of gold (Plate 4). In acuteness of
observation and psychological penetration, then,
Raphael continued precedents in papal portraiture
which, at the same time, he surpassed in subtlety
and concentration. The patron presumably approved
or even insisted. It was not only in politics that
Pope Julius was determined to outdo his predecessors, above all his Borgia rival Alexander VI.

The disposition of the figure on a chair or throne
gathered up, without being strictly limited to, variations on another papal portrait type. With an ances-
try extending back to imperial Rome, seated statues
of the pope were customarily placed over a city gate
or on a cathedral facade or, beginning with Leo X,
on the Capitoline Hill to symbolize the temporal and
spiritual powers of the papacy. The first major portraits of Pope Julius—the sculpture by Michelangelo
for the facade of San Petronio at Bologna (1506–8)
and that at Ascoli Piceno (1507–10)—belonged to
this tradition and were probably influenced by the

example of his uncle Sixtus IV at Assisi. These front-facing, hieratic images, usually larger than life and dressed in full pontificals, were very different from the intimate and obliquely turned figure in Raphael's *Julius*. But there were close similarities between Raphael's pope and the seated popes in votive paintings, dedication pictures, and scenes of papal audiences which had branched out from the strict honorific type by the mid-fifteenth century. It has been suggested that several of these variations derived from a lost *Portrait of Eugenius IV* painted by the French artist Jean Fouquet in Rome between 1443 and 1445. If the evidence of later engravings and the apparent borrowing by Filarete for his doors at St. Peter's are any indication, Fouquet's Eugenius was seated full length at an oblique angle in nonliturgical dress; his entourage stood around him and the "cloth of honor" of French royal iconography hung behind him (Plate 5). Whether through Fouquet's example or otherwise, these motifs had appeared repeatedly by the early sixteenth century in painting, manuscript illumination, reliefs, and medals representing the pope.

Raphael's first painted portrait of Pope Julius as *"Pope Gregory IX" Receiving the Decretals* shows that he was aware of these developments just before beginning the London panel (Plate 6). On the other hand, the grand scale and romanizing, even archaeological, effect of this fresco suggests that he looked farther back than the fifteenth century to classical art. He might well have been inspired by the *Liberalitas* relief on the Arch of Constantine. Or he might have

learned from the relief of an emperor receiving captives which Julius had placed in the Belvedere
sculpture court. The Roman prototype of an en-
throned and angled central figure was obviously not
lost on Raphael (Plates 7–8).

Two additional motifs of the London portrait—
the knee-length view and the casual dress in *camauro*
and *mozzetta*—figured neither in the mainstream of
papal portraiture nor in Raphael's slightly earlier fresco of Julius-as-Gregory-IX for the Vatican
Stanze. But there were precedents here too, precedents so specific and so rare in all but portraits of
Julius's uncle Sixtus IV that Raphael and his patron
must have had them in mind. The only knee-length,
seated papal likeness known to us is that of Sixtus IV
painted about 1474 by Justus of Ghent for the *studiolo*
in the ducal palace of Urbino (Plate 9). This painting
belonged to a series of twenty-eight famous men
from antiquity to the present—Sixtus represented
the up-to-date theologian—chosen to inspire the beholder with lessons of wisdom and virtue. As in the
London *Julius,* the likeness that hung in Raphael's
hometown was turned partially to one side and
seated three-quarter length. The figures in both pictures filled the corner of a room draped with a
cloth of honor. The lowered head of Pope Sixtus
wore a contemplative expression; one hand was active, the other passive—as head and hands were
to be rendered in Raphael's *Julius.* Apart from differences in size and scale, the principal distinction between the two portraits was the costume.
Another Sistine precedent suggests itself among

the very few known paintings before Raphael's of
a pope in informal attire. For, dressed in *camauro*
and *mozzetta,* none other than Sixtus IV appeared
in Melozzo da Forlì's fresco of *Platina's Appointment as Prefect of the Vatican Library* (1476–77) and
the crude fresco variant of this scene for the Hospital
of Santo Spirito in Rome (Plate 10). Melozzo's fresco included, with other papal nephews, the future
Pope Julius, who, as cardinal, had supervised his uncle's projects at Santo Spirito. The Sistine lineage behind Raphael's panel could hardly be more direct.

Formally, then, as a papal portrait, the *Julius* was
at once a creative synthesis and an innovation. Traditions of papal portraiture have carried us far enough
to suggest that painter and patron depended on certain choices within a repertory of inherited possibilities. At the same time, the papal precedents
were partial and particular—nothing so much as a
ready-made prototype. What they have not prepared
us for is a naturalness and intimacy so complete as to
set the London panel apart from the relatively iconic
quality even of Pinturicchio's Alexander VI or of its
own immediate predecessor in the Vatican *Stanze* by
Raphael himself (cf. Plates 4 and 6). And then—it is
odd that this has not, at least to our knowledge, been
observed before—Raphael's *Julius* was the first independent painting of a single pope in the history of
art. So far as papal portrait traditions were concerned,
these characteristics defined something of the formal
inventiveness in Raphael's work. But here again
synthesis was involved, in this case the consolida-

tion of important debts to another Renaissance tradition—the independent secular portrait.

It is possible that Raphael's *Julius* was a direct, if distant, descendant of the late medieval ancestors of this
genre. Independent portraits seem first to have been
used to represent the kings of France. The earliest
surviving example is the small, quarter-length
profile (c. 1360–64) of the French king John the
Good (Plate 11). Angled against a green cloth of
honor, Fouquet's *Portrait of Charles VII* illustrates
elaborations on the basic pattern at the middle of the
fifteenth century (Plate 12). Together with his influential seated-figure-with-entourage in the lost
painting of Eugenius IV, the French painter may
have brought this royal portrait type to Rome. The
bearded profile of Pope Julius in winter dress,
painted by an anonymous artist and known only
from a later copy, seems to have reproduced the
prototype (Plate 13). In any case, if precedent were
needed for an intimate view of an exalted personage,
there was none better than the unabashed revelation
of royalty by Fouquet and other northern artists.
Then too, portraits such as Fouquet's were meant,
like Raphael's, to hang on walls; still more sugges-
tively, Fouquet's *Eugenius IV* hung in the sacristy of
Santa Maria sopra Minerva, just as Raphael's *Julius*
may have hung, when not on display for feast days,
in the sacristy of Santa Maria del Popolo.

But there were much closer connections between
Raphael's work and the development of indepen-

dent portraiture in Florence. The panels of private
persons which began to appear in Florence during
the 1430s and 1440s were evidently painted to hang
in the palaces of Florentine families to keep alive
the memory and the inspiration of their ancestors
(Plate 14). These characteristically rigid, highly idealized profiles suited their commemorative, even
ritual, purpose. By the third quarter of the fifteenth
century painted portraits and sculpted busts began to
take on the features of living persons over a wider
range of poses, and so began to convey a far greater
sense of naturalness and personal presence. Botticelli's *Portrait of a Man with a Medal of Cosimo de' Medici*
from the 1470s is an especially revealing example of
the new type, since the combination of a commemorative medal of the dead Cosimo with the
image of a living man seems to capture its development in a moment of transition (Plate 15). Around
the turn of the century the transition was virtually
complete, and it was then, between 1504 and 1510,
that Leonardo painted the *Mona Lisa* (Plate 16).

Leonardo's example was crucial not only for the
Julius but also for most of Raphael's later Florentine
and Roman portraits. Through infinitely subtle gra-
dations of tone and modelling, a prodigious understanding of the workings of anatomy and nature,
and a keen sense of an underlying harmony pervad-
ing all things, Leonardo created an image of such
graceful animation that previous portraits looked
wooden by comparison. To accommodate the pose
of the first explicit "sitter" in the history of independent portraiture he invented a new half-, almost

three-quarter length format. But despite the aura of life, Leonardo was not interested in the particularity of the sitter. The setting was obviously an imagined one, its loggia seemingly suspended in a cosmic landscape. Mona Lisa became an archetypal mother-goddess through the geometrical perfection of her form, her preternatural mass, and the abstract clarity of the architectural framework against a god's eye view of the world. She could hardly be imagined on the streets of Florence.

From Raphael's two Doni panels (c. 1506) to his *Portrait of a Cardinal* (c. 1510) we see the apprentice absorbing the impact of Leonardo while attempting to invest his own work with the observation of physical and psychic uniqueness (Plates 17–19). One *could* imagine Maddalena Doni in sixteenth-century Florence. Yet the sharply rendered details of her costume and physiognomy seem superimposed on the highly abstract design, thick torso, and generalized landscape derived from Leonardo. The pendant *Portrait of Agnolo Doni* was more vivid for the looser geometry of its composition, the varied silhouette and topography of the face, the angled and asymmetrical placement of the figure in space. Still incompletely absorbed, however, the Leonardesque ideal forced itself into the contradictory impulses of the stabilizing balustrade, the bent right arm tying the sitter to the format despite the extension of the torso beyond it, and the broad handling of costume, landscape, and color. The disjunction between the ideal and the real remained, and it was only in the *Portrait of a Cardinal* that Raphael achieved a fully effective and harmonious balance of intentions.

The formula for the *Cardinal* set the standard for many Renaissance portraits that came after it, Raphael's own *Portrait of Julius II* among them. The example of Leonardo was apparent in the central placement of the figure, the rendering of the silhouette in simple geometrical forms, the anchoring arm parallel to the bottom edge of the panel, and the palette of limited range unifying the interplay of forms. But Raphael also adopted certain devices to overcome the conflict between general and particular, between abstraction from and representation of appearances, which had been so conspicuous in the Doni portraits. Reduced to a neutral foil, the background cooperated with the strongly focused light to project the turned bust of the sitter forcefully into space. The painted surface displayed a newly won technical virtuosity which served to communicate a physical and psychological presence perhaps no more real but certainly less remote than Mona Lisa. The positioning of the figure in the *Cardinal* was more casual, the geometry less regular, the color more intense than Leonardo would have allowed. The intermingling of an idealized and a contingent vision may have been less exalted in Raphael; but it was also more accessible.

For the London *Julius,* Raphael refined the formula of the *Cardinal* by adding a backlight to enliven the background and create a spatial ambience for the sitter. In contrast to the *Mona Lisa,* the setting became a real-seeming corner of a room. The rendering of sur-

face and psyche were now of a nuanced subtlety equal
to Leonardo's, but even more individualized than in
Raphael's earlier work. Rather than the murky light
and labored execution of the *Mona Lisa,* rapidly executed finishing touches of thickly painted but finely
lined highlights created a far more convincing illusion
that the observer views the portrait with the sitter
bathed in natural light. But for all the freedom and
vivacity, Raphael employed a clearer, grander, and
more stable structure than he had contrived for any of
his previous portraits. The chair, the corner of the
room, and the pope's body were carefully composed
to form a solid pyramid locked within a grid of verti-
cals. The refined modulation of detail, the convincing
anatomy, and the sculptural presence of the forms
testify to much painstaking effort, several days at least
and probably longer judging from the revisions, or
pentimenti, disclosed by X-ray photographs.

The fusion on the National Gallery panel of spon-
taneous creation, careful concentration, and attention
to precedent can be put to one final visual test.
Raphael was probably not so intimate with the pope
as Vasari wanted to believe. But his wonderfully
fresh, quickly sketched Chatsworth drawing of
Julius's head suggests that the harried pontiff did
"sit" at least once, just as Federico Gonzaga was to
do a few months later, when the painter "made a
charcoal sketch for later use" in a room in the Vatican Palace (Plate 20). On the other hand, if what appears to be a heavily reworked cartoon for the *Julius*
in the Corsini Gallery in Florence is authentic, it was
among the first ever made for a portrait—and one

more indication that a period of careful calculation preceded the moment when Raphael first laid his brush on the London panel.

Contemporaries noted the simultaneous interplay of precedent and invention in Raphael. Already in the 1520s Paolo Giovio was writing of the painter's quick powers of assimilation—and of what Giovio chose to consider a conflict between artifice and nature in his style. Vasari elaborated in his *Lives*. Raphael had been the great and gracious inventor, but also an artist "who, studying the works of ancient masters and those of the moderns, took the best from all and, having assembled them, enriched the art of painting. . . ." Ludovico Dolce varied the theme but slightly: Raphael "did not paint at random, or for the sake of practice, but always with much application." The painter's first aim had been to imitate the best models—*la bella maniera delle statue antiche* was Dolce's example. The second was "to contend with nature."

These judgments are revealing in themselves. They help describe and confirm what we have seen on our own. But they should also lead us from considerations of motif and form to questions about their cultural context. What were the enabling circumstances and available categories for what we have seen and now, from contemporaries, have heard about Raphael? What was there, after all, in the Julian setting that permitted or positively encouraged the blending of synthesis and invention, or of the calculated effect and of naturalness, which seems to define the individualism of Raphael's *Julius?*

These are difficult questions, but they are at least questions of a sort that would have been understood in the High Renaissance. The special character of any culture reveals itself along the interface between received conventions and the particular instance, and this was an especially self-conscious concern in the Renaissance world. Whatever was "Renaissance" depended, by definition, on both the prescriptive authority of models from the past and the commitment to make them live—or re-live—in the present. As a result, tensions between past patterns and present possibilities, archetype and experience, prescription and invention, norm and nature became the underlying calculus of creativity in the Renaissance style. If the style of Julian Rome can be described at all accurately as *High* Renaissance, it is largely because these tensions were so intensely felt and acted out in the prevailing culture. Raphael's *Julius* was clearly no exception.

But there are quite specific points of cultural access to what we have seen so far in the portrait. The principle of imitation in literature and art, for one, was a favorite theme of Renaissance scholars and writers after Petrarch, not least among *literati* close to Raphael and the Julian court. This is understandable, in the first place, because a central Renaissance issue was at stake: how could the language, the imagery, and so the culture of antiquity be appropriated for the uses of the present? In the second place, the ancient authors so much admired in the Renaissance had practiced and prescribed a rhetoric of imitation. Traditions transmitted by Cicero and Quintilian emphasized the need to balance the formalism of training in approved models *and* an inventive openness to observation and discovery. "Rhetoric," Quintilian had explained, "would be a very easy and small matter, if it could be included in one short body of rules, but rules must generally be altered to the notions of each individual case, the time, the occasion, and necessity itself."

By the early sixteenth century the question of whether to imitate had long since been resolved; what had been the imaginative discovery of a few had become a commonplace of humanist studies and schoolrooms and, eventually, a habit of mind. The question was rather how to imitate—whether, for example, to stress the absolute authority of precedent over invention; or, again, whether to follow many or only a few models. The stricter formalist position had gradually centered on a quite un-Ciceronian insistence on the authority of Cicero as opposed to the free imitation of a wide range of ancient authors. Opinion divided along similar lines over *la questione della lingua*. The vernacular had come to have its classics too. Should the "good Tuscan" of Petrarch and Boccaccio be imitated exclusively then? Or should one write in the polyglot Italian of the courts, drawing on the best models from different times and places?

A famous controversy on these questions broke out in Rome just after the completion of Raphael's *Julius*. Preliminary skirmishes may have begun while Raphael was actually at work on the London panel; both parties to the dispute must have been well known to the painter and his patron. The exchange of letters *de imitatione* between Gianfrancesco Pico and Pietro Bembo reads, in any event, very much like commentary on the creative processes Raphael's *Julius* seems to presuppose. The case for combining many models with one's own ingenuity was precisely Pico's challenge to Bembo. "I have decided," he wrote in Rome on 12 September 1512, "that there should be some imitation but not continual, and that all good writers should be imitated, not some exclusively nor wholly but just as each one thinks safe." This had been the practice of the ancients; they "took from any source whatever and as much as seemed to strengthen or adorn their phrase and was recognized as appropriate to the theme." It was also natural, "since Nature distributes her gifts to one and all in such a way that the standard of beauty is established from the variety." Besides, it was the technique of good teachers to "place many models before us." Pico clinched his case with the tale of the Greek painter Zeuxis, who had painted the features of many maidens in creating the perfect image of one beautiful woman. This was a cliché, a well-worn link between literature and art. In literature and in painting—*ut pictura poesis* in the famous formula of Horace—Pico expected writers and artists to follow many examples with the guidance of their own innate judgment and the standards they had learned in practice.

Pico might have been describing the making of Raphael's *Julius*. But Bembo's reply should not be passed over as an irrelevant Ciceronian exercise. The arch-Ciceronian appreciated the power of the eclectic ideal. Replying in Rome to Pico on 1 January 1513,

Bembo admitted to having practiced it himself for years. Only after "much thought and through many steps" had he concluded that nothing but the best and most complete models—Cicero in prose, Virgil in poetry—should be imitated. Granting the premise that imitation was desirable, Bembo's argument was forthright, even compelling. And, even more than Pico, Bembo drew support from the analogy of painting. Ancient artists, he argued, could copy from pictures by Polygnotus and Thymantis, but they had learned most from Apelles, the greatest master of them all. One thinks of the decisive role Leonardo's example played for Raphael. One thinks too of the impact of Pope Julius's actual presence in Bembo's assertion that even artists who learned by imitation, "when they desired to fashion the portrait of Alexander, kept their mind and eyes on him alone." Finally, Bembo offered a rationale for what the most careful tracing of precedent must in the end confirm in Raphael's *Julius:*

I limit the method so that if anyone is superior, industrious, or fortunate enough to surpass his master he ought to do so. Indeed, I quite approve of Phidias who excelled Eladus in sculpturing. Polyclitus who surpassed his master in painting, and Apelles, who left his teacher far behind.

This network of ideas running close by (and surely through) Raphael's *Julius* did not stop at Pico or Bembo. It extended back to early humanist discussions of art which, as Michael Baxandall has shown, were predicated on the application of classical rhetorical theory to the visual arts. In his treatise *On Painting* (1435) Leon Battista Alberti had already recommended to painters Pico's eclecticism, Bembo's concentration on one model, and the lessons of nature; in his short work *On Sculpture* (after 1443) he adapted rhetorical distinctions between the general category and the particular case in an analysis of verisimilitude—truth to type and to the specific instance—in portraiture. Closer to Raphael and his patron, Mario Equicola, writing from Julian Rome in defense of a courtly vernacular, singled out the Roman court as an ideal center for imitation with distinguished results, since there were in Rome "outstanding and most excellent men from every region [of Italy]." If encouragement to master one model *and* to draw on many models were necessary, Baldassare Castiglione would have provided it. Castiglione was Raphael's friend and correspondent; he had been a companion of Pope Julius at the siege of Mirandola and was a familiar figure at Della Rovere courts in Urbino and Rome. In the *Book of the Courtier* he advised "the good pupil . . . to transform himself into his master"; then "to observe different men of his profession and, conducting himself with that good judgment which must always be his guide, go about choosing now this thing from one and that from another." It seemed no contradiction to Castiglione that such studied imitation could be made to appear perfectly natural. That was the essence of the desired effect of *sprezzatura,* that double duplicity which transformed nature into art and art into the appearance of naturalness.

Only one more variation on these themes could bring us still closer to Raphael and his *Julius*. It was Raphael's own. In 1514, in a famous letter to Castiglione, the painter took up the great commonplaces for himself:

To paint a beautiful woman, I would need to see many beauties, with the condition that your Grace join me to choose the best. But lacking good judges and beautiful women, I make use of a certain idea that comes into my head. Whether it has any excellence as art I don't know; at least I try very hard to have it.

This has been called "a curious notion." Roots in Neoplatonic or Aristotelian philosophy have been solemnly proposed for it. Raphael's letter was wonderfully playful, but it was "curious" only if the painter and his culture were; and it was not so much a philosophical argument as a bow to the impulses of a common culture. Fifteenth-century writers on art had often emphasized observation of the natural world, just as, in practice, artists such as Leonardo or Pollaiuolo had often chosen to concentrate on the workings of nature. Half a century after Raphael, theorists of the Ideal were drawing sharp contrasts between ideal and actual visions of the world. It seems somehow characteristic of the culture of Raphael and his patron that creativity seemed still so flexible, that "ideal" and "real" perceptions, or the play of precedent and of inventiveness, could still be held in balance.

Similar combinations in contemporary ways of perceiving an individual derived from another set of attitudes and ideas. Raphael's contemporaries were used to reading the underlying character of an individual in his physical appearance. They owed this skill in the most general sense to the old commonplace of a pneumatic psychology that physical attributes were related to the actions of the soul. This assumption had been refined by a literature on physiognomics and by still other inheritances from the classical rhetoricians—for example, their views on expressing "the spirit in the letter"; and the standard topic of the "living likeness" or the "speaking image" in their discussions of art. The physical codes of mental and spiritual qualities were a major theme in the treatises on painting by Alberti and Leonardo. "Let the attitudes of men and the parts of their bodies be disposed in such a way that these display the intent of their minds," wrote Leonardo on one of many pages analyzing "the movements of the soul in bodily appearances." Otherwise painting would be a lifeless thing, since it "is not in itself alive . . . and if it does not add the vivacity of action, it becomes twice dead."

A chapter on physiognomy from Pomponius Gauricus's dialogues *De Sculptura* (1504) can be read as a Julian guide to physiognomical lore. Since the thirteenth century, scholastic philosophers in the universities had drawn from a rich tradition of Greek and Arabic writing on physiognomics. The original, pseudo–Aristotelian texts (Gauricus based his chapter on one of these) were recovered and reexamined by humanist scholars, while artists applied rule-of-thumb versions with a frequency and familiarity that Alberti and Leonardo only begin to suggest. This

confluence of precedent and practical exploration describes a characteristic pattern in Renaissance culture.
By bringing these strands together, Gauricus, who
may have been in Rome while Raphael was painting
the National Gallery panel, played his part in an
equally characteristic High Renaissance, and Julian,
kind of culmination.

Rather than the *tabula rasa* of Burckhardtian individualism, Raphael and his contemporaries had these
cultural cues and categories to bring to the spectacle
of Pope Julius. It is true that, where literally applied,
Renaissance physiognomics produced grotesque ex-
aggeration or stereotype, not Raphael portraits. But
diffused, as a habit of mind, the common stock of
physiognomical ideas did sustain a conviction in the
substantive reality of particular physical appearances
and in the significance of physical differences among
individuals, both in themselves and as mirrors of individual temperament and the individual soul. The
physiognomical mask reflected the man; the man portrayed the mask.

This may help us understand how the aspect of a
"choleric" type and the features of a pope at a particular moment could seem practically indistinguish-
able in Raphael's *Julius*. The flushed complexion
of the likeness and the strong forehead and nose
signalled, in a physiognomical key, high spirits in
general, irascibility in particular. The dark eyes,
moderately recessed, confirmed and extended this
interpretation. According to a passage from Gauricus,
"[such eyes] will betray a huge spirit, a great soul
for effecting great deeds, but then too those prone

to rage, the drunkards, and those who strive for glory over mankind. . . . " Beards too—beards quickly grown at that—had a place in physiognomical lore as a sign of fiercely determined character. There was even room for one of the subtlest effects of Raphael's characterization: the ruddiness which signified a propensity to wrathful passion was also held to reflect pain and profound meditation.

The overall impression could have been seen as at once accurately descriptive and "leonine." The leap by analogy from men to the animals they were supposed to resemble was a commonplace of physiognomical literature and, as has been shown for the leonine type at least, of Renaissance artists. Alberti's deliberately leonine mask on a self-portrait medal, Verrocchio's experiment with the warrior's snarl in the Colleoni monument, and the lionlike visage of imperial majesty on Cellini's *Bust of Cosimo I* are telling examples. Between the rigidity of experiment in the Quattrocento and of propagandistic intent in the Cinquecento a medal of Julius, struck perhaps in 1511, gave him a conspicuously leonine appearance. One wonders about the square face and hanging cheeks, the clamped mouth and the prominent forehead, with its suggestion of a "clouded" brow, in Raphael's portrait. Do these features of his *Julius,* however subtly modulated, betray the lion's mask? We can only be sure that the conventions of the leonine type were such and, furthermore, that the significance attributed to them would have suited the Julian image. The leonine individual was taken to be strong, virile, inclined to anger and fury, but also, with the brooding power of the lion, capable of mastering terrible passions. The lion-man merged with the archetypical classical hero, with Hercules, and with his Christian transformation already discussed by Lactantius and elaborated by Renaissance writers as a symbol of Christlike righteousness. It is a tempting network of associations, the more so because it is easy to imagine them tempting Julius himself.

Where did the "norm" end and "nature" begin? The point—the High Renaissance point—is that such distinctions were not sharply drawn in the Julian world. In creativity and in perception, commitments to categories and experience or to prototype and invention were widely held to flow into, not against, one another. What we see in Raphael's *Julius* had, in short, its cultural vocabulary and rationale.

It also had its metaphysic. Raphael had scarcely finished his work when Machiavelli expressed the hopeful wisdom of his contemporaries that the creative power, the *virtù,* of great individuals might master the circumstances and precedents, the *fortuna,* that faced them. Pope Julius was one of Machiavelli's prime examples. In sermons the Julian court heard preached in the Sistine Chapel, and could see illustrated in Michelangelo's vault above, man was proclaimed made in the image of God but pronounced free to fashion the likeness he chose for himself. Within a few months of Raphael's portrait Pope Julius convened the Fifth Lateran Council, where the doctrine of individual immortality was first officially established. The Aristotelian position that the soul was universal and indivisible among merely mortal men was rejected. If the Fifth Lateran decree was logically and perhaps biblically dubious, its historical relevance was not. For the aspirations of Julian culture, like Raphael's *Julius,* depended on the conviction that the identity of the individual was at once beyond time and of the moment, that the soul, as the Lateran fathers decreed, was immortal, but only "in the bodies in which it is infused and capable of multiplication in the multitude. . . ."

Yet culture is not strictly a matter of ideas, and we would miss much in the individualism of Raphael's *Julius* by supposing its cultural significance limited to intellectual principles for their own sake. The London panel, like any artifact, can also be said—and seen—to have contents derived from institutional, political, and in the broadest sense, social circumstances of its making. This need not commit us to a heavy-handed material determinism to explain the particular sort of individualism—the fusion of precedents, invention, and naturalness—we have found so far in Raphael's portrait. But it should lead us to expect those qualities to have referents and relevance as products, if also as conditions, of the society inhabited by the painter and his patron.

Consider the fact that Raphael's *Julius* represents a papal *persona* and the utterly particular person of the pope. General type and specific instance merge in a masterful way. This combination can be read simply as one more variation on what should seem by now a familiar pattern. Our analysis could stop there. But a moment's reflection suggests further possibilities,

not least that the *Julius* recorded and, indeed, depended upon the kind of individual presence Renaissance society tolerated or actually demanded in a
pope.

Something like a cult of personality was deeply
rooted in the history of the papal institution, especially in its development during the fourteenth and
fifteenth centuries. To the extent that a pope was
thought to embody the powers of his office in succession from St. Peter, the office could be identified
with the man, for all the attempts of conscientious
theorists to keep them distinct; and to the extent that
the pope was absolute, as papalist writers insisted in
proportion to the intensity of contradiction, there
was little in theory to gainsay the style, effective or
not, of a strong-willed individual in office. Ernst
Kantorowicz devoted key parts of a great book to
the ideology behind this process of personification.
In the early Middle Ages, he observed, the "mystical
body of Christ" had designated the host consecrated
in the Mass; by the middle of the twelfth century the
formula was being applied to the institutional organization and administrative apparatus of the
ecclesiastical hierarchy. What had been liturgical and
sacramental in meaning became a sociological description in response to the elaboration of institutions within the Church and challenges from secular
powers without. The next step was to associate the
"mystical body" with the head of the hierarchy—the
pope himself.

This association was not a mere debating point,
interesting only to theologians and lawyers. It was

an efficient political weapon in times of trouble for
the papacy after the early fourteenth century. Bon-
iface VIII and his supporters were testing it at
the beginning of the century in their hard-fought
confrontation with Philip the Fair of France. To
show that popes surrendered nothing for their long
residence at Avignon (1305–78) the claim was repeated over and over again that "the mystical body
of Christ is where the head is, that is, the pope." Not
only Rome, but Jerusalem, Mt. Sion, the "dwellings
of the apostles," and the "common fatherland" of
Christians—*all* these were where the pope was, papal
apologists proclaimed, "even were he secluded in a
peasant's hut."

That the Church was drawn still more closely
around the hierarchy, the curia, and their single head
was the most lasting, if most paradoxical, effect of
the division of Christendom among rival heads between 1378 and 1417. By the mid-fifteenth century,
the period of the Great Schism and the church councils, with the "parliamentary" resistance growing
out of the conciliar movement, could be made to
seem an unfortunate aberration which might be laid
to rest. The pope had been reestablished once and for
all in Rome; the central institutions of the Church
were more dependent on him than ever. Speaking
for the hierarchy in the person of the vicar of Christ,
Pius II's famous bull *Execrabilis* (1460) condemned
any presumption of appeal to a General Council
"from the ordinances, sentences, or mandates of ourselves or of our successors. . . ."

Half a century later the theme of Christian unity

in the body of the pope was often invoked. The fathers of the Fifth Lateran, warding off yet another time of crisis, referred to it again and again. When Cipriano Benet dedicated a treatise on the Eucharist to Pope Julius, he associated the miracle of the Mass with the presence of divinity in the pope. So did Raphael in the *Mass of Bolsena* (Plate 21) and in the *Disputa,* where Julius was probably depicted in the guise of St. Gregory the Great and was, in any case, named in two inscriptions on the altar. Julius contemplated and adored the host. He witnessed and confirmed the miracle of Transubstantiation which sanctioned in turn his spiritual power and his office as Christ's vicar.

In important ways, then, the self-display of Renaissance popes was not an inroad of secular society on religious values and institutions. But it *was* that too. No exaltation of the papacy, even (perhaps especially) when meant to shield the Church from secular ambitions, could conceal how much the popes had compromised or lost; on the contrary, ideals of papal supremacy promoted worldly interests at the center of the Catholic world. Although Denys Hay has most recently reminded us how little is known about the actual workings of the Renaissance papacy, the secular orientation was glaring enough. Stories of "bad Renaissance popes" have, if anything, been told too often, with little regard for the pressure of historical circumstances. Economically and politically vulnerable abroad, Renaissance popes were thrown back on their Italian possessions, where they were often forced, if they did not choose, to play politics as Italian princes

did. Their revenues had fallen sharply as a result of the
Schism and the councils, and by the 1470s they depended on the Papal States for more than half their
income. Clerical discipline was lax, a casualty in part of
generations of distraction and lay interference. The
shambles Rome had become could not be rebuilt on
pure spirit. And if papal politics were blatantly dynastic (not for the first time, it should be remembered), it
was partly because the growing monopoly of Italian
families on the papacy and the highest offices of the
Church had linked ecclesiastical affairs to an insatiable
system of secular demands.

Whether for sacred motives or profane, by 1511–12
the personal touch and presence of Renaissance popes
had broken openly through and merged into an official
persona which had itself become ever more exaggerated. The anthropologist Mary Douglas observes that
any "physical experience of the body, modified by the
social categories through which it is known, sustains
a particular view of society." It is a notion papal
apologists, courtiers, image makers, and quite ordinary Christians were equipped to understand. The
more a society is segmented and divided by hierarchical distinctions, Douglas maintains, the more the ego
of its leaders will have full play. Her analysis of the
leader relatively unchecked by bonds of group solidar-
ity might have been intended for Pope Julius:

He sees the powers which dominate [the cosmos] as available to anyone for the grasping. Courage, determination
and cunning are the list of respected virtues. To his own
personal endowment of these he owes his own success. But

there is no rational explanation of how he came to earn or deserve his advantages.

Moving from the leader to his followers in a divisive social setting, Douglas describes how they must seek a center and a focus to compensate for disunity in society as a whole. The figure at the top comes to epitomize the separate and self-serving disposition of the various levels of society; at the same time, his authoritative (and authoritarian) presence guarantees and legitimates the social hierarchy through the subordination of its parts to him. In such a world—for the sake of argument, in the world of Pope Julius—social interests speak, and show, through the individualism of the ruler, which is far from being his alone.

We should not be surprised that Raphael's *Julius,* image that it is of charismatic papal leadership, would seem tangibly real and authoritatively ideal. The believable presence in an idealized form was one more means through which society could be persuaded to believe in itself. Like deeper miracles, it could authenticate existing arrangements and aspirations, and analogies with the "mystical body," the Real Presence in the celebration of the Mass, or even the Incarnation did not seem blasphemous to many inhabitants of the Julian world. Papal display could sanction the official functions and sacred mystique of the ecclesiastical hierarchy; it could stand surety for bankers' credit on "Saints Albinus and Rossus," white silver and red gold, to the Holy See. Through the person of the pope patronage could be extended,

provincials made cosmopolitan, and Romans assured
that pilgrims, profits, and high style would flow to
the city. Had the greatest artists not glorified the
papal image, lesser ones would surely have been
called to do so.

While Raphael's representation of the *persona* and
person of Pope Julius presupposed both old uses
of charisma and the new Renaissance environment
in the history of the papacy, the London panel also
incorporated another presence at least as individualized as its subject's. As surely as Pope Julius, Raphael
was there, unseen but actively establishing the
perspective of the beholder, monumentalizing an
otherwise fleeting image of nature, investing *his*
portrait with a unity of conception greater than the
sum of its parts.

This self-conscious mediation by the painter would
hardly have been possible if artistic enterprise had been
organized as a strictly corporate, more or less utilita-
rian form of manual labor on the guild model. As a
social type, the guildsman strives to conform to traditional standards and so to merge his creative identity
into impersonal rhythms of work and rewards. He
provides a social service. In his world, paintings,
sculpture, or buildings are produced in the same manner as shoes or hardware, or the banners, furniture, and
costumes still made by Renaissance artists. Raphael
could never have remained an ordinary apprentice
even if he had stayed in Urbino. The point is worth
making, however, that by the end of the Quattrocento

the circumstances in which works of art (or at least of painting) were made positively encouraged artists to develop a personal style.

It is true that the craft tradition persisted much longer than Renaissance writers would have us, or their own contemporaries, believe. Recent studies have qualified the notion that Renaissance artists adopted a modern pattern of work—what is tempting to call the garret model, according to which artists operate as creative individuals, cultivating a more personal style and a more cosmopolitan culture than the craftsman in the workshop. Few, if any, artists met Alberti's ideal of the learned and virtuous painter; none could match him at citing the classics—certainly not Raphael, who apparently did not know Latin. And, as Peter Burke has shown in an analysis of the creative élite in Renaissance Italy, painters, sculptors, and architects continued to come mainly from the artisan and shopkeeper class; the writers and scholars were, like Alberti himself, mostly descendants of nobles, merchants, and professionals. Nevertheless, the elevated personal and professional status Renaissance writers envisioned for artists did not remain altogether theoretical or wishful thinking. It was only after contacts with Florentine artists in the 1430s that Alberti wrote *On Painting,* confident in the power of art to master nature through individual minds and eyes. Artists themselves may not have put the practice of perspective construction on a theoretical footing or set the arts in the mainstream of humanist culture, but many came to associate, as Alberti thought they must, with learned men who "have many ornaments in common with the painters" and "are full of information about many subjects."

The growing prestige accorded to personal style and invention can be documented in the few hundred contracts between patrons and artists which have survived for the fifteenth and early sixteenth centuries. For all the variations due to time, place, and medium, there is considerable evidence of a few overarching trends. Provisions for expensive materials for the sake of sheer display, or fixing style and subject matter ready-made to the patron's order, gave way gradually, if not altogether consistently. Patrons of painting were more and more likely to buy the artist's brush than showily expensive gold or ultramarine. The high cost of pictorial skill was widely discussed and, more impressively, paid for. By the end of the Quattrocento it was not unusual for contracts to discriminate sharply between the individual master and his workshop and to demand works of his own design and execution. E. H. Gombrich's formula—from "commission" to "mission" —seems apt. In effect, artists were being subsidized to surpass their rivals and themselves for their own greater glory, the renown of their patrons, and the realization of the heady new ideal fostered by these developments—progress in art.

From the middle of the fifteenth century, Rome was a vital center for the redefinition of the artist's social place and professional function. The Renaissance campaign of building and decoration in Rome began after a century and a half of more than the usual neglect. It was partly a response to the need to restore the physical fabric of a city of cow pastures; winding, dilapidated streets; broken aqueducts, and a population reduced from a million or more inhabitants in the time of the Roman empire to as few as 25,000 in 1420. To renew the city was also to refurbish its image in line with the restoration of a self-conscious papal supremacy and a *Kulturpolitik* based on the Renaissance recasting of traditional principles attributed to Nicholas V, the pope responsible for the great jubilee of 1450:

. . . to create solid and stable convictions in the minds of the uncultured masses, there must be something which appeals to the eye; a popular faith, sustained only on doctrines, will never be anything but feeble and vacillating. But if the authority of the Holy See were visibly displayed in majestic buildings, imperishable memorials and witnesses seemingly implanted by the hand of God himself, belief would grow and strengthen from one generation to another, and all the world would accept and revere it.

In this atmosphere, popes and prelates, aristocrats and international bankers drew artists and architects from all over Italy to Rome with that special sort of atavism inspired by new ambition and wealth. Even Pastor, who resorted to counting works of religious art in his *History of the Popes* to prove the Catholic sincerity of the Quattrocento, was staggered by their apparent quantity and cost in Rome.

It was like Pope Julius and like Raphael to make the most of their chances in what had become a boom town for art. Julius had been schooled in its uses by the most extravagant papal patron of the fifteenth century, his uncle Sixtus IV. He seems to have become a kind of artistic adviser to Innocent VIII, and he plainly meant to surpass Alexander VI as a patron of art. His expectations as pope for the greatest artists on the most grandiose projects are a matter of record; otherwise we could only consider him, as satirists were quick to do, a Renaissance patron in caricature. But Raphael himself, already *the* Renaissance painter in 1511–12, was practically a living myth in his own right. He had been summoned to Rome in 1508 at the age of 25 after a kind of triumphal progress through commissions at Urbino, Perugia, Siena, and Florence. With stunning facility he had learned at every stop and adapted his style to the lessons of important sources wherever he found them. Once in Rome, he was chosen to complete the painting of Julius's own apartments, where, by 1511, he had inserted his own portrait among the pagan and Christian immortals of the *Stanza della Segnatura*. Through painting he became more than a painter—courtier and familiar of the great, connoisseur of antiquities, prospective son-in-law of a cardinal, builder of his own palace, and a wealthy man. It measured his own special genius but also how far an artist could rise that near-contemporaries thought of him in terms they applied to his patron. Raphael, too, was a "prince," "divine," "a mortal god."

But there were limits. Artists in Julian Rome were certainly not free agents, as even the greatest among them were reminded on more than a few occasions.

Julius quashed Bramante's plan to reorient the new
St. Peter's on line with the Vatican obelisk. Michelangelo was forced to submit to Julius with the
symbolic noose around his neck after fleeing from a
real or imagined papal insult in Rome, and arbitrary
changes in his plans for Julius's tomb by the pope
and then his heirs tormented the sculptor to the end
of his life. Payments rarely kept pace with the artist's
or the patron's ambition. The very scope of Julius's
projects was a source of frustration because, as in the
famous case of St. Peter's which took more than 100
years to build, it was rarely possible to see them
through to completion. With all the willfulness and
the power of humiliation a prince could command
the court obviously lay between the Guild and the
Garret. The obverse side of the artist's new dignity
and freedom was a new kind of servitude. Even
Raphael, ever able and adaptable, complained with
feeling from Rome that an artist knew "what it
meant to be deprived of one's liberty, and to live
obligated to patrons. . . . "

Even so, Julian commissions were of unrivalled
scale and opportunity. The pope listened to artists as
he did to few other men, and he did not hesitate to
raise his terrible stick against the unfortunate *monsi-
gnore* who dared to say against Michelangelo that
artists were "ignorant of everything except their
art." Raphael's portrait was one of many rewards of
the vision—and the historical experience—behind
his patron's blows.

In the end, it is true, we are left to imagine what the
encounter between Pope Julius and Raphael was re-

ally like. Of experience as it was actually lived we have only outcomes, objects, and rather inadequate terms for describing them. And since the creative process ultimately escapes analysis, we can only suggest how much even the individualism of Raphael's *Julius* was conditioned by a Renaissance stock of motifs and forms, ideas about the creative process in art, modes of perception, and circumstances of what it meant to be a painter or a pope. Certainly *Renaissance* individualism had little to do with much later manifestations, equally historical in their own time, of free artistic inspiration and outright rebellion against cultural traditions and social norms. If the term is meaningful, perhaps it is because Renaissance individuals—say, Pope Julius and Raphael—could choose and act self-consciously to draw together, and sometimes to extend, the conventions of their culture.

2
Roles of a Renaissance Pope

While a sense of individuality may be immediately striking in Raphael's *Julius,* the fact that we are looking at a Renaissance pope is hardly less so. This is not simply a matter of illustration; it is also a result of those coexisting meanings which make communication more than a mechanical exchange of propositions in one dimension. We all know from everyday experience that whatever a message says on the surface seems always to be qualified and framed by other messages which amplify, diminish, or actually negate it. Depending on how and where they are spoken, the most stylized greetings tell us a good deal more than "good morning" or "good night." If this is true of ordinary experience, it is truer still of the complexly transmitted experience in a work of art, particularly of art in a culture accustomed to perceiving various levels of significance in things. In this chapter we turn from individualism to the further, if not necessarily the second, impression we have on viewing the London panel, that this is, of course, a Renaissance pope. Here again we shall have to proceed on a variety of levels, not only because art does so, but also because Raphael's portrait contains references to so many roles played by Renaissance popes—none more grandly than Pope Julius himself.

To confirm the need and take our bearings for this sort of analysis let us look again at contemporary responses to what we might suppose to be only a high touch of Julian individualism—the famous beard. The diary of Paris de'Grassis tells us that the pope let his beard grow from the time of his siege of illnesses at Bologna beginning in October 1510. But even the pragmatic master of ceremonies could not limit himself to mundane explanations such as weakness or lack of hot water. Messer Paris went on to suggest that the beard had something to do, perhaps "through a vow," with the losses the pope had recently suffered at the hands of the French. As a Bolognese chronicler recounted it, Pope Julius "was wearing a beard to avenge himself and said that he did not want to shave it again until he had driven King Louis of France from Italy." Reports from Rome and abroad agreed, and when Julius appeared clean-shaven, it was, according to Marino Sanuto, following Venetian dispatches from Rome in April 1512, "because he saw things were going well." Sources closer to the pope observed that his beard had actually disappeared by degrees in March 1512, as if to mark and conjure up in stages the fulfillment of his vow. The Fifth Lateran Council had been summoned (July 1511) to address the call for reform—and to counter the French-inspired Council of Pisa. Against all expectations Julius had recovered from another nearly fatal illness in time to put down an uprising in Rome (August 1511). The Holy League (October 1511) had consolidated his position in alliances with Spain, Venice, the Swiss Confederation, and England. With the all but miraculous rout of the French after their illusory victory at Ravenna on 11 April 1512 the success of the papal cause—and the beard—was complete.

That the beard was a symbolic gesture seems quite certain. In contemporary eyes and quite likely in his own the bearded Julius assumed, at one level, the identity of warrior prince and even of an emperor. Erasmus's devastating satire *Julius Excluded from Paradise* would soon spread this image all over Europe, and the Erasmian picture of the pope as a soldier king and new Caesar, banging on St. Peter's gate, was not so far off target. Almost all the very few Italians shown with beards before Julius in Hill's corpus of Renaissance medals were ruling princes and nobles; after Julius's time and, according to at least one source, with his specific encouragement beards became a standard attribute of the determination and majesty proper to princes. They were no less suited to the aspect of an emperor. Among other soldiers and rulers the most celebrated to have sworn by his beard was none other than that first Julius who, as Pope Julius could have read in the copy of Suetonius in his private library, grew a beard in mourning after a defeat by the Gauls (!) and vowed not to cut it until he had taken vengeance. So strong were the imperial associations in Julian Rome that the Emperor Justinian, traditionally represented as clean-shaven, was shown with a beard in the *Pandects* fresco—Raphael's fresco—for the *Stanza della Segnatura*.

There were other associations and other roles encompassed by the gesture of growing the beard. Although Erasmus's St. Peter was reluctant to grant Pope Julius even the appearance of a priest, let alone the virtues of piety and holiness, others took the beard as a distinctive sign of priestliness. That bored bureaucrats in the curia may have joked about Julius's beard as the beard of St. Peter does not mean that the comparison was not taken seriously. Julius's other namesake, the first Pope Julius, was shown bearded in a twelfth-century mosaic, and for at least one Roman, who could not recollect ever hearing of a bearded pope, the image of a holy hermit sprang to mind. Giles of Viterbo, addressing the assembled cardinals at Bologna in May 1511, likened Julius's beard to that of the high priest Aaron in the Old Testament. It was an analogy drawn from a text recited in papal coronation ceremonies, and a reference that fit the needs of the moment. The authority of Aaron's succession to Moses and so, analogously, of the succession of St. Peter and the popes to Christ had been confirmed when God destroyed Corah and his followers for attempting to usurp the office of high priest. Botticelli had illustrated the punishment of Corah by the bearded Aaron in the frescos which Sixtus IV, in his own campaign for papal supremacy, had commissioned for the Sistine Chapel. Analogies between Pope Julius and Aaron would be drawn again in a triumphal float for the Roman carnival procession of 1513.

This did not exhaust the spiritual significance of the papal beard. Raphael's own *Expulsion of Heliodorus* (c. 1512) in the Vatican *Stanze* linked the old dispensation in the East and the new in the West by representing the bearded Julius observing and, one imagines, identifying with the bearded high priest who prayed for deliverance in the Temple of Jerusalem (Plate 22). Renaissance allegories converted the bearded sun god Serapis into a Christ-type. And there was of course the ultimate allusion to the bearded Christ himself. By 1529 Piero Valeriano, once a member of the Julian court, could write an entire treatise in defense of priestly beards. Citing precedents pagan and biblical, ancient and modern, he argued that nothing was more pleasing to God or appropriate to the priesthood. Could there be any higher authority, he wondered, than Raphael's likeness of Pope Julius, "made with a beard in the sight of all men?"

Prince, emperor, and priest—the implications of the beard alone warrant a closer look at the roles of a Renaissance pope and their expression in Raphael's London portrait.

In Erasmus's *Julius Excluded from Paradise,* St. Peter was sure what he saw in the pope:

JULIUS: What the devil is going on here? Doors won't open, eh? Looks as if the lock has been changed. . . .

ST. PETER: . . . what monstrosity is this: while you wear on the outside the splendid attire of priest, at the same time underneath you are altogether horrendous with the clatter of bloody weapons? And then how fierce are your eyes, how nasty your mouth, how baleful your expression, how haughty and arrogant your brow!

I suspect that the most pestilential pagan Julius has returned from the underworld to mock me; so completely is everything in you consistent with him. . . .

JULIUS: Though it is degrading for the famous Julius, hitherto invincible, to submit now to Peter, who is, to say the least, a fisherman and practically a beggar; nevertheless, so you'll know what sort of a prince you're insulting, listen. . . .

Erasmus's imperious warrior prince was *the* Pope Julius for many in his own time. We find this characterization no less savagely turned in the tracts of hostile propagandists and in doggerel complaints from Venice and Rome; we find it acted out in *tableaux-vivants* staged in Paris and broadcast in woodcuts to the wider world (Plate 23). An early sonnet by Michelangelo, the most Julian of artists, played on the imagery of chalices turned into sword and helmet, cross and thorn into shield and blade, in his patron's Rome. "It was," remarked Francesco Guicciardini, ever cautious, "as if Julius were a secular prince." After his election, the pope's Ligurian countrymen were already congratulating him for his "Caesar-like soul," and inscriptions at the coronation ceremonies celebrated "Caesar reborn." More than 400 years later Ludwig von Pastor felt obliged to apologize for what was still the dominant impression.

But apologies were a post-Reformation, not Julian, style. Quite apart from his own actions and the reactions of others, Pope Julius styled himself "royal pontiff." To his followers on a military compaign he recited passages from the *Aeneid,* as if to remind them of his own imperial destiny, and to the world at large his spokesmen proclaimed his attributes as builder, liberator, peacemaker, provider, and legislator in imperial language and on an imperial scale.

Projected by Julius himself, reflected from the culture around him, these images were pieces of a picture which clearly informed Raphael's own. It would be fanciful to suspect armor under the display of red velvet and white silk on the London panel. But the bull neck, youthful hands, seemingly powerful arms and legs, ready to spring into action, might well have flattered any Renaissance prince and *generalissimo.* Whether in Erasmus's adjectives or more generously, the face portrayed, as we have already suggested, the reality and the mask of the "choleric" temperament—the temperament of leaders of men and of the god of war. Such a figure could be imagined as his own *condottiere,* the fortress builder who constructed or restored at least nine strongholds in the Papal States, the pope who pushed the boundaries of the territories of the Church to the farthest limits they had ever reached, or would ever reach again. Regal in life, and in Raphael's portrait, so too after death Julius was to have been placed in a tomb designed by Michelangelo (1505) in the free-standing form of tombs for northern royalty and their upstart imitators in Italy. We might well believe that the subject of Raphael's *Julius* was determined, as he and others for him claimed, to liberate Italy as but the first step toward the conquest of the Holy Land and the unification of the world under his leadership. The themes were those of the Renaissance papacy; the pitch was wholly Julian.

Much in the London portrait quite specifically declared the likeness to be princely and regal. Or so it would seem if we allow iconographical significance to certain motifs we have already considered in purely formal terms. We saw in the first chapter not only that the obliquely seated figure and the background cloth of honor could be traced to traditions of French portraiture, but also that these motifs had been elaborated in depictions of royalty. Relatively informal in contrast to full pontifical or liturgical dress, even the ermine-trimmed cape and the cap—*mozzetta* and *camauro*—seem to go back to royal origins. These garments apparently evolved from the long, fur-trimmed robe and helmetlike hat which the popes first began to wear in the manner of French kings while resident at Avignon (Plate 24). Robes of similar type were worn with the tiara, symbol of the pope's temporal authority, by Eugenius IV at the middle of the fifteenth century (Plate 25), and secular princes in Italy were shown wearing them later in the Quattrocento. Sixtus IV adopted the shortened version of the robe and more bowl-shaped hat used later by his nephew (Plate 10), but it may be that the implication of royalty had not been lost. While modern eyes may still read the thronelike chair as royal furniture, contemporaries probably saw much more of the "royal pontiff" in Raphael's *Julius*.

Raphael's apparent references to costume and forms which had figured in portraits of Sixtus IV were themselves a tribute to the dynastic thrust of princely rule in Renaissance Italy and elsewhere (Plates 9–10). The large, luminous acorns of the Della Rovere oak on the back of the papal chair were altogether explicit. They signalled, among other things, the closest approximation to genuine dynasticism possible in an institution whose head was elected at the instigation of the Holy Spirit. In a world of power politics where the available means commonly fell short of the ends proposed for government, a firmly established dynasty was looked upon as a source of continuity and some measure of effective control. The opportunities and obligations of the individual in the context of his household and lineage—a major concern of recent historians of Italian Renaissance society—were thus projected into the highest political arenas. Nepotism had particular attractions for a pope, faced with entrenched institutional structures and, very likely, with the hostile clients of his predecessor. Medieval commentators, not Renaissance apologists, had developed the stock excuses for those "who build Zion with the help of blood relations."

No previous pope had favored his nephews more lavishly, or shown his nepotism more conspicuously in art, than Sixtus IV (Plate 10). And no papal *nipote* stood by family traditions or, despite disclaimers from Pastor, exercised his own position as family

head more completely than Julius II. The testimony
is overwhelming that he viewed himself as the loyal
nephew of Pope Sixtus and a faithful member, however humble its origins, of the Della Rovere clan
from the Ligurian town of Savona. Inscriptions proclaimed the dynast everywhere: on Julian medals,
coins, manuscripts, fresco cycles, and buildings. Paris
de'Grassis concluded that Julius sought "in many,
almost in all things, to imitate his uncle Sixtus."
The London panel was true to form.

Not that Julius stopped at princely conceptions of his
role. Neither his followers nor his enemies doubted
that he possessed—or was possessed by—what a
medal commemorating the submission of Bologna
called "imperial virtues." His building projects alone
would have sufficed for an emperor. There was
Bramante's Belvedere—"eighty feet high and 1000
feet long," trumpeted an inscription. Comprising a
new imperial palace and villa, with sculpture court,
theater, garden, fountains, nymphaeum, and por-
ticoed walkways which have been called a *via tri-
umphalis,* the architectural ensemble boasted a scale
and coherence unequalled since the Roman empire.
Michelangelo's "royal" tomb was also imperial, re-
calling, as has been suggested recently, Pliny's account of the Mausoleum of Halicarnassus and imperial funeral pyres known from Roman coins which
depicted rites acclaiming the emperors as gods. "I
am certain," Michelangelo announced to his patron,
"that if it is made, the whole world will not have its
equal"; "in beauty and splendor," added Vasari,

"and in the grandeur of ornament and the richness of statues, [the 1505 design for the tomb] surpassed all ancient and imperial sepulchres." For his design of the new St. Peter's, Bramante is reported to have acknowledged his debts to the Basilica of Constantine and the Pantheon. But Sigismondo de'Conti, the pope's private secretary and historian, believed that the new church, too, was planned to surpass all its ancient prototypes. "By the inspiration of Vitruvius," exulted the papal protonotary and court poet Evangelista Capodiferro, "Ancus Marcius and Caesar Augustus were reborn in Julius." The imperial architect, an early founder of the city, and the builder of imperial Rome were to live again as one.

Inscriptions, poetry, and prose expanded the list of "imperial virtues" in elaborate epithets—Expulsor of Tyrants; Author of Peace; Custodian of Tranquillity; Restorer of Public Liberty; Defender of Justice; Recoverer of Justice, Peace, and Faith. Words were acted out in processions *all'antica*. Specific references were made, or implied, to identify Julius with some particular emperor, not only with his namesake or with Augustus but also with Tiberius, Trajan, and Constantine. The identification with Caesar was important for the Julian name and for the archetype of empire-building; the *pax romana* of Augustus had prepared for the *pax Christi,* the reign of Christ, born in the Augustan Age. Trajan had been wisely victorious, and by his conversion and supposed donation of the western empire and imperial regalia to the pope, Constantine had accomplished the union of the temporal authority of the Roman empire and the spiritual dominion of the Church—the *respublica christiana*. Even in darker moments of recognition Julian Rome would not settle for less than the analogy between its pope and Tiberius.

The spell of Constantine was especially powerful. Believed to commemorate the providential victory over Maxentius which had led to the establishment of Christianity in the Roman empire, the Arch of Constantine had already appeared as a prominent symbol of papal supremacy in the frescos commissioned by Sixtus IV for the Sistine Chapel. For the triumphal Julian entry into Rome in 1507 a replica illustrating the pope's military exploits was erected directly in front of St. Peter's. Pope Julius was, in effect, the new Constantine. The following year Michelangelo envisaged the Sistine Chapel as a kind of triumphal arch for his ceiling frescos, the organization and structure of which have been shown to be a creative reordering of nearly all the component parts of the Arch of Constantine. Raphael's frescos for the *Stanza d'Eliodoro* quoted freely from the same source and, in one of the window embrasures, illustrated Constantine's donation to Pope Sylvester. Julius himself issued several coins inscribed with a cross and the prophetic words of the emperor's dream on the eve of his battle with Maxentius—*In hoc signo vinces*. Lorenzo Valla's famous treatise of 1440 proving that the Donation of Constantine was an early medieval forgery had obviously been discounted; or rather, reacted against with the insistence of challenged belief. In 1510 favor-seekers were still sending the pope their works on the Donation, including the text of the "original" in Greek.

But of course Julius had to outrank the ancient

emperors. "Never had any Caesar or any Roman commander" equalled him, declared one witness to the celebrations in April 1512 after the collapse of the French army so recently victorious. Giles of Viterbo could compare ancient emperors unfavorably with Julius, whose sway ran over the Old World *and* the New. Julius Caesar had depended on sheer military power, but Pope Julius, insisted Giles, drew on the power of piety. "The pope wants to be the lord and master of the world," reported the Venetian ambassador in 1510. As a Mantuan agent put it two years later, he was, at any rate, "a man capable of ruining a world."

Emperor in the imagination and in life, Julius was imperial too, as we could only expect him to be, on the London panel. We suggested earlier that Roman reliefs of seated emperors influenced the *form* of Raphael's Vatican fresco of Julius-as-Gregory-IX and the slightly later London likeness; but imperial *content* was hardly likely to have been unintended— or missed—in Julian Rome. One possible source, the Aurelian relief of *Liberalitas,* was assumed (because transferred to the Arch of Constantine) to represent Constantine distributing coins after his victory over Maxentius (Plate 7). It was the pose that Julius himself had imitated at Bologna in 1506, and in 1511–12 one especially charged with symbolic hope amidst the challenges to his authority. The other possible imperial source, the Vatican sarcophagus of an emperor crowned by a winged victory, was installed beneath the so-called Cleopatra in the Belvedere sculpture court just at the time Raphael was painting the London panel (Plate 8). Julius Caesar and Augustus, both conquerors (and one a conquest) of the Egyptian queen, were obvious associations. This was precisely the kind of understanding a courtier set to verse: just as Julius Caesar, conqueror of the Nile, had loved Cleopatra, so too Pope Julius, "second only in time," symbolically loved Cleopatra and would be victorious by bringing her effigy into the Belvedere. It was known that Augustus had placed a golden likeness of Cleopatra in the Temple of Venus after his victory at Actium; so too could Pope Julius, another Augustus, bring her image to the sacred precinct of the Vatican in anticipation of victory. With Raphael's imperial sources, then, came the imperial allusions which could make his subject out to be a new emperor, confident of mastery, ruler of a universal empire over the West and the East.

Particular details in the portrait had the potential for reinforcing such allusions—even so innocent a prop as the cloth in Julius's right hand. In classical antiquity a cloth, or *mappa,* held in the hand had been a mark of status. As illustrated on Roman ivories, it was the particular insignia, when held in the right hand, of consular rank, a position often occupied by the emperor (Plate 26). By the mid-fifteenth century historians knew that Constantine had taken the consular title four times and that consular diptychs often showed the *mappa* in connection with scenes of *liberalitas.* Beyond these associations with imperial authority and with the kinds of formal sources Raphael may have used for his portrait, it was also understood that the great cycle of games marking

the beginning of the new year in the ancient calendar
was opened by throwing down or lowering the *mappa*.
Could there be some hint of renewal and regeneration,
too, in the cloth of the London *Julius?*

If not the cloth, then certainly the dynastic acorns
were standard equipment in Julian visions of universal renewal through imperial (and Della Rovere)
dominion. The iconographical resources of those
family totems grew as many-branched and as dense
as the tree they represented. Consider the following
stock of (to the Renaissance) commonplace associations:

—acorns as the food of the golden age in Arcadia;
—the holy oak which grew from the staff of
  Romulus on the Capitoline Hill, so to mark the
  caput mundi;
—the oak under which Venus gave armor made
  by Vulcan to Aeneas in a symbolic translation
  of imperial authority from the East to Rome;
—the oak as a symbol of the cardinal (and imperial) virtue of fortitude;
—the oak of the tree-of-life;
—and so of the Cross, which brought renewed
  life to the ends of the earth and time.

The image makers—and the iconoclasts—of the Julian world could hardly have been better provided
for. The imagery of oak and acorns could be man-
aged in vast productions of theme and variations always a little mysterious but never quite secret. The
allegorical oak would have had to be created if it had
not already existed.

Since it did exist, it was used to the fullest.
Preachers and writers such as Giles of Viterbo,

Marco Vigerio, Girolamo Vida, and Pietro Bembo drew on its implications of a kind of Christian imperialism of renewal. Julian medals showed the Good Shepherd directing his flock from a large oak through the strait but triumphal gate into paradise. On the Sistine Ceiling garlands of oak and acorns were entwined in a message of salvation and redemption through the Church Universal. Sublime in Michelangelo, the empire of the oak was only ridiculous in papier-mâché and gilt pageantry. Or so it would have been, had these ceremonies, like all ceremonies, not been so fraught with the deeper intentions and the needs of their time and place. Even on a Julian scale it would be hard to conceive of a joke so colossal as Julius's entry into Orvieto (1506), where little boys hung as angel-acorns on the branches of an oak, exchanging praising choruses with a costumed Orpheus on the *piazza* below; or as the parade of 100 youths in Bologna, each with an acorn-tipped staff.

Nothing was spared in Rome. Here is a scene from Julius's entry, 27 March 1507, after his victorious campaign for the recovery of papal territory in northern Italy. Near the Castel Sant'Angelo stands a float, round in shape, drawn by four white horses. Ten youths are dancing with palms of victory—it is Palm Sunday; they sing to the glory of the divine Julius, *expulsori tyrannorum*. Above the dancers' heads the celestial sphere of universal dominion; above the sphere, between two palm trees, reaching higher than the church of Santa Maria in Traspontina, a golden oak filled with acorns. The inscription runs: "Under Julius the palm has grown up from the oak.

No wonder—for these are the works of Jove." On
what was believed to be the site of the supposed
tomb of Romulus the oak has risen over the very
foundations of Rome; the oak reigns over the youths
of a new generation, the globe, the inscription to the
head of the Roman pantheon, and even the palms of
Christ the King. In another scene, the oak appears
on the last car in the carnival procession of 1513. At
the top of the tree, within a circle of branches, there
is an effigy of the pope. Beneath it hang likenesses
of the signatories of the Holy League—Emperor
Maximilian, Ferdinand of Spain, Henry VIII of England. Swords are drawn for the defense of the
Church and the conquest of the Holy Land. The oak
is the symbolic scaffold of a papal utopia.

Julius's critics did not set their sights on the oak
because such spectacles were not taken seriously. Satire, as Burckhardt pointed out, was the obverse
side and antidote of Renaissance pretensions to fame.
Erasmus's St. Peter ostentatiously ignored the golden
oak. Others accepted the rules of the allegorical
game in order to overturn it. In the punch line of a
pasquinade of 1506, acorns were "little valued, now
that the golden age has passed." Jean Lemaire,
apologist of the schismatic cardinals at Pisa in 1511,
mocked a pope who "will not succeed in creating
the new and abnormal world he hopes for; for pigs
will always eat acorns, and oaks will shed their
leaves at the proper time, and where wood is
wanted, wood will be used." Clearly, the oak and
acorns were not a mere dynastic label, still less simply interior decoration. Followers and foes alike

might have agreed that the golden acorns in Raphael's *Julius* had much larger purposes than framing the head of the figure. With other trappings in the portrait they could also frame the princely and imperial callings of the pope in the expectation of triumphant renewal and universal dominion even at the brink of desperation and defeat.

Prince, king and emperor—Julius was all of these in the context of his culture, and his portrait. But in the most exalted visions of Julian Rome he also remained what his detractors have insisted, and even sympathetic observers have feared, he was not— high priest, Supreme Pastor, true believer. Raphael suggested as much. The attributes and the formal traditions in his portrait denoted the high priest of the Roman Church. The beard had what we have seen to be Old Testament, apostolic, and votive implications. And there was much else besides to confirm the sacred character of the likeness and of the panel itself.

Let us look again at a few details. Beneath the red cape the figure wears a flowing white dress, or rochet—a liturgical vestment. More than differences in climate or changes in fashion may have shortened the cape after the popes returned to Rome from Avignon. The abbreviated *mozzetta* worn by Sixtus IV, Pope Julius, and virtually all later popes uncovered more of the rochet; at a time when the popes were especially concerned to reaffirm the sacred character of their office perhaps this was deliberately meant to distinguish them from secular princes, who affected

the long robes of the French royal style. Removing
the cape and donning the elaborately embroidered
stole over the undergarment, the pope was dressed
for the celebration of the Mass; with the heavy cope
over the rochet and his high, pointed mitre he
moved in sacred procession. Paris de'Grassis worried
a great deal about keeping Pope Julius in appropriate
dress. It was his business as master of ceremonies to
do so because Renaissance audiences noticed such
things, down to the tilt of a cap and the cut of a jer-
kin, a tabard, and—we may be sure—priestly attire.

For the same reason they probably attributed
more than regal pretensions or merely ornamental
show to the rings in Raphael's *Julius*. Certainly the
rings were conspicuous for their number—all six of
them—and for their impressive gems—diamonds,
rubies, and emeralds, so far as we can tell. We know
that there were many more treasures in the Julian
hoard, including a laminated gold and silver ring
carved with the four doctors of the Church, set with
a diamond, and reportedly worth the enormous sum
of 22,500 golden *scudi*. A memorable outburst of Julian *terribilità* ensued on the loss of a diamond, and
Paris de'Grassis related how Julius commanded from
his deathbed that he be buried wearing two precious
rings. Despite the princely, not to say parvenu,
touch, rings could have peculiarly clerical meanings
quite apart from whatever happened to be carved on
them. They had long been symbols of marriage and
fidelity, a symbolic usage emphasized by the Church
around 1500. The ring of a bishop sealed his own
symbolic marriage to Christ and the Church, and

had a liturgical function, too, when held for the communicant to kiss during the Mass. Within a few months of Raphael's portrait the image of Pope Julius as the Bridegroom was to be much favored among those who spoke at the Fifth Lateran Council. Something of that image may well be preserved for us on the London panel. We cannot really be certain—but neither should we be so sure, as the satirists might have been, that his rings were simply one more mark of worldliness.

Popes were entitled, in fact, to wear at least three rings, and a book on protocol dating from 1516 ruled that they could wear as many as they wished. Which, if any, of the rings in the portrait may have been specifically papal is unclear. But it may be worth noting that the colors of the jewels shown on the right hand were, like those of the painting overall, colors prescribed for the theological virtues: white for faith, green for hope, red for the fire of charity. A few years earlier Raphael had arrayed the personification of Theology for the *Stanza della Segnatura* in those colors, and it is probable that symbolic meanings were intended for the London panel as well. Nor does this seem so far-fetched when we remember that color symbolism was fashionable enough for the sharp-tongued humanist critic Lorenzo Valla to make fun of it around the middle of the Quattrocento.

The possibility of multiple references to Julius's priestly role prompts another look at the cloth he holds in his hand in the portrait, for here too marriage symbolism and liturgical implications may

have been layered together with quite different
meanings. In more or less contemporary marriage
ceremonies the bride and groom could be united by
covering their joined right hands with a ritual cloth.
A so-called care-cloth was sometimes held by the
priest over the heads of a newly married couple as a
sign of their union. Judging from Botticelli's Villa
Lemmi frescos (c. 1484), where the figures hold
cloths in scenes which have been thought to commemorate a marriage, this kind of symbolism was
understood by artists and their audiences. The same
claim can be made with rather more confidence for
the quasi-liturgical meaning of purifying and
sanctifying the hands with a cloth. The silk band, or
maniple, on the forearm of a priest in liturgical dress
is known to have evolved from the ancient *mappa,*
and the general sense of purification and sanctification clearly underlies the holding of a cloth in paintings as distant from Raphael's as Giotto's *Stefaneschi
Altarpiece* in the Vatican (c. 1330) or as close as Botticelli's Uffizi *Adoration* (c. 1472–75) and Ghirlandaio's *Visitation* (1485–90) for Santa Maria Novella
in Florence. The cloth of the pope imperial, the cloth
of the Holy Bridegroom, held in what seems after all
a gesture of blessing—these were far from being impossible combinations in the Julian world.

When we turn from the portrait to the culture
around it, we find such combinations everywhere. If
Julius's name was imperial, it was pontifical as well.
In 1505 he issued a brief promoting the cult of his
other namesake, the first Pope Julius, the fourth-
century lawgiver and martyr whose relics had just

been recovered. In April 1510, reported the Venetian ambassador, the pope "went to S. Maria in Trastevere, where the body of Pope Julius is, and there performed certain ceremonies," and on 26 May he announced a plenary indulgence to all who visited the church. Again, if Julius entered Bologna like a triumphant emperor, dressed in purple, throwing coins to the crowds, he also appeared as bishop, wearing a mitre, with the Host carried before him. The coins he dispensed in imperial style included the image of St. Peter. On his return from Bologna to Rome in 1507 he passed through an arch bearing Caesar's own motto, "I came, I saw, I conquered," and the medal struck for the occasion was inscribed *Julius Caesar Pont[ifex] II* (Plate 27). But the medal showed Julius in a papal cope; the obverse carried the Della Rovere and the papal arms and the words "Blessed is he who comes in the name of the Lord" (Psalms 118:26) from the processional hymn for the Feast of the Tabernacle in the Mass of Palm Sunday, the day the pope, in imitation of Christ, chose to enter Rome. In the minuscule space of one single medal Julius could be at once emperor and pope, prince and priest.

In the greatest spaces of Julian Rome, Christian foundations and spiritual aims were not forgotten. "Let the profane keep out": this inscription near the entrance to the sculpture court in the Belvedere defined that space as holy ground. If so, it was of another religion, complained Gianfrancesco Pico, surveying the pagan gods and demigods assembled there; even the warning notice came from Virgil.

Nevertheless, in the allegorizing vein of long-standing traditions and of the Julian court, the *Apollo Belvedere* could be read as Christlike; Hercules wrestled with Antaeus, as Christ had struggled with sin and death; *Venus Felix* foreshadowed the Virgin and the Church, and *Laocoön,* as a contemporary poem made clear, the fate of those who resisted divine authority. Allegory was unnecessary in the case of the new St. Peter's. Pope Julius, already custodian of St. Peter's name and relics as cardinal of San Pietro in Vincoli, allowed St. Peter to come first. He would not permit Bramante to reorient the church at the risk of tampering with the apostle's tomb. And for all the kingly and imperial elements in the design for his own burial place, a crucial fact in its conception was that it was meant to stand close to the remains of the prince of the apostles. In the *Stanze* and the Sistine Chapel, too, the doctrinal and even sacramental lessons were probably of a far more conventional kind of Christianity than has usually been supposed.

Even that least credulous observer, Niccolò Machiavelli, concluded that Pope Julius "did everything to aggrandize the Church. . . ." Certainly the pope's position as Supreme Pastor and successor to St. Peter was not left to inscriptions and to art. Nothing infuriated him more than assaults on the "liberty of the Church," and no one who faced his tongue and his stick on this point doubted that he meant to vindicate the Church at all costs. Warrior cardinals, papal mercenaries, and, in Cesare Borgia, the son of a pope had been seen in the field before, but never a pope in armor, rushing into the breach. A crusade against the Turks had been promised by every pontiff-elect since the early fifteenth century, but no pope, with the exception of Pius II after the fall of Constantinople in 1453, took his pledge more seriously than Pope Julius. The threat was real enough as Turkish pressure increased against Hungary, Austria, and even the coasts of Italy, and so was his response. Julius's fortifications at Ostia as cardinal (1483) and at Civitavecchia as pope (1508) were directed primarily against Ottoman attacks. In 1506 he ordered Giles of Viterbo to preach before the cardinals that Constantinople and Jerusalem would be liberated after the conquest of the Papal States, and in 1507 he sent a cardinal-legate to promote the crusade at the court of Emperor Maximilian. With the king of Portugal he looked to ventures on land and sea in the Orient as part of a great crusading effort. These projects were discussed to the very end of the Julian Age—in sermons in the Sistine Chapel and in Santa Maria del Popolo; in the papal bull (25 July 1511) announcing the Fifth Lateran; in any number of diplomatic dispatches and reports. The mission of conquest in the West and the East had become no less apostolic than princely or imperial.

The same could be said of papal administration in the city of Rome and the Church at large. The pope's menacing stick became "the sacred rod of justice" in the eyes of one contemporary, who added that it had always been used "to acquire and maintain the welfare of the Holy Roman Church." Julius issued some

40 papal bulls, more than his three immediate predecessors combined. Reform of the religious orders
was a special preoccupation. Despite his own dubious election, strongly worded provisions against
simony were announced on at least two occasions. In
his presence and in the words read in his name at the
first session of the Lateran Council the desperate
need for reform was openly and eloquently recognized. Julius appeared not as an emperor but as the
canonist-pope Gregory IX on the south wall of the
Stanza della Segnatura (Plate 6). A medal probably
struck in connection with his peace with his rebellious Roman subjects in 1511 adopted the biblical
phrase "Justice and peace now embrace" (Psalms
85:10). The unfinished Palace of Justice which would
have consolidated judicial institutions on the pope's
model street, the new Via Giulia, was a project as
much in the spirit of an Old Testament priest and
king as of a Roman emperor. (Ever ready with an
analogy, Giles of Viterbo called Julius another Solomon and David.) It may tell us something about
the importance of the holy lawgiver's role to the
pope that the building would have been second in
size only to the Belvedere and St. Peter's in the sacred precincts of the Vatican.

In the milieu and in the subject of Raphael's portrait we have found worldly roles edging everywhere into spiritual ones. Classical forms carried
Christian convictions; images from mythology and
Scripture or from history, ancient and medieval,
figured and prefigured the unfolding of divine pur-

poses. This synthesizing kind of spirituality seems perfectly consistent with our suggestion that certain details shown on the London panel can be referred as much to the sacred as to the profane callings of the pope. So much so that we have only to go a little farther to suspect that the multi-levelled conception and, for want of a better word, the "mood" of the portrait rested in very fundamental ways on the religious outlook which seems to have prevailed in Julian circles.

One of the overriding characteristics of the faith articulated by preachers, theologians, and writers close to the pope was the ideal of continuity and unity in time and in type. Julian Rome and very often Pope Julius himself were understood to represent and to embody the holy cities and the divine messengers of the old and new dispensations. All roads did lead to Rome, the New Jerusalem, and all preordained roles to the pope, the new Adam; in the city and through God's vicar what had been established and gradually revealed from the beginning of time would be fulfilled. Cajetan, Master General of the Dominicans, opened the second session of the Lateran Council (May 1512) with such comparisons. But one did not need to be a theologian to grasp what was being heard and, as it seemed, enacted in Julian Rome. For those in Julian circles not to see, or not to pretend, that there were many divinely charged dimensions of identity in the pope was more difficult.

Julius himself brought much of his willful urgency to this all-embracing spiritual mission. On his deathbed he spoke of his "martyrdom" as pope. According to one source, he had his reward, for "at his death he was adored as if he were a saint." Other reports added that he died "constant and strong toward God"; "with so much devotion and contrition that he seemed a saint"; as if his were "the true body of St. Peter." It is true that there is something of the canonical "good death"—of a pope in the final proof of piety or even of the old sinner saved in the nick of time—about these accounts. They convey something, too, of the religious aura inspired by power and good luck, especially in a Mediterranean culture used to associating the Hero and the Holy Man. On the other hand, the position of the pope and all his other *personae* hinged on his capacity to represent, channel, and use divine authority. Since doctrines that linked spirit and flesh were particularly important to validate the mystery of the pope's own powers, Julian piety and Julian art had good reason to feature such orthodox and mediating themes as the Incarnation, Transubstantiation, the Trinity, and the cult of the Virgin—vessel and symbol of revelation and the Church. To think of the *papa terribile* as a saint may offend nothing more than a quite peremptory squeamishness about the limits of what can be truly pious. What is certain is that in his piety, as in most things, Pope Julius was not one to be lukewarm or altogether conventional.

But the fervor of apocalyptic and millenarian zeal was another major current in Julian spirituality. Not only was history believed to have reached a fullness in Rome and in the pope; it was widely expected in Julian circles that history would end there. Visions of that glorious new time to emerge from turmoil and tribulation at the end of the old time run deep in Western consciousness; how deep in Renaissance Italy recent studies have finally been able to show. A wave of acutely anxious and hopeful expectation peaked around the turn of the Quattrocento. The mood of hope and fear gripped the powerful and the lowly. We know that men of learning and quite orthodox religion were affected as intensely as the marginally learned or the heretics real and imagined.

The signs were closely watched in Julian Rome. For the great troubles always foreseen in prophetic visions Julian seers could point to the continuing scourge of the foreign invader, the horror of a new schism impending in the Church, the threat of the Turk; any number of moral offenses and doctrinal failings (especially the Aristotelian denial of the soul's immortality) were always easy for prophets to turn up and to magnify in Renaissance Italy. The official pronouncement read in Julius's own name at the opening of the Fifth Lateran Council acknowledged that "every institution has collapsed" and "a great upheaval of morals has occurred." On the other hand, positive signs of renewal seemed to be drawing nigh on an unheard-of scale. A plenitude of peoples, time, and doctrine—always a mark of the coming millennium—could be read into the voyages of discovery, the conquests of Pope Julius, and the Fifth Lateran Council, which together, it was believed, presaged the conversion of the en-

tire world and the return of the true faith to its
roots in the East. The days before the millennium
were supposed to witness battles to end all battles
against the Unbeliever—as perhaps, in the Great
Crusade preached under Pope Julius. In the flour-
ishing restoration of learning, literature, and art
Rome seemed to have become once more the *caput
mundi,* ready again for the mission millenarian
traditions had assigned to the Holy City even from
Etruscan times to the Julian Age. If there was to
be an angelic pope to lead the elect or an antipope
to resist them, his identity could hardly have been
in doubt.

The insistent themes of spiritual ripeness and
apocalyptic intensity found their most powerful expression in the great fresco cycles of Julian Rome.
Raphael's own frescos in the *Stanza della Segnatura*
(1508–11) united and integrated the major spokesmen of wisdom from past to present in the continuous quest for knowledge through reason, revelation,
poetic inspiration, and law. Their very presence in
what was evidently Julius's private library attested to
the return of a Golden Age of understanding delivered from the beginning of time to the Vatican and
the pope, who himself appeared in the guise of one,
probably two, of his greatest predecessors. On a
tremendous scale Michelangelo's Sistine Ceiling
(1508–12) began with the Creation and summarized
the history of mankind "before the Law" to form,
according to standard Christian chronology, a continuous sequence with the earlier Sistine frescos beneath illustrating the eras "under the Law of Moses"

and "under the Grace of Christ." Leading up to the message of providential continuity, the lunettes and spandrels depicted in alternating pairs the unbroken lineage of Christ from Abraham to Joseph; above them Old Testament prophets and pagan sybils saw signs of salvation yet to come. The enormous panels from the Book of Genesis in the center continued the tale of the future in the story of the most distant past. Man fell into original sin, death, and disgrace in the *Temptation of Adam,* the *Flood,* and the *Drunkenness of Noah.* But there was hope in the Days of Creation and the visionary prophets and sybils. Many references to water, wine, and redeeming acts of sacrifice and penance suggested the promise of salvation through the sacraments. The presence of paired couples, children, and greening garlands, hills, and vines hinted everywhere at regeneration. The enemies of the true faith were undone on the accompanying medallions and pendentives, nowhere more violently than in the pendentive figures painted in 1511–12. The commonplace association of Eve with the Virgin and of the Virgin with the Church made the *Creation of Eve* at the very center of the vault the fulcrum of a salvific history: the institution of the Church was already prefigured in the founding of the human race.

Although completed in part after the death of Pope Julius, the murals by Raphael for the *Stanza d'Eliodoro* (1511–14) were the most explicit visual machine of the Julian outlook. In the vault, Old Testament histories alluded to Christ's incarnation, sacrifice, redemption, and foundation of the Church;

scenes in *grisaille* were taken mostly from the Arch of Constantine, as if to link the divine plan with the Roman empire. The window embrasures showed Constantine and Pope Sylvester founding the *respublica christiana,* challenges to the authority of Christ, and the final challenge and triumph of the Apocalypse. The walls themselves began with the Old Testament (*Expulsion of Heliodorus from the Temple of Jerusalem*) and continued counterclockwise to the New Testament (*Liberation of St. Peter*), the Early Christian Era (*Repulse of Attila*), and the Middle Ages (*Miracle of the Mass of Bolsena*). In each case divine intervention came to the aid of priest or apostle, moving clockwise against the direction of "mere" human chronology. In each case the bearded Julius (or a surrogate) was a participant in the action or an observer. The panorama of time played itself out in and for the *papa terribile;* foreshadowing his aspirations, his trials, and his victories, history projected through him into the future. In Raphael's *Sistine Madonna* (c. 1512–13) Julius's apotheosis was complete (Plate 28).

We could continue in detail. The blend of late medieval, pro-papal, and (from Florentine circles) humanist versions of a rapidly approaching fullness of time pervaded Julian culture and Julian art. Clearly we are not dealing with two opposing outlooks—medieval prophecies of gloom versus Renaissance optimism hailing the new Golden Age. For many in Julian circles great tribulation and great beatitude seemed juxtaposed in history and in their own experience.

But we may already feel that we have somehow seen this perspective at work before. A sense of trial but of deep-seated faith in blessings soon to come would very nearly describe the characterization of Pope Julius by Raphael. Was there not a profound cultural and, ultimately, a profound religious resonance to the intense expectation *and* weary dejection we see in Raphael's *Julius?*

Erasmus would have none of this—or rather, his Renaissance dreams of renewal and his ideal Church were cast in another mold. In his Julian dialogue St. Peter countered every defense. Pope Julius protested that "the whole Christian state would collapse if it could not protect itself against the power of its enemies"; it would have been better, retorted St. Peter, if Christendom could see in its head "the true gifts of Christ—namely, holiness of life, sacred learning, burning love, prophecy, virtues. . . . " Julius spoke of enlarging, adorning, defending the greatness of the Church; St. Peter of "earthly sway," "destructive wars," runaway pleasures, extravagance, vice. If Julius was so mighty, challenged the saint, let him take his gang of men and hoarded wealth to build a new paradise. There was little room for compromise—perhaps there still is not. *Tout comprendre, c'est tout pardonner* has probably never been a very true or possible principle.

What we can suggest, and see in the papal roles reflected in Raphael's portrait, is the pressure of historical circumstances and aspirations. Over the long term the popes responded to a deteriorating political

and economic situation for the Church by taking a
princely part in the affairs of Italy. They drew support from late medieval and Renaissance theories of
papal monarchy and from the political example, the
legal structure and the lore of imperial Rome. The
sense of continuity from the Roman empire not only
legitimized papal claims to universal sovereignty and
plenitude of power; it also ensured that, as the recovery of the literary and artistic remains of antiquity accelerated, the propaganda campaign waged
in defense of the papacy would be increasingly
clothed in the form and imbued with much of the
spirit of imperial Rome. But the spiritual authority
and sacred mystique of the Roman Church and the
papal institution, newly charged with millenarian
zeal, were never far from the roles assumed by Renaissance popes. At few moments could the stakes
have seemed higher or the pope's mission as prince,
emperor, and high priest more compelling than in
1511–12. Not the least of the miracles of the Julian
age was that Raphael and Pope Julius undertook
their portrait encounter in that fullness of time.

3

The Setting and Functions
of a Renaissance Portrait

We first hear of what must have been the London
panel when, early in September 1513, a portrait of
Pope Julius was displayed for eight days on the altar
of Santa Maria del Popolo (Plate 29). The Venetian
ambassador who is our source tells us that the pope
had commissioned the likeness sometime before his
death eight months earlier and had given it to the
church of the Augustinian friars. There the ambassador left it, as art historians have by and large been
content to do. But the church of Santa Maria del
Popolo was not neutral wallspace, simply one
church among the 300-odd churches of Renaissance
Rome lucky enough to receive a random gift from
the pope. Many of the deepest concerns of Pope
Julius and his age led to and from the Popolo. In its
physical fabric and in its significance the church became a Julian temple, sanctuary, showcase, and theater. To preserve, museums deprive art of its original setting and function. To confirm and extend
what Raphael's *Julius* has already let us see in the
Julian world, we must try to restore it to the place
it has lost.

Between 1506 and 1512, Pope Julius came to Santa Maria del Popolo on several notable occasions. His first campaign for the recovery of papal territories as far north as Bologna was launched there on 26 August 1506, and there the victorious expedition ended on the vigil of his Palm Sunday procession to the Vatican, 27 March 1507. Four years later (26 June 1511) the bearded Julius reentered Rome at the Popolo from his second campaign in the north, this time defeated by the French and deprived of Bologna. The Virgin (it was thought) had delivered him from a cannon shot, a near miss, on the front lines at Mirandola, and in her church at the gates of Rome Julius offered prayers in which downcast passion and expectant faith must have been mixed—as they seem to be in the closely contemporary London portrait.

Two key maneuvers in his strategy for revenge brought the pope to the church again during the following months. On 5 October 1511 the Popolo resounded with the solemn proclamation of the Holy League which united Julius, Ferdinand of Spain, the Venetians, and, a few weeks later, Henry VIII of England against the French. Then, after the surprise retreat of a winning but shattered French army from Ravenna, the virtual collapse of the French-inspired Council at Pisa, and the sacrifice of the emperor's Venetian enemies to papal *Realpolitik,* the church served to stage the ceremonial adhesion of the Emperor Maximilian to the League on 25 November 1512. In the time between the great public spectacles we know that, early in September 1508, Julius appeared in the Popolo as a grieving and tearful pilgrim to appeal for the recovery of his favorite nephew Galeotto della Rovere from what turned out to be a fatal illness. During the same general period the pope must have come as patron to inspect Bramante's new choir (c. 1505–10), with its ensemble of tombs, frescos, stained glass, and, eventually, the *Madonna of the Veil* and his own portrait by Raphael.

While Pope Julius drew on Santa Maria del Popolo at the high points of his reign and the low, from public ceremonies to private devotions, the Popolo drew from him in turn the impulses we have come to expect in his presence. Certainly the individualism we have seen before was on full display there. The diary of his master of ceremonies was a perfect foil. Paris de'Grassis, with his hovering valet's eye, was quite sure to note good form and equally certain to grumble if Julius chose to have his own way. When the pope broke with convention, it was sometimes because, in life as in art, the nature of the case and good sense required it. For example, he would have preferred Matthäus Lang, the imperial ambassador on whom so much depended in November 1512, to accept the proper dignity and attire of a cardinal— Lang's reward for the emperor's adherence to the League. But the ambassador, self-important like his master, and wanting to be wooed, arrived at the Popolo in his ordinary bishop's robes. How could he possibly be seated among the assembled cardinals, wondered the harassed master of ceremonies? "Why not!" demanded the pope, and there, over the pro-

tests of Messer Paris and offended dignitaries, the affair of the ambassador's new clothes ended. At other
moments Julius remade ritual in the Popolo because
it was his prerogative to do so. His entourage could
only murmur in consternation on the eve of Palm
Sunday 1507 when he saw fit to bless not the cross
but the altar of the Virgin—where his portrait would
be placed. Again, he could order the church decorated with fronds of palm and olive branches to suit
the occasion or, in November 1512, adapt the liturgy
so that prayers would be said for the Holy Spirit, for
himself, and for the emperor. He could be the model
pilgrim at the Popolo nevertheless, distributing alms
to the friars, humbly petitioning their prayers for his
nephew. These actions will not seem out of character
in the subject of Raphael's *Julius*.

At Santa Maria del Popolo, too, the particular, and
particularly mixed, roles of a Renaissance pope were
intensely exposed. A princely Julius arrived at the
church for his Palm Sunday vigil of 1507 as Raphael
would show him, in *mozzetta* and *rocchetto*. Only
when a stole replaced the red cape at the church door
was it quite clear that he was a priest; to the obvious
relief of his master of ceremonies the *Te Deum
Laudamus* could then be sung within. The next day
the pope heard Palm Sunday Mass before proceeding
in triumph to St. Peter's. Palm fronds and olive
branches filled the church; Bramante's romanizing
choir was rising at the end of Sixtus IV's nave, one
of the prototypes for which was the Basilica of
Maxentius and Constantine—the presumed "Temple
of Peace" commemorating the Emperor Vespasian's

victory over Jerusalem. Through recollections of Jerusalem and imperial Rome, the church became a symbolic sign and seat of the union of both divinely chosen cities in the greater empire of Christ and His vicar. The long-standing Della Rovere connection and the family's monuments hinted in no uncertain terms at dynastic claims to this inheritance. It comes as no surprise that Julius's Palm Sunday procession to the Vatican fused the reenactment of Christ's entry into Jerusalem with the pageantry of an emperor's triumph in Rome.

But there was also room for the pious priest in Pope Julius at the Popolo, particularly for his devotion to the Virgin. It was the Virgin's altar that he blessed in March 1507, and it was to her he turned to heal his nephew (Plates 29–30). In June 1511, no matter how late the hour or how dispirited the papal party, Julius paused to kiss the cross at the door to the church and offer prayers at the altar before retiring for the night. Against this background, much about the portrait Raphael was soon to paint suddenly comes clear in ways that will need to be considered in some detail. It may suffice for now to point out that the week of early September 1513 when the portrait appeared on the altar was the octave of the Nativity of the Virgin. The old devotee had thus returned, "as if he were alive," to witness and to share the reverence due his great protectress.

Julius made what was probably his last appearance in the flesh at Santa Maria del Popolo on 25 November 1512 to celebrate the reception of the emperor into the Holy League. The ceremony was the occasion for Giles of Viterbo's valedictory to the Julian Age. Fifty-two diplomatic envoys and fifteen cardinals, including the obstinate imperial ambassador, filled Bramante's choir to the right and the left of the pope and in front of the altar. The Augustinian general introduced his theme: in the hour of darkest calamities yet had God worked a great liberation of his Church. Schism had raised its serpent's head at Pisa; the massed forces of the League had been overwhelmed at Ravenna by the basilisk of war, and Rome itself had trembled in the fear that God had abandoned His people. In this very night before Creation, this gloom of unenlightened souls to which the Platonists and St. John the Evangelist bore witness, only "Julius Pontifex Maximus, with all the firmness of his [oak] tree, never ceased to bear his burden, never gave in. He, following the example of Almighty God, whose place he occupies, said 'Let there be light. . . . ' " The calling of the Lateran Council was like the light of Creation on the First Day; the condemnation of the schismatic Pisan council took the place of the creation of the sky and the separation of the waters on the Second Day. The Third Day brought forth the fruits of the earth as the third session of the council produced the first harvest of a Church trusting to the power of its sanctity. To Rome, in the Holy City, the message was proclaimed: *fugit impius nemine persequente.* Now, as at the midpoint of Creation when the sun was made, the Holy League had gathered in the temple of the Mother of the Greatest Son, and the work of reform and renewal would beam from the Lateran Council with His light.

Near the end of his oration Giles turned to Julius himself. The pope and the emperor had joined to bring about a New Age of unity and peace, but there could be no mistake about the location of supreme authority, and the last word:

All men have seen you choosing nothing if not great deeds, acting against the unjust, the robbers, the tyrants, constructing eternal edifices, raising up the admirable mass of the temple, adding to the Holy See so much territory, so many peoples, so many splendid cities. And although these things might seem altogether great in themselves, how much greater still are those gifts which Almighty God has this year granted to you to overwhelm those two monsters which, striking out among peoples, had almost brought Italy and the Church to perish— Schism, I say, and War. . . .

O new day! O longed for day—never before seen by our ancestors, as never to be believed by posterity and its children! Who, I ask, does not see that God has never given any other Pontiff such deeds to perform as to you?

Such phrases, among the last Pope Julius was to hear in Santa Maria del Popolo, might well have been spoken of his portrait in the church. Light contrasted with the dark, despair close to deliverance, authoritative traditions adapted creatively to the present, a pope made out to be the special object and the summation of divine Providence once and for all time—the words of Giles and brush of Raphael worked strikingly similar effects.

The particular suspended moment of Raphael's *Julius* had passed before Giles began to speak, but not the character of the pope, the perspective of his culture, and the stimulus of his special church.

But why the special attachment to Santa Maria del Popolo? We know enough by now about the retrospective sweep of Julian culture to be sure that the answer must begin far back in the history of Rome.

At the base of the Pincian Hill, near the Flaminian Gate at the northern edge of the city, the site of Santa Maria del Popolo was steeped in memories of imperial Rome. These traditions had become, if anything, more vivid and more compelling in the course of the Quattrocento. It was not so much the medieval myth maker as the Renaissance antiquarian who transmitted tales of the Emperor Nero buried in the vineyard where the altar of the church was to stand; or the more historical picture of candidates for imperial office passing the site in white robes on their ritual descent from the Pincio. Renaissance accounts continued, too, the kind of exorcism which, in medieval legends, had turned such ground to Christian and specifically papal purposes. When medieval Rome receded to cluster close-knit around the River Tiber, the site was left a rural outpost, guarding the gate, marking boundaries, channeling the passage between the city and the world. It was territory which had to be resettled physically and reclaimed spiritually by the people and the bishop of Rome.

The name and the early history of the church reflected this dual reclamation. *Popolo* derived most likely from the term (*pieve* or *plebs*) for rural parish churches staking out Christian space in areas unsettled or adjacent to older civic centers in the early Middle Ages. But the legends of the place were no less revealing. One tradition related the naming of the church to an appeal by the Roman people that the pope rid the site of the demons molesting settlers near and travellers through the Flaminian Gate. Then, there was the association with a nearby poplar tree or grove, the *pioppo,* which became in the fullest elaboration of the legend a sinister nut tree growing from the bones of Nero. In 1099, according to a fifteenth-century text, the Romans went to Paschal II seeking relief from these afflictions. The pope prayed with all his clergy to God and the Blessed Virgin. On the third night the Virgin appeared to him, commanding that the tree be cut down and a church to her honor be founded in its place—which in grand procession and ceremonies at the spot was done to the dismay of the Enemy. Pope Paschal raised with his own hands an altar to the Virgin; he endowed it with indulgences and relics, among them relics of the Virgin and St. Sixtus (and so of the chief saints of Sixtus IV and Julius II). In the thirteenth century, the account continued, Gregory IX (again the pope whose part Julius took in Raphael's *Segnatura* fresco; Plate 6) brought to the place one of those miracle-working icons supposedly painted by St. Luke. The Virgin of the Popolo (Plate 30) continued to work her Julian miracles nearly 300 years later, the power of her church enhanced by relics of her dress, veil, hair, and milk.

By the fifteenth century, on the strength of much legend and a little history, Santa Maria del Popolo was a link to traditions of the empire, the people, and the bishops of Rome, a gatehouse to the material and the spiritual city, a junction point of Marian majesty and miracles. To these attributes Sixtus IV and the Della Rovere set about making claims for themselves in the manner of the restoration-minded culture of Renaissance Rome. So much the better that the medieval church-with-cloister seems, in contrast to the site, to have been undistinguished. It suited the stylish new magnificence of the upstart clan of Ligurians to borrow prestige without encumbrances. Between about 1472 and 1480 Pope Sixtus rebuilt the church from the foundations up—or at any rate altogether transformed it.

Among his motives there is no reason to doubt that the Virgin came first. We would expect as much from the old Franciscan whose mother had told of dreams of Mary summoning him to the Order (Plate 31). Francesco della Rovere had made much of his reputation as a polished theologian in writings on the Immaculate Conception; as pope, he granted privileges to the cult of the Virgin at the Popolo—two of them were inscribed on either side of the principal entrance—and built other churches and altars for her. "Moved by piety and the singular devotion he had always toward the Blessed Virgin he erected from the foundation the church of Santa Maria del Popolo"—the original inscription on a fresco celebrating the building of the church made the Marian motive quite explicit (Plate 32). Other motives could not have been far behind for the papal monarch, dynast, and self-styled *Restaurator Urbis*. The family needed, in effect, their pantheon, mausoleum, and royal chapel, where their piety might be treasured up in this life and for the next. If Rome was to see new days as *caput mundi* under the Della Rovere, then the Via Flaminia and Santa Maria del Popolo were a necessary artery and northern lobe. This was the route of pilgrims, supplies, and the expected reconquest of papal territory. With overtones of rising millenarian expectancy, another commemorative inscription suggested that pious works such as building the Popolo also "prepared the way for the kingdom of Heaven."

Buildings are often deceptive, but Renaissance applications of the supposedly modern principle that "form follows function" may not be at all irrelevant at Santa Maria del Popolo. The Sistine church, much obscured by later additions, was a three-aisled, vaulted basilica in the form of a Latin cross, with an octagonal drum and cupola at the crossing and polygonal chapels extending off the side aisles (Figs. 1–4). For a family reliquary and mausoleum Sixtus could not have done better than to commission the side chapels, the first in Renaissance Rome to be designed as an integral part of the structure. Before the end of the first Della Rovere pontificate three members of the family occupied the chapels under monuments built in the best instant classicism of the Roman funerary style. Perhaps the half octagons of the chapels and the full octagon of the cupola-bearing drum over the crossing were employed to convey the traditional association of the eight-sided figure with the eight days of Christ's passion and

1. Rome, Santa Maria del Popolo. Facade, c. 1477.

2. The Sistine Nave, c. 1472–80.

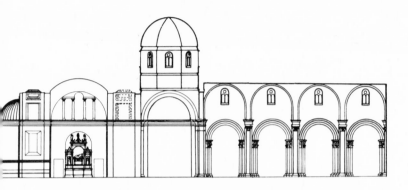

3. Section of Santa Maria del Popolo as it appeared in the reign of Julius II.

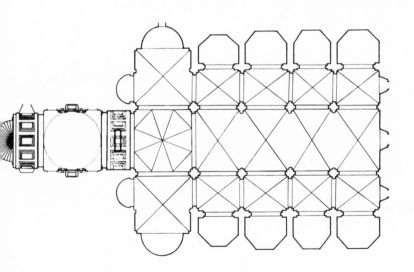

4. Plan of the Sistine Church with the Julian additions of c. 1505–10.

5. Rome, Santa Maria del Popolo. The Julian Choir, 1505–10.

resurrection. Domes were a standard architectural
metaphor for the vault of heaven, where Della Rovere dead surely expected their reward. Symbolically
or not, the dome of the Popolo, the first of the Renaissance in Rome and the first glimpse of the city
for travellers from the north, was obviously calculated to impress. So was the pure (and purloined)
Roman articulation of the interior. Augustinian
churches in Lombardy probably influenced the plan,
but in Della Rovere hands the church became a

monument to the New Rome, the Virgin, and themselves.

In 1509, Francesco Albertini's new Roman guidebook saluted Pope Julius in phrases which fairly describe his own apparent intentions at Santa Maria del Popolo: "Sixtus IV began the restoration of the City, his successors followed in his footsteps, but your Holiness has outstripped them all." Julius was very much the good *nipote* when, around 1505, he began where his uncle had left off—at the choir. The dating and sequence of the additions and extensions to the choir are not altogether certain between the general dates 1505 and 1510. We are not sure to what extent the project evolved by steps or was conceived as a totality by Bramante, Julius's premier architect and chief artistic adviser during this period. What is clear, and consistent with Della Rovere traditions, is that Julius concentrated on the area of the Virgin's altar and the rites performed in her honor. Julian patronage also developed the Roveresque concern for the funerary function of the church and, as Sixtus had done at the Popolo and elsewhere, brought together a team of the best artists available for the undertaking. It was as much the family as the Julian manner, too, for the outcome to fuse a classicizing style and vocabulary with conservative Christian symbolism and iconography.

Bramante's project moved from a barrel-vaulted space off the crossing to a square mausoleum area before ending in the choir proper, with its own coffered barrel vault and scallop-shell apse (Figs. 3–5).

The first barrel vault contained the Virgin's altar, behind which, under the second vault, Julius apparently sat for the ceremonies of November 1512. Between the vaults, the mausoleum was designed with the central plan and geometrical harmony equivalent to divine perfection and eternity in Renaissance architectural theory. Two facing tombs were commissioned for the niches of this center section (Plates 33–34). Here Julius buried his nephew and adopted son Cardinal Girolamo Basso della Rovere (d. 1507) and, with a gesture of magnanimity and political calculation, an old enemy, Cardinal Ascanio Sforza (d. 1505). Sforza support from Milan was an important consideration in any papal strategy in northern Italy, but Julius could afford to be magnanimous, since Cardinal Ascanio, who had provided for the church shortly before his death, died intestate, so that the pope was entitled to his inheritance in accordance with canon law.

For the Julian building campaign, too, despite recent arguments for earlier origins, Bramante seems to have constructed a low-hanging sail vault over the altar in order to create more prominent space for frescos by Pinturicchio. Whether included in the original design or added as a brilliant afterthought, three-part windows *all'antica* were used to penetrate the wallspace between vault and tombs and light the ensemble. The choir itself occupied a rectangular space of its own, yet provided tombs and altar with an appropriate visual and functional backdrop. The barrel vaults, with their Pantheonlike coffering, established a triumphal and specifically Roman passageway to the great scallop shell of the apse, with its classical and early Christian allusions to redemption and eternal life.

These themes were fully elaborated in the more or less traditional and predominantly Marian iconography of the tombs, windows, and vault. In the central lunettes over the tombs, the Virgin and Child mediated between God the Father and the reclining effigies surrounded by personifications of the cardinal and theological virtues (Plates 33–34). Placed as if to intercede for the dead cardinals by reason of the attributes figuratively claimed for them, Mary was represented as the model of their love and substituted, in fact, for the otherwise missing virtue of charity; she was also the symbolic object of their love and, again, the channel of grace between heaven and earth. All the other elements of the tombs expressed a similar conjunction, or transition, between the material and spiritual worlds. The effigies seemed to hover between life and death. Used in funerary contexts since antiquity, the shells, the flaming candelabra, and the swags and vines bore witness to the triumph of death—but also to the anticipation of immortality, light, and renewed life. Decorated with angels and cherubim, the arched forms of the tombs designated the way of release from terrestrial existence and the triumphal entrance into paradise. Even the bold signature of the sculptor centered on each tomb boasted of earthly skill in a bid for eternal fame.

Links between spirit and flesh were likewise the traditional message of the episodes from the lives of the Virgin and of Christ narrated in the stained glass windows (Plates 35–36). The narrative unfolded in two rows arranged in chronological sequence from left to right. The top band of the Virgin cycle—*The Meeting at the Golden Gate, The Birth of the Virgin, The Presentation of the Virgin*—illustrated the birth and sanctification of Mary as the instrument of divine love. Incarnation was the theme of the lower band—*The Marriage of the Virgin, The Annunciation, The Visitation of the Virgin and St. Elizabeth.* In the Christ cycle of the window opposite, all three of the upper scenes referred to the Nativity, while the incidents beneath prefigured the essential aspects of Christ's redemptive purpose. Christ was first consecrated in the *Presentation in the Temple; Christ among the Doctors* marked the beginning of his teaching and preaching mission. The central episode, *The Flight into Egypt,* was understood in standard exegesis to foreshadow Christ's sacrifice and ultimate salvation. Needless to say, the patron did not conceal his contribution or implied connection to the glittering lesson in light. The coat of arms, the oak, and the name of Pope Julius appeared prominently in both windows.

On the vault the sybils painted by Pinturicchio revealed their prophecies (Plate 37). The accompanying inscriptions told of the incarnation and redemption foreseen long before the Advent: "The invisible Word will become known"; "The offspring of the Virgin will be the salvation of mankind"; "The Son of God will become flesh and judge the world"; "In the last age God will become man." The four sybils were combined with the four evangelists, who were complemented in turn by the four Latin doctors of the Church—Ambrose, Jerome, Augustine, and Gregory. The message of salvation, ordained from the beginning and valid for all time, could thus be seen in its passage through the pagan mysteries, the revealed truth of the gospels, and the authoritative interpretation of the Church Fathers. At the center of the vault the *Coronation of the Virgin* showed the resolution of the distance between spirit and flesh when the human creature became divine.

Marian and family space, a self-conscious adaptation of antiquity to Christian uses—the requirements of the good nephew were well met at the Popolo. Concern for precedent extended into matters of detail. The new choir seems, for example, to extend and complete the interior of the Quattrocento church, for a massive apse and tripartite Serlian windows figured in Renaissance renderings of the "Temple of Peace" quite as much as in structural features appearing in the Sistine nave. The new tombs echoed the style of the earlier tombs. The octagonal aperture for the *Coronation of the Virgin* at the center of Pinturicchio's frescos on the sail vault repeated the shape of drum and cupola over the crossing, and the artist of the vault was the painter of the decoration in the family chapels.

But the dutiful heir followed precedent only so far. The scale and style of the choir showed up the Sistine church for its rather halting classicism. In important respects the new choir did not even need the old church. The Julian additions could be perceived as virtually self-sufficient through any number of formal devices—the closed symmetry of the two tombs sharing the cardinal virtues and linked by the orientation of the effigies to the apse; the repetition of a tripartite structure in the tombs, the high altar, and the windows; the diagonal turn of the fresco layout to join the burial spaces; the self-referencing response of the niches of the four doctors of the Church frescoed in the vault to the niches of altar, tomb, and apse; the reappearance of the four doctors on the altar and the vault. St. Luke shown on the vault painting an image of the Virgin implied a link to the actual icon on the altar beneath. Balance, rhythmic variation, and subtle modulations of tone unified and animated the overall composition. The symbolic content reflected the liturgical functions of altar and choir in the themes of death, sacrifice, salvation, and immortality.

Building on and yet out from tradition, then, new standards were set in the choir. Bramante's architecture was a pace-setting essay in the evocation of antique space and form. Testing Renaissance conceptions of universally authoritative principles of design, his work became a scale model of many elements in the choir for the new St. Peter's. Sansovino's development of basic Florentine prototypes became the norm in funerary monuments for the rest of the century. In the final design (1542–45) for the tomb of Pope Julius himself the new motif of the half-reclining effigy poised ambiguously between life and death was adopted by Michelangelo. Marcillat's stained glass introduced French standards of excellence in a medium which had been little known in

Rome. Raphael and his followers departed from Pinturicchio's archaeological reconstruction of Roman ceiling decoration. The impressive integration of media—architecture, sculpture, and painting—looked forward to Raphael's Chigi Chapel in the Popolo and far beyond it to the Baroque.

We can now return to Raphael's *Julius* with a very full sense of its setting in time and space. The portrait dates from the period between the completion of Pope Julius's new choir at Santa Maria del Popolo and his culminating appearance there, for God and the Holy League, on 25 November 1512. The painting signalled, accordingly, the end of commitments beginning early in his reign and, still earlier, in the generation before him; it signalled, too, the beginning of the end of the Julian Age. More than merely marking time, however, Raphael's *Julius* was marked in turn by much of what was believed and enacted in the physical and chronological space to which it once belonged. As Raphael made him out to be, so Julius often was, or seemed, in his special church. What remains to be suggested is that the relationship between portrait and setting was not a passive connection; that the portrait, if it was acted upon, was also an actor with supporting roles to play. For like the places for which they were made, Renaissance portraits had functions to perform.

It is true that we do not really know where Raphael's portrait hung. Our closest reference puts the papal likeness and gift on the altar for the Feast of the Nativity of the Virgin shortly after the death

of the pope. That is all—just enough to imply that
the position was temporary. At least for the high
holiday of the Nativity we can picture the image at
the place of honor on the Virgin's right, which is to
say, somewhere to the left of the icon in the center
of the altar (Plates 29–30). The next references, from
the 1540s and later, seem to confirm the occasional
hanging for feast days, now on a pillar, apparently
paired opposite Raphael's *Madonna of the Veil* (Plate
3). We could wish, as patron and painter might well
have done, for a still more Julian location. At the
center of Bramante's apse, under the shell-shaped
symbol of immortality, the portrait would have been
highly visible on axis with the altar. Like Julius himself in November 1512, his image would have pre-
sided over prayers from the apse and would have
been situated to receive them; it would also have
been ideally lighted by windows on the upper right,
as if by design, the *only* apsidal windows. In the
empty wreath now at the crown of the apse a Julian
insignia could have labelled the subject of the picture
and the builder of the choir. The fit seems perfect.
Unfortunately, it also seems quite unlikely, since
the migration to the altar for feast days would hardly
have been necessary with the portrait already in so
central and conspicuous a position. Other papal portraits are known to have hung in sacristies, and we
are left, however reluctantly, to imagine Raphael's
Julius hanging in the sacristy of the Popolo on all but
special occasions.

Still, the brief appearance on the altar had its Julian
touch. So far as we know, it was unprecedented to

locate such a portrait on an altar. Or rather, this was still another Julian (and Raphaelesque) leap from precedents and purposes which conditioned the meaning of the commission.

A patron was entitled to be noticed before his works. In *his* choir, in *his* family's favorite church, Julius took his place in Raphael's portrait as patron and donor. The portrait reinforced coats of arms and inscriptions; it put the face of the individual and his roles on what was to be seen unmistakably as a Julian enterprise. Small wonder that we found ourselves tracing formal sources for Raphael's work to representations of donor types—Renaissance popes, French kings, Roman emperors, and Sixtus IV. Here again Renaissance form was probably following Renaissance function. With a difference, however. In the portrait at the Popolo the donor and the artist emerged on their own. Sponsoring saints have been dismissed; the donor, no longer reduced to appearing in profile, commanded the picture space. The object of the donation was outside, not within, the picture frame, and the portrait could be valued in itself and for its value as art.

Even so, Julius did not come to the Popolo simply as a high-spending and rather possessive patron of art; he came there as the special patron and client of the Virgin. Donor portraits sprang from the desire for salvation and the rather more tangible benefits expected from pious works, and there is every reason to believe that Raphael's *Julius* was no exception. Julius had put himself under the Virgin's care in painting before. As cardinal, he knelt before the Vir-

gin in the right wing of a provincial altarpiece
painted before 1484 by Giovanni Mazone (Plates
38–39). He was his uncle's creature, sharing the
hometown chapel of Sixtus IV in the Cathedral of
Savona. It was Sixtus's patron saints, Francis and
Anthony, who were shown, and it was Sixtus who
took the honorary place at Mary's right, receiving
the Christ Child's benediction and monopolizing the
light. The conventional kneeling posture and relatively small scale of the donor in a sacred presence
remained in another Savona polyptych by Vicenzo
Foppa, dated August 1490 (Plate 40). But Cardinal
Giuliano moved from joint to sole patron and
petitioner, from his uncle's chapel to the high altar,
from the wings into the central panel with Virgin
and Child. The place of honor and the light were
now his; advanced by his own angel, he alone received the attention and the benediction of Christ. In
effect (and as usual), Raphael simultaneously continued and went beyond the cues of tradition on the
London panel. In the church of the Virgin of the
Popolo and on her altar the likeness must have been
seen as the portrait of her donor and devotee, mag-
nified now in proportion and significance by the
papal office and Raphael's skill.

Raphael's portrait must have been, in fact, nothing
less than a votive image, one of a series of interlocking Julian offerings and acknowledgments to the
Virgin culminating only with Raphael's *Sistine
Madonna* (c. 1512; Plate 28). In 1473 the sculptor
Andrea Bregno completed the so-called Borgia Altarpiece to encase the miraculous icon at the Popolo

(Plate 29). The evidence for a Borgia commission is problematic, because it rests on the inconclusive testimony of much later documents and a pair of Borgia arms on a base which appears to have been added to the altar. It is at least as likely that the future Pope Julius may have begun to do his duty by the Virgin of the Popolo (and she by him) at the very outset of his career in Rome. Sixtus IV was just beginning his building campaign at the church in 1473—one year after the Virgin was believed to have interceded to halt an outbreak of plague and little more than a year after naming his nephew Giuliano a cardinal. The circumstances would have been right for a Della Rovere and a Julian gift to the altar. It is clear that the future pope made some sort of early claim on the miracle-working altar near the Flaminian Gate. For at the top of Bregno's work we find the coat of arms of none other than Cardinal Giuliano della Rovere.

Subsequent Julian transactions with the Virgin usually came back to the Popolo. As if in gratitude for his victories in the north, Pope Julius gave pontifical sanction in 1507 to the shrine of Loreto; in the same year he founded the church of Santa Maria di Loreto near Trajan's column in Rome. The Della Rovere had already revived the cult and opened accounts on the legend of the little town in the Marches where the house of the Virgin had miraculously appeared in the thirteenth century, delivered intact from the Holy Land. The Carmelites had been called to the spot by Cardinal Girolamo Basso della Rovere, bishop of nearby Recanati. Cardinal Girolamo had also received the dedication (1489) of

the official account of the miracle; in 1500 he had
completed the church Sixtus IV had begun to build
around the Holy House. It was this same Della Rovere nephew and adopted son whom Julius buried
beneath the Marian iconography of Sansovino's
tomb and Marcillat's stained glass in the choir of the
Popolo (Plates 34–35). And it was Bramante, architect of the still unfinished choirs at the Popolo
and St. Peter's—both dedicated to the Virgin—to
whom the pope entrusted both his plans for the
newly founded church in Rome and his wish "to do
great things" at Loreto.

The interchange between Rome and Loreto continued. As the project at the Popolo neared completion, work at Loreto began in earnest. New privileges
for the *Lauretana* were published in March 1509; later
that year a medal was issued with Bramante's design
for a new facade on one side and a profile of the
donor, *Iulius Ligurus Pontifex Maximus,* on the other.
Soon afterward, at the time of his second expedition
in northern Italy, Julius was alternately increasing
and drawing upon his credit with the Virgin in
Loreto and in Rome. Before marching north, he
made the long detour to the Marches. Celebrating
the Nativity of the Virgin in the church of the Holy
House, he gave the shrine a silver cross, a chalice,
and a special indulgence. On his return in June 1511,
again by way of Loreto, he hung on a silver chain
over the altar the cannon shot he believed the Virgin
had deflected at Mirandola. Then, as we have seen,
he carried his prayers to the Popolo in Rome. One
can easily imagine the bearded Julius intoning the

prayers attributed to him for the Queen of Heaven and Mercy.

This brings us just to the edge of the period between June 1511 and March 1512 when Raphael evidently painted the London panel. In June 1511 the pope had offered his gifts at Loreto *voti et devotionis causa;* in August he took the nourishment that brought him through his nearly fatal illness "out of love for the Madonna of Loreto." In December 1511 he gave a portrait of himself to San Marcello, a Roman church of the Servants of Mary, or Servites, "because of a vow made to an image of Our Lady." The obvious inference is that Julius also meant, "because of a vow," to add a portrait by Raphael to his offerings at one of the most important and familiar seats of the Virgin in Rome, to place himself by that famous "image of Our Lady" in which he had so much at stake. And since there is no further evidence to connect Raphael with San Marcello or to suggest any tradition of independent portraiture of Julius other than that stemming from the painter's work at the Popolo, the San Marcello likeness (apparently burned in a fire of 1519) was probably one of many copies after Raphael. If so, the Popolo's original must have been finished by December 1511.

Something of this tale is told, after all, by the portrait itself. The beard as a sign of mourning and of appeal, the expression of reflection and readiness— the features we have tried to characterize so often would take on a far more exact meaning as a specific offering for grace recently received and still urgently needed. Even the immediacy of the likeness would have been demanded in a votive image. To a Marian church such as the Annunziata in Florence thousands of lifelike effigies in wax and paint were presented at the altar by the humble and the great, including Sixtus IV. From no less a patron than Isabella Gonzaga or critic than Vasari we know that these likenesses were prized when "natural and so well made that they represent not men of wax, but life itself." There was no room for mistaken identities where such serious interests were concerned. In a votive setting, too, we can understand more clearly why Raphael's *Julius* appeared on the Virgin's altar, perhaps even why the portrait seems intentionally to respond to the presence of the icon. The oblique arrangement of the figure and the direction of light from the right side suggest as much; so do similarities in the disposition of head and torso, the linearity of fabric and hem, the counterpoint of closed and open hands, the rings (cf. Plates 2 and 30).

Starting from conventions in the imagery of dedication and donation, then, the pope and his painter defined a special relationship and a new equality with the Virgin and *her* painter. In the *Sistine Madonna* Julius knelt as an interceding St. Sixtus before the Virgin, finally occupying the same celestial space, as if sanctified by her dazzling display of power and special favor. It would be one more anticipation of this ultimate triumph over life through art if, as has sometimes been supposed, the *Julius* was meant to complement Raphael's slightly earlier *Madonna of the Veil* (c. 1508–9; Plate 3). The two paintings were very nearly the same size; they were strongly vertical in composition. The figures in each were obliquely turned as if to one another, and were lighted from the right and the left as if to be hung flanking the high altar and illuminated from the central dome. Both works were set off by a green background cloth; closed, cloth-holding right hands and open left hands figured in each. The eyes were similarly downcast, the expressions contemplative. We cannot tell whether the Child wakes or sleeps, whether the veil is a coverlet or shroud; we do not know whether Julius awaits deliverance or death in his portrait. These connections can be made on grounds of formal and iconographical relationships, similar date, identical place, and the documentary evidence of at least a later pairing from the 1540s onward. It is the functional logic of an encounter of patron and protectress, vicar and vessel of divinity, which supplies a missing motive.

Until Raphael's *Julius* was discovered to be by the hand of the master himself, it was relegated to the storerooms of the National Gallery. Now it hangs in a place of honor, an object of aesthetic devotion. In its own time and place the portrait was, as we have seen, much more than a work of art. Yet it was an object of devotion—of a Renaissance kind. In three-quarter length the image of the pope can be imagined whole only by the willing beholder. At Santa Maria del Popolo, beholder and worshipper merged in the crowd which, after the death of the *papa terribile,* admired his likeness "as if he were alive" and adored him "as if he were a saint." The very accessibility of Raphael's *Julius* must have mirrored its special setting and function.

Epilogue

The Julian Image and High Renaissance Culture in Rome

In order to understand the making of a masterpiece, a scholar in a tale by Jorge Luis Borges tried to re-write *Don Quixote* as if it had never been written, word for word. Anyone who has looked at all seriously at Raphael's *Julius* since its restoration ten years ago to something like its original brilliance will understand the fascination of the attempt, and why it must have failed.

A work of art is obviously something greater and other than the sum of its parts. For all their analyses, the wisemen of Hindustan, "to learning much inclined," still failed to see the elephant. The levels of our Renaissance likeness remain distinctions of analysis and of language, not those the eye or the artist would necessarily have made. We would dispense with them if we could. But of course we cannot. It does not matter how good our vision may be. We need analytical distinctions to differentiate and bring into focus what might otherwise remain indistinct or be altogether missed; we also need them because, in its actuality and immediacy, the making of a work of art is no more recoverable than the living experience of Pope Julius and Raphael. But we should not be satisfied with accepting bits and pieces in lieu of something whole. What we must try to do is see our portrait and our levels in the round, to consider how distinctions might be pieced together again. Although we cannot recreate the larger context of an original reality, we can create a larger context of interpretation. This is a fundamental task—and dilemma—of cultural history.

It is some help that we have been dealing with a work and a culture in which synthesis was a characteristic quality and often a quite deliberate aim. This synthetic aspect has taken many different forms at many different points in the preceding pages. Already at the outset we found that the individualism of Raphael's *Julius* was inclusive and integrating, not an exclusive or isolating trait. In formal and quite technical ways we saw that the painter seems to have drawn together motifs from various traditions of portraiture. Visually, the individualism of Raphael's work was synthetic twice over—a fusion of portrait types and an exercise of inventiveness on (and beyond) the available stock of precedents. Contemporaries who understood this in Raphael confirmed our own impressions and gave them a cultural rationale.

There were different emphases, but it was generally agreed, on the one hand, that true creativity was imitative and, on the other hand, that truly creative spirits would surpass received standards and respond to the unique challenges of nature and experience.

The creative process was a precarious balance between ideal and actual, convention and contingency, past and present. Extended to the reading of individual character, this view of things meant that any given individual was likely to be perceived not only as a particular person but also as an approximation to type. Physiognomical theory and practice reflected and encouraged this sort of double vision. So did prevailing philosophical and theological doctrines—for example, the conception made official at the Fifth Lateran Council that everyone possessed an individual soul which transcended nevertheless, by reason of its immortality, any particular temporal condition. Together with the intellectual justifications, the synthesizing thrust in Julian culture and in Raphael's portrait was sustained by the ideological and practical needs of the Renaissance papacy, developments in the practice of art and the premium that patrons were increasingly prepared to pay for artistic achievement. In this environment the best talent, the most advanced techniques, and the widest possible range of traditions could come together in Rome for what contemporaries themselves regarded as a fullness of time.

Looking to what we called the papal "roles" represented in Raphael's *Julius* or to the setting and function of his portrait at Santa Maria del Popolo, we saw this capacity for combinations everywhere. Julian culture was unwilling, or unable, to draw sharp distinctions where we would insist on them. Since the boundaries between sacred and profane, spirit and flesh, Christian and pagan were often blurred at best, it was perfectly possible for the pope to play prince, emperor, and priest. Conversely, since the pope did play a composite part, it was perfectly possible and even necessary for such lines to remain indistinct. Whether they liked it or not, contemporaries had come to expect as much of a pope. The staging, the masks, the language of this mixed identity had developed deep in the traditions and the history of the papal institution; Renaissance popes had learned to mobilize and so to exaggerate every possible defense in reaction to the challenges against papal authority during the fourteenth and fifteenth centuries. It was not so much the roles as the sweep, the intensity, and the extravagance of the performance that must have impressed Raphael not least among the contemporaries of Julius II. By returning his portrait of the pope to Santa Maria del Popolo we were able to locate that impression in a place and time where it was thoroughly and purposively exposed.

Of course all cultures and their artifacts are to some extent synthetic. It is a second quality in Julian culture which makes the characterization especially apt—the consciousness and actuality of a kind of cultural culmination in Julian Rome. Culmination does not necessarily mean conclusion; if it were a matter of endings, a better case might be made for the death of Leo X in 1521, the sack of Rome in 1527, or the years after midcentury when one can begin to speak of a Counter Reformation and eventually a Baroque Rome. What the term does suggest well enough is the sense of cultural fulfillment, of arrival, of accomplishments long since anticipated and finally reached. We have seen something like culmination in this sense in

Raphael's weaving together of different portrait styles at a level of integration and equilibrium that neither he nor any other Renaissance painter had ever achieved before. We saw, too, that this technical feat was accompanied and surely conditioned in turn by a fully mature awareness of some of its basic presuppositions. There was nothing new about the doctrine of imitation, the psychology, at once deductive and experimental, of physiognomical teachings, or the definition of man as creature and creator in the image of God. But these Renaissance commonplaces had never been articulated more completely, shared more widely, or used more actively than they were in Julian Rome.

The "real" world did not, for once, lag far behind. The revival of Rome and the papal Counter Revolution beginning early in the fifteenth century came to a head in the policies and power, if also in the vulnerability, of Julius's pontificate. The high standing and heady opportunities of the creative élite in Julian Rome brought Quattrocento possibilities to a new pitch. No wonder Julian culture dreamed of the greatest heights and depths in its myths of itself.

Synthesis and culmination . . . both are familiar but extremely problematic terms for characterizing High Renaissance culture. They imply conceptions of development and criteria of judgment as old as Vasari, or even as the Roman author Pliny, from whom Renaissance writers learned most about tracing the history of art and of culture more generally. In his *Lives,* Vasari interpreted what he was the first to call the *Rinascita* of the arts in Italy as a process of cumulative improvement handed down from one generation to the next. First in the Trecento, then in a second age during the Quattrocento, Italian artists had broken through the "darkness" and "decay" of the Middle Ages to the achievements of the Ancients. But the masters of the first two ages were only forerunners of still greater things to come from the third age of Leonardo, Raphael, and Michelangelo. "If [the former] were not altogether perfect," Vasari wrote, "they came so near the truth, that the third category . . . profited by the light they shed, and attained the summit of perfection. . . ." Studied reproduction of nature, proportion and design, lessons recovered from the best examples of ancient art—the results of two centuries of development were harmonized in the grand manner of the geniuses of the third age and elevated to such heights that "decline must now be feared rather than any further progress expected." The language has been changed, or only toned down and refined. The process no longer seems so clear or continuous or the outcome obviously authoritative. But at least for the first two High Renaissance or classical decades of the Cinquecento the Vasarian paradigm has survived more or less intact.

The problem with the traditional framework is not that it is *déjà vu*. The terrible verdict of a nineteenth-century reviewer—"What's true is not new; what's new is not true"—has lost none of its point in a time when the latest fad is only too likely to count for wisdom. If anything, like fashions old enough to become interesting again, the notion of a

Renaissance synthesis and culmination may even seem quite fresh and provocative. It challenges a modern loss of sympathy and touch with the formally balanced harmonies of rule and representation in classicizing traditions of Western culture. We no longer really care about the specific formal types developed in classical Greece and Rome and elaborated by generations of *epigoni*. The classics have become an excuse for nostalgia, or a subject for specialists, "archaeologists" in a general sense. We would no longer know a barbarian if we saw one. More than tastes have changed. It is the view of reality implicit in a classical style—ostensibly confident, orderly, and authoritative—which is profoundly at odds with whatever is restless, relativistic, and science-struck in the modern temper.

But the pride of place long enjoyed by High Renaissance culture and art has been undermined in quite specific ways. Art historians these days would hardly dare to dismiss Quattrocento artists as Pre-Raphaelites or Italian Primitives. Historians for their part have tended to push back the date of the greatest vitality and creativity in the Italian Renaissance to an ever earlier period. As a result, the picture of a society living off capital, losing its nerve, increasingly static and hollow by the later fifteenth century stands in the way of the trajectory toward perfection that once seemed so inevitable and so clear. And where the older view simply shrugged off or found enlightened benevolence in the authoritarian impulses of the later Renaissance, some historians have been inclined to limit the true flowering of the Renaissance spirit to what they regard as the relatively pluralistic and dynamic republican cultures of Florence and Venice. The aftermath of the High Renaissance has assumed a different aspect too. Both Vasari's sense of continuity and the once-fashionable charge of decadence after Raphael have given way, for example, to a general revaluation of Mannerism as an experimental and expressive style, or a series of styles, with close affinities to modern movements in the arts. One common impulse behind these shifts of outlook may be a belated, almost a vindictive, recognition that the Renaissance has lost its traditional historiographical standing as the origin and Heroic Age of the modern world.

We are probably better for the loss. It forces us to look again and calls for a renewed sense of inquiry where few questions used to be asked or needed. The old assumptions of virtually inevitable progress to a determined end can certainly go unlamented. As the case of Raphael's portrait should suggest, it is the contingency and complexity of a cultural artifact that make it historically rich and revealing. We can also dispense with the secular orientation, the academic taste, and the high-minded idealism so often characteristic of the grand tradition of criticism. Had we supposed that the Julian world was rather unmindful of traditional religion or altogether committed to a new view of man as the measure of all things, we might have missed the intensity of conventional, even archaic, religious content and purposes in Raphael's work and the culture in which it was made. The assumption that the world of the painter and

his patron aimed at a pure classicism or understanding of antiquity would have been equally misleading. Eclecticism and allegorical representations
of Christian content in secular or classical dress were
not shortcomings but essential features and, indeed,
accomplishments of Julian culture. And then, the
view that art exists "for art's sake" could only dis-
tort or diminish the significance of Julian art. That
art belongs to a self-sufficient and higher realm beyond mundane interests, that it is somehow valuable
in proportion to its uselessness, is open to question
in most periods of history. Raphael's *Julius* was
hardly pedestrian for having what were clearly practical functions to perform.

But after qualifications have been made, we are
still left with the themes of synthesis and culmination. Here, if anywhere, we may be close to seeing
the elephant after all. We do seem to be able to piece
together many patterns in Julian culture under those
rubrics; they give the evidence recognizable shape
and form. There may be more to this than fitting the
phenomena. In the end the traditional themes lead us to
a still more general proposition they expose and share.

If there was one central ideal in the culture of Julian
Rome, it was that culture was a kind of epiphany, a
"showing forth" in particular forms of the precepts,
ultimately of the divine principles, which particular
things were taken to exemplify. Something like this
understanding of culture made synthesis a possible,
even a necessary, cultural aim in the sense that it po-
sited appropriate categories by which experience
should continually be subsumed and measured. In-

sofar as experience was necessary to the categorical display and the measurement in the first place, it was in history and tradition that the principles behind (and in) all creation would be more or less fully revealed. One sought in history accordingly culminations in one time of what could be and had been, and one charted the course of history in terms of progress toward or decline from those Golden Ages when the ideal and the real were thought to be fully one.

Other corollaries to the notion of culture-as-epiphany have become familiar in these pages. The analogical and allegorizing modes of expression we have so often encountered were a likely consequence of seeing revelations of type in the existence of detail. When appearances must always be referred to categories that contain them, the world we perceive, or as perceived for us in texts and artifacts handed down over time, becomes an arena of similitudes, of signs corresponding to and resembling the deep-seated structures they are taken to indicate. As in the sixteenth-century *episteme* reconstructed by the French philosopher-historian Michel Foucault, so in Julian Rome "to know must therefore be to interpret: to find a way from the visible mark to that which is being said by it and which, without that mark, would lie like unspoken speech, dormant within things." If God had revealed and guaranteed the principles in nature and in history, to interpret had also to be to divine, to seek in the past, present, and future the innermost and most universal dimensions of spiritual meaning through the transparency of all creation. It followed that to interpret was to value and arrange things in an ideal order according to their apparent truth to type. As reflections of divine realities, which were constant, types did not change. But since they might be neglected or obscured, closeness to their original form and Originator became an index of degrees of perfection and height of place among the works of this world. The great object of human inquiry in theory and in practice was to activate the archetype.

If all this may seem remote and abstract, its implications were anything but that. Translated into conviction, expressed in action, this cluster of assumptions incited the creative imagination, called for demonstrations from the leaders of men, and even projected an image of governance ideal for the human community. Hidden truths and underlying principles of significance were neither true nor significant for men until they were brought to the surface and made known. Since the visible world was a house of mirrors, of signs relating and related to what they signified, the imaginative faculty became the human instrument most suited to the need to make meaning manifest. It was for his ability to make symbols and to appropriate them in nature and his own activity that man was most like God. The power of the imagination was such that it could supersede and actually substitute for external reality. Improving on the data of experience from nature or the historical record, the image had in this sense magic enough to become the world as it ought to be. Representation *of* reality edged into representation *as* reality. At the extremes of this process, as Northrop Frye has put it, "a stupid and indifferent nature is no longer the container of human society, but is contained by that society and must rain or shine at the pleasure of man." The creative imagination could not be less than what we have found it to be in Julian Rome—"apocalyptic," always at the edge of some, revelation which had to be spoken out or shown beyond the sum of nature and of tradition.

Where imagination was knowledge and power, politics could not be far behind. More than a special virtue, patronage of art and literature became an obligation of leadership. Patronage validated a ruler's claims to further the best interests and to use the material resources of the community at his disposal. It connected him with the highest purposes and products of the human condition. His services were amply rewarded, to be sure. The leader became the subject and hero of the imagination, not simply because he had paid for it, but also because the mirroring of precept in particular guise which structured all creation could be identified and focused in him. For his power, for the encyclopedia of virtues and antecedents embodied in him, he occupied, as Giles of Viterbo said of Pope Julius in 1512, the place of God on earth.

In Frye's terms a "high mimetic mode" grants the ruler "authority, passions, and powers of expression far greater than ours," while subjecting him, like the heroes of epic and tragedy, if not of myth or romance, to the expectations of his society and the order of nature. The high mimetic has its central theme—"the theme of cynosure or centripetal gaze, which . . . seems to have something about it of the court gazing upon its sovereign, the court-room gazing upon the orator, or the audience gazing upon the actor." In Julian Rome that contemplation soared highest in the vision of an earthly utopia as universal and triumphant as its faith in the conjunction of spirit and flesh. At least in the massive centering operation of a classical style the Julian world could deny the ambiguities of its own existence.

Pope Julius riveted the gaze of his contemporaries. His *terribilità* gave a real presence to the mysterious energies radiating through the particular things of this world. He activated the archetypes of the institution and the city he represented and ruled. In him the old prescriptions and prophecies that there would be "one flock and one shepherd" when Christ would "draw all things" to Himself seemed to spring to life. At times, however brief, the mirrors of his culture, and Raphael's, became windows.

References

GUIDE TO ABBREVIATED TITLES

Ademollo   A. Ademollo. *Alessandro VI, Giulio II, e
                 Leone X nel Carnevale di Roma, Documenti
                 inediti (1499-1520).* Rome, 1967.

Albertini   F. Albertini. *Opusculum de Mirabilibus novae
                 urbis Romae.* Edited by A. Schmarsow.
                 Heilbron, 1886. Also in *Five Early Guides
                 to Rome and Florence.* Edited by Peter Mur-
                 ray. Farnborough, England, 1972.

Angelis   P. de Angelis. *L'Ospedale di Santo Spirito in
                 Saxia.* 2 vols. Rome, 1960 and 1962.

Bentivoglio   E. Bentivoglio and S. Valtieri. *Santa Maria
and Valtieri   del Popolo.* Rome, 1976.

Bernardi   A. Bernardi. *Cronache Forlivesi, Monumenti
                 istorici pertinenti alle provincie della Romagna.*
                 Ser. 3, *Cronache* (R. Deputazione di Storia
                 Patria). Bologna, 1897.

Brummer   H. Brummer. *The Statue Court in the Vati-
                 can Belvedere.* Stockholm Studies in the
                 History of Art 20. Stockholm, 1970.

Bruschi   A. Bruschi. *Bramante architetto.* Bari, 1969.

Buchowiecki   W. Buchowiecki. *Handbuch der Kirchen
                 Roms.* 3 vols. Rome, 1967-74.

Chevalier   U. Chevalier. *Notre-Dame de Lorette.* Paris,
                 1906.

Cian   V. Cian. Review of L. Pastor, *Geschichte der Päpste seit dem Ausgang des Mittelalters*, 3. Freiburg, 1895. In *Giornale storico della letteratura italiana* 29 (1897), 403-52.

Conti   Sigismondo dei Conti. *Le storie de' suoi tempi dal 1475 al 1510*. 2 vols. Rome, 1883.

Di Cesare   M. Di Cesare. *Vida's Christiad and Vergilian Epic*. New York, 1964.

Dussler   L. Dussler. *Raphael*. London, 1971.

Erasmus   *The "Julius exclusus" of Erasmus*. Translated by P. Pascal. Introduction and notes by J. Sowards. Bloomington, 1968.

Ettlinger   L. Ettlinger. *The Sistine Chapel before Michelangelo*. Oxford, 1965.

Frommel   C. Frommel. "Die Peterskirche unter Papst Julius II im Licht Neuer Dokumente." *Römische Jahrbuch für Kunstgeschichte* 16 (1976), 59–136.
               ———. "'Capella Iulia': Die Grabkapelle Papst Julius II in Neu-St. Peter." *Zeitschrift für Kunstgeschichte* 40 (1977), 26-62.

Gilbert   C. Gilbert. *Complete Poems and Selected Letters of Michelangelo*. Edited by R. Linscott. New York, 1963.

Golzio   V. Golzio. *Raffaello nei documenti, nelle testimonianze dei contemporanei e nella letteratura del suo secolo*. Vatican, 1936.

Gombrich   E. Gombrich. "Hypnerotomachiana." *Journal of the Warburg and Courtauld Institutes* 14 (1951), 119–25.

Gozzadini   G. Gozzadini. "Di alcuni avvenimenti in Bologna e nell'Emilia dal 1506 al 1511. . . ." *Atti e memorie della R. Deputazione di Storia Patria per le Provincie di Romagna,* ser. 3, VII (1889), 161-267.

Grassis   Paris de'Grassis. *Le due spedizioni militari di Giulio II.* Edited by L. Frati. Bologna, 1886.

Grassis (Döllinger)   J. Döllinger. *Beiträge zur Politischen, Kirchlichen und Cultur-Geschichte.* Vienna, 1882 (reprinted Frankfurt, 1967).

Guicciardini   F. Guicciardini. *Storia d'Italia.* Edited by S. Menchi. 2 vols. Turin, 1971.

Hartt   F. Hartt. *"Lignum vitae in medio paradisi:* The Stanza d'Eliodoro and the Sistine Ceiling." *Art Bulletin* 32 (1950), 115-45, 181-218.

Hill   G. Hill. *A Corpus of Italian Medals of the Renaissance before Cellini.* 2 vols. London, 1930.

Huelsen   C. Huelsen. *Le Chiese di Roma nel Medio Evo.* Florence, 1927.

King   A. King. *Liturgy of the Roman Church.* London, 1957.

Klaczko   J. Klaczko. *Rome in the Renaissance: Pontificate of Julius II.* New York, 1903.

Legg   J. Legg. *Ecclesiological Essays.* London, 1905.

Lotz   W. Lotz. *Studies in Italian Renaissance Architecture.* Cambridge, Mass., 1977.

Luzio   A. Luzio. "Federico Gonzaga ostaggio alla
                 corte di Giulio II." *Archivio della R. Società
                 Romana di Storia Patria* 9 (1886), 509-82.
                 ————. "Isabella d'Este e Giulio II (1503-
                 1505)." *Rivista d'Italia* 12 (1909), 837-76.
                 ————. "Isabella d'Este di fronte a Giulio
                 II negli ultimi tre anni del suo pontificato."
                 Archivio storico lombardo 17 (1912), 244-334,
                 and 18 (1912), 55-144, 393-456.
                 ————. *Le letture dantesche di Giulio II e di
                 Bramante.* Genova, 1928.

Machiavelli   N. Machiavelli. *The Chief Works and
                 Others.* Translated by A. Gilbert. 3 vols.
                 Durham, N.C., 1965.

Miniature del   Miniature del Rinascimento. Quinto Cen-
Rinascimento*   tenario della Biblioteca Vaticana. Vatican,
                 1950.

Minnich   N. Minnich. "Concepts of Reform Pro-
                 posed at the Fifth Lateran Council." *Ar-
                 chivum historiae pontificiae* 7 (1969), 163-251.
                 ————. "The Participants at the Fifth Lat-
                 eran Council." *Archivum historiae pontificiae*
                 12 (1974), 157-206.

Moroni   G. Moroni. *Dizionario di erudizione storico-
                 ecclesiastica da S. Pietro ai nostri giorni.* 103
                 vols. Venice, 1840-61.

Norris   H. Norris. *Church Vestments: Their Origin
                 and Development.* New York, 1950.

Oberhuber   K. Oberhuber. "Raphael and the State
                 Portrait—I: The Portrait of Julius II." *Bur-
                 lington Magazine* 113 (1971), 124-30.

O'Malley   J. O'Malley. "Man's Dignity, God's Love,
                 and the Destiny of Rome: A Text of Giles

of Viterbo." *Viator* 3 (1962), 389–416.

———. "Giles of Viterbo: A Sixteenth-Century Text on Doctrinal Development." *Traditio* 20 (1966), 445-50.

———. "Giles of Viterbo: A Reformer's Thought on Renaissance Rome." *Renaissance Quarterly* 20 (1967), 1-11.

———. "Historical Thought and the Reform Crisis of the Early Sixteenth Century." *Theological Studies* 28 (1967), 531-48.

———. *Giles of Viterbo on Church and Reform: A Study in Renaissance Thought.* Leiden, 1968.

———. "Fulfillment of the Christian Golden Age under Pope Julius II: Text of a Discourse of Giles of Viterbo, 1507." *Traditio* 25 (1969), 265-338.

———. "Erasmus and Luther: Continuity and Discontinuity as Key to Their Conflict." *Sixteenth Century Journal* 5 (1974), 47-65.

———. "Preaching for the Popes." *The Pursuit of Holiness in Late Medieval and Renaissance Religion.* Edited by C. Trinkaus and H. Oberman. Leiden, 1974, pp. 408-40.

———. "The Discovery of America and Reform Thought at the Papal Court in the Early Cinquecento." *First Images of America: The Impact of the New World on the Old.* Edited by F. Chiappelli. Berkeley, 1976, pp. 185-200.

———. "The Vatican Library and the School of Athens: A Text of Battista Casali, 1508." *The Journal of Medieval and Renaissance Studies* 7 (1977), 271–87.

Pastor   L. von Pastor, *Storia dei papi dalla fine del medio evo,* 16 vols. Rome, 1943–63.

Pauly–   A. Pauly and G. Wissowa, *Real-encyclopädie*
Wissowa   *der classischen Altertumswissenschaft.* Berlin, 1894–1963.

Pope–   J. Pope-Hennessey. *Italian High Renaissance*
Hennessey   *and Baroque Sculpture.* 3 vols. London, 1963.
                  ————. *Italian Renaissance Sculpture.* 2nd ed. London, 1971.

Rodocanachi   E. Rodocanachi. *Histoire de Rome, Le Pontificat de Jules II.* Paris, 1928.

Sanuto   *I Diarii di Marino Sanuto.* 58 vols. Edited by F. Stefani, G. Berchet, N. Barozzi, and M. Allegri. Venice, 1879–1903.

Steinmann   E. Steinmann. *Die Sixtinische Kapelle.* 2 vols. Munich, 1901 and 1905.

Tedallini   Sebastiano di Branca Tedallini. *Diario romano.* Edited by P. Piccolomini. *Rerum italicarum scriptores,* N.S., XXIII, Pt. 3. Città di Castello, 1907.

Tomei   P. Tomei. *L'architettura a Roma nel Quattrocento.* Rome, 1942.

Valla   *The Treatise of Lorenzo Valla on the Donation of Constantine.* Translated and edited by C. Coleman. New Haven, 1922.

Vasari   *Le vite de' più eccellenti pittori, scultori, ed architettori scritte da Giorgio Vasari.* Edited by G. Milanesi. 1568 ed. Florence, 1878–85.

Weisbach   W. Weisbach. *Trionfi.* Berlin, 1919.

Weiss   R. Weiss. *The Medals of Pope Sixtus IV
               (1471-1484)*. Rome, 1961.

               ————. "The Medals of Pope Julius II
               (1503-1513)." *Journal of the Warburg and
               Courtauld Institutes* 28 (1965), 163-82.

PREFACE

Art and History

M. Baxandall, *Painting and Experience in Fifteenth-
Century Italy* (Oxford, 1972); P. Burke, *Culture and Society
in Renaissance Italy, 1420–1540* (London, 1972), 3–21; E.
Castelnuovo, "Per una storia sociale dell'arte," *Paragone*
27, no. 313 (1976), 3-30 and 28, no. 323 (1977), 3-34; C.
Geertz, "Art as a Cultural System," *Modern Language
Notes* 91 (1976), 1473-99; S. Alpers, "Is Art History?"
Daedalus (Summer 1977), 1-13.

1. RAPHAEL'S *JULIUS*
AND RENAISSANCE INDIVIDUALISM

Raphael's Julius

Sixteenth-century notices: Sanuto XVII, 60; *Il codice ma-
gliabechiano,* ed. C. Frey (Berlin, 1892), 128; Vasari IV, 338
(for the 1550 edition see H. Grimm, *Das Leben Raphaels*
[Berlin, 1886], 133–34); R. Borghini, *Il Riposo* (Florence,
1584), 388-89; G. P. Lomazzo, *Idea del tempio della pittura*
(Milan, 1590), 132.

Modern studies: C. Gould, *Raphael's Portrait of Pope
Julius II: The Re-emergence of the Original* (London, 1970);
idem, "The Raphael Portrait of Julius II: Problems of Versions and Variants; and a Goose that Turned into a Swan,"
Apollo 9, (1970), 187–89; Oberhuber, 124–30; Dussler,
29–30.

124 References to Chapter One

Date: The *Decretals* fresco was probably completed by 16 August 1511 (see Golzio, 24), and it is likely on grounds of style that the *Mass of Bolsena* portrait was executed before mid-1512 (see Oberhuber, 128). The London *Julius* belongs stylistically between these two works; for a fuller discussion of its date, see chapter three.

Drawings: A chalk study of Julius's head from life is in the Devonshire Collection at Chatsworth (36 x 25 cm.); see O. Fischel, *Raffaels Zeichnungen,* 8 vols. (Berlin, 1913–41), V, 257. A full-scale chalk and charcoal cartoon, perhaps authentic, is in the Galleria Corsini, Florence, no. 148 (109 x 82 cm.); illustrated in Klaczko, frontispiece. See also Dussler, 30.

Contemporary Characterizations of Julius

Beard: Scadinari (5 Nov. 1510), in Gozzadini, 181; Grassis (15 Dec. 1510 and 18 Feb. 1511), 213, 241; Antonio Gatico (3 Jan. 1511), in Luzio, "Federico Gonzaga," 569; Peter Martyr (March 1511), *Opus epistolarum* (Paris, 1670), Lib. XXIV, ep. 451; Giles of Viterbo (3 May 1511), in L. Pélissier, "Pour la biographie du Cardinal G. de Viterbe," *Miscellanea di studi critici edita in onore di Arturo Graf* (Bergamo, 1903), 809; Ubaldino Friano (7 May 1511), *Cronaca di Bologna,* in Gozzadini, 182; Evangelista Capodiferro (24 June 1511), in O. Tommasini, "Evangelista Maddaleni de' Capodiferro accademico . . . e storico," *Atti dell' Accademia dei Lincei,* ser. 4, I (1892), 15; Tedallini (27 June 1511 and March 1512), 321, 327; Cardinal Bibbiena (13 March 1512), in Rodocanachi, 126 n. 3; Stazio Gadio (16 March 1512) and Grossino (25 March 1512), in Luzio, "Isabella d'Este di fronte," 69–70; Capello (April 1512), in Sanuto XIV, 86; and Erasmus, 53. M. Zucker, "Raphael and the Beard of Pope Julius II," *Art Bulletin* 59 (1977), 524–33, arrived independently at an interpretation of the beard which parallels our own in many respects.

Appearance: Francesco Gonzaga (30 Nov. 1503), in Luzio, "Isabella d'Este e Giulio II," 845 n. 1; Grassis (Döllinger), 492; and Andrea Bernardi (1507) in *Monumenti istorici pertinenti alle provincie della romagna,* ser. 3, *Cronache* (Bologna, 1896), II, 190.

Gout, syphilis, and drunkenness: Lucido and Cattaneo (7 Feb. 1504), Francesco Maria della Rovere (3 March 1505) and Brognolo (13 Jan. 1506), in Luzio, "Isabella d'Este e Giulio II," 845–46, 850; Scadinari in Gozzadini, 181; Grassis (Oct. 1506), 63; Trevisan (April 1510) and anonymous epitaph (Feb. 1513) in Sanuto X, 80 and XV, 564; Erasmus, 110, 112 and *passim;* Rodocanachi, 81–82 n. 4; and Guicciardini, Bk. VII, Ch. III, 645.

Personality: Marcantonio Casanova (1503), in Cian, 442; Grassis (1 June 1505), in P. Mashanaglass, "Une ambassade Portugaise à Rome sous Jules II," *Revue d'histoire diplomatique* 7 (1903), 58; Brognolo (28 Nov. 1505), "Isabella d'Este e Giulio II," 848; Albertini (1510), Bk. III, "De nova urbe"; Capello (April 1510 and 13 Jan. 1511) in Sanuto X, 73 and XI, 741; Lippomano (14 Nov. 1510 to 5 March 1511), in Sanuto XI, 642, 722, 724–25, 729–30, 745, 772–73, 776, 778, 781, 843 and XII, 12–14, 32; Archdeacon of Gabbioneta (4 and 7 Nov. 1510), Stazio Gadio (18 and 27 Nov. 1510), and Ippolito d'Este (4 Dec. 1510), in Luzio, "Isabella d'Este di fronte," 262, 266n, 270n, 273; Brognolo (22 Feb. 1510), Stazio Gadio (6 and 11 Nov. 1510, 25 Aug. 1511, and 18 Dec. 1512) and Cardinal of Mantua (20 Feb. 1513), in Luzio, "Federico Gonzaga," 510, 516n, 525–26, 546, 555; Giles of Viterbo (ca. 1513), in O'Malley, *Giles,* 6 n. 1, and K. Höfler, "Böhmische Studien," *Archiv für Kunde österreichischer Geschichts-Quellen* 12 (1854), 382–87; Tommaso In-

ghirami, in Erasmus, *Il Ciceroniano,* ed. A. Gambaro
(Brescia, 1965), 131; Giorgio Anselmi and Antonio
Flaminio in Hartt, 216 nn. 208, 209; Vasari VII, 187;
Machiavelli, 91, 254, 523, 905, 910, 1459; P. de Nolhac,
Erasme en Italie, Étude sur un épisode de la Renaissance (Paris,
1888), 14. See also Steinmann II, 29–40; Rodocanachi, 7
n. 3; and A. Fabroni, *Leonis X pontificis maximi vita* (Pisa,
1797), 280.

Terribilità: J. Białostocki, *Stil und Überlieferung in der
Kunst des Abendlandes. Akten des 21. Internationalen Kongres-
ses für Kunstgeschichte, Bonn, 1964* (Berlin, 1967), III, 222–
25.

Renaissance Individualism

J. Burckhardt, *The Civilization of the Renaissance in Italy*
(many eds.), especially Pt. II, "The Development of the
Individual"; much subsequent interpretation and bibliography in W. Ferguson, *The Renaissance in Historical
Thought* (Cambridge, Mass., 1948); F. Chabod, "The
Concept of the Renaissance," *Machiavelli and the Renaissance* (New York, 1958), 149–247; and D. Hay, *The Italian
Renaissance in Its Historical Background,* 2nd ed. (Cambridge, 1976).

Renaissance Portraiture

General: K. Wörmann, *Die italienische Bildnismalerei der
Renaissance* (Esslingen, 1906); J. Burckhardt, "Das Porträt
in der italienischen Malerei," *Beiträge zur Kunstgeschichte
von Italien,* 2nd ed. (Berlin, 1911), 163–337; Hill, *passim;*
A. Warburg, "Bildniskunst und florentinisches Bürger-
tum," *Gesammelte Schriften* (Leipzig, 1932) I, 89–126;
J. Pope-Hennessey, *The Portrait in the Renaissance* (New
York, 1966)(important review by C. Gilbert, *Burlington
Magazine* 110 [1968], 278–85); E. Castelnuovo, "Il si-

gnificato del ritratto pittorico nella società," *Storia d'Italia* V, Pt. 2 (Turin, 1973), 1033–94; L. Sleptzoff, *Men or Supermen? The Italian Portrait in the Fifteenth Century* (Jerusalem, 1978).

State portraiture: M. Jenkins, *The State Portrait: Its Origin and Evolution* (New York, 1947); Oberhuber, *passim;* and *idem,* "Raphael and the State Portrait—II: The Portrait of Lorenzo de' Medici," *Burlington Magazine* 113 (1971), 436–43.

Papal portraits: H. Werner, *Die Ehrenstatuen der Päpste* (Leipzig, 1929); G. Ladner, *Die Papstbildnisse des Altertums und des Mittelalters,* 2 vols. (1941 and 1970); A. Haidacher, *Geschichte der Päpste in Bildern* (Heidelberg, 1965); K. Schwager, "Über Jean Fouquet in Italien und ein verlorenes Porträt Papst Eugens IV," *Argo, Festschrift für Kurt Badt* (Cologne, 1970), 206–34; Hill, *passim;* M. Meiss, "The Altered Program of the Santa Maria Maggiore Altarpiece," *Studien zur toskanischen Kunst. Festschrift für Ludwig Heydenreich zum 23. März 1963* (Munich, 1964), 169–90; Émile Gaillard, *Sano di Pietro, 1406–1481, Un Peintre Siennois au XVe Siècle* (Chambéry, 1923), pl. 6; E. Carli, *Il Pintoricchio* (Milan, 1960), 49–51, 69–79, pls. 84–85, 122, 132, 134, 136–37, 139, 141; *Miniature del Rinascimento,* cat. 97, pl. 17; J. Pope-Hennessey, *The Portrait in the Renaissance* (New York, 1966), 11; *idem, Fra Angelico* (New York, 1952), pl. 116; P. Albright, "Pollaiuolo's Tomb of Innocent VIII" (Master's thesis, University of California, Berkeley, 1977); J. Pope-Hennessey, *Italian Renaissance Sculpture,* 317–19, fig. 115; A. Cinagli, *Le Monete de' Papi descritte in tavole sinottiche* (Fermo, 1848), nos. 66–67; M. Kahr, "Jean le Bon in Avignon," *Paragone* 197 (1966), 3–16; and P. Bonanni, *Numismata Pontificum Romanorum Quae a Tempore Martini V usque ad annum MDCXCIX,* 2 vols. (Rome, 1706).

Portraits of Sixtus IV: L. Ettlinger, "Pollaiuolo's Tomb of Sixtus IV," *Journal of the Warburg and Courtauld Institutes* 16 (1953), 239–71; idem, *The Sistine Chapel,* pl. 34c; R. Weiss, *The Medals of Pope Sixtus IV (1471–1484)* (Rome, 1961), 28, figs. 10, 11; *Miniature del Rinascimento,* cat. 72; P. Rotondi, *Il Palazzo Ducale di Urbino,* 2 vols. (Urbino, 1950), 337–56; B. Biagetti, "L'Affresco di Sisto IV e il Platina," *Melozzo da Forlì, Rassegna d'arte romagnola* 5 (1938), 227–29; A. Schiavo, "Profilo e testamento di Raffaele Riario," *Studi Romani* 8 (1960), 414–29; P. de Angelis II, 378–516; M. Petrassi, "I Fasti di Sisto IV," *Capitolium* 48 (1973), 13–23; and E. Howe, *The Hospital of Santo Spirito and Pope Sixtus IV* (New York, 1977).

Portraits of Julius: G. Zanghieri, "Il ritratto di Giulio II di Grottaferrata presumibile copia di un Raffaello perduto," *Capitolium* 30 (1955), no. 7, 209–14; Klaczko, *passim;* O. Fischel, "Due ritratti di Giulio II," *Bollettino d'arte* 28 (1934), 195; idem, "Due ritratti non riconosciuti di Giulio II," *L'Illustrazione Vaticana* 7, No. 11 (1936), 514; C. de Tolnay, *Michelangelo* (Princeton, 1943), I, 219–23; N. Huse, "Ein Bilddokument zu Michelangelos 'Julius II' in Bologna," *Mitteilungen des kunsthistorischen Instituts in Florenz* 12 (1966), 355–58; W. Lotz, "Sixteenth-Century Italian Squares," *Studies in Italian Renaissance Architecture* (Cambridge, Mass., 1977), 80–81; L. Hautecoeur, *Le peinture au Musée du Louvre, II, Écoles Étrangères, École Italiennes (XIIIᵉ, XIVᵉ et XVᵉ Siècles)* (Paris, 1941), 99–100, pl. 100; G. Carotti, "La gran pala del Foppa nell'oratorio di Santa Maria di Castello in Savona," *Archivio storico dell'arte,* ser. 2, I (1895), 449–65; Hill, nos. 222, 224–49, 395, 445, 659–61, 817, 843, 866–72, 873–77; Weiss, "The Medals of Pope Julius," *passim,* Sanuto XIII, 350; Dussler, 36–37; and Hartt, 118.

Florentine portraiture in general: E. Schaeffer, *Das Floren-*

tiner Bildnis (Munich, 1904); J. Alazard, *The Florentine Portrait* (London, 1938); I. Lavin, "On the Sources and Meaning of the Renaissance Portrait Bust," *Art Quarterly* 33 (1970), 207–66; J. Schuyler, *Florentine Busts: Sculpted Portraiture in the Fifteenth Century* (New York, 1976); and J. Lanyi, "The Louvre Portrait of Five Florentines," *Burlington Magazine* 84 (1944), 87–95.

Florentine independent profile portraits: G. Pudelko, "Florentiner Porträts der Frührenaissance," *Pantheon* 15 (1935), 92–98; J. Lipman, "The Florentine Profile Portrait in the Quattrocento," *Art Bulletin* 18 (1936), 54–102; R. Hatfield, "Five Early Renaissance Portraits," *Art Bulletin* 47 (1965), 315–34; J. Mambour, "L'évolution ésthètique des profils florentins du quattrocento," *Revue Belge d'archéologie et d'histoire* 38 (1969), 43–60; and M. Ritter, "The Sources and Meanings of the Profile Portrait on the Italian Renaissance Tombs of the Fifteenth Century" (Master's thesis, University of California, Berkeley, 1976).

Independent portraits of French kings: C. Sherman, *The Portraits of Charles V of France (1338–1380)* (New York, 1969); M. Vale, "Jean Fouquet's Portrait of Charles VII," *Gazette des Beaux-Arts* 110 (1968), 243–48; and O. Pächt, "Jean Fouquet: A Study of His Style," *Journal of the Warburg and Courtauld Institutes* 4 (1940/41), 89.

Leonardo's "Mona Lisa": K. Clark, "Mona Lisa," *Burlington Magazine* 115 (1973), 144–50; and R. Huyghe, *Léonard de Vinci, La Joconde* (Fribourg, 1974).

Raphael's portraiture: M. Burkhalter, *Die Bildnisse Rafaels* (Laupen bei Bern, 1932); S. Freedberg, *Painting of the High Renaissance in Rome and Florence,* I (Cambridge, Mass., 1961), 65–66, 177–78, 333–46; Dussler, *passim*; and F. Gruyer, *Raphael, Peintre de Portraits,* 2 vols. (Paris, 1881).

Raphael's portrait of Federico Gonzaga: Golzio, 24–28.

Contemporary judgments on Raphael: Golzio, 191–93 (Giovio), 195–232 (Vasari), 294–306 (Dolce; see also M. Roskill, *Dolce's "Aretino" and Venetian Art-Theory of the Cinquecento* [New York, 1968], 205–7).

On Imitation

Ancient and Renaissance traditions: P. A. Duhamel, "The Function of Rhetoric as Effective Expression," *Journal of the History of Ideas* 10 (1949), 344–56, where the traditions behind the quotation from Quintilian (Inst. II. xiii.2) are discussed; R. Sabbadini, *Storia del Ciceronianismo* (Torino, 1885); H. Gmelin, "Das Prinzip der Imitatio in der romanischen Literatur der Renaissance," *Romanische Forschungen* 46 (1932), 85–360; M. Vitale, *La questione della lingua* (Palermo, 1960).

Pico-Bembo controversy: Le epistole "De Imitatione" di G. F. Pico della Mirandola e P. Bembo, ed. G. Santangelo (Florence, 1954) (I. Scott, trans. *Controversies over the Imitation of Cicero* [New York, 1910], 1-18).

Applications to art: E. Panofsky, *Idea: A Concept in Art Theory* [1924] (New York, 1968); R. Lee, *Ut pictura poesis: The Humanistic Theory of Painting* (New York, 1967); M. Baxandall, *Giotto and the Orators: Humanist Observers of Painting in Italy and the Discovery of Pictorial Composition, 1350–1450* (Oxford, 1971), 33ff, 65–66; E. Battisti, "Il concetto d'imitazione nel Cinquecento," *Rinascimento e Barocco* (Torino, 1960), 175–215; and M. Kemp, "From 'Mimesis' to 'Fantasia': The Quattrocento Vocabulary of Creation, Inspiration and Genius in the Visual Arts," *Viator* 8 (1977), 347–98. The texts on imitation collected in *Scritti d'arte del Cinquecento,* ed. P. Barocchi (Milan/Naples, 1973), II, 1523–607, include Raphael's letter to Castiglione, 1529–31 (also in Golzio, 30–32), and the relevant passages from Castiglione's *Book of the Courtier,* Bk. I, chaps. 26 and 53.

Physiognomics

   Theory: R. Foerster, *Scriptores Physiognomici Graeci et Latini,* 2 vols. (Leipzig, 1893); P. Gauricus, *De Sculptura,* ed. A. Chastel and R. Klein (Geneva, 1969), "De Physiognomia," 128–63 (on dark eyes, 141); Leonardo da Vinci, *Treatise on Painting,* ed. and trans. A. P. McMahon (Princeton, 1956), I, 147–57 ("twice-dead" painting, 150–51).

   Leonine portraits: P. Meller, "Physiognomical Theory in Renaissance Heroic Portraits," *The Renaissance and Mannerism: Acts of the 20th International Congress of the History of Art* (Princeton, 1963), II, 53–69; R. Watkins, "L. B. Alberti's Emblem, the Winged Eye, and His Name, Leo," *Mitteilungen des kunsthistorischen Instituts in Florenz* 9 (1960), 256–58; K. Forster, "Metaphors of Rule: Political Ideology and History in the Portraits of Cosimo I de' Medici," *Mitteilungen des kunsthistorischen Instituts in Florenz* 15 (1971), 65–103; and L. Ettlinger, "Hercules Florentinus," *Mitteilungen des kunsthistorischen Instituts in Florenz* 16 (1972), 119–42. The most leonine of Julian medals is Hill, no. 877.

High Renaissance Definitions of Human Potential

   F. Gilbert, *Machiavelli and Guicciardini: Politics and History in Sixteenth-Century Florence* (Princeton, 1965), esp. 179ff, 326–28; O'Malley, "Preaching for the Popes," 408–40; C. Trinkaus, *In Our Image and Likeness: Humanity and Divinity in Italian Humanist Thought* (Chicago, 1970); W. J. Bouwsma, "The Two Faces of Humanism: Stoicism and Augustinianism in Renaissance Thought," *Itinerarium Italicum,* ed. H. Oberman and T. Brady (Leiden, 1975), 3–60; and P. O. Kristeller, "The Immortality of the Soul," *Renaissance Concepts of Man* (New York, 1972), 22–42.

   The Lateran decree on immortality: J. D. Mansi, *Sacrorum*

Conciliorum nova et amplissima collectio 32 (Paris, 1902), col.
842–43; cf. F. Gilbert, "Cristianesimo, umanesimo e la
bolla 'Apostolici Regiminis'," *Rivista storica italiana* 79
(1967), 967–90; Thomas de Vio (Cajetan), "On the Immortality of Mind," in *Renaissance Philosophy,* ed. L. Kennedy (Paris, 1973), 46–54.

Late Medieval and Renaissance Papacy

General: E. R. Labande and P. Ourliac, *L'église au temps
du grande schisme et de la crise conciliaire,* 2 vols., *Histoire de
l'église* 14 (Paris, 1962–64); P. Prodi, *Lo sviluppo dell' as-
solutismo nello stato pontificio (secoli xv–xvi)* 1 (Bologna,
1968); W. Ullman, *The Growth of Papal Government in the
Middle Ages* (London, 1955); and now (with extensive bibliography) D. Hay, *The Church in Italy in the Fifteenth Century* (Cambridge, 1977).

Particular aspects: E. Kantorowicz, *The King's Two
Bodies: A Study in Mediaeval Political Theology* (Princeton,
1957), 194–206; Cipriano Benet, *De sacrosancto eucharistie
sacramento* (Nuremberg, 1516), A[1]; E. Lewis, "The Structure of Authority in the Church," *Medieval Political Ideas*
2 (1954), 357–429; P. Brezzi, "Lo scisma occidentale come
problema italiano," *Archivio della Deputazione Romana di
Storia Patria* 67 (1944), 391–450; H. Jedin, *History of the
Council of Trent* (St. Louis, 1957), I, 5–135; P. Partner,
"The 'Budget' of the Roman Church in the Renaissance
Period," *Italian Renaissance Studies,* ed. E. F. Jacob (London, 1960), 256–78; M. Douglas, *Natural Symbols: Explo-
rations in Cosmology* (London, 1970), Ch. 5, "The Two
Bodies," esp. 65, and Ch. 7, "Sin and Society," esp. 104.

Social Status of Artists and Conditions of Patronage

M. Wackernagel, *Der Lebensraum des Künstlers in der
florentinischen Renaissance* (Leipzig, 1938); R. and M. Wittkower, *Born under Saturn: The Character and Conduct of Ar-*

tists (London, 1963); P. Burke, *Culture and Society in Renaissance Italy, 1420–1540* (New York, 1972); and M. Baxandall, *Painting and Experience in Fifteenth Century Italy* (Oxford, 1972).

Artistic "Progress": E. Gombrich, "The Renaissance Conception of Artistic Progress and Its Consequences," *Norm and Form: Studies in the Art of the Renaissance* (London, 1966), 1–10.

The quotation from Alberti is in *On Painting and on Sculpture: The Latin Texts of De Pictura and De Statua,* ed. and trans. C. Grayson (London, 1972), 94–95.

Raphael: Stylistic development: R. Wittkower, "The Young Raphael," *Allen Memorial Art Museum Bulletin* 20 (1963), 150–68; J. White, "Raphael: The Relationship between Failure and Success," *Studies in Renaissance and Baroque Art Presented to Anthony Blunt on his 60th Birthday* (London, 1967), 18–23; S. Freedberg, *Painting of the High Renaissance in Rome and Florence,* 2 vols. (Cambridge, Mass., 1961), *passim.* Courtier: Vasari IV, 383. Antiquarian: Golzio, 78–92. Prospective son-in-law of Cardinal Bibbiena: Vasari IV, 380. Palace builder: Vasari IV, 353; A. Bruschi, *Bramante architetto* (Bari, 1969), 1040–46; and C. Frommel, *Der römische Palastbau der Hochrenaissance,* 3 vols. (Tübingen, 1973), II, 80–87. Wealth: Vasari IV, 381. Mortal god, prince, and divine: Vasari IV, 316, 385, 594; and Golzio, 284–292. Raphael's self-portrait is to the extreme right in the *School of Athens.* Raphael's complaint about his loss of liberty is in a letter to Francesco Francia dated 5 Sept. 1508; see Golzio, 19–20.

Bramante: For the plan to reorient St. Peter's, see Pastor 3, 1121–22, doc. 135.

Michelangelo: Submission to Julius in Bologna, see Vasari, *La vita di Michelangelo nelle redazioni del 1550 e del 1568,* ed. P. Barocchi, 5 vols. (Milan, 1962), I, 33 and II, 387–88. For the "tragedy of the tomb," see *ibid.*; A. Condivi, *Life of Michelagnolo Buonarroti,* in C. Holroyd, *Michael Angelo Buonarroti* (London, 1903); and the letters of Michelangelo in E. Ramsden, *The Letters of Michelangelo,* 2 vols. (Stanford, 1963).

Quattrocento Revival of Rome

T. Magnuson, *Studies in Roman Quattrocento Architecture* (*Figura* 9) (Stockholm, 1958); Tomei, *passim;* V. Golzio and G. Zander, *L'arte in Roma nel secolo XV* (Istituto di Studi Romani, Storia di Roma 28) (Bologna, 1968); L. Gabel, "The First Revival of Rome, 1420–1484," and R. Kennedy, "The Contribution of Martin V to the Rebuild-ing of Rome, 1420–1431," *The Renaissance Reconsidered: A Symposium* (Smith College Studies in History 44) (North-hampton, Mass., 1964), 13–25, 27–39; E. Müntz, *Les arts à la cour des papes pendant le XV*^{e} *et XVI*^{e} *siècle,* 3 vols. (Paris, 1878–79, 1882); C. Seymour, *Sculpture in Italy, 1400 to 1500* (Harmondsworth, 1966); C. Westfall, *In This Most Perfect Paradise: Alberti, Nicholas V, and the Invention of Conscious Urban Planning in Rome, 1447–55* (University Park, Pa., 1974); G. Urban, "Die Kirchenbaukunst des Quattrocento in Rome," *Römisches Jahrbuch für Kunstge-schichte* 9/10 (1961–62), 73–289; L. Heydenreich and W. Lotz, *Architecture in Italy, 1400 to 1600* (Harmondsworth, 1974); P. Partner, *Renaissance Rome, 1500–1559* (Berkeley, 1976); and Pastor, *passim.* The speech of Nicholas V is from Pastor, *History of the Popes* 2 (St. Louis, 1902), 166.

2. ROLES OF A RENAISSANCE POPE

Beards

Julius's beard: See references to chapter one, "Contem-porary Characterizations of Julius."

Princely connotations: Representations of bearded Italians before Julius include Francesco Gonzaga, Giovanni Sforza,

Albertino Papafavo da Carrara, Doge Agostino Barbarigo, Doge Niccolo Tron, and Cesare Borgia. See Hill, *passim;* C. Gilbert, "Piero della Francesca's *Flagellation:* The Figures in the Foreground," *Art Bulletin* 53 (1971), 43–46; and A. Heiss, *Les Médailleurs de la Renaissance* 5 (1885), 51; 7 (1887), 145–46; 8 (1891), 73. A painted panel in the Louvre representing five famous Florentines purportedly shows Uccello and Donatello as bearded, but the identifications, and whether or not they are even portraits, are open to question. Almost all bearded foreigners on Italian medals before Julius are of the highest rank—emperors, sultans, kings, or lords. Julius's encouragement of others to grow beards is mentioned in a letter of 30 Dec. 1511 from Stazio Gadio to the Bishop of Ivrea.

Imperial connotations: Suetonius, I, LXVII, 2; and L. Dorez, "La bibliothèque privée du pape Jules II," *Revue des bibliothèques* 6 (1896), 97–124.

Priestly connotations: For Pope Julius I, *New Catholic Encyclopedia* (New York, 1967), VIII, 52; but cf. G. Ladner, *I Ritratti dei Papi nell'antichità e nel Medioevo* (Vatican City, 1941), I, 34–35. Botticelli's fresco of the *Punishment of Corah,* Ettlinger, *The Sistine Chapel,* 66–70. The 1513 carnival procession, Ademollo, 41, and Luzio, "Federico Gonzaga," 580. For the bearded Serapis, Pirro Ligorio, *Del significato del dracone,* cited in M. Fagiolo and M. Madonna, "La casina di Pio IV in Vaticano, Pirro Ligorio e l'architettura come geroglifico," *Storia dell'arte* 15/16 (1972), 259. The references to Valeriano's *Pro sacerdotum barbis* are from the 1533 English edition (London) 22v–23r and 26v.

Julius as Warrior Prince

General: Erasmus 18–19, 45, 48, 50, 110, and *passim;* Sanuto XV, 562–66; Gilbert, no. 10, 8; and Guicciardini, Bk. XI, Ch. VIII, 1115.

Tableaux-vivants: C. Brown, "Language as a Political Instrument in the Work of Jean Lemaire de Belges and Other Poets of the "Rhétoriquer" Tradition" (Ph.D. Diss., University of California, Berkeley, 1978), 95–165.

Woodcuts: R. Bainton, *Erasmus of Christendom* (New York, 1969), 105, and Rodocanachi, pl. 20.

Julian fortresses: Pastor III, 721, 919, and *passim;* E. Bentivoglio, "Bramante e il geoglifico di Viterbo," *Mitteilungen des kunsthistorischen Instituts in Florenz* 16 (1972), 168; Bruschi, 909–10, 938–45; and Hill, nos. 224b and g, 816 ter., 817 and 872.

Camauro and mozzetta: See references, chapter one, "Renaissance Portraiture" and subsections "Papal portraits," "Portraits of Sixtus IV," "Independent portraits of French kings," and Moroni XLVII, 27–36. Pius II might have worn the short *mozzetta* before Sixtus IV, but it is impossible to tell from his portrait on medals; see P. Bonanni, *Numismata Pontificum Romanorum,* I, 65. Examples of Italian nobles wearing long French-styled robes are Lodovico Gonzaga frescoed in the Camera degli Sposi by Mantegna in the Palazzo Ducale in Mantua (1474) and a miniature of Ercole d'Este in *De origine domus estensis* in the Biblioteca Estense of the second half of the fifteenth century. For the latter see Oberhuber, Fig. 9.

Dynasticism: E. Lee, *Sixtus IV and Men of Letters* (Rome, 1978). In Melozzo's fresco, Giovanni della Rovere, Prefect of Rome and Duke of Montefeltro, and Girolamo Riario, Count of Imola and Forlì, stand to the left; Cardinal Giuliano della Rovere (the earliest known portrait of the future Julius II) and Raffaele Riario, apostolic protonotary, later cardinal, stand to the right. Julius is in a more prominent position, directly facing Sixtus, than any of the others and is emphasized by the background elements of a column, an arch, and a silhouetting back light. For the inscriptions of dynastic significance, Tomei, 157, 176; Weiss, "The Medals of Pope Julius II," and *The Medals of*

Pope Sixtus IV; Hill, nos. 222, 229, 445, 659–61, 816 ter., 866–74; M. Cruttwell, *Antonio Pollaiuolo* (London, 1907), 192–93; Steinmann II, 56, n. 3 and 58 nn. 2, 5; and Golzio, 23, 26. For the quotation by Paris de'Grassis see Steinmann II, 176, n. 2.

Julius as Emperor

General: O'Malley, "Discovery of America," 192; *idem, Giles,* 126; Sanuto VII, 63–65; Hill, no. 875; Weiss, "The Medals of Pope Julius II," pl. 31j; *Corpus Nummorum Italicorum* 15 (Rome, 1934), pl. 17, no. 13; and B. Horrigan, "Imperial and Urban Ideology in a Renaissance Inscription," *Comitatus* 9 (1978), 73–86.

Julius Caesar: Pastor III, 663 n. 4; Sanuto VII, 64; Albertini, "Epistola"; Weisbach, 68–69; Gombrich, 119–22 (in hieroglyphics Julius was to have been represented by a profile of Julius Caesar); *Die Chronicken der Deutschen Städte* 23 (Leipzig, 1894), 103; M. Vattaso, *Antonio Flaminio e le principali poesie dell'autografo vaticano 2870* (Rome, 1900), 50–51 (also Brummer, 220, n. 22); and Hill, no. 874.

Augustus: J. Shearman, "The Vatican Stanze: Functions and Decorations," *Proceedings of the British Academy* 57 (1971), 382–83, where the *Stanza della Segnatura* is related to the Palatine Library of Augustus. When Julius established a special office concerned with the Tiber and had the Tiber dredged for the first time since antiquity (Rodocanachi, 46; Bruschi, 633–34; P. Frosini, "La liberazione dalle inondazione del Tevere," *Capitolium* 43 [1968], 227), he was following the example of Augustus (Suetonius, II, xxx, 1, and xxxvii, 1). The treaty between Julius and the rebellious Roman nobles in 1511 was glorified as the Augustan *Pax Romana;* see C. Gennaro, "La 'Pax Romana' del 1511," *Archivio della Società Romana di Storia Patria* 90 (1967), 17–60. For Julius citing the Aeneid

(I, 204ff.) on the road from Imola to Tossignano en route
to Bologna in 1506, see Pastor III, 716; Marcantonio Vida
wrote an epic (unpublished) lauding Julius's martial ac-
complishments entitled the *Juliad,* based on the *Aeneid;* see
M. Di Cesare, 3. For further Virgilian references in Julian
Rome, Brummer, 166, 229–30; O'Malley, *Giles,* 121, 128;
Vat. Lat. 1682, 28v; the inscription, *Numine afflatur*
(*Aeneid,* VI, 50), with the personification of Poetry, and
the grisaille fresco of *Augustus Preventing Virgil from Burning the Aeneid,* both in the *Stanza della Segnatura;* and the
Cumean sibyl, Virgil's prophetess of the Augustan Golden
Age through the line of Iulus (!), in the center of the Sistine
Ceiling. For Capodiferro's reference to Julius as Augustus
and Ancus, Steinmann II, 59, n. 1. (The inscription on the
fortress at Ostia also links Julius to Ancus, the 4th king of
Rome [642–17 B.C.], by stating that it was completed in
"1486, 2,115 years from the foundation of Ostia, 2,129
from Ancus Marcius founder of the city"; see Weiss, *The
Medals of Pope Sixtus IV,* 33. Paris de'Grassis, opening his
diary in 1504 after his appointment as master of ceremonies, wrote that in order to insure that religious obser-
vances be done correctly it was necessary to record all
ceremonies just as Ancus Marcius had ordered the pontifex to copy out the commentaries of Numa for public
consultation [Livy, I, xxxii, 1–2]; see Grassis [Döllinger],
364.)

Trajan: The medal inscribed *Centum Celle* (Hill, no.
872; see also nos. 244b and g) suggests a parallel between
Julius, the founder of the fortress of Civitavecchia in 1508,
and Trajan, the original founder of the Roman port.

Tiberius: Steinmann II, 786–87.

Constantine: Ettlinger, *Sistine Chapel,* 66–70, 90–93,
112–16: Grassis, 176; S. Sandström, "The Sistine Chapel
Ceiling," *Levels of Unreality: Studies in Structure and Construction in Italian Mural Painting during the Renaissance*

(*Figura, Acta Universitatis Upsaliensis,* new series IV) (Uppsala 1963), 173–91 (also in C. Seymour, Jr., *Michelangelo: The Sistine Chapel Ceiling* [New York, 1972], 207–21); J. Traeger, "Raffaels Stanza d'Eliodoro und ihr Bildprogramm," *Römisches Jahrbuch für Kunstgeschichte* 13 (1971), 29–99; A. Cinagli, *Le monete de' Papi descritte in tavole sinottiche* (Fermo, 1848), 66–67; *Corpus Nummorum Italicorum* 15 (Rome, 1934), 249–56; Chevalier, 270; F. Falk, "Beiträge zur Pastors Papstgeschichte," *Zeitschrift für katholische Theologie* 22 (1898), 189; and E. Savino, "Ad Julium P. M. de donatione Constantini," *Un curioso poligrafo del quattrocento, Antonio de Ferrariis (Galateo)* (Bari, 1941), 429–42.

Julius greater than any emperor: Sanuto X, 80 and XIV, 457–58; Conti II, Bk. XV, 360; O'Malley, *Giles,* 127; *idem,* "Discovery of America," 191; and the centrally placed tondo in the Sistine Ceiling showing Alexander the Great submitting to the high priest of Jerusalem (who is dressed in papal regalia!); Sanuto (XV, 561) said that Julius "sta causa di la ruina de Italia," and Bramante, known as *ruinante,* was considered capable of destroying the whole world (Pastor III, 892).

Cortile del Belvedere: J. Ackerman, "The Belvedere as a Classical Villa," *Journal of the Warburg and Courtauld Institutes,* 14 (1951), 70–91; *idem, The Cortile del Belvedere* (Vatican, 1954); Bruschi, 291–433, 865–82; Brummer, *passim;* L. Grisebach, "Baugeschichtliche Notiz zum Statuenhof Julius' II im vatikanischen Belvedere," *Zeitschrift für Kunstgeschichte* 39 (1976), 209–20; and Hill, no. 876. The Vatican Loggie project by Bramante of ca. 1508–9 is also of imperial scale, articulation (cf. the Colosseum), and function (cf. the Septizonium of 203 A.D. which similarly screens an agglomeration of earlier buildings to present a unified facade).

Julius's tomb: Frommel, "Capella Iulia," 26–62; A.

Frazer, "A Numismatic Source for Michelangelo's First Design for the Tomb of Julius II," *Art Bulletin* 57 (1975), 53–57; Gilbert, 192; and Vasari VII, 163.

St. Peter's: Pastor III, 889; and Conti II, Bk. XV, 344.

Triumphal entries into Rome and Bologna: L. Frati, "Delle monete gettate al popolo nel solenne ingresso in Bologna di Giulio II per la cacciata di Gio. II Bentivoglio," *Atti e memorie della R. Deputazione di Storia Patria per le Provincie di Romagna,* ser. 3, I (1883), 474–87; Grassis, 84–96, 169–76; Weiss, "Medals of Pope Julius II," 163–82; Sanuto VI, 492–93 and VII, 64; Albertini, ed. Schmarsow xxii, and ed. Murray Book II, "De triumpho nonnullorum"; and Hill, no. 874.

Cleopatra and the East: Brummer, 153–84, 216–51; and E. MacDougall, "The Sleeping Nymph: Origins of a Humanist Fountain Type," *Art Bulletin* 57 (1975), 357–65. Additional links to Egypt, implying Julian connections with the earliest sources of human wisdom and dominion over the East, are the hieroglyphics intended for the Cortile del Belvedere and used in St. Peter's and the 1513 carnival procession. See Gombrich, 119–25; R. Wittkower, "Hieroglyphics in the Early Renaissance," *Developments in the Early Renaissance,* ed. Bernard S. Levy (Albany, 1972); Frommel, "Die Peterskirche," docs. 197, 209, pp. 111–12; Ademollo, 40; and Luzio, "Federico Gonzaga," 580. Julius's connections and dominion over Greece and the Holy Land are implied by Battista Casali (see O'Malley, "The Vatican Library," 271–87) and the following visual representations: *Parnassus, Alexander the Great Placing the Iliad of Homer in Safekeeping, School of Athens, Blinding of Zaleucus,* and *Justinian Receiving the Pandects* in the *Stanza della Segnatura; Expulsion of Heliodorus* in the *Stanza d'Eliodoro; Submission of Alexander the Great to the High Priest of Jerusalem* and *Judas Maccabaeus Defeats Nicanor* on the Sistine Ceiling; and the illumination in a Vatican manuscript by Michele Nagoni (see Weisbach, 68–69). In addition, the central plan of the new St. Peter's was derived ultimately from the martyria of the Holy Land.

Cloth

Imperial mappa: Pauly-Wissowa, XIV, Pt. 2, 1414–15; C. Daremberg, *Dictionnaire des antiquités grecques et romaines* (Paris, 1877), 1593–95; R. Delbrueck, *Die Consulardiptychen u. verwandte Denkmaler* (Studien zur Spätantikenkunstgeschichte 2) (Berlin, 1929). For the Virgin holding the *mappa* in early Christian art, see O. Montenovesi, *Le Madonne antiche delle catacombe e delle chiese romane* (Rome, 1904), 37, 39, 53. For fifteenth-century knowledge that Constantine was consul four times and that the office was assumed on the first of January, see Valla, 137–39.

Marriage context: Legg, 191–95; E. Mellencamp, "A Note on the Costume of Titian's Flora," *Art Bulletin* 51 (1969), 174–77, especially figs. 1, 5–8, and 177, n. 17; E. Verheyen, "Der Sinngehalt von Giorgiones 'Laura'," *Pantheon* 26 (1968), 220–27; and E. Panofsky, *Problems in Titian: Mostly Iconographic* (New York, 1969), 137–38 (but cf. J. Held, "Flora: Goddess and Courtesan," *De Artibus Opuscula XL: Essays in Honor of Erwin Panofsky,* ed. M. Meiss [New York, 1961], 216). Although dating from the 1560s, the report that Pietro Carnesecchi went to his execution "fashionably dressed in a white shirt, with a new pair of gloves and a white handkerchief in his hand as though to a wedding," would certainly seem to put the *mappa* into a marriage context (see D. Cantimori, "Italy and the Papacy," *New Cambridge Modern History* [1967], II, 267). For the Villa Lemmi frescos, see H. Ettlinger, "The Portraits in Botticelli's Villa Lemmi Frescoes," *Mitteilungen des kunsthistorischen Instituts in Florenz* 20 (1976), 404–6.

For purifying the hands: R. Hatfield, *Botticelli's Uffizi "Adoration": A Study in Pictorial Content* (Princeton, 1976), 35–41.

Maniple: Norris, 92–94; King, 214–17; J. Legg, *Church Ornaments and Their Civil Antecedents* (Cambridge, 1917), 63–66; and F. Bock, *Geschichte der liturgischen Gewänder des Mittelalters* (Bonn, 1866), II, 62–83. Other examples in the Renaissance where persons hold a cloth seemingly in either a quasi-liturgical or imperial context are Ghirlandaio, *Portrait of Lucrezia Tornabuoni* (see J. Lauts, *Domenico Ghirlandaio* [Vienna, 1943], fig. 103); Michelangelo, *Lorenzo de' Medici* in the Medici Chapel; Scipione Pulzone, *Portrait of Cardinal Alessandro Farnese* in the Galleria Nazionale, Rome (see F. Zeri, *Pittura e Controriforma, L'arte senza tempo di Scipione da Gaeta* [Torino, 1957], colorplate II); and two portraits of Eleanora da Toledo in Berlin and the Palazzo Vecchio in Florence (see Venturi *Storia dell'arte italiana* [Milan, 1901–39], IX, Pt. 6, 21, fig. 3, and 341, fig. 193).

Acorns and Oak

Food of Arcadia: for example, Plutarch, *Moralia* 4, "Quaestiones Romanae," 92; further, Pauly-Wissowa, V, 2027, "Eiche."

Capitoline oak: Livy I, X, 5; and Ovid, *Metamorphoses* XV, 560–64.

Aeneas's oak: Virgil, *Aeneid* VIII, 615–16.

Oak as fortitude: E. Wind, "Platonic Justice: Designed by Raphael," *Journal of the Warburg and Courtauld Institutes* 1 (1937/38), 70.

Tree-of-life and cross: P. Berchorius, *Ovidius Moralizatus* (Paris, 1509), fol. 92, and Hartt, 133.

Golden age and renewal: O'Malley, "Fulfillment"; Hartt, 133, n. 128; Di Cesare; and A. Capelli, *Lettere di L. Ariosto* (Milan, 1887), 345. Pomponius Gauricus, Giovanni Au-

relio Augurello, Lancino Corte, and Antonio Mancinelli
all wrote poems celebrating the return of the Golden Age
under Julius, on the occasion of his election to the papacy;
see Cian, 442. For the long tradition of trees and reform
see G. Ladner, "Vegetation Symbolism and the Concept
of Renaissance," *De Artibus Opuscula XL: Essays in Honor
of Erwin Panofsky,* ed. M. Meiss (New York, 1961), 303–
22.

Oak and good shepherd: Hill, 661.

Entry into Orvieto: Grassis, 34, 89.

Float in front of S. Maria in Traspontina: Grassis, 175,
and Sanuto VII, 64. For the *meta* of Romulus in front of
the church, see R. Valentini e Giuseppe Zucchetti, *Codice
Topografico della Città di Roma* (Rome, 1953), IV, 497.

Holy League float of 1513 apotheosis: Luzio, "Federico
Gonzaga," 580–81, and Ademollo, 41.

Hostile use: Sanuto VI, 463, and Pastor III, 784.

Gems and Rings

Julian: Moroni II, 66; F. Cancellieri, *Notizie sopra
l'origine e l'uso dell'anello pescatorio e degli altri anelli ecclesiastici e specialmente del cardinalizio* (Rome, 1823), 15; M.
Tafuri, *Via Giulia, una utopia urbanistica del '500* (Rome,
1973), 431–32; Luzio, "Federico Gonzaga," 525, 542; *idem,*
"Isabella d'Este di fronte," 327; Grassis (Döllinger), 429,
432; Grassis, *passim;* Rodocanachi, 82–83; Sanuto X, 283;
Bernardi, 190; L. Baldiserri, "Giulio II in Romagna (1 set-
tembre 1510–26 giugno 1511)," *Rivista storico-critica delle
scienze teologiche* III (1907), 570; Pastor III, 716, 718; and
Raphael's *Decretals* fresco.

Function and symbolism of rings: F. Bock, *Geschichte der
liturgischen Gewänder des Mittelalters* (Bonn, 1866), II,
205–12; A. Fourlas, *Der Ring in der Antike und im Christen-
tum* (Munster, 1971); Moroni II, 58–71; G. Kunz, *Rings for
the Finger* (Philadelphia, 1917), 249–87; J. Legg, 181–218;

P. Castelli et al., "Le virtù delle gemme, Il loro significato simbolico e astrologico nella cultura umanistica e nelle credenze popolari del Quattrocento. Il recupero delle gemme antiche," *L'oreficeria nella Firenze del Quattrocento* (Florence, 1977); F. Murphy and J. Nabuco, "Rings," *New Catholic Encyclopedia* (Washington, 1967), XII, 505–7; J. Jungmann, *The Mass of the Roman Rite,* rev. ed. (New York, 1959), 480–81; H. Leclerq, "Anneaux," *Dictionnaire d'archéologie chrétienne* (Paris, 1904), I, 2174–223; King, 146–47, 368; and Norris, 183–86. In a colloquium (January 1979) for the Department of History at Berkeley on marriage rites in Renaissance Italy, Dr. Christiane Klapisch-Zuber illustrated "the triumph of the ring" around 1500.

Julius as Priest

General: Since Julian roles overlapped, many of the references above for "Julius as Warrior Prince" and "Julius as Emperor" are also relevant here.

Julius I: Bibliotheca Sanctorum 6 (Rome, 1965), cols. 1235–36; Sanuto X, 159; and papal bull of 26 May 1510 (Santa Maria in Trastevere, Archivio del vicariato, Liber I, Instrumentorum, fol. 127r. ff.), for which references, our thanks to Prof. Dale Kinney.

Church liberty: Machiavelli I, 46; Weiss, 164–66; and Conti II, Lib. XV, 296. Julius first articulated his policy of "church liberty" by the inscription on a medal of the 1480s by Sperandio (Hill, no. 395) made in connection with his appointment as bishop of Bologna: *Iulianus Ruvere S. Petri ad Vincula Cardinalis Libertatis Ecclesiastice Tutor.* On the reverse is an allegory of the Church as the agent of salvation inscribed "Celestial Life." The ship evidently symbolized the Church; the pelican of piety on the bow, as well as the mast and yard, Christ's redemptive sacrifice that gave the Church its authority; and the water, the rite of baptism by which the fruits of Christ's sacrifice were channeled to the faithful. Within the *navicella* the dog (?) represented faith, and Minerva (?) holding a spear, the strength and divine wisdom of the Church.

Crusades: O'Malley, "The Vatican Library," 277; *idem,* "Fulfillment," 324–28, 334–35, 338; *idem, Giles,* 14–15; *idem,* "The Discovery of America," 190; Frommel, "Die Peterskirche," doc. 216; Weisbach, 68–69; Grassis (Döllinger), 390; Minnich, "Concepts of Reform," 166; Luzio, *Le letture,* 4–5; Steinmann, "Chiaroscuri in den Stanzen Raffaels," *Zeitschrift für Bildende Kunst* 10 (1898/99), 169–78; Pastor III, 662, 711, 728–29, 786–87, 821.

Justice, peace, and reform: Bernardi, 395; O'Malley, *Giles,* 154 and *passim; idem,* "Discovery of America," *passim;* Minnich, "Concepts of Reform," *passim;* Sanuto VII, 64; Pastor III, 848–49; Grassis (Döllinger), 432; Steinmann II, 786–87; and Hill, nos. 222, 877.

Palace of Justice: L. Salerno, L. Spezzaferro, and M. Tafuri, *Via Giulia, Una utopia urbanistica del '500* (Rome, 1973), 15–152, 314–22; C. Frommel, "Il Palazzo dei Tribunali in Via Giulia," *Studi Bramanteschi, Atti del Congresso internazionale* (Milan, 1970), 523–34; S. von Moos, *Turm und Bollwerk, Beiträge zu einer politischen Ikonographie der italienischen Renaissancearchitektur* (Zurich, 1974), 83–88; and Hill, nos. 225, 227.

Julius as Solomon and David: Pastor III, 900–901; Frommel, "Die Peterskirche," *passim;* and *idem,* " 'Capella Iulia'," *passim.*

Historical Continuity, Millenarianism, and Rome in Julian Spirituality

Especially useful in a vast literature, R. Brentano, *Rome before Avignon* (New York, 1974); N. Cohn, *The Pursuit of the Millennium* (Fairlawn, N. J., 1957); J. Comblin, "La liturgie de la nouvelle Jerusalem," *Ephemerides theologicae lovanienses* 29 (1953), 5–40; C. Davis, *Dante and the Idea of Rome* (Oxford, 1957); R. Folz, *The Concept of Empire in Western Europe from the 5th to the 14th Century* (London, 1969); W. Goez, *Translatio Imperii: Ein Beitrag zur Geschichte des Geschichtsdenkens und der politischen Theorien im Mittelalter und in der frühen Neuzeit* (Tübingen, 1958); A. Graf, *Roma nella memoria e nelle immaginazioni del medio evo* (Turin, 1915); R. Konrad, "Das himmlische und das irdische Jerusalem im mittelalterlichen Denken: Mystische Vorstellung und geschichtliche Wirkung," *Speculum Historiale,* ed. C. Bauer, L. Boehm, and M. Müller (Munich, 1965), 423–41; Minnich, "Concepts of Reform," 163–251; O'Malley, "Fulfillment," 265–338; *idem,* "Giles of Viterbo: A Reformer's Thought"; *idem,* "Giles of Viterbo: A Sixteenth Century Text," 445–50; *idem, Giles, passim; idem,* "Historical Thought," 531–48; *idem,* "Man's Dignity," 389–416; *idem,* "Erasmus and Luther," 47–65; *idem,* "The Discovery of America," 185–200; *idem,* "The Vatican Library," 271–87; M. Reeves, *The Influence of Prophecy in the Later Middle Ages* (Oxford, 1969); P. Schramm, *Kaiser, Rom und Renovatio* (Leipzig, 1929); M. Seidlmayer, "Rom und Romgedanke im Mittelalter," *Speculum* 7 (1956), 395–412; A. Walz, "Von Cajetans Gedanken über Kirche und Papst," *Volk Gottes,* ed. J. Hofer (Freiburg, 1967), 336–60; D. Weinstein, *Savonarola and Florence* (Princeton, 1970); and M. Wilks, *The Problem of Sovereignty in the Later Middle Ages: The Papal Monarchy with Augustinus Triumphus and the Publicists* (Cambridge, 1963). For further bibliography, see L. Partridge, "Divinity and Dynasty at Caprarola: Perfect History in the Room of Farnese Deeds," *Art Bulletin* 60 (1978), nn. 172–82.

Julius's "good death": Luzio, "Federico Gonzaga," 55; *idem, Le Letture,* 6; O. Raynaldi, *Annales ecclesiastici,* n. 9; *Memorie perugine di Teseo Alfani dal 1502 al 1527,* ed. F. Bonaini, *Archivio storico italiano,* ser. 1, XVI.2 (1851), 263 and n. 1; Pastor III, 844–45; Grassis (Döllinger), 432; Bernardi, 394–97; Tedallini, 338–39; and O. Tommasini, *La vita e gli scritti di Niccolò Machiavelli* (Rome, 1911), II, 1113.

Integrity and piety: Conti 2, Bk. XV, 296; Steinmann I, 580, n. 3; Sanuto XIV, 458; and Pastor III, 847–48.

Themes in the Stanze and Sistine Ceiling: it must suffice to refer for an enormous bibliography to the suggestive discussions in works by Hartt, Sandström, Seymour, Shearman, Steinmann, and Traeger cited above, under "Julius as Emperor," "Julius as Priest." Cf. also H. Pfeiffer, *Zur Ikonographie von Raffaels Disputa, Egidio da Viterbo und die christlich-platonische Konzeption der Stanza della Segnatura* (Rome, 1975).

Julius and Erasmus

Erasmus, introduction and 88–90; and J. McConica, "Erasmus and the 'Julius': A Humanist Reflects on the Church," *The Pursuit of Holiness in Late Medieval and Renaissance Religion,* ed. C. Trinkaus and H. Oberman (Leiden, 1974), 444–71.

3. THE SETTING AND FUNCTIONS OF A RENAISSANCE PORTRAIT

Santa Maria del Popolo

Julius's appearances: Grassis, 21–22, 169–72, 291–93; Grassis (Döllinger), 385, 412; Sanuto XIII, 76; Pastor III, 794; and C. O'Reilly, "'Maximus Caesar et Pontifex Maximus'," *Augustiniana* 22 (1972), 80–117 (the direct quotations from the 1512 address of Giles are on pp. 102–3 and 110–12).

History: T. Ashby and S. Pierce, "The Piazza del Popolo, Rome: Its History and Development," *Town Planning Review* 11 (1924), 75–96; E. Lavagnino, *Santa Maria del Popolo (Le Chiese di Roma Illustrate* 20) (Rome, 1925); Huelsen, *passim;* P. Rotondi, *La Chiesa di Santa Maria del Popolo e suoi monumenti* (Rome, 1930); R. Valentini and G. Zucchetti, *Codice Topografico della Città di Roma* 4 (Rome, 1953); and Buchowiecki III, 102–51.

Architecture: Tomei, 117–22; G. Urban, "Die Kirchenbaukunst des Quattrocento in Rom," *Römisches Jahrbuch für Kunstgeschichte* 9/10 (1961/62), 73–289; Angelis II, 407–516; Bruschi, 435–62, 911–21; L. Heydenreich and W. Lotz, *Architecture in Italy, 1400–1600* (Baltimore, 1974); S. Valtieri, "Santa Maria del Popolo in Roma," *L'Architettura* 236 (1975), 44–55; S. Bentivoglio, "Il Coro di S. Maria del Popolo e il Coro detta 'Del Rossellino' di S. Pietro," *Mitteilungen des kunsthistorischen Instituts in Florenz* 20 (1976), 197–204; Bentivoglio and Valtieri, *passim;* Frommel, "'Cappella Iulia'," 49–50, n. 97.

For a Renaissance reconstruction of the "Temple of Peace," which includes vaults, apse, and serlian windows similar to those of the Popolo, see Lotz, 53, fig. 16. For an earlier example of a citation of the temple, another reconstruction drawing, and its New Jerusalem connotations in a fifteenth-century fresco cycle, see E. Borsook and J. Offerhaus, "Storia e leggende nella cappella Sassetti in Santa Trinità," *Scritti di Storia dell'Arte in Onore di Ugo Procacci,* ed. M. and P. dal Poggetto (Milan, 1977), 289–310, esp. fig. 288.

The empty wreath in the shell of the apse probably contained the Julian arms, as suggested by the analogy with the tombs. At the top of the tombs the papal arms are placed in front of a shell at the feet of God the Father. The suggestion by Bentivoglio and Valtieri, 26 and 35–36, that the wreath contained the arms of Alexander VI is not convincing.

Sculpture: Rome. S. Maria del Popolo. Archive 2: 15th and 16th Century Sculpture in Italy, ed. I. C. Hill, Courtauld

Institute Illustration Archives (London, 1976); E. Panofsky, *Tomb Sculpture* (New York, 1964), 82; Pope-Hennessey, *Italian Renaissance Sculpture,* 66, 287, 322–23; idem, *Italian High Renaissance and Baroque Sculpture,* I, 41, 54–66 and III, 45–51; and Bentivoglio and Valtieri, 69, 164–65 (Ascanio Sforza).

Icon and high altar: J. Wilpert, *Die römischen Mosaiken und Malereien der kirchlichen Bauten vom IV bis XIII Jahrhundert* (Freiburg, 1916), IV, 299, no. 2; and Bentivoglio and Valtieri, 28, n. 19, 30, n. 27, 175–77 , 198–99.

Sixtus IV, Andrea Bregno, and Julius II were not alone in responding to the Popolo Madonna as a miracle working icon. Pius II paraded the image as part of his campaign against the Turks in 1463. Alexander VI gave thanks at the Popolo for narrowly escaping death when a chimney fell in the Vatican during a storm (Bentivoglio and Valtieri, 28 nn. 18, 54).

Painting: A. Schmarsow, *Bernardino Pinturicchio in Rom* (Stuttgart, 1882); J. Schulz, "Pinturicchio and the Revival of Antiquity," *Journal of the Warburg and Courtauld Institutes* 25 (1962), 35–55; E. Carli, *Il Pintoricchio* (Milan, 1960), 83–85.

The inscriptions of the sibyls in the vault are *Germen virginis erit salus gentium* (Persian); *In ultima etate humanabitur deus* (Erithean); *Dei filius incarne veniet ut iudicet orbem* (Crimean); *Invisibile verbum paleabitur* (Delphic).

Stained glass: G. Mancini, *Guglielmo di Marcillat* (Florence, 1909).

Relics: Dizionario delle reliquie e dei santi della chiesa di Roma (Florence, 1871), 170, and Huelsen, 150–51.

Virgin Mary

Sixtus IV: Pastor 2, *passim;* Chevalier, *passim;* Ettlinger, *Sistine Chapel,* 14–15; Angelis II, 407–516; Lotz, 68; and H. Ost, "Santa Margherita in Montefiascone: A Centralized Building Plan of the Roman Quattrocento," *Art Bulletin* 52 (1970), 373–89.

Julius II: See references, chapter one, "Renaissance Portraiture," subsection "Portraits of Julius"; E. Motta, "L'Università dei pittori milanesi nel 1481 con altri documenti d'arte del Quattrocento," *Archivo storico lombardo,* ser. 3, 22 (1895), 424; and N. Nilles, *De rationibus festorum sacratissimi Cordis Jesu et purissimi Cordis Mariae* (Oeniponte, 1885), II, 481–82.

Loreto: Chevalier, 233–34, 241–50, 251–71, and *passim;* Bruschi, 252–667, 960–69; Hill, nos. 868, 869; Pope-Hennessey, *Italian High Renaissance and Baroque Sculpture* III, 48–50; Pastor III, 760–61, 769 n. 2 and 785; Grassis, 190; and Luzio, "Federico Gonzaga," 526.

S. Maria di Loreto, Rome: S. Benedetti, *S. Maria di Loreto (Le chiese di Roma illustrate,* 100) (Rome, 1968).,

Raphael's "Madonna of the Veil": S. Vögelin, *Die Madonna von Loretto* (Zurich, 1870); F. Gruyer, *La Peinture au Château de Chantilly* (Paris, 1896), 91–93; L. Pfau, *Die Madonna von Loretto* (Zurich, 1922); F. Filippini, "Le vicende della Madonna di Loreto di Raffaello," *L'Illustrazione Vaticana* 5 (1934), 107–9; A. Scharf, "Raphael and the Getty Madonna," *Apollo* 79 (1964), 114–21; Dussler, 27–28; and B. Fredericksen, "New Information on Raphael's *Madonna di Loreto," The J. Paul Getty Museum Journal* 3 (1976), 5–45.

Ex votos: J. von Schlosser, "Geschichte der Porträtsbildnerei in Wachs," *Jahrbuch der kunsthistorischen Sammlungen des allerhöchsten Kaiserhauses* 29 (1911), 171–258; A. Warburg, "Bildniskunst und florentinisches Bürgertum," *Gesammelte Schriften* 1 (Leipzig, 1932), 89–126; Vasari III, 274; Arcangelo Maria Giani, *Annalium Sacri Ordiniis Fratrum Servorum B. Mariae Virginis* 2 (Florence, 1622), 46 (*ex voto* of Sixtus IV in SS. Annunziata); Sanuto XIII, 350 (S. Marcello portrait of Julius; for the burning of S. Mar-

cello see Buchowiecki II, 344); and R. Trexler, "Florentine Religious Experience: The Sacred Image," *Studies in
the Renaissance* 19 (1972), 7–42.

EPILOGUE: THE JULIAN IMAGE AND
HIGH RENAISSANCE CULTURE IN ROME

Perspectives on High Renaissance Culture

Vasari IV, 7–15; W. Ferguson, *The Renaissance in Historical Thought* (Cambridge, Mass., 1948), 59–67; *Storia
d'Italia* (Torino, 1974), I, 329–85; R. Lopez, "Hard Times
and Investment in Culture," *The Renaissance: A Symposium* (New York, 1952); W. Bouwsma, "Changing Assumptions in Later Renaissance Culture," *Viator* 7 (1976),
421–40; M. Foucault, *The Order of Things* (New York,
1973), 32; and N. Frye, *Anatomy of Criticism* (Princeton,
1957), 33–34, 119–120.

Credits for Photographs

Alinari/Anderson: 5, 6, 8, 10, 12, 15, 16, 17, 18, 19, 21, 22, 28, 29, 33, 34, 37, and 40.

Archives Photographiques: 3, 9, 11, 14, 24, 38, and 39.

Archivio Fotografico delle Gallerie e Musei Vaticani: 4 and 25.

R. Bainton, *Erasmus of Christendom* (New York, 1969), 105: 23.

Courtauld Institute: 20.

R. Delbrueck, *Die Consulardiptychen* (Berlin, 1929), Pl. 32: 26.

G. Fontana, *Raccolta delle migliori chiese di Roma e suburbane* (Rome, 1855), Pl. LVIII: 35 and 36.

Fototeca Unione, Rome: 7.

Gabinetto Fotografico Nazionale, Rome: 31 and 32.

G. Hill, *A Corpus of Italian Medals of the Renaissance before Cellini,* 2 vols. (London, 1930), No. 874: 27.

J. Klaczko, *Rome in the Renaissance: Pontificate of Julius II* (New York, 1903): 13.

The National Gallery, London: 1 and 2 (reproduced by courtesy of the Trustees).

J. Wilpert, *Die römischen Mosaiken und Malereien,* IV (Freiburg, 1916), Pl. 299, No. 2: 30.

Index

158   *Index*

Designer:	Eric Jungerman
Compositor:	Interactive Composition Corporation
Printer:	Thomson-Shore, Inc.
Binder:	Thomson-Shore, Inc.
Text:	VIP Bembo
Cloth:	Holliston Roxite B 53538
Paper:	60 lb. P&S Laid Offset

Plates

1. Raphael, *Portrait of Pope Julius II* (detail), 1511–12. London, National Gallery.

2. Raphael, *Portrait of Pope Julius II,* 1511–12. London, National Gallery.

3. Raphael (?), *Madonna of the Veil*, c. 1508–9. Chantilly, Musée Condé.

4. Pinturicchio, *Pope Alexander VI* (detail from the *Resurrection*), c. 1492–94. Fresco. Vatican, Borgia Apartments.

5. Filarete, *Pope Eugenius IV Receives Emperor John Paleologus*, c. 1440–45. Bronze Doors (detail). Vatican, St. Peter's.

6. Raphael, *Pope Gregory IX (as Pope Julius II) Receives the Decretals in 1234,* 1511. Fresco. Vatican, Stanza della Segnatura.

7. Aurelian Relief, *Liberalitas Augusti,* 161–80 A.D. Rome, Arch of
Constantine, 312–15 A.D.

8. Roman Sarcophagus, *Roman Emperor Crowned by Victory Receives Captives*. Vatican Museum.

9. Justus of Ghent, *Pope Sixtus IV*, c. 1474. From the *studiolo* in the Palazzo Ducale, Urbino. Louvre, Paris.

10. Melozzo da Forlì, *Pope Sixtus IV Appoints Platina Prefect of the Vatican Library*, 1476–77. Fresco. From the Vatican Library. Vatican, Pinacoteca.

11. Anonymous, *Portrait of John the Good,* c. 1360–64. Paris, Louvre.

12. Fouquet, *Portrait of Charles VII,* mid-fifteenth century. Paris, Louvre.

13. Anonymous, *Portrait of Julius II in 1510–11.* Mid-sixteenth-century copy. Tarquinia, Museo Nazionale.

14. Uccello (?), *Portrait of a Man,* 1430s. Chambéry, Musée des Beaux-Arts.

15. Botticelli, *Portrait of a Man with a Medal of Cosimo de' Medici,* 1470s. Florence, Uffizi.

16. Leonardo, *Portrait of Mona Lisa,* 1504–10. Paris, Louvre.

17. Raphael, *Portrait of Maddalena Doni,* c. 1506. Florence, Pitti.

18. Raphael, *Portrait of Agnolo Doni,* c. 1506. Florence, Pitti.

19. Raphael, *Portrait of a Cardinal,* c. 1510. Madrid, Prado.

20. Raphael, *Portrait of Pope Julius II,* 1511. Drawing. Chatsworth, Duke of Devonshire Collection.

21. Raphael, *Mass of Bolsena*, c. 1512. Fresco. Vatican, Stanza d'Eliodoro.

22. Raphael, *Expulsion of Heliodorus*, c. 1512. Fresco. Vatican, Stanza d'Eliodoro.

23. Anonymous, *Pope Julius II Excluded from Heaven*. Woodcut. Title page of the 1522–23 German edition of Erasmus, *Julius Exclusus*.

24. After Matteo Giovanetti of Viterbo (?), *Portrait of Pope Clement VI Receiving a Diptych in the Presence of John the Good,* c. 1342. From the sacristy of St. Chapelle, Paris. Paris, Bibliothèque Nationale, Estampes, Oa 11, fol. 85.

25. Anonymous, *Antonio da Rho Presents His Three Dialogues on the Errors of Lactantius to Pope Eugenius IV,* c. 1431–47. Vatican, Lat. Vat. 227.

26. Consular Diptych, *Consul Orestes*, 530 A.D. Ivory.
London, Victoria and Albert Museum.

27. Anonymous, *Portrait of Pope Julius II* inscribed IVLIVS
CAESAR PONT II, obverse; *Rovere and Papal Arms*
inscribed BENEDI[CTVS] QV[I] VENIT I[N] NO[MINE]
D[OMINI], reverse; 1507. Bronze medal.

28. Raphael, *Sistine Madonna*, c. 1512–13. Dresden,
Gemäldegallerie.

29. Andrea Bregno, *Altarpiece,* 1473. Marble. From the high altar of Santa Maria del Popolo. Rome, Santa Maria del Popolo, Sacristy.

30. Anonymous, *Virgin and Child*, c. 1300. Rome, Santa Maria del
Popolo, high altar.

31. Anonymous, *Before the Birth of Pope Sixtus IV, an Icon of the Virgin and Child and SS. Francis and Anthony Appear to His Mother Luchina*, 1478–84. Fresco. Rome, Hospital of Santo Spirito.

32. Anonymous, *Pope Sixtus IV Founds Santa Maria del Popolo*, 1478–84. Fresco. Rome, Hospital of Santo Spirito.

33. Andrea Sansovino, *Tomb of Ascanio Sforza,* 1505. Marble.
Rome, Santa Maria del Popolo, Choir.

34. Sansovino, *Tomb of Girolamo Basso della Rovere,* 1507. Marble.
Rome, Santa Maria del Popolo, Choir.

35. After Marcillat, *Life of the Virgin,* c. 1509–10. Stained glass. Rome, Santa Maria del Popolo.

36. After Marcillat, *Life of Christ,* c. 1509–10. Stained glass. Rome, Santa Maria del Popolo.

37. Pinturicchio, *Vault,* c. 1509–10. Fresco. Rome, Santa Maria del Popolo, Choir.

38. Giovanni Mazone, *Holy Family with SS. Francis and Anthony of Padua and Donors Pope Sixtus IV and Cardinal Giuliano della Rovere,* before 1484. From the Chapel of Sixtus in the Cathedral of Savona. Paris, Louvre.

39. Mazone, *Holy Family* (detail with Cardinal
Guiliano della Rovere).

40. Vicenzo Foppa, *Virgin and Child with Donor
Cardinal Giuliano della Rovere,* 1490. From
the high altar of the cathedral at Savona.
Savona, Oratory of S. Maria di Castello.

Sexual Ethics

Liberal vs. Conservative

Bruce Fleming

University Press of America,® Inc.
Dallas · Lanham · Boulder · New York · Oxford

Library of Congress Control Number: 2004102177
ISBN 0-7618-2864-8 (paperback: alk. ppr.)

Contents

Preface

Why are people embarrassed to talk about sex? Why do arguments about sexually-related subjects like abortion and pornography raise the ire of the debaters to such a fever pitch?

Sex is different. It is neither completely part of the personal realm nor completely part of the social. Though sexual relations all start in the social realm, as they intensify they go increasingly by the seat of their pants, throwing away the rule book. This makes them impervious to ethics, which offers general rules in the social realm. Precisely because sexual relations ultimately slip from the grasp of ethics, ethics clutches ever more desperately after them. The personal realm is completely beyond the reach of ethics. If ethics has a say, the issue is no longer purely part of the personal realm.

The most heated debate regarding sexual matters, as well as others, is between liberals and conservatives. Conservatives rejoice at (say) setting up carvings of the Ten Commandments in public places; liberals see the end of democracy. Conservatives are for military action as a solution to countless problems; liberals counsel reflection.

Nowhere is the head-butting more intense than around the age's flash-point topic: abortion. Conservatives insist that "life begins at conception"; liberals insist on the mother's right to choice. "It's a Child, not a Choice," respond the conservatives. The logjam is complete.

Liberal and conservative are patterns of thought, underlying structures. The particular tenets of liberals and conservatives are the result of the patterns. The only hope for breaking the jam is by understanding the underlying structures. On the surface is only disagreement. In the underlying structures, we find divergence, but we will at least avoid the disagreement.

Conservative ethics expresses its general rules in terms of actions. "Thou shalt not X" is an intrinsically conservative pronouncement. Liberal ethics expresses its general rules in terms of actors. For this reason liberal thought must always consider the specific circumstances. Liberal thought will, when possible, avoid doctrinaire assertions altogether. When it does utter them, they come out with a list of caveats. Conservatives snort in derision. "May I steal?" is a conservative question, a question to which conservatives know the answer already. "May I steal this bread to feed my family?" is a liberal question.

Conservatives see individuals as being guided by rules outside themselves. As a result, conservatives get to see themselves as firm and pro-active. They practice tough love. They are not wimps.

Liberals see conservatives as stupidly stubborn. Why not allow abortion for the victims of rape? ask liberals. Why not for young women whose lives would otherwise be blighted? Why not for couples that want a baby later? No abortions, no exceptions, no waffling, rejoin conservatives. Rules are rules, and rules must be followed.

A liberal bumper sticker sums up the fundamental disconnect between liberals and conservatives. "Against Abortion? Don't Do It" it taunts. It's snide because liberals know perfectly well that what conservatives want is not merely that conservatives should not practice abortion, but that no one should. Conservative thought expresses itself in a rule of action, which means, action for everyone.

The disconnect between liberals and conservatives on sexual topics is almost complete in the America of the early twenty-first century. Whether or not liberal and conservative can continue to co-exist under the umbrella of American democracy will depend on whether or not they ultimately give their primary obedience to the larger structure of which they are both a part.

Bruce E. Fleming
Annapolis, Maryland
September 15, 2003

Chapter One

The Problem with Sex

Sex is Different

Sex is theoretically problematic in our lives in a way that other things or activities are not. It's simultaneously something many of us spend countless hours thinking about, and a subject we are almost forbidden to refer to in polite company. It's the most intimate of activities yet, in recent decades, it's all over the West in the images of commodified consumption: sex sells.

We all like sex, but we still call pictures or books with sexual content "dirty." We still use a vast vocabulary of words implying physical decay (the opposite of "pure") associated with people, especially women, who engage in sexual activities outside of narrowly circumscribed situations, usually marriage. The double standard here is alive and well: a woman with many partners is a "whore," a man with many partners is a "stud." The concept of a "fate worse than death" for women as a synonym for rape, especially pre-marital virginity-destroying rape, may have disappeared, yet rape counseling nowadays deals largely with the woman's own sense of having been humiliated and defiled.

Sex is fundamental to our lives, yet it's shot through with taboos. It's anti-social, sometimes causing us to betray our friends as well as the objects of our desires—though of course this means it involves other people. It's completely personal, yet at the same time impersonal. We can never answer the question, Are we attracted to this person for him/herself? Or merely an instantiation of his or her sexual possibilities?

Sex doesn't fit with the other things we do. It has nothing to do with the rules for getting along with other people that we are supposed to have learned in kindergarten. How, many people have wondered, can we spend most of our time talking rationally with other people, treating them with respect, deferring to the wishes we anticipate them having, and suddenly, with the exchange of glances, a few words, perhaps a few minutes over white wine, be grappling in a sweaty twist on the floor, one person pinning the other down, the pinned down one begging to be overwhelmed? How can it feel so right to throw (say) the woman we promised to love, honor, and cherish, to the bed and enter her in great lunging thrusts? Is this an extension of cherishing, or its Janus face? How can she be so eager to have us do this? And then we talk normally when it is over, offer the other person the bathroom first, get a towel, or discuss tomorrow, next week, the weather, or the logistics of our next encounter—like a shifting of gears, a new beginning. Was the person who did all that the same person as ourself?

No wonder, when we catch our breath, the whole thing seems somewhat strange, as if we had been grabbed by the scruff of the neck by a great hand coming out of the sky and made to do things we otherwise would never have done. And then, at least temporarily, it's all over and we return to normal.

Sex teeters uneasily between the social and the personal realms, with aspects of both and defining features of neither. The oddness of sex is that we don't have a rule book for it. We're flying by the seat of our pants: what we do is made up in each individual case. At the same time, what we do is quite abstract, following the rules for similar situations. We re-negotiate the combination in each particular case, and so the action itself seems neither.

Because ethics is a social expression form, ethics finds itself particularly uncomfortable with sex. This is so for what we may call structural reasons; that's just the way sex is. We may engage in sex, but we cannot justify it ethically to others, or indeed talk about it in a social vocabulary at all.

In his Sonnet 129, Shakespeare expresses this sense of the strange power of sex to control us, to pick us up like a tornado and whirl us around before, abruptly, dropping us with a bump. The poem's subject is simply "lust"—carnal lust, we assume, rather than lust in any metaphoric sense, say, for money, or for power. More specifically, it's an excellent description of male, rather than female, lust. Women still are not typically the sexual aggressors, in a position to engage in the lying, cheating and stealing the poet says we do engage in to get at the object of our lust.

What characterizes lust in this poem is an astonishing divergence of attitude on the part of the person caught up in it between the way he (the pronoun seems inescapable) feels before the act, and the way he feels after. According to the poem, a man will do anything to get sex. Lust "till action," the narrator (or poet) tells us, "is perjured, murderous, bloody, full of blame, savage, extreme, rude, cruel, not to trust." Of course, he concedes, having sex—what he calls "lust in proof"—is "bliss." Yet we repent immediately: we "despise" it as soon as we have enjoyed it. What we despise is apparently lust itself, the subject of the poem. After the fact, it's a "woe." This is another reason to assume that male lust, in particular, is the subject of this poem. The nature of the female orgasm seems different from the male—not the abrupt drop-off from the cliff that leaves the man completely uninterested for a certain period, but something more wave-like.

After we've given in to lust, we wonder what that was all about— at least for a short period. The act goes from seeming, before the fact, "a joy proposed," to afterwards merely being a "dream." Certainly men will understand this one. Jokes abound about the intensity of male disinterest in the woman after orgasm—a disinterest that, to the woman, seems paradoxical when compared with the intensity of male interest before. And women probably would have preferred cuddling anyhow. At least that's what 74% of the respondents to a poll taken by the late advice columnist Ann Landers said, according to her *Washington Post* obituary.

Lust in all three of its phases is out of the ordinary: "Had, having, and in quest to have, extreme." Not that we can do anything to avoid it. We have it inside us. Lust according to Shakespeare is like "a swallowed bait/ On purpose laid to make the taker mad." Nowadays we'd say, we're born with the pre-programming for the hormones. What to do? Nothing, except accept it. "All this the world well knows; yet none knows well/ To shun the heaven [orgasm?] that leads men to this hell"—where hell, presumably, is the whole endless cycle of mad desire and the depths of repentant abnegation afterwards.

To be sure, the narrator's extremes here may seem a bit too extreme to be completely true to life. How many people really kill and perjure to get at their sex objects? How many of us collapse into the abyss of despair after the fact? We may suspect that the narrator is exaggerating for dramatic, almost comic effect.

Yet though we see a caricature of the life we know, we will probably at least shake our heads ruefully in acknowledgment that Shakespeare has got the basic oddness of sex right, the way it clouds our senses and then makes us think.

For some people, sex is firmly excluded from the rest of life, relegated to an "other" world whose clearest quality is that is not the waking full-lit world of talk and social interaction. Sex is associated with the night, with beds, with the private spaces of life. The euphemism "to sleep with," with variants in all European languages, means to have sex with.

Most of the vocabulary the social world has for sex is that of the un-social, or completely private one. It is the world not only of our thoughts and feelings that rarely if ever find direct expression to the outside, but also of things known which no one else is ever aware of. For example, waiting to enter a line of traffic, the precise moment at which there is a large enough space for us to slip in. This is what I call "disposable knowledge," used up in a single action. A purely private question slips from the bounds of ethics. Shall I have vanilla or chocolate ice cream? No one cares; this one is up to us. Shall I watch TV or read a book? Probably, it doesn't matter, and we get to make the choice based on what we call inclination or whim.

To be sure, some apparently private questions and choices can be found to have public ramifications, and at this point they enter the world of ethics. Let us say it turns out the flavoring used in vanilla ice cream is found in the rain forest, which is being destroyed for its harvest. Or that TV rots my brain and so makes me less able to keep down my job. Or my SUV is contributing to global warming. There may be a reason why I should read the book rather than watch TV, or the reverse.

The boundary between the public, ethical realm and the private is fluid, but at any given time we can usually say where it is. Over time, general conceptions of where this boundary is may change. There are micro-worlds consisting of a few people, such as the family unit that at one time would have fallen under the sphere of the father's personal world, with all decisions made the affair of the father alone. Now, increasingly, they are relegated to the social side of the line, with strict limits regarding what kinds of actions are permitted on his part. All ethical pronouncements encroach on the private sphere like civilization on the desert; all find their limits in the boundless and uncharted vistas of the personal.

Not that all of the choices of the personal realm are as trivial as the choice between vanilla or chocolate. Most of the great realizations of our life are in the personal realm. We realize that we are, say, afraid of life, or fulfilled, or sexually unsatisfied, or have fallen in or out of love. Or our fleeting memories of great hopes that have foundered on the rocks of reality, or family, or economic necessity: it may be that no one at all will ever hear about these things. Or our so-vivid sense of a family member, now dead: there may be no one alive who wants to hear about this person, and so we guard him or her in a world of our own. The personal realm is composed of all those things we keep to ourselves, for whatever reason.

This is part of one person's personal realm: One August day, I drove into Washington, D.C. to go to the Hirshhorn Museum. I went alone. During the two hours I spent in Washington, I spoke to no one. I drove to the shaded street in front of the U.S. Capitol where, on weekends, parking spaces usually taken up by government employees' cars are available, and felt myself lucky to get an ideal parking spot in the shade. It was hot.

On the way to the Hirshhorn, I was overwhelmed by the dry grass, turned whitish, under the inadequately shading rows of trees. The buildings by my side, the East Wing of the National Gallery of Art, and then the West Wing, were equally white, so that the dry grass and whitish dirt their dessication revealed seemed unified with the buildings around them, as if I had entered a blanched world. The world was all of a piece with the white pathways on which a few tired joggers moved in a way that it is not here in the spring, when the grass, still flush with green and moisture, makes such a contrast with the paths. No one shared my pleasure at this world transformed, the way the brilliant colors of a New England autumn alter the familiar, or snow that turns things to white shapes.

In the museum, I stood in an exhibit of photographs of cityscapes, transfixed at the way the highly polished gray floors with the interrupted trapezoids of light entering from doorways reflected blurred versions of the pictures on the walls, as if the world did not end at the floor but only continued downward, and myself suspended at half-height within it.

A few minutes later, I looked out the window at the transitory patterns of the spume of water in the central courtyard that reaches to the top story of the museum, where we are equal or slightly above its apogee, as if seeing it frozen in mid-air. There was a rainbow at its base, probably invisible from the ground.

As I watched, a little girl, miniaturized by distance, moved ahead of her mother and began to run, then fell. I watched the mother pick the child up in miniaturized dumb-show, dust her off, comfort her, and set her on her feet again, at which point she darted forward again and then was lost under the underhang of the building. This was a small drama both from her life, that of her mother, and mine, as well (of course) as part of the social world of the family below. They did not know I watched them, or that I smiled, thinking that such moments occur billions of unremarked times all around us every day.

The exhibit I had come to see included photographs by William Eggleston that were more delicate than the ones I associated with his name, his earlier ones almost like merciless colorized Diane Arbus-like dissections of Middle American objects in all their garishness: cars, billboards, clocks. These were subtler. A ray of sun that drew from shadow an uneven stone wall and so created a symphony of browns with two passing cars. An alleyway that, because of a passer-by's coat and the light, became shades of the same pale yellows. The juxtaposition of a hotel sign with the paving of a street that made clear they were from the same family of darks. Had the framing been a bit different, the angle changed slightly, the color film only a bit less sensitive, the moving object not frozen in this place, there would have been no coordination, none of the sense of the world falling, if only briefly, into place. By having the technique to make these photographs of these chance color convergences of such minute shades, Eggleston had found a way of allowing them to enter the public realm

Up the street, the entrance hallway to the National Museum of African Art was more beautiful than I had ever seen it. Partly roped off, lined with unidentifiable semi-industrial shapes abandoned in crippled postures, the long hallway with light flooding it from the garden outside had been primed for an application of paint but was still unpainted: Please Excuse Our Appearance, a sign read, We Are Installing A New Exhibition. Nothing to excuse, I thought. How beautiful they were, these unfinished walls in light brown, with the seams painted in long slightly uneven white lines with a few floating rectangles of white made by the same brush beside them.

If I had the technique of an Eggleston, and my camera with me, I could have probably somehow captured this strange world of beiges, the lighter soft-shaped shapes both regular and irregular on the walls. To an artist, these walls, this hallway, would have been the artwork. As interesting things, however, they were clearly part of the private realm. Not intended as ends in themselves nor meant to be looked at in their current state, they gave me a private pleasure like that I got from watching the evanescent patterns of the Hirshhorn fountain. Such things were the basis of the Eggleston photographs, which had taken things with no importance for anyone but the individual and made them public.

How am I feeling today? Melancholy? Excited? It may not matter to anyone but myself, unless it does. Others can ask me, or I can volunteer this information, but the vast majority of such things of which our lives are made are born and die in the confines of the self. Does my getting this particular parking space that day in Washington matter? Whom can I share this with? Perhaps my wife, for whom my whole day is something to share. Perhaps with my patron saint, if I believe she was responsible for my serendipity.

Everyone has such tiny successes or failures; things like these simply do not, usually, make it to the big stage. Occasionally, though rarely, some of the things of which our private worlds are composed have greatness, so to say, thrust upon 'em. Suddenly we find ourselves in court, with an army of lawyers focusing on the minutest details of a day we had completely forgotten. Who knew that someday someone would be interested in this? Or one day a family member asks us about a departed person, or a television crew arrives to interview us as the Last Living Whatever and demands our recollections. Suddenly, we might say, somebody cares. Or alternately, for whatever reason we are suddenly willing to share things that we have kept for ourselves for decades. The private realm is the ocean on which float the islands of the social.

Earlier centuries tended to demand an absolute line between social and private, insisting that many private realizations had no public ramifications at all. A woman might realize she wasn't in love with her husband, but what she was supposed to do about it was precisely nothing. Nowadays people seem so eager to make all aspects of their lives part of the private realm there is a tendency to believe that we must all be constantly in search of a stage to perform on, that all of the private sphere exists only to be valorized in the public.

Yet even people who are happy to wash their dirty laundry in public (as we say, using a metaphor that reveals a more rigid conception of private and public than may be operative today, comparing our experiences to the unsightly and private fact of clothing full of the odors of our bodies) do not look on all the things in their personal realms as amenable to public sharing. Did the coffee taste good this morning, or bitter? Did I sleep well, or not so well? Am I getting my hair cut today or tomorrow? Typically, no one but we ourselves will care, so we do not think of these things as candidates for social expression.

Much of sex is relegated to this personal realm. Yet a great deal of what we do in the service of sex, as Shakespeare pointed out, is very social indeed. To begin with, we should note, as Shakespeare did not, that we typically we do it with another person, who must be found, plucked from the social continuum. In most cases we must move from the "How do you do?" world of the social to the sexual world, which is very different. All of us know what it feels like to pass this boundary, to re-negotiate the givens of a relationship with someone. Only with prostitutes, defined by their availability for sex, can we dispense with the transition from social to personal realm.

Though to a large degree, we associate sex with the private realm, it is ultimately unsatisfying to relegate sex too absolutely to the world of the private and the night. This is undoubtedly the source of the extreme erotic charge for some people of sex in public, and hence forbidden, places. We are constantly negotiating the boundary of sexual acts with the social sphere. Indeed, we will never be able to come up with a definition of what is sexual and what is not. Under certain circumstances, a touch on the arm may be sexual, in others not. Even the views of the people involved as to whether an interaction was or was not sexual may diverge, or change. Did he mean it this way? Or the other? The question itself may be a torment.

In sexual interaction, rules can fly out the window. We make things up as we go along. If the other person gives us the right look, we realize instantly that politeness or deference is the last things we should offer. The man, generally, is expected to know how to proceed, and the woman wants him to—to use the terms of the most common form of sex. Or at least this is true in many cases: sometimes one partner wants something not so "vanilla," as we say. This must be negotiated, and usually this cannot happen right away. If the basic game plan of a sexual encounter is not so easily assumed for whatever reasons, negotiations are carried out which determine how and whether things will proceed.

Sex escapes absolutes. In sexual relations, there don't seem to be any completely right or wrong answers, at least not ones we can know beforehand. As we get deeper and deeper into a sexual relationship, we are increasingly in uncharted waters, one thing leading to another, lost without a guide book. If something feels "right," we are likely to do it, with diminishing thoughts of what the world considers proper. We go with our instincts, reading our partner's reactions and correlating them with our own desires, or offering desires and trying out fits with our partner's reactions, reacting to our partner's desires with sometimes surprising discoveries about ourselves. This is information that matters to no one but ourself and our partner. It can never be shared and is applicable to no other circumstances in the world, unless in generalized form.

Sexuality is the most personal of all the social relationships and the most social circumstances of the personal world. Frequently, there is a long checklist of conditions that sexual relations must satisfy first before they are allowed to leave the social sphere where they begin. Are both parties willing? Are they of age? Some people would add questions like, Are they of opposite sexes? Will they avoid specific practices X, Y, and Z or engage in specific practices A, B, and C? The checklist can be applied at any time. If we get a negative response to a question, the deal is off, the sex comes to an end. A woman may initially welcome a man's advances and stop herself only subsequently—on the grounds that she is married, for example. A woman may be drawn to another woman and stop herself for precisely that reason: she isn't "supposed to be" doing this.

Other situations may hit the wall of the socially (im)permissible on behalf of those involved in the sexual relation, as in the case of pedophile priests, or rape, or sexual favors curried under duress. Those being victimized (as we say) may not be in a position to object. If they are, they may not be able to do anything about it. Other people may be the ones to determine how much of the interaction should be expressed in social terms, which is to say in terms of generalities. Most people would say it is never right for a grown man to molest (as we say) a 12-year-old boy, even if the boy is unaware that there is anything wrong with it.

The Ambiguous Nature of Sex

We haven't ever figured out what role sex should play in life. Is it private? Social? If something in between, why is it still something we don't talk about in front of strangers, and even most friends?

Most people would associate sex with our "animalistic" side, one of the physical needs that embarrass us to because we would like to believe ourselves "beyond" such things. Perhaps for this reason, the taboos associated with sex are similar in some ways to the taboos associated with defecation. However, we see that defecation ends up being classified as part of the personal sphere, whereas the position of sex is much more ambiguous.

To be sure, we both defecate and engage in sex behind closed doors, use terms from both as sources for the transgressory speech we call swearing, and don't speak of either in polite company. In some ways, indeed, sex is the more publicly acceptable subject; we cannot imagine a Broadway show devoted to defecation, in the way that *Oh! Calcutta* was devoted to sex.

In the nineteenth century, women were discouraged as strongly from expressing their sexuality as they were from exercising. Ladies didn't "sweat," they "perspired." Men, by contrast, were allowed to sweat, even to exercise if they were of a mind to, and could talk about their sexual exploits, though not of course with ladies. Nowadays women may sweat and express their sexuality to the same degree as men; greater freedom has made it clear that exercise is something that may be done in public for both sexes, whereas sex is not. Greater gender equality has allowed differentiation between "animalistic" activities lumped together in earlier eras because of gender differentiation.

The master Spanish filmmaker Buñuel, in a movie from his later years entitled *The Discreet Charm of the Bourgeoisie* consisting of a series of semi-surreal skits, ruminates on the relation between the two bodily functions of eating and defecation. In one segment, proper bourgeois sit on toilets grouped around a table and chat, then retire to tiny airless rooms (in France, the toilet is still typically segregated from what is more literally the "bathroom" and relegated to a "water closet") to gulp down food, stuffing the entire chicken leg in their mouth in their haste to get this distasteful activity behind them. Why, the film seems to be asking, do we privatize the one and not the other?

Some cultures do privatize eating. In Rwanda, for example, where I lived for a time, male strangers are not invited for meals, only for beer and peanuts with the men. Meals are more intimate, involving both the protected members of the family and acknowledgement of private needs to a greater extent than the more sedate drinking and quick cupping to the mouth of hard peanuts. Nor is American food consumption so public as Mediterranean; not so much time is spent at it, and it is not considered good manners to partake too heartily. "Fast food," after all, is Anglo-Saxon in origin, and utterly antithetical to the Latin aesthetic. Think of the French insistence on *gastronomie*, or the Italian proverb that "*a tavola, non si invecchia*": time spent at the table doesn't count against one's mortal span of fourscore years and ten.

Most of the etiquette associated with eating aims to eradicate animalistic feeding, replacing it with polite "dining." Eating has been covered over with so many rituals that its fundamentally biological nature has all but disappeared; it seems to have been integrated, in Western cultures at least, into the social world.

Defecation has been steered to the private. Sex, alone among the bodily functions, teeters uneasily between these realms. Defecation is a means to an end, not an end in itself. Since it requires only one person, and usually has a place devoted to it, it "fits" with the rest of life as something we do alone, like the rest of our personal hygiene. Most of us don't like to look at images of defecation or think about it, as we do sex.

We can imagine a switch similar to Buñuel's of sex and conversation with strangers, where what once was called "free love" is the initial level of contact between unknown people, whereas conversation is engaged in only with select people behind closed doors. Indeed, people *have* imagined such worlds; they are the stuff of dystopias including Huxley's *Brave New World* and Margaret Atwood's cautionary tale about reproductive freedom, *The Handmaid's Tale.* Clearly sex is not an unalloyed part of the social sphere. At the same time it is not merely private.

The more we try to relegate sex to the completely private sphere the way we have relegated defecation, the less comfortably it occupies that space. Even nowadays when we may believe ourselves unshockable about so many things, the presence or absence of sexual relations determines the nature of a relationship between two people in others' eyes in a way that completely private activities do not. Sexual activity of other people holds a power to change our social view of them that other activities do not have. Is X "sleeping with" Y or not? It is the big definer of our view of relationships in a way that the answer to the question, "is X having coffee with Y?" or "is X playing golf with Y?" is not.

We may find somewhat archaic the world of Henry James's *The Ambassadors*, where the virginal narrator Lambert Strether is prepared to defend the unconventional friendship of Chad, the young man he has gone to France to bring back to America, with a Frenchwoman—until the day when Strether realizes that the relationship is precisely what others had been assuming it to be, or at least asserting it had the appearance of being: a sexual one. At that point his defense evaporates. His attempt to be *moderne* and in touch with new ways is revealed as a pitiable attempt of old age to play a game that was far beyond his capabilities.

Most young men in America today would have no compunctions telling even their parents (to whom most sexual things cannot be said, though it was precisely these people who copulated to produce us) that they were having a "relationship" (if not an "affair"—too old-fashioned) with an older woman. The notion that young people have a string of sexual relationships before marriage does not upset us any more, unless we preach abstinence until marriage.

Yet sexual intercourse or its absence is still as much of a binary relationship-definer now for a relationship as it was for Henry James's world, even if the subject is not so shocking. The "modernity" of Strether's daring leap, which (in his own view) turns out to be a leap into the abyss, lies in accepting the possibility of a Platonic friendship between a man and a woman. We may be more ready than he or his world to accept a sexual relationship, but we still want to know the same thing that mattered so much to Henry James's characters: is the relationship sexual or is it not? The default position is still to assume that if a man and a woman are spending a lot of time together, they are sexually involved. It still takes a leap of faith to persuade us that a young man and an attractive woman can merely be "friends." At the very least, accepting this state of affairs raises suspicions regarding the young man's virility. Sex or its lack matters socially.

My claim is that we can explain our squeamishness with sex by its structural qualities alone, without recourse as an explanation to the obviously circular difference that the sexual relationship includes sex. There must be something different about our relationships with people in friendship and in sexual encounters. At the same time, clearly there are some similarities.

Both can involve either many or few people, depending on our circumstances: we can spend our whole life with a single sexual partner, or with a few friends. And of course some very personal social situations share the no-rule-book aspects of sexuality. One of them is parenting. No parent knows who his or her child is; this is something that has to be discovered. This starts at birth. Each mother or father learns the meaning of the child's various cries: wet, hungry, tired. This is half-private, half-public information relevant for no one else but the three people involved, and information moreover with a limited half-life. By the time the child is two years old it may be useless, but until then it is something that must be learned and retained.

In the same way, we can learn things about someone we live with but are not involved with sexually: a roommate, say. We learn whether or not s/he is likely to do the dishes, what his/her likes and dislikes are, and so on. A marriage, no matter how much or how little sex we are having within it, involves aspects of learning about the other person— how s/he likes coffee or tea, where his or her back is to be scratched, and so on. After the roommate leaves, or after a divorce, this information becomes orphan information. Assuming a child grows up and remains in contact with us, the new things we learn about him or her "grow over" the old, and our sense of loss is kept to a minimum. But let us say we lose contact with the child, perhaps through divorce or another sort of rupture. The information we had about the (say) ten-year-old floats in a vacuum, left behind as surely as if from the roommate who has moved away, becoming once again part of the private sphere.

What's personal is also private, but the fact that something is private isn't what makes it personal. Social relations, whether with one person or many, are highly codified; personal relationships are not. Because the degree of predictability can vary minutely from relationship to relationship, the distinction between personal relations and the social world is not absolute, which means the relationship between sexual relations and other relations is not absolute either. Still, sexual relations are different from all others, even if they bear some similarity to certain specific non-sexual relationships.

Our social lives are lived along a spectrum of social situations varying from the most rigid and codified to those we are allowed to make up as we go along. In the more structured relations of the social world, such as our interactions with the mail carrier or the person who checks out our groceries, we follow unvarying rules for interactions. In more unstructured circumstances of the social world, we interact with another person in a more supple way, but still according to rules of what we call politeness. These rules include that we allow the other to speak first, offer our opinions but do not force them on the other, listen for their views, offer things to say that are appropriate and interesting but not overbearing, and so on.

Many relationships change nature in the middle from less personal to more so (and occasionally the reverse), and we must (and are able to) change gears with them. Even when we stand in the grocery line, expecting only the question of "paper or plastic?," we are probably prepared to engage in some more personalized conversation with the checker, which either of us might initiate. And if a more personal situation developed—say, it turned out we knew the woman when she was a girl, or that she had baby-sat us when we were a child—we would not insist on keeping the relationship within the expected boundaries.

Our interactions with other people are like a complex machine with interlocking wheels of many sizes and degrees of predictability, some of which may in turn intersect with the sexual realm or the personal.

We have relationships with only one other person, say our spouse; with several, say our children; with a group, say our students or colleagues; and with the vast mass of other individuals, in which people like the checkout person usually falls. We usually switch from one to another without problems, excusing ourselves from a meeting to deal with a family emergency, asking less pressing matters to wait, and so on. The fact that we are simultaneously juggling many balls can produce collisions between these groupings, or even total collapses.

We in the West, for example, are currently resolving the intrusion of personal telephone conversations into the social sphere that the cell phone has made possible. Instead of slipping into a telephone booth to take care of our phoning needs, or doing this in the privacy of our office or home, some people carry on lengthy conversations with friends and family within earshot of perfect strangers who willy nilly are forced to follow along. In the same way the appropriation of public land for the erection of private mourning symbols in the United States, usually roadside crosses bedecked with flowers at the sight of an automobile accident, has begun to drift north from Latin Mexico, where it has long been the custom. Perhaps hospital rooms will soon be filled to bursting with plastic flowers in memory of those who have died there, leaving no room for the beds of people being treated.

In what way does a death at this particular spot transfer the land use rights to the family of the dead person? This makes clear that the study of interpersonal relationships has many variables. Some cultures demand less in terms of personal space than ours does. In addition they share the sense that public land is alien, rather than belonging to the collective, and so can and should be appropriated as an entitlement, at least under the abnormal circumstances of sudden death. The fact that a member of my family died here on this public land makes this my land.

Consideration of the transitions between eras or geographically-defined places give us many examples of mutations between the personal and the public. A person from a different part of the world or from a different position in society, or a time traveler, will all be perceived as odd, lacking in manners. Indeed, the rules of etiquette of whatever time and place are designed to uphold the barrier between personal and social in that particular time and place. The precise rules of etiquette are precisely what change over time. The act of reading in the Medieval world, for example, was almost universally a public activity: one person read aloud to many. The alteration to silent reading was a cultural shift making reading more personal. Nowadays it is acceptable for people to walk around in public in clothing that only decades ago would have been reserved for private spaces.

Yet sexual encounters, though similar to many of the more personal social situations, as well as to aspects of our personal life, are still neither fully one nor fully the other of these. They are different from, say, relationships with our children, which can be arranged on a scale ranging from personal at one end (typified by the autocratic parent: children are merely emanations of the parents) to the very social (children must be respected), but are rarely the strange hybrid that typifies sexuality. Nor is a sexual relationship the same as same-sex Platonic bonding, which exhibits many of the elements of a sexual relationship, without giving up the respect that characterizes social interaction and that becomes beside the point in sexual relationships.

Take male bonding as an example. Men don't push their buddies; all interactions take place if and only if the other man wants to do something of his own volition. Male friendships strain when the other man is asked to do something he doesn't want to do, just because the other man wants him to. This means, almost inevitably, failing to treat him as a free agent. The relationship becomes too intimate for most men. It breaks all the social rules of male bonding and begins to reek of the sexually intimate. Men who feel that their buddies are beginning to pressure them will always protest.

Shakespeare's Sonnet 129 also captured what makes sex different from any other social relationship, and why it has elements of the personal world without being part of that world either. It's the way sex takes over our lives for briefer or longer periods of time like an alien force commandeering our bodies. Sexual desire has elements of the obsessive need to eat that have been drummed out of social dining, the fact of our being willing to tear others apart if they get in the way, and the way we fall on our prey. In the case of eating after great hunger, we tear our food apart with our hands and teeth; in the case of sexual desire we copulate. The two actions seem equally intense, to take us over and crowd all other things off the stage. Animalistic eating has been all but eliminated by regular access to food. Sex has developed its own rituals: candles, white wine, candles. But sex loses its point if the animalistic center is toned down. This obsessive quality of sexuality, the way it takes over the system, is what makes sexuality in some ways part of the personal world and also articulates its fundamental paradox: we give way, but to our own desire. It is also what puts its other foot in the social realm, the realm of other people.

In his metaphor of desire as the chariot's horses from the *Symposium,* Plato famously stressed the necessity for rationality, the charioteer, to keep tight control of the otherwise wild horses. In my schema, the charioteer comes from the world of the social, the wild horses are from the world of the personal. Yet the metaphoric fit isn't very tight. Personal desire in my structure isn't intrinsically suspicious, nor intrinsically in need of control. It is merely irrelevant with respect to the social world, in the same way that no one cares whether I order vanilla or chocolate (at least, I know of no reason why anyone cares), or (to take a non-trivial example) whether or not I wake up one morning with the realization that all is vanity—unless I decide that I must somehow act on this realization, make it enter the social sphere.

Of no other two-person social relationship is this obsessive "doing it for myself and the devil take the hindmost" quality so determinative. Kant, whom I consider below, was clearly right in his intuition that at least to a degree sex uses the other person as merely a walking version of a blow-up sex doll—as we might say from a vantage point he could not have imagined. The other person is to some degree merely a means to an end, furniture of my personal world.

Because sex is neither wholly social nor individual, neither completely specific nor general, we cobble together a vocabulary to speak of it in the same language we use for expressing other things, made partly of the vocabulary of one realm, partly of the other. The line between what is social and what escapes the social in the sexual interaction is a fine one. Disagreements will always arise regarding where it will be drawn, precisely because the territory is fundamentally liminal, at the edge of social expressibility.

Antioch College's "Sexual Offense Policy" of the 1990s, which required that each stage of sexual interaction receive a verbal affirmative from the other partner, usually the woman (the assumption was the traditional one that the man was initiating the encounter) was met with such derision because most people felt that it left very little of the sexual situation that was not amenable to social codification. The College rules, after all, did not apply to situations most people would have agreed required policing, those involving underage people, nor to a situation of unequal power—save insofar as the male-female pairing always, according to some commentators, expresses unequal power. If this most "normal" situation of a consenting male and consenting female was as amenable to social codification as all other sexual encounters, the implication was that there was nothing in sex that escaped the social. And this seemed counter-intuitive to most people. It is as if Antioch thought it could transform sex into something that even Kant would approve of, subject to the same rules for fairness as the rest of (social) life. (Alan Soble provides an entertaining consideration of some of the reactions to this, "Antioch's Sexual Offense Policy."[1])

In mapping the landscape of our sexual desire, the distinction between inductive and deductive ceases to be operative, the same way the general situation of individual knowledge completely escapes the scientific paradigm that otherwise holds sway in our life. In order to say whether or not I am drawn to people of a certain type because I possess the inclination towards that sort of sexual object or whether I am merely describing what I have noted—whether the type is really a type in the world, with validity for others, or whether it is merely the category of my objects of desire—I would have to compare my particular situation with a particular situation like mine in all save one detail, and so on. Clearly this is not the way life works; we live the life we live.

Ethics

Ethics is the language of the social world, the attempt to make human actions predictable. Sex always escapes the predictable, at least to some degree. This is why both conservative and liberal ethics disapprove of sex. Conservative ethics, as I consider in greater detail below, is expressed in terms of actions, liberal in terms of actors. But both issue general statements.

Conservative ethics disapproves of sex because the couple, alone with each other—as we say, to capture the strange nature of sex—may well engage in actions that conservatives would like to prohibit for everyone, under all circumstances. Conservatives have the list of proscribed actions ready. In recent decades, conservatives have been impelled to man the barricades against many specific sexual actions: oral sex, anal sex, same-sex sex, and many other actions.

The viewpoint that fueled the Antioch policy is the liberal's equivalent of this conservative love of forbidding. Liberal ethics disapproves of sex for another reason than conservative ethics, but it still disapproves. It does so because sex lacks, at least to a certain degree, rules that put the individual first. Kant offers a cohesive statement of this liberal disapproval, and much of contemporary "political correctness," insisting on politeness and not hurting anyone's feelings, is generated from the same liberal point of view. Even the most conventional forms of male-female sex fly in the face of political correctness because they fail to "respect" the more submissive partner.

There is little defense against liberal charges that even conventional sex is depersonalizing. Of course this is so, and most of us can only laugh uncomfortably when it is pointed out to us. Our only defense of Stanley Kowalski in Tennessee Williams's *Streetcar Named Desire,* when taxed with the same thing by his sister-in-law Blanche, is Stanley's own: that his wife Stella wanted to be pulled down off her pedestal in this way. She is lowered, he agrees, but defends himself by saying that she loves it. Perhaps she shouldn't be allowed to do this, any more than (as liberal ethicists have held) the individual has the right to sell him- or herself into slavery, thereby alienating his or her own freedom.

Of the two ethical groups I consider, liberals and conservatives, it is liberals who come off as more concerned with the rights of the woman in sex, as it is liberals who come off as more concerned with the rights of the woman in the case of pregnancy. This is not because they are more concerned with women *per se* (this is what I call a second-level position), but rather because of their expression of ethical rules in terms of actors in general, which does not allow the sub-categories of gender to play a determinative role. For liberals, what's sauce for the goose is sauce for the gander, and this because of the structure of liberal thought. Rules are expressed in terms neither of goose nor gander, but of fowl. Whence the conservative male sense that liberals are trying to emasculate them, stop their fun.

Conservatives, by contrast, express their rules in terms of actions. X, Y and Z are prohibited. Because some of this list may be actions only men can do (have sex with other men, for example), or only women can do (be a woman having sex with multiple partners), conservative thought allows gender differentiation in its rules. This is why conservatives look like the great prohibitors.

Before turning to traditional explanations for the uneasiness we feel towards sexual topics, I consider briefly the notion that "sex is a language." This is a much-repeated semi-witticism, usually followed by a judgment about the fluency or lack of fluency of a particular person in that language. In the academic world, the thesis that sex really is a language is associated with the theories of Robert Solomon ("Sexual Paradigms")[2].

All metaphors break when pushed too far. It isn't surprising that the half-joking assertion that "sex is a language" cannot sustain the full barrage of academic analysis, any more than any other metaphor can. Metaphors emphasize the one or two qualities that two divergent things have in common. Of course the next step of nay-sayers will be to point out the many other qualities they do not share.

The metaphoric connection of sex to language is strongest in the transition from the social sphere to the sexual. We are always surprised at the transition from the social realm to the realm of the sexual, and may express this surprise by noting that the other person "speaks" the language of sexuality. Abruptly it seems that the other person has a whole other side, a set of capabilities of which we had been unaware, and that we have a way of connecting with that person that we lacked before. This is comparable to the way that two people who speak incompatible languages suddenly discover that they can communicate in a common third language.

But once we are past the discovery of these capabilities, the metaphoric connection of sex to language weakens. Why is sex a language more than (say) a skill, or a game? Why, specifically, a language? It isn't, particularly. Solomon's technical theses have been attacked on equally technical grounds: What is the relationship between syntax and semantics in this "language"? Can sex be analyzed with the tools of linguistic analysis? We don't even agree on how languages with words work, so it's hardly surprising that the debate on a metaphoric "language" rapidly becomes convoluted. The connection of sex with a language rather than with other things seems fanciful, or arbitrary, once we are over the shock of seeing that some communication at all is possible.

The religious and Freudian explanations

The notion that sex is something we do but don't talk about, as well as the realization that it does not play a clearly defined role in the larger scheme of our lives, are firmly anchored in the Judeo-Christian story of the Garden of Eden found in the Biblical Book of Genesis, or at least our Modern Age interpretations of that detail-poor document. The widespread sense that the sex organs are hidden and shameful, and the sexual act as well, is taken by most commentators to be definitory of the post-Lapsarian human condition. Milton puts it as follows, describing the easy nudism of the first couple before their sin, in order subsequently to contrast it with the way their descendents instinctively cover up:

Nor those mysterious parts were then conceal'd,
Then was not guilty shame: dishonest shame
Of nature's works, honour dishonorable,
Sin-bred, how have ye troubl'd all mankind

With shows instead, mere shows of seeming pure,
And banisht from man's life his happiest life,
Simplicity and spotless innocence.
So passed they naked on, nor shunn'd the sight
Of God or Angel, for they thought no ill. [3]

Interestingly, in Milton's view, Adam and Eve weren't celibate. His justification for this entangles him in some of the logical difficulties endemic to his project of explaining the life we know by comparison with things we can never know, such as life in the Garden of Eden, or life among the angels. Clearly these beings have to be enough like us to have us use the same words to describe them that we use for ourselves. At the same time they have to be different in some fundamental way.

How to achieve both goals simultaneously? This is Milton's ongoing problem. When given the choice between distancing his non-human entities or using the same human terms we use for ourselves, Milton always chooses to humanize them. His angels are as petty as the Homeric gods who were his prototypes. This humanizing makes the poem come alive, but entangles it in unsolvable logical paradoxes.

According to Milton, angels eat like humans. Do they excrete? Do they have to cook their food? Milton tells us there was a cyclical alternation of light and dark in Heaven even before day and night were created, kept in a little cave. But how are we to understand light and dark in alternation before day and night?

The problems with using terminology of the world we know extends to descriptions of Adam and Eve. Milton wants to use Adam and Eve before the Fall as the prototype "how-to" couple in sexual matters: we should aim at being like them. If they didn't have sex, we might well conclude that Eden was missing something, and that Falling wasn't without its compensations. If they did have sex, that would seem to be a go-ahead for any two other naked people finding themselves alone in a garden. If Adam and Eve are (in this sense) just like us, then Falling diminishes in importance.

According to Milton, Adam and Eve are sexual creatures like us. At the same time, their sexual intercourse has none of the aura of shame he believes attaches to our sex. We'd expect him to say that this was because Adam and Eve had not yet Fallen. Yet the disadvantage for him of choosing this option is that this quality distances them from us absolutely. Thus he chooses another course, itself not without disadvantages (there is no perfect answer, given the problem). Milton says that sex between Adam and Eve lacked the quality of shame that attaches to it otherwise because they were married—a quality we can share with them. He fails to explain how we are to understand this notion of marriage without benefit of clergy, but if pressed for an explanation he would probably say that Adam and Eve were "naturally" married, whereas we post-lapsarian creatures must somehow institute a ceremony to return to this state.

The poet invokes Adam and Eve lying together, and proposes coyly that Adam probably did not "turn . . . from his fair Spouse," nor that "Eve the Rites/Mysterious of Connubial Love refus'd."[4] Connubial love between spouses, such as he suggests Adam and Eve were, is not the same as mere lust, given that the purpose of sex in marriage was procreation. (This position continues to be the official dogma of the Catholic Church; I consider it below.) Only the Devil tells us not to have children. "Our Maker bids increase, who bids abstain/ But our destroyer, foe to God and Man?"

Sex in marriage, therefore, isn't merely sex in marriage; it's a different thing entirely than sex outside marriage, and it's something we too have access to. "Hail wedded Love, mysterious Law, true source/ Of human offspring, sole propriety."[5] Only "hypocrites," moreover, "defam[e] as impure what God declares/Pure." Yet this choice on Milton's part to say that Adam and Eve had sexual intercourse comes at a price. If Adam and Eve could procreate before the Fall, what is the meaning of God's subsequent curse that Eve would bear children in pain? Could she not have gotten pregnant? Would she have borne children without pain?

According to many people before and after Milton—as I consider more fully below—sex is related in some fundamental way to marriage. Certainly the two are very close to each other in the spectrum ranging from the social on one end and the personal on the other. Marriage is a situation where two people are put in a room and told to sort things out. They find out what works and what doesn't. Sometimes this knowledge comes easily, sometimes not so easily. What they learn isn't applicable to anyone else, or at least need not be. They can generalize these things and offer them to others, but the particulars of the relationship are useful only to them in that they help solve particular problems.

Yet the uncomfortable fact is that the "fit" of marriage and sex is not very good. There is some evidence it may be particularly bad for men. As those who stay in marriages for any length of time discover, the lack of variety endemic to limiting sex to a single partner almost always acts as a soporific upon desire. Those couples who avoid what is sometimes called "bed death" must constantly look for ways to vary circumstances or the sexual menu. The cover of one recent issue of *Newsweek* magazine was devoted to the topic of sexless or virtually sexless marriages, which anecdotal evidence suggests are more typical than people had hitherto been willing to admit.[6]

Why this coupling of sex and marriage? Marriage is the structure where sex has lodged in practice because, like sex, it combines aspects of the social with the personal. In a more finely delineated world containing many other alternatives to the purely social sphere, it is conceivable that we might be able to separate sexuality from marriage. Theoretically they are already separate. Marriage in practice is a different matter than marriage in theory, functioning as well as any cut-to-your-own-size institution functions, which is to say, fairly well so long as the freedom to find individual versions of it is preserved. Marriage may be a theoretical mess, but individual marriages frequently end up working out in practice. The fact of the ambiguity of sex in our lives is not, however, solved by marriage.

Religion tells us that we're uncomfortable with sex because of the Fall. In effect this translates as: that's just the way things are. It's an acknowledgement of the phenomenon more than an explanation. Yet we moderns have failed to be satisfied with this lack of an explanation. Most of us have accepted the only major candidate we have for an explanation, that offered by Freud. For most people today, Freud's explanation for the anomalous quality of sex has become so quotidian they hardly see the quality itself any more, only the explanations he offered. If we nowadays ask, Why are people embarrassed to talk about sex? we are likely to respond immediately that of *course* we're embarrassed. That's the way society has ordered things in order to get us to go to work in the morning rather than following out our natural sexual urges. We see ourselves as the victims of quasi-personalized forces larger than ourselves.

The keystone of Freud's non-religious explanation for the strange nature of sex was his theory of societal repression, laid out in most compact form in *Civilization and its Discontents*.[7] According to Freud, all of society is like a vast locomotive powered by the furnaces of unexpressed sexual urges. This image was later captured in Fritz Lang's film *Metropolis*, where subterranean workers sacrifice their lives among turbines so that the effete children of the rich can play on the surface of the Earth. Ultimately, in Lang's movie (script by Thea von Harbou) the workers revolt, the turbines overheat, and the machinery necessary for the idleness of the rich blows up. Freud, however, thinks society has regulated things so the machinery doesn't blow up: "Sublimation of instinct is an especially conspicuous feature of cultural development; it is what makes it possible for higher activities . . . to play such an important part in civilized life. . . . it is impossible to overlook the extent to which civilization is built up upon a renunciation of instinct." [8]

Like all influential thinkers, Freud thought in patterns. Repeating patterns are what allow one individual to achieve the feat of apparently subsuming a great deal of the world in his/her theory; I consider below whether and how theories ever subsume the world. The basic Freudian trope is to explain a perceived equilibrium of 0 with respect to whatever he is considering by postulating an underlying force of + 10, kept down by a counter-force of - 10 that sometimes slips up. Apparent equilibrium is for Freud always evidence of a clash of unseen Titans. This is why so many of Freud's theories of normalcy are based on extreme or pathological cases where, through rifts in the ground, the messy disputes he postulated as the rule rather than the exception spill out into the light of common day.

Childhood for Freud, for the same reasons, cannot in fact be an absence of any real sexuality, for this would belie his basic trope of usually neutralized conflict. Instead, for him, childhood is a great plain of war between impulses attempting to break out and those holding them back. This pattern of thought will always result in an extreme view of sex rather like Shakespeare's in Sonnet 129. To sympathize with Freud, or with Shakespeare, we have to see our faced normal lives merely as weaker versions of the great struggles they postulate.

Freud's theories, being based on images of things that by nature can be intuited only by their effects, either buried deep in the psyche or deep in the sub-strata of societal structures, are made so as to be unverifiable. Intellectuals discovered they liked this sort of unverifiable assertion, perhaps because people living the life of the mind are attracted by self-contained worlds which make such neat packages, tie up so many loose ends. Indeed, so self-contained is Freudian thought that its similarity to what we now call conspiracy theories, which base their "proof" on the very lack of evidence for their assertions (the Martians not only came, they took away the evidence of their coming), has struck more than one contemporary critic.[9]

Freudian reliance on a version of conspiracy theories makes us think of Tennyson's "Morte d'Arthur," where Tennyson treats the mythical King Arthur like a real person, insisting that he did too exist—and, at the same time, provides a reason for the utter lack of any evidence for this existence. Arthur, according to Tennyson, commanded that the sword Excalibur, which might have provided evidence of the glory of Camelot to a later generation, be thrown back into the lake from whence it came by Sir Bedivere, the last of his knights. The things evoked, for Freud as well as apparently for Tennyson, are really real, and the reason we don't see this is that they are being repressed, hidden under the visible surface of things.

Some commentators have attempted to explain the extreme nature of Freud's picture as being merely a description of the particularly rule-bound world of the Austro-Hungarian Empire before the first World War. The implication is that we no longer need any theory because we have gone so far to removing the conditions that led to it. Would Freud recognize the society he would encounter in the West of the early twenty-first century? Surely he would, despite the predominance of half-naked torsos, both male and female, towering above pedestrians in cities, filling glossy magazines, and forming the stable of television advertising.

For even if suddenly everyone in society is "getting some" rather than not "getting some"—or at least talking about it—the problems with sex do not disappear. Sex remains something we do in private or are titillated by in public, hide from children, and fail to talk openly to our friends about. Public interest in sex is not the same as integration of sex into our daily lives, in our small group or one-on-one encounters. Indeed, the relegation of sex to the anonymous world of advertising and television is only the flip side of public taboos on all things sexual, not an alternative to them.

Something like Herbert Marcuse's *Eros and Civilization*, proposing a world where sexuality is somehow de-genitalized, diffused equally throughout life, might have been a real alternative to the world of the West in the new millennium that Freud would still find so familiar.[10] Yet this has not yet even begun to be achieved. Indeed, we can't even conceive of what a world without genital sexuality would look like.

Freudian theories, with their assertion that what seems calm to us is really only momentary stasis in a great struggle, postulate wildly improbable explanations for life as lived since we must accept that apparent stasis is really furious, if submerged, battle. Yet, bizarrely enough, these explanations have become commonplaces. Perhaps this is so precisely since it took a great gulp for us collectively to swallow a theory such as Freud's whose intellectual interest is precisely that it is so counter-intuitive. Having gotten it down, however, we are loath to cough it up: this would imply we were chumps to begin with.

Freud is an intellectual bully, and this too tends to have its effect in suppressing dissent. Not for Freud the forgiving notion that other people may be making sense in their own terms, or working out their own destinies in words. No, everyone had to be at the place he is, verbally speaking, accepting his formulations when he is offering them. Ultimately too, Freud is one of history's great naïfs in appearing to believe that people will do what he says they should merely because he says it.

If we question Freud's view of things, no matter how faintly, he immediately retaliates with theory: our denials are more evidence of the very thing he was talking about, the fact that we're denying shows precisely how right he was, and so on. We may think of the hollow bull Daedalus created for Minos, King of Crete, in which people being roasted alive were hidden so that the cries of their agony would be transmuted into gentle and appealing lowing. Freud has made such a bull so that, object though we might, all our voices turn from being a chorus of objection to his theories to hymns of praise, or at least substantiating threnodies.

The problem with Freud

I share with Freud what I take to be his initial intuition that sex does not jibe with the rest of life. But this is a fact of how we articulate our social relationships, not the result of ignorant armies clashing by night. Sex is an activity that, when described in the only developed vocabularies we have, those of (on one hand) the social or (on the other hand) the private spheres, seems merely negative, a not-thing. Sex has aspects of both and is completely neither. This is the reason it has failed to find a home either in the social sphere or the completely private one.

Freud's explanation for this phenomenon, however, is too dull a tool to be ultimately useful. Freud clearly thought societal intolerance of sex absolute and undifferentiated, a structural fact. What to make of the fact that there are some situations more resistant than others to acknowledgement of sexual activity? Sexually active young men in a locker room, for example, rate each other more highly for sexual talk and sexual action with women, not less highly. Even in those circumstances where sexual congress is frowned upon, men give each other high points for the very aggressiveness and masculinity that would, under other circumstances, be useful in attracting and keeping women.

Yet it is not surprising Freud failed to acknowledge that some social circumstances are more tolerant of sexual relations than others, having himself apparently had a tin ear for the ramifications of social situations. For someone advocating a talking cure, Freud seemed puzzlingly deaf to the fact that the action of saying things out loud to the therapist changes their nature, pulls them out of the private realm and makes them public. Why resort to theories of repression and the super-ego to explain why the person on the couch wasn't saying what the analyst thought s/he should be saying? One reason for our unwillingness to tell our innermost secrets is so much more easily explained by the fact that articulating the private makes it public, and so changes it. Besides, what the analyst wants us to say may not be true. The intellectual interest of Freud is that he figured out a way for this not to matter.

It is true that, because sex is a social relationship with so large a component of the personal (and the reverse), it fits very badly indeed into the situations where the social fabric is tightest, those places on the spectrum of relationships farthest from the personal realm. In such situations we are, or feel ourselves to be, responsible for specific groups of people, and demand absolute predictability from them. These situations include relations with children under our guardianship, our children's relationship with us, members of action-oriented institutions like the military, or same-sex groups of adolescent friends who spend great amounts of time together. In all these cases we become distressed at the idea of someone we are supposed to keep tabs on or whose actions we need to be predictable engaging in an activity that is not in the same way amenable to codification. That person is off on his or her own journey for which we have no map.

Sex creates bubbles, mini-worlds that stand as alternatives to the close-knit world of these tight connections, made self-enclosed by the aspect of obsession and total concentration on the object of desire that is missing from other relationships with people. If you're concentrating on a single individual, you're not available for a social situation that demands your attention. The more your attention is demanded, the more your absence is condemned. But this is a fact of the micro-structures in which we may find ourselves, not some over-arching fact of socialization in general. There are equally many circumstances under which mental or physical absence from the group is neither here nor there. The urge to eradicate sexual relations is thus not a uniform fact of the social structure. It is the logical result of those particular social situations where we demand that the other people be available to us at all times for the metaphoric or literal equivalent of a "roll call."

People in the military, to take an example of such a situation, are by the nature of the structure they are involved in, supposed to be completely social creatures. What they do has to be predictable, or the structure doesn't "work." At least this is true while on duty. While off duty, the sky is the limit. Because fathers of daughters have in the past felt responsible for keeping them "pure" until they are handed off to other, younger, males, the fathers have traditionally been much more intolerant of sexual activity from their daughters than from their sons. As the sense of responsibility for keeping daughters chaste has diminished in recent decades, paternal acceptance of their daughters' sexuality has risen as well.

Sex slips the bounds of the predictable, and the predictable is what we demand of people under our supervision or tightly accountable to us. For this reason, whether or not we feel sex is a good thing for ourselves, we almost universally sense that it is bad for children, whom we feel we must keep very close tabs on indeed—our own children closest of all, but generally, as part of the collective, all children. This sense that there are some relationships that must be kept free from sexuality is the way we express the need to hold people accessible to us in a social situation. Virtually all of us make a distinction between "wholesome" and "un-wholesome" play among children, between actions by children that bear scrutiny and those that do not. How horrified even the most sexually active of us would be to find that another child had been proposing genital exploration to our children, or swearing in front of them using sexual terms. Worst of all would be to learn that this person had penetrated our child sexually.

These impulses to eradicate sex in people under our control or from whom we demand predictability may continue when our children become adults. Many parents impose restrictions on sexual activity on adult children living at home. It is also operative with young adults only marginally under our supervision, as part of the collective. We are pleased to think of high school students doing something in a "nice clean way," which means without sex. We are happy to see a gym-full of a boys' high school football team engaged in practice, or in lifting weights, or to see them spill on the field to crash into each other for our entertainment. Things get questionable when they go after girls, or more upsetting still, "fool around" with each other.

The demand for "purity," which is to say social availability, is made in the opposite direction as well. Children are usually reticent to think of their parents in sexual terms because this implies an unpredictable aspect to their being, even if this aspect is expressed only with the marital partner. Children typically don't want to think of their parents doing "those things" with each other because children selfishly tend to see parents as existing only in the social context of parenthood. Children resist acknowledging that their parents exist in other contexts as well, in a way they do not resist acknowledging this about other adults they have not grown up with.

The need for predictability can even extend to other people like us whom we would normally allow to be sexual. Men tightly bonded with other men can regard involvement with women as a betrayal of the bond, based on the need for absolutely predictability and presence. From this comes the almost universal male conviction that nothing breaks up a male friendship faster than a woman: it distracts the other man, and takes him away from his buddies.

Sex fits equally badly into a realm held inviolate as personal—for example, into the world of the painfully shy person, or the person who resists touching or physical involvement. Such attempts to interject sexuality into a completely personal realm are disasters of their own sort, like the attempt to interject sexuality into very social ones. Yet attempts to force the sexual into the private realm are played out as private tragedies, and only rarely find expression. It is usually the attempt to force the sexual into the social realm that occupies society's attention—logically so, as this attention is the attention of the collective, not the personal.

Purely private actions do not challenge such tight social situations in the same way that sex does. The personal can assume with no intrinsic problems a relationship of complete subjugation with respect to the public sphere. Officers in a submarine get what sleep they get between watch calls: the bell can interrupt them at any moment of the night and day. Private lives can be simply assumed away in the context of a very social one, or carried on in pieces, on what the military calls a "non-interference" basis.

When we move out of such hyper-social, because hyper-intimate, relations to another category, that of people we are not responsible for and do not have to keep tabs on, sexual activity of others becomes irrelevant to us. Conservatives put many other adults in this category of adults they have to keep tabs on. Thus the sexual activity of adult strangers becomes relevant to conservative thought. We can sometimes bracket out sexual relations if they are held to be with a sort of person not of our world: women, say, or women not our sisters. But we need to have access to labels that separate off groups of people, and in many cases the labels of society are not very finely delineated. In common parlance we have only two groups, men and women, with sub-groupings being only the vocabulary of these sub-groups themselves. The need to keep the boundaries clear-cut is behind the unease a man typically feels when he learns an intimate male friend, who he thought would never be sexually involved with another man, is involved in this way. Because what protected the friendship relation before was the conviction of the first that the second would limit his sexuality to outside the group, being involved with another man seems to the first to be a sort of pollution, posing a threat to the friendship relation (sexuality does pose such a threat to more social relationships). He may possibly accept it only if the gay friend assures him that of course he would never think of *him* in those terms, or that he only likes (say) smaller men, or older, or younger, or limits himself to certain specific sexual actions he doesn't want to engage in with his friend. If the friend can accept these as types or groups to which he does not belong, he may be mollified, feel unthreatened in the same way he would if his friend were sexually involved with a woman.

Because it is not all circumstances that fail to tolerate sexuality, but only those where predictability is at the highest premium, the expression of sexuality poses the fewest problems for someone with no relatives and few friends, and not a member of an organization such as the military. Such a person can with little problem spend all his or her life in sexual pursuits without bumping his or her nose very often—a fact that should by rights be impossible if Freud's explanations in terms of sacrifice and repression were correct. Think of Casanova, say, or Fanny Hill, or perhaps sexually promiscuous gay men of the 1970s, that post-Stonewall, pre-AIDS era.

For most people, therefore, it is theoretically possible for sexual relations to play a much larger role than they do. Freud's mistake was to assert that because the larger proportion is possible, those who settle for a smaller must be being denied something. But percentages are by definition a zero sum game. A Casanova, in exchange for more sex, has fewer societal relations, friendships, or familial relations.

All of us can choose: the domain of sexuality is there to be entered if we wish. Entering it more often means giving up other things, such as social relationships. Each of us has felt or will feel the tension between the two domains, yet this is a tension that can in each case be resolved, in one way or another.

Nobody knows who I am going to be attracted to, not even me. This does not show that I am somehow denying that knowledge to myself, or to others. I can't know until I try things out with my own body. The knowledge I obtain is in all cases merely a reaction to what I in fact do and don't do.

Chapter Two

Does Sex Have a Purpose?

Liberal vs. Conservative

Ethics offers prescriptions for action expressed in terms of generalizable rules. Most people encounter ethics negatively, in a conflict situation, through someone telling us what we may not do. Indeed, sometimes it may seem that ethics has a power of its own, attempting actively to beat people into submission to its dictates. There is always tension between the particular and the general; this is what produces the possibility of guidance by the general. But it is people who make weapons of ethics, not an intrinsic expansionist urge. Ethics alone is powerless, because it is merely an abstraction.

The reason sex causes us so many problems in our social lives is that it is only partly amenable to articulation in the terms of the social realm. For this reason, ethical debate regarding sexual matters is loud and long. The issues of whether or not homosexuality or pre-marital sex are wrong, which American liberals may well have thought dead issues, have revealed themselves as very much alive in the early years of the twenty-first century. So too the debate regarding abortion, given the emergence of clinic protesters hurling vindictive epithets, and occasionally shooting bullets, and the U.S. government refusing federal money to perform abortions in overseas military hospitals.

Debates regarding sexual ethics are so shrill because both sides are trying to stake their claim in territory that is not completely amenable to expression in ethical terms. Sexuality and its related issues delineate a territory that straddles two well-defined realms, the social and the personal. The shrillness comes from the social realm, whose defenders are trying to take as much of this un-attributed land as possible, each in its own way. Because each version of the social is fighting a losing battle with one leg on the solid land and the other leg dangling over the cliff, the polemics increase in force to cover the fundamental indefensibility, and instability, of their positions.

Liberal and conservative are versions of ethics, which is to say, of the social realm. Yet we should ask, what do we mean by these two labels? Is the distinction between these two groups, which collectively fill most of the political spectrum, absolute? Assertion of absolute distinctions between groups is the intellectual lingua franca of our day. A great deal of contemporary thought begins by postulating prima facie differences between groups of people, asserted to be such in advance: white people, people of color, heterosexuals, homosexuals, first-world and third-world denizens. If we do not see these distinctions as absolute, we can be tarred with various brushes. Assertion of absolute difference between the two parties of the non-existent discussion by definition puts an end to communication. If we want liberals and conservatives to speak to each other, we may not hold the distinction between their groups to be primary.

Most people would distinguish liberals and conservatives by listing the tenets each group tends to espouse. Conservatives tend to oppose abortion and support the use of military action. (After the destruction of the World Trade Center, this last became attractive to both sides of the spectrum.) Liberals tend to support government programs aimed at rectifying inequities within society. Conservatives tend to believe in a form of social Darwinism: those on top, economically speaking, deserve to be there. Re-allocation of their resources is theft, and contrary to societal interests.

The problem with differentiating groups such as these by reference to a list of their tenets is that there is no visible pattern behind the lists. Why should conservatives be so concerned with the "right to life" of a fetus (or, as conservatives prefer to say indicatively, an unborn child) and be apparently so unconcerned with the lives of soldiers on the battlefield, or with the civilian casualties wars invariably inflict, or with the lives of criminals condemned to capital punishment? To liberals, this seems a contradiction. Why should liberals be the ones who are, generally speaking, more concerned with industrial pollution of streams and air and the effects of drilling for oil? To the liberal, it looks as if conservatives are denying the real cost of their actions. To the conservatives it looks as if liberals are trying to constrain their freedom.

Each side vilifies the other. As *Washington Post* commentator Charles Krauthammer puts it, "conservatives think liberals are stupid. Liberals think conservatives are evil."[11] Krauthammer is a self-identified conservative, so he characterizes liberals from the conservative point of view. "Liberals tend to be nice, and they believe—here is where they go stupid—that most everybody else is nice too." "Liberals, who have no head . . . , believe that conservatives have no heart." For Krauthammer, conservatives are the realists, liberals the dreamers.

Looked at as a list of tenets, each side's position will seem incoherent to the other. I call these tenets secondary qualities of each position. Understanding, though of course not necessarily acceptance, of both positions can only come if we look at primary qualities. We may call these the deep-structural nature of each position, debasing Chomsky's rather odd theory of language into general use in much the same way Freud's questionable assertions have provided us with an entire vocabulary for expressing relationships with ourselves. All morality expresses itself in terms of generalized absolutes. If everything in the world is a particular, there is no possibility of establishing precepts, and no possibility of influencing actions through rules.

Conservative thought conceptualizes in terms of actions. Liberal thought conceptualizes in terms of actors. Each way of thinking operates in a preferred field of issues because these are more congenial to expression in terms of a specific conceptual pattern. Yet at the same time, each way of thinking must interact with the other. When it does so, the interaction also takes place in terms of predictable patterns.

Conservatives express their moral absolutes in terms of actions. "Thou shalt not x" is a prototypically conservative pronouncement. For conservatives, particular situations may not influence the general rule. Whatever the specifics of thy situation, thou *still* shalt not x.

Conservatives start with the more general rule, say "Thou Shalt Not Steal," and usually deny that any further qualities added to the particular situation are relevant. "Should I steal this loaf of bread to feed my family?" is a liberal question; "Should I steal?" is a conservative question. We may very much want, or in our view, need, to steal this particular loaf of bread, but for conservative ethics, particularities of the situation do not override the general prohibition against stealing.

Catholic ethics, a conservative ethics, is categorical on the subject of actions with absolute value: we can never allow individual circumstances to undermine principles. A sin is a sin. We will always want to find excuses for not avoiding them in the particular circumstances, and will always have to resist. Debate in terms of actions is, thus, debate on the conservative home field. Liberal ethics reacts to this inductively, starting with the particular, or at least conceiving of the general as having been derived from the particular.

The relation of specific to general is reversed when what is at issue is a rule expressed in terms not of actions, but of actors. There the liberal position is doctrinaire, which is to say general, on what is owed all individuals. The quintessential expressions of liberal ethics, say Kant or John Rawls, are based on some form of the Golden Rule, and deny differences between people, even between one's self and others. Conservatives object to liberal ethics by insisting that there are *too* legitimate differences between groups of people. The conservative demands, Must we treat all people the same? Are there no distinctions, such as family or nation, which may influence our actions? The doctrinaire liberal shakes his head and says emphatically though perhaps somewhat defensively, "no." Still, even the most liberal of commentators tend to allow a distinction between the self and all other people in situations of extreme physical threat to the self. We may, according to almost all commentators, always save ourselves.

The primary difference between liberals and conservatives is that their general rules are expressed in terms of actors and actions, respectively. These are two ways of cutting the same cake. Liberal and conservative are complementary ways of thinking. In order to see this, take one topic which currently makes people hot under the collar (under the choler, in the original expression): abortion, a subject to which I turn in greater detail below. The fury of the debate between liberals and conservatives regarding abortion comes from the fact that secondary tenets are espoused without understanding what their deep-structural causes are.

Arguments between liberals and conservatives on the subject of abortion are predictable, and end up being the equivalent of an argument between, say, an American and a Frenchman, where each asserts that his or her own national cuisine, flag, or national anthem is better than the other. The only difference is that in such situations as this, we have labels which help us to understand why ultimately we must agree to disagree; we begin by identifying ourselves as American or French.

We have no such labels, understood as categories, to mark the distinction between liberals and conservatives, a distinction which is much more absolute in many ways. The closest we have in the US is self-identification by affiliation with one of the two major political parties. But the divergences between each respective party and a designation of it as "liberal" or "conservative" is sufficiently loose as to make party affiliation a poor substitute for a more useful label. If we would only announce at the beginning of a discussion, "I'm a liberal" or "I'm a conservative" to mean something other than "I am likely to hold certain views," the way we unashamedly announce "I'm American," a great deal of time would be saved. Subsequent arguments might be reduced, and in any case would be understood as expressing an underlying way of thinking, not as providing new information that required hashing out.

Anyone who limits discussion to the particular instance when the subject is actions—such as insisting that the discussion be carried out on the level of "Should I steal this loaf of bread?"—would be merely showing his liberal credentials. With regards to actions, liberals insist that the particular situation is always relevant. The person who insisted that the question must be, "Should I steal?" would merely be showing that s/he is a conservative. When what is at issue is actors, conversely, the liberal will always insist on situation-blindness; the conservative will demand that individual differences be taken into account.

In a conflict between upholding a category and doing something more individualized, the conservative will always support the first and the liberal will always support the second. This is so even though the particular positions these imply may well be subsequently abandoned, as when what in the first conflict played the role of the particular plays the role of a general in a subsequent conflict. Conservative and liberal are not absolute positions, but instead take their nature by relation to each other. Conservatives tend to believe that men should always do X and Y during the sexual act: only with women, for example, only (say) on top, perhaps no giving of oral sex. If men allow the women on top, and allow the man to give oral sex, this is only "masculine" with respect to something else even more particular, say sex with other men. If conservatives could somehow be brought to accept sex with other men, they would typically consent to the more "masculine" role of "top" but not the "bottom," and so on.

The world of what is sometimes called "genderfuck," whereby each person gets to decide his/her spot on the spectrum of possibilities, is deeply repellent to conservatives, because this is allowing, in their view, the monkeys to run the zoo, the individual to determine the general rule. Indeed, for liberals exultant at the range of possibilities open to the individual, there are no rules, and it is in this anti-conservative format that their rejection of conservative doctrine is expressed. But of course liberal ethics does not lack rules, any more than the now-*passé* deconstruction and decentering, that provided American academics with a vocabulary for several decades, lacks rules. For liberal ethics, the rules are expressed in terms of actors.

Does Sex Have A Purpose?

One quality in particular allows us to schematize liberals and conservatives with respect to sexual ethics: their divergent position with respect to teleology, theories of the ultimate purpose of sex. The question that allows us to sort out these positions is simply, Does sex have a purpose?

Conservatives inevitably assert that it does, and that this purpose is procreation, as we saw for Milton in *Paradise Lost.* Usually conservative thought appeals to writings by Saints Augustine and Thomas Aquinas to justify this view. From it arise a slew of prohibitions of particular actions. Homosexual sex is prohibited, masturbation is prohibited, pre-marital sex is prohibited, extra-marital sex is prohibited, abortion is prohibited, birth control is prohibited . . . the list goes on, until liberals are rolling their eyes and holding their heads.

For conservatives, liberals are anything-goes degenerates deserving, and sometimes incurring, the wrath of God. Liberals hold that not merely does sex not have the purpose conservatives say it does, but that it doesn't have any purpose at all. It merely is.

Yet it is clear that liberal and conservative are complementary. This means, for each position of a given side, the other has a sort of shadow position, a reaction to the other, written into it from the start. Not all these shadow positions are articulated at any given time, but all are possible.

The secondary position regarding sexual morality held by conservatives is the view that all people should at least pay lip service to the value of monogamous marriage and, if they do marry, abstain from all sex before and non-marital sex afterwards. Predictably, the emphasis is on the action here, the absolute expressed with respect to it. The Catholic Church now holds that to this is added, inseparably, the "unitive" function of sex. Further, this function is only to be exercised in marriage, which is defined as a union between a man and a woman contracted for life.

From the conservative assertion of one function of sex, or at most two inseparable ones, follow many things. Most egregiously for many in our post-Stonewall post-1968 age follows a disapproval of homosexuality and rejection of homosexual marriage, as well as disapproval of contraceptive measures other than scheduling sex at those times of the month when reproduction is least likely. There are fewer apologists for adultery, and people tend to "support" pre-marital sex by doing it rather than defending it. In this, as in all things, the issues we think important are defined as such by our current preoccupations. At another time, others may come to the fore and those that once so obsessed us fade into the background. Positions which remain unarticulated or undeveloped still retain their places as shadow positions; it seems almost chance that certain other positions are pushed to the forefront.

Section 12 of Pope Paul VI's *Humanae Vitae* asserts that God willed the inseparable connection between two meanings of the conjugal act (sex), procreation and the unification of the couple.[12] To someone who questions the assertion of "that's what it's *for*" that is the starting place of conservative thinking on these topics, it seems ludicrous to posture at a position of knowledge greater than the one we actually have. "How do we know that's what it's for?" the liberal asks. The conservative does well to point to some objectively extant evidence, usually the Bible. God tells us so, the response sometimes is. We don't have to understand it, but there it is.

The argument from Holy Writ at least has the virtue of offering an answer to the question, How do we know what God wants us to do? Presumably everyone agrees that we should do what God wants us to do, assuming this is a real thing and that it is knowable; in any case this is a separable issue. Written evidence seems something quite different from yet another preacher asserting that s/he knows what God wants.

To this the liberal can respond only by questioning the status of this purportedly Holy Writ. Usually s/he evokes difficulties in interpretation, misinterpretations, human action necessary for the canonization of the Christian Bible, and so on, all of which are complex enough topics that it is usually quite some time before the discussion returns to the subject of sexual morality. In any case, the objections are broad they determine many other topics as well, and the specific question of sexual morality is almost inevitably lost in the din.

This is the point at which conservatives, assuming they are still willing to argue rather than simply re-asserting the tenets of their beliefs, typically produce what we may think of as an Aristotelian form of teleology, in keeping with Aristotle's definition of things by considering their place in the world: what they are is somehow to be defined by how they function among other things, taking their existence for granted.

This argument says, we have only to open our eyes to "see" what sex is for, only to think about it to realize what the purpose of the penis is. We can have access to God's plan in ways other than merely by appealing to perhaps-arbitrary-but-there-it-is Holy Writ. Likewise, it may seem clear to the conservative that sex with love is so clearly superior to sex without love as to be not merely different in quantity but in quality. Thus people should reserve themselves for this higher thing, even if this means that everyone gets less sex than they would if their standards were not so high, and some people, apparently, get none at all.

The liberal argument at this point is usually to attack the conclusion of teleology from the evidence offered by conservatives. This means accepting the fact that having sex sometimes produces children, but denying the conclusion that this is what sex is for. Since incalculably more ejaculations or egg releases fail to result in the production of children than do, liberals ask: What is the basis of saying that the purpose of an event that so rarely has this outcome is this thing that almost never occurs? Liberals object to the conservative argument from functionality on the grounds that there are other possible uses of sex organs besides begetting children or the establishment of married "unity."

The conservative side need not be unaware that these functions exist. Indeed, the Church acknowledges that these are possible sexual expressions. Why spend all that time inveighing against homosexual sex, birth control, or masturbation if these aren't activities many people want to engage in? To make a consistent argument, we would have to spell out the submerged reasoning of this reaction. It is the implicit argument that secondary functions should be avoided in the pursuit of primary, or sacrificed to them. Why this should be so is only rarely articulated. Perhaps this is because they take our attention away from achieving the primary ones. Perhaps, in the case of situations where any given individual will in any case not seek the primary goals even if s/he refrains from seeking the secondary ones (a 100% gay man will not engage in sex with a woman even if he is prevented from having sex with men), it is still good in terms of the collective if not in terms of the individual if the honor of the primary goal is upheld through sacrifice of secondary possibilities.

This notion that sacrifice of less than optimal options is good is frequently heard even in the mouth of liberals defending monogamy: we have other sexual outlets open to us, but freely renounce them in favor of a principle, in this case the fidelity of monogamy, which may go contrary to our personal desires. Few people argue that we should follow all our individual desires: sacrifice to something or other is widely accepted as a good.

Yet there may be a reason why the conservative side by and large keeps this argumentation hidden. Acknowledging that there are other secondary purposes to actions or body parts would require an explicit justification for their prohibition. And this would be to acknowledge that the actions it wishes to privilege are not self-evidently superior. Conservatives would have to begin to bargain, discussing whether or not more than a certain amount of quality X, whose lack had led to the conclusion that action Y was impermissible, might not make Y permissible after all. The conservative side is far better advised simply to refuse to negotiate. Permissible sexual acts are qualitatively different from impermissible ones: this is the point of departure, not the conclusion. No "compassionate conservative" view that takes as its point of departure a mere quantitative difference between permissible (optimal, natural) sexual acts and others can win its case against liberals able to come up with cases where such an act might not in fact seem immoral. Far better, as *Humanae Vitae* does, to identify one set of actions as simply being good and all others as not good.

Even liberal attempts to confound the Church's Thomistic assumptions tend to accept its implicit view that the definition of sex is the ejaculation of male semen. It is much more difficult to argue that the purpose of egg-release is not ultimately the propagation of the species than it is to argue that male ejaculation does not evidently have as its purpose the same thing. After all, female orgasm is completely separate from egg release, as well as female pleasure.

It is at least arguable that in the male, the act of sex is dual, as there are clearly at least two elements in female sexuality, pleasure and propagation of the species. We could therefore have one action, ejaculation, that at certain times served one function and at other times another. There is no chance of the Church accepting this reasoning, however, since the Church, like all conservative viewpoints, expresses rules regarding actions in terms of invariable absolutes. This insistence that there be no sub-distinctions between actions leads to the Church's rejection, for instance, of a couple wanting some children over the course of their marriage but not right now.

For someone making an evolutionary argument (considered below), the link between female pleasure and reproduction may be stronger. The argument is usually that because sometimes procreative sex includes female orgasm, women globally seek orgasm and achieve, at least some percentage of the time, procreation. The problem would therefore be that the male is a "two-fer", combining business with pleasure, not with the intrinsic notion of teleology, or purpose, in itself.

When the liberal position goes even further than this and denies the possibility of arriving at the inductive conclusion that sex has a purpose, it argues as follows. Even if results Y were correlated to act X 100% (if every act of intercourse produced a baby), we would not be able to conclude a purpose, only 100% correlation between X and Y. If this is logically necessary, the correlation is empty, as when we say the purpose of teeth is to be teeth, or to sit the mouth. If it is not a logical connection, the correlation might be caused by other factors entirely. Ultimately, as I will be pointing out below, the conflict here seems to be an example of the problem Kant set out to address, that we do not perceive purpose in the world, only events. Kant would call this conflict an antinomy.

An evolutionary version of the conservative argument from teleology exists as well. It is captured in an article by Michael Levin called "Why Homosexuality is Abnormal."[13] Levin's argument is based on the bio-evolutionary claim that heterosexuality, serving better to propagate the species than homosexuality, must in some evolutionary way be normatively "normal" as well as statistically so. It's a thing we should do, not just a thing that happens the majority of the time.

All bio-evolutionary arguments are circular. Such arguments identify a behavior we engage in now, and assert that the fact that this behavior has survived since the cave man days shows that it was a "winner" of a behavior, something we ought to do. This requires our articulating the behavior we engage in now in a way that makes it plausible cave men could have engaged in it.

Nobody says that playing Nintendo or wearing ties is biologically determined, but we may argue that wearing clothes and keeping ourselves amused are. But the fact remains I put on a tie rather than another adornment; I play Nintendo rather than another game. Who says the particular qualities of these things we do today are irrelevant? We are simply removing all un-caveman-like qualities in order to establish the identity of what we do to what cave men did. Which is to say, we are presupposing precisely what we seem to be proving.

In the case of heterosexual sex it seems we circumvent this problem. Heterosexual sex is the only way (so far) of propagating the species, the ostensible point of all evolution. Without it clearly the species dies out. But we haven't circumvented this problem at all. We've called the activity "heterosexual sex" since cave men presumably engaged in the same activity. We've chosen not to call it "romance," or "expressing ourselves sexually," or "worshipping at the altar of Venus" because those things seem in our view of cavemen foreign. We've called it precisely the thing that emphasizes the continuity of the species, the highest good (indeed, the only good) of evolution.

Bio-evolutionary arguments are selective in nature. This disguises the circularity of their presuppositions. They always choose certain things we do nowadays and work backwards to cave men. The claim is always that if both we and cave men did X, then X is consonant with evolution. It is justified for us to do X. The point is never to justify the cave men, only us. And it is never to call something unjustified. If it were unjustified in terms of evolution, we wouldn't do it.

The same argument can be made with a version of anything we do, which means that everything we do is justified according to this argument. We are perfect.

Such arguments selectively target behavior for justification. If we aren't arguing for the behavior today (as wearing ties and playing Nintendo are not usually under attack), we don't look for the earlier behavior that justifies it, indeed don't claim that it is species-enhancing at all. We do not claim that every quality about ourselves collectively or individually (some of us like lobster, some don't) is hard-wired into us with the proof being that we are here to have such qualities. Or do we? Chomsky seems to claim that everyone contains the prototype of every word yet to be invented. This means that in (say) the year 100 (1000?) BCE all living human beings somehow contained in embryo the word "computer" and the structures of twenty-first century American jive talk. People who understand evolution as a justification of what is would have to claim that the fact that some of us like lobster (and, presumably, that some of us don't) must by definition in some way be species-enhancing.

Such arguments also betray a misunderstanding of the concept of evolution. Continuation of qualities or propensities alone proves nothing: this may be (see above) not evolutionary choice of a quality, but merely unchanged qualities that haven't had to be addressed yet because there was no alternative to them in reality. Nobody says that evolution works in an optimally efficient way, with all qualities or traits disappearing as soon as they are no longer necessary, only that the animals that survive have more of a species-enhancing quality than those who die. The comparison of better with less good is not with a perfect situation, only with what failed to be. We have to wait for something to die out to conclude, in a circular fashion, that it was not species-enhancing. The mere fact of possessing a quality doesn't mean that evolution has "voted" for this quality. It may mean that it hasn't had to express an opinion about it yet. There may be many of our qualities that have simply never been tested out and so are either neutral to evolution, or actually noxious—albeit not so noxious as to have caused us to die out. How do we know which qualities have contributed to our survival? Perhaps we have survived despite some of them, not because of them. Some may be neutral.

Besides, evolution isn't finished yet: we're not the final product. What served cave men might not be serving us now; at some point in the far distant future we be destined to lose this tendency.

Bio-evolutionary arguments confound a micro-sense of "normative" with a macro-usage. Because such arguments are conservative in nature, they insist on behavior being expressed in terms of absolute rules for action. In practice this means, the same action every time. If enough people are heterosexual, clearly the species doesn't die out. This doesn't tell us how many people should be heterosexual, or how much homosexual activity should be allowed to people who do propagate the species. It may be enough to beget 2.1 children to propagate the species; all the rest, it could be argued, is up to the individual. Women can be lesbians in college so long as they end up in suburbia in a mini-van full of children (a fairly common pattern in some circles).

Bio-evolutionary arguments are intrinsically about groups, not individuals, and so cannot give guidelines for individual behavior. But this is because they are expressed in terms of rules for actions. Establishing the likely results of (here) heterosexuality doesn't imply that anybody should necessarily be heterosexual, only the likely results if they are. There is no reason we should try to carry out what we perceive to be the evolutionary imperative—it is blind to our desires, and carries itself out. This sort of argument is the attempt to abrogate some of God's qualities for Darwin.

Pangloss and Co.

The debate regarding the question of whether the universe as a whole or its constituent parts are "going" anywhere, have a purpose, is part of the core of Western post-Renaissance philosophy—as we might expect, given the predominance of the Christianized version of Aristotle in the Medieval world. Kant, that philosopher who seems to both summarize the past and presage the future for the Modern age in the same way Aquinas did for the Medieval world, found himself obliged to delineate the relationship between the world of things as they are, the world of perception, and the world in which we can postulate the patterns behind them, their teleology. Kant was trying to clear space for a middle ground, his "synthetic *a priori*," which he held to be the basis of valid scientific assertions as well as of judgments of aesthetic taste. He succeeded only in making clear the impossibility of ever mediating between the realm of concepts, the noumenal realm, and the lived world. This conclusion caused a crisis in more than one thinker or poet of the early nineteenth century and led finally to full-blown Romanticism, a hymn of despair at the impossibility of ever achieving the upper realm, the realm of freedom and purpose.

Kant was responding to Leibniz's belief that teleology could be proven in the visible world, and to Hume's banishing of it to the realm of "human nature," something we are condemned to believe in without foundation. Voltaire too, in his enduring *Candide, or Optimism*, pilloried Leibnitzian teleology, not as being false, but as leading to unacceptable conclusions. Voltaire couldn't disprove Leibniz, he could only make fun of him. In this I think Voltaire was right. Ultimately there is no way to argue down either the conservative or the liberal side, and Kant's compromise doesn't silence either one. We can only point out their commonality and suggest that the problem is larger than the position of either side.

Liberal sexual ethics finds itself in something of the same bind as Voltaire did, disapproving of where a belief in teleology leads, but not knowing how to break free of it. Liberal teleology is rarely expressed. It exists as a kind of shadow-reaction to the too-hard conservative version, and for this reason isn't called upon to justify itself. Indeed, as a teleology, it fails, so it's probably a good thing that it's more a pragmatic alternative than a theoretical one.

The running joke in *Candide* is the response of the buffoon-like Pangloss to all of the horrors Voltaire visits upon him and his associates, including his naïve student, the eponymous Candide. Whatever happens, Pangloss quickly assures those willing to listen, is for the best, and this by definition, in this "best of all possible worlds." Yet how, Voltaire asks, can this be, given the degree of misery which human beings suffer? Still, Pangloss's position is philosophically unassailable, and Voltaire is unable to puncture it.

If we believe in a good, omnipotent God, we are forced to the conclusion that all the apparent ills that befall us are in fact not ills at all, at least not in the larger scheme of things. Perhaps they have a good outcome beyond our immediate ken, and in any case they are fully under the control of this good, omnipotent God, hence by definition for the best. If God, being omnipotent and good, could have created a better world, S/He would have done so. This world must be as good as they come, which is to say, the best of all possible worlds. Voltaire can point out the absurdities this position leads us to, but he cannot—or at least does not—attempt to take it on head on. I do not see any way in which he could.

Voltaire begins his skewering of Pangloss by allowing the philosopher to speak for himself in Chapter 1:

> —It is clear, said he, that things cannot be otherwise than they are, for since everything is made to serve an end, everything necessarily serves the best end. Observe: noses were made to support spectacles, hence we have spectacles. Legs, as anyone can plainly see, were made to be breeched, and so we have breeches. Stones were made to be shaped and to build castes with; thus My Lord has a fine castle. . . . Consequently those who say everything is well are uttering mere stupidities; they should say everything is for the best. [14]

The relevance of this reasoning to the debate regarding sexuality becomes clear when we consider once again the Augustinian/Thomstic belief that the definition of sex is the emission of semen, and hence, the female half of the zygote not having been intuited at that time, procreation. Why, liberals ask (repeating arguments outlined above), can we not conceive of semen as emitted for other purposes, starting with the orgasmic pleasure that inevitably accompanies it? Who says the purpose of the penis, aside from urination, is the production of new children? Or is the teleology in question not that of the body part but the act? Even if we choose to acknowledge the production of children as the primary purpose or function of the penis (or sex), who says we cannot also exploit non-secondary functions?

Is the problem here that Pangloss has postulated a single function, or that he has gotten his single postulate wrong? It seems likely that Voltaire's answer would be the second, that common sense tells us noses are made "for" smelling, and legs "for" walking. It seems likely too not to be chance he had Pangloss avoid examples such as fingers. Noses and legs seem to have a clearer "real" purpose than fingers, hence Pangloss's assertion that what for most people is a minor function is in fact the only one will be amusing. Perhaps Pangloss could have been made to seem equally ridiculous claiming that the function of fingers was, say, to wear rings, but this might have already seemed the slippery slope to a reader wondering what, in that event, the function of fingers actually was. To shake hands? To eat? To write? To speak in American Sign Language? To say that the purpose of fingers is to wear rings may not be so ridiculous after all, especially if the rings are not merely decorative but somehow informative or symbolic, as wedding rings are. And the "function" of such things as hair or male nipples? (St. Augustine gave up on nipples, saying finally that they were only for decoration. This is a function of sorts, if rather a weak one. Of course in some men nipples are the source of sexual pleasure, which is not something St. Augustine might have been eager to admit.) If it is ridiculous to say that the function of noses is to hold up spectacles, it is so because we see that there is another function to noses, not because we reject the notion of function *per se*.

At first glance it might seem that the tolerant Voltaire would allow each person, in the words of his patron Frederick the Great of Prussia, to be *"selig nach seiner façon"*—holy in his or her own way, even as regards, perhaps, the "function" of legs. If someone has decided his or her legs look good in stockings, then who is to say this is not a legitimate "function" of legs? Voltaire's did not look good, by all accounts, but the allure of more "well-turned" male legs as shown off in stockings and red-heeled shoes was well-known to his contemporaries.

Had Voltaire articulated this position, it seems probable he would have ended by rejecting it, given that it is very close to Pangloss's. It is vacuous to assert as a philosophy that a function of noses is to hold up spectacles given that we put spectacles on noses. For this implies that whenever we come up with something new, this is retroactively written into the deep structure of the object. And this conception seems to trivialize the restrictions implied by the notion of function.

Could Voltaire have defended the position that there is in fact no teleology at all? That we are merely atoms in a void? If so, the book is pointless. For really, the book is a great cry of rage at this omnipotent, good God that nonetheless allows His creatures to suffer. If there is no God, there is no point in the cry of rage: Voltaire is brandishing the ills of the world in God's face and demanding redress. Thus the point seems somehow to be the very inscrutability of the world.

Here it is useful to return to "Why Homosexuality is Abnormal." Levin echoes but ultimately goes further than Voltaire when he considers the case of a Mr. Jones who pulls all his teeth to string them around his neck; Levin thinks we will find it "natural to say the Mr. Jones is misusing his teeth".[15] But this is comparable to a case of someone who not only says that the nose is meant for putting glasses on, but who stops it up with an unremovable substance to make it stronger for the glasses, or to the case of someone who cuts off his penis to use as a gruesome necklace ornament on the grounds that this is its proper function. Such actions make impossible something that most of us would agree is at least one use, which is not the case with someone who supplements the procreative function of his penis with the pleasure function, or indeed combines the two.

Both Levin and, I suspect, Voltaire, would object to this as being against common sense. So it would be, because it made impossible an important (*the* important?) usage of this body part. Levin ought to be considering the case of South Sea Islanders who file and decorate their teeth while the teeth are still anchored in their mouths. For that matter, teeth are a beauty sign here in the West too and are cleaned partially for that reason. Or the way we aim for both beauty and function with almost all of our body parts. Do we even know what the function of hair on our head is? We use it almost exclusively for decoration.

The notion of revisable teleologies leads to Pangloss, and, so, is nonsensical. But revisable teleologies is not the only form a liberal alternative to the over-arching a priori teleology of the conservative side can take. We can also propose individualized teleologies. And this, I think, is what most liberals do in fact believe in, even if they tend not to articulate them as such.

This is so because liberal conceptions are expressed in terms of actors rather than actions: the person, we may say, always comes first. But this is not so most primarily in terms of the tenets this leads to, which in my conception here are secondary instantiations of more fundamental patterns. I am not talking about the Enlightenment tenets of individual self-realization, individual rights, and so on. Rather the very conception is in terms of the actor rather than the action, regardless of what liberals subsequently assert is the appropriate thing to do for or with this individual.

On the secondary level, the conservative question is always, What ought we all to do? The liberal question is always, What does the individual want to do? Sometimes even liberals agree that "ought" trumps "want," but this is not their point of departure. We might express the most fundamental liberal position as empathy for the individual. This sets up the playing field, whatever the game played upon it.

My articulation may seem counter-intuitive to conservatives who hold that liberals most fundamentally think in terms of the group: removing impediments from the advancement of the individual is a conservative agenda, not a liberal one. But conservative defenses of the individual always mean, not all individuals, only some. This is the reason I say the liberal position makes its general out of the individual, whatever the specific content of that individual.

The liberal's standard is something closer to the notion of what is "healthy" or "right" or "good" in a more than merely hedonistic way. Who has not sat by the fire with his or her loved one, united in a relationship of trust at the end of a long day, and felt, "this feels so right"? Who has not sat back in the sun of a winter's day, watching children (whether or not his/her own) playing on a playground, and thought, "this is the way things are supposed to be?" And who, by contrast, has not found him- or herself in a relationship that produced the thought that "this isn't good for me"? Who has not felt that something s/he was doing was not "right," say excess grieving for a lost loved one, or the repeated attempt to make friends with people incapable of returning interest?

The parting of the ways between liberals and conservatives on issues of sexual morality is not around whether we should think in terms of purpose. Instead it is around whether the purpose is something common to all, or more individually defined. This is no small difference, for it means that the conservative can tell all people before knowing them how they should act; whereas the liberal assumes that an articulation of "how they should act" is individual to the person as well as something each person must seek out when he or she becomes aware of a problem.

This parting of the ways echoes the difference between "classical" (conservative) and "romantic" (liberal) as expressed so cogently by T.E.Hulme.

> [The] root of all romanticism [is] that man, the individual, is an infinite reservoir of possibilities; and if you can so rearrange society by the destruction of oppressive order then these possibilities will have a chance and you will get Progress.
> One can define the classical quite clearly as the exact opposite to this. Man is an extraordinarily fixed and limited animal whose nature is absolutely constant. It is only by tradition and organization that anything decent can begot out of him.[16]
>   . . .
> To the one party man's nature is like a well, to the other like a bucket.[17]

The conservative thinks people should try to live up to a set of constant moral standards which allow no fine-tuning for the individual. The liberal believes in each person defining his or her own standards.

The conservative misrepresents the liberal position in presenting it as lacking standards; the liberal misrepresents the conservative in presenting it as repressive. Conservatives get to feel tough, and to look down on liberals. Liberals see conservatives as masochists. Conservatives, clearly aware that they are giving up pleasure, revel in self-denial and tar liberals with a lack of self-discipline.

The liberal assumption is that all of us have a kind of inner moral gyroscope which keeps us doing the right thing, unless it is broken in individual cases. I take this image of the gyroscope from its use in another context entirely in David Riesman's and Nathan Glazer's classic *The Lonely Crowd.*[18] Problems therefore arise in individual cases and must be defined in individual terms. The conservative notion of teleology is, by contrast, a one-size-fits-all standard external to us to which we must aspire: the problem, which is to say our insufficiency, goes beyond individuals. The Church's doctrine of Original Sin may be only the most far-reaching of conservative positions, or it may be the Ur-form of such positions.

This not inconsiderable difference aside, the two types of standards are similar in at least one way. The notion of "healthy" (taking this as a rough synonym for all of the various ways we express contentment with the fact that we are living out the innate structure of things) can be dissected with precisely those tools liberals train on the notion of "purpose." Yet at the same time the standards are dissimilar, as we see from the fact that liberals never do this. How do we know that X is right except our intuition? We sense that this was, as even liberals sometimes say, "meant to be." The liberal's inner sense plays the same role as the assertion of Papal infallibility.

There would seem to be a better answer, namely that "healthy" in relationships works like "healthy" in medicine, from which after all it is derived. Still, were liberals as intent on dissecting this assumption that what is "healthy" is what we should do as they are on attacking conservative versions of teleology, they could begin by questioning the validity of the metaphor. So let us do it for them, filling in a conservative argument that is rarely made. (This is another example of a shadow argument for which a place is reserved by the nature of the conflict between liberal and conservative, whether or not it is actually made with any strength.) We may demand that liberals be as hard on their own version of teleology as they are on the conservative one.

Such a position would argue like this: It is not at all clear that we can take the temperature of a relationship in the same way we can take that of the human body. Indeed, even the apparently more secure ground of medical pathology gives us no more certain access to values. Even if 98.6 (with small variations) is the "healthy" human body temperature; who is to say that the overwhelming statistical norm holds any value? (This echoes the liberal insistence that the statistical norm in the case of heterosexuality holds no normative value.) Who says feverish, though abnormal, is in any sense worse than not feverish? Perhaps the "right" of people with fevers of 104 and above to run any temperature they want has not been defended simply because there are so few of them around who stayed at this temperature for any period of time to do the defending. Perhaps conservatives should be more assiduous in defending the right of the ill to their illness.

Liberals seeking a foundation for using illness as an example of a state that permits of no such defense might argue back as follows: Medical pathology is usually accompanied by pain. From this we can tell in some sort of objective sense what is healthy and what is not. But the same argument has been made in sexual ethics, as for example in Levin's claim, in the article I have been considering here, that homosexuals are unhappier than heterosexuals. The weaker of the possible liberal responses is to say that yes, this is currently true, but this unhappiness is caused by society rather than the intrinsic condition. The stronger response denies that homosexuals are unhappy. An even stronger response views the whole discussion as academic and refuses to enter into it. Whatever the result of being homosexual, if one is, one is, and one lives with it.

The liberal interest, therefore, is in establishing a difference between being homosexual and having a temperature of 104. Such a difference might well be that being homosexual is constitutive of the person and cannot be changed, whereas the temperature of 104 is a temporary state (whether or not it is aberrant in any but a trivial sense is precisely what is under discussion). This difference can be questioned—we don't know if homosexuality is constitutive of the person or not. Or it can be made relative: expressed in terms of time units, being homosexual is the same as having a temperature of 104 in that both control the person in question, only for different proportions of his or her life, different lengths of time.

In any case, as Levin suggests, the issue may not be the effectiveness of attempts to alter the state at all. "Calling homosexuality involuntary does not place it outside the scope of evaluation. Victims of sickle-cell anemia are not blameworthy, but it absurd to pretend that there is nothing wrong with them".[19]

Apart from such devil's advocate liberal positions, or mocking conservative ones, it is difficult to conceive of a sincere defense of the right of the ill to remain so. Almost no group, not even Christian Science, is an adherent of this point of view. In this particular issue, there is no liberal/conservative split (contrast this with the case of abortion, considered below), though logically there could be. Liberals have carried the day.

This is so because the notion of medical pathology that is currently mainstream jibes perfectly with the liberal view of teleology as something that kicks in in cases where the internal gyroscope that normally keeps us on course is broken. We are only infrequently aware of being healthy; we are always aware of being sick. We naturally have health except when it is taken from us. And when it is taken from us, the situation must be rectified.

The liberal position is determined *ex post facto*, the conservative *a priori*. Both, however, are based on the assumption that everyone knows, simply knows, when the world is in order and when it isn't. Even liberals who say what feels "right" are not eager to relativize this: they might add, right "for me," but only as a reflex. Watching children play in the spring sun, we may be aware that not everyone has access to this good. But I do not think we doubt that it is an unalloyed good— perhaps it is enjoyed by fewer than 100% of the population, but it is a good nonetheless. In a marriage with someone we love, surrounded by energetic but respectful children with body temperatures of close to 98.6, surely we have some justification for thinking that this is deeply right. Not, perhaps, everyone's cup of tea, but surely right in more than merely a subjective way.

Liberals, under such circumstances, probably come close to uttering what Kant would think of as synthetic *a priori* judgments of taste. Kant is after all the liberal philosopher *par excellence*. These judgments are more than the purely subjective "this tastes good to me," yet less than logical concepts. They do not exclude the possibility of there being other ways to instantiate concepts; but that these surely do so, there can be no doubt. In aesthetic terms, for Kant, this leads to the assertion that something is beautiful—not just for me, but for everybody. But it is a something in the world that is beautiful, not a logical concept.

Liberals are not well advised to attack conservatives on issues of sexual ethics on the grounds that conservatives offer no ultimate justification for their assertions of ultimate purpose. Neither do liberals, though liberal teleology is personal teleology. Personal teleology is enough of a contradiction in terms for us to say that the very concept of teleology more naturally belongs to the conservative side.

The divergences between liberals and conservatives are based, as T. E. Hulme would say, on the fact that conservatives apply common standards, which means external standards. Liberals, by contrast, assume that if we simply leave things alone we will conform to our more individual, and more internal, gyroscopes. Divergences in the realm of sexual ethics seem only an expression of this more fundamental split, which cannot be mediated by addressing the secondary issue of its working out around this particular argument.

Actors are not completely absent from conservative thought; the self is clearly an actor. Antagonisms, however, are not cast in terms of other actors, but in terms of impersonal forces. This single acting self tends to silhouette against a blurry background of forces. No particular defeat by these impersonal forces will ever wipe this "I" from the conceptual map of conservative thought, which thus by definition lives to fight another day.

Other people in the conservative universe are either versions of one's self—which is why conservative thought is attracted to constellations of hierarchically-arranged allied units, such as family members, or the military—or they blur into the status of the inhuman. This last is another reason why conservatives generally have less trouble accepting military action, for this in their view only targets "the enemy." Typically, liberals will see other people rather than "the enemy."

Liberal and conservative argue so vociferously because of the fundamental connection of their positions. The assertion that the purpose of sex (or anything else) is X, where X is unrelated to individuals, is a quintessentially conservative assertion; procreation is simply the purpose that holds conservative front and center at the present time. Yet putting "procreation" in the space of X in this case, though currently a conservative position, is in fact quite a liberal notion, since procreation at least refers to some degree to the people involved. We can imagine many other candidates for the position: fulfilling God's plan, perhaps, or punishing man- (or woman-)kind. In something of the same way, the contemporary liberal viewpoint regarding purposefulness in sex is tinged with the conservative viewpoint: liberals may not talk in terms of overall purpose, but they do seem to think in terms of a more individualized version of purpose. It is in the nature of things, however, that liberal and conservative argue so vociferously despite the strong admixture of the other position in what they maintain to be the case. For "despite" should be "because": we argue with those we are related to, not with those so far away we have nothing in common with them.

Chapter Three

Sexual Definition

One of the most enduring conflicts between liberals and conservatives of the twentieth, and now twenty-first, century, is that over sexual definition. We are very concerned with the categories of heterosexual and homosexual. Who is each? Liberals and conservatives give very different answers. Added to this divergence is that between those placed on one side of the division or the other: gay thinkers see the world in one way, straight ones in another. Why is it that typically gay thinkers will align with the liberal position and vociferously straight ones with the conservative? How, in any case, is reconciliation possible—assuming it is so?

Do any generalizations about sexual attachment make sense? If so, which ones, and why? Let us start with the fact that for the individual, such generalizations are hard won and constantly being revised. This brings us back to Milton.

Despite his hymn to married love, Milton was clear about the intensely individual, and intensely unpredictable, nature of sexual attachment, in marriage or out of it, as well as the fact that people find sexual "matches" only with great difficulty, if they find them at all. One of the results of Adam's Fall, responsibility for which the poet places squarely on Eve's shoulders, is that men will, heretofore, have no more "straight [simple, uncomplicated] conjunction with this Sex," women. One result of the Fall is that we can never be sure of getting our mate. In this we are unlike Adam, for whom a perfect mate was created.

Milton goes on to lay out the pitfalls of looking for a partner. People after the Fall, which is to say all of us, have to look hard for a partner. Whole lives can be wasted looking for the "right one," who, if ultimately found at all, may well turn out to be married or worse, out of bounds (here, she is married to his enemy).

> ... Either
> He never shall find out fit Mate, but such
> As some misfortune brings him, or mistake,
> Or whom he wishes most shall seldom gain
> Through her perverseness, but shall see her gain'd
> By a far worse, or if she love, withheld
> By Parents, or his happiest choice too late
> Shall meet, already linkt and Wedlock-bound
> To a fell Adversary, his hate or shame.[20]

One of the facts of what we call the human condition, Milton realized, is that there is no hard and fast, easy answer to the question of whom we will be attracted to, much less whether or not a person we are attracted to will be available. Milton intimates that Adam was both the first and last man for whom there was a perfect mate.

We learn things about our sexual selves by devoting time and energy to their exploration, and we are always in the process of getting to know ourselves. Let us imagine a young man called Benjamin on his voyage of sexual self-discovery.

Benjamin's Story

First off, we should consider that the entrance into the sexual arena is a big step for most people, who can say years later what their "first time" was. Certainly our bodies impel us to try to contact other people, but the bestial nature of the sexual act is so at variance with the social world we are taught to function in that many barriers must be breached. Those who find entering the sexual arena hardest are typically those without the precedent of easy physical contact, say with others of their own sex, in sports, that renders bodily contact normal. Men who have been taught to respect women too greatly find it difficult to engage with them sexually and must be taught to do so, usually by the women themselves, or indirectly by older men, who must reassure these shy young men that women really do want them to do these things done to/with/for them. Those men who think the least of women seem to find it easiest to have sexual contact with them. That aggression plays a role in sexuality is a given; the line is fine between too little or too much.

Yet sex is always new the first time. We all start our trajectories at different places. Someone sitting on the outside would be absolutely unable to predict how things are going to work out. It need not ever start at all. Some people, if only very few, die virgins, and not young. But let us say our Benjamin, at whatever age, finally takes the plunge. Perhaps he has been eyeing one particular woman for months, trying to work up the nerve to ask her out. We'll call her Sally. Perhaps he does; things go well and lead to a second date.

Perhaps Benjamin decides for whatever reason he cannot define he doesn't like Sally. Perhaps she decides the same. Perhaps he does like her but has been taught that sex is dirty and she must initiate things, either directly or by lowering her eyes and bringing her breasts close to him so he can feel their warmth and smell her perfume. Perhaps he has assumed he will land in bed with her after the first date and thinks something is wrong if he doesn't.

Let us take follow one possible scenario. Say Benjamin and Sally do end up in bed. What will their encounter be? Fulfilling? Not fulfilling? What each had expected? Monumental? Trivial? And when it is over, things can go in many directions. Perhaps Benjamin feels things have been successful but Sally, upon further reflection, doesn't, as Benjamin has no notion of how to please her and is interested, Sally reflects, only in his own orgasm. Perhaps Benjamin has shocked her by "going down" on her. Or annoyed her by not doing so. Perhaps she didn't have an orgasm. Perhaps she doesn't usually but was suddenly overcome by, say, Benjamin's muscular back and, for the first time in her life, has one. Perhaps she decided, when she sees him with no clothes on, that he was not her type. Perhaps she isn't at the point where she has even a working hypothesis for a type, but knows only that she is not aroused by his (pick one) pasty skin, too-dark skin, too-small shoulders—or, as is more likely with women, by his lack of smile, his words, his hands, his sneer, or his inability to listen to her.

From Benjamin's perspective, her breasts may be too small or too large, identifying a taste he didn't know he had, at least to this degree; her reactions to him satisfying but not too satisfying, or very satisfying indeed.

Because Benjamin is Benjamin, that is to say, in the middle of his own story, he will not know beforehand what he finds satisfying: he will have to find out by doing. The same thing is true of Sally. Nothing says that she will be in a position to articulate her feelings, especially not after a single encounter. Perhaps what Benjamin is looking for is a strong reaction on the woman's part, though (as he might later say) he didn't know it at the time. Perhaps, by contrast, he decides he wants something more low-key. It is at least as likely that he doesn't know what he wants as that he does. How much has he thought about his fantasies? How introspective is he?

Let us say both Sally and Benjamin are happy with the first encounter. Since this is the first time for Benjamin, he is likely to be very happy indeed, assuming biology cooperated. Yet it is possible to feel completely comfortable about each of a whole series of sexual encounters and only later see in them what, with time, turns out to be a negative pattern. After many sexual episodes, Sally may seem to Benjamin (say) too yielding. Let us say she is quiet during sex, and makes him do almost all the work. The first several times, he may be unaware that this is a pattern. These may simply seem the particularities of the individual circumstances. Indeed, it is unlikely he knows about himself that he is looking for more of a tigress. He may be aware of a certain disinclination to continue the relationship. Whether or not he identifies the source of this is up in the air. Let us say he thinks about the fact that he is less than enthusiastic about continuing. He realizes only then that he was looking for more of a challenge. He decides things aren't working with Sally.

It is unlikely that by this point he will have developed adequate break-up skills, so he lets things trail on for months, making Sally miserable. She asks for help from a girlfriend, who suggests she press the question. She does, and Benjamin blurts out his unhappiness. The relationship ends. At this point we leave Sally, who continues on her own trajectory.

Where does Benjamin go from here? Perhaps this relationship with Sally has made Benjamin shyer than he was before about approaching women. Perhaps it makes him bolder. We cannot say. For that matter, Benjamin himself probably cannot say; only what in fact happens decides the effect. Let us choose the alternative that Benjamin is emboldened. He comes across Rachel, flirts with her, is looking for a woman who responds quicker than Sally and so is aroused when Rachel flirts back and signals her willingness to sleep with him on the first date. They do.

For a while Benjamin is besotted with Rachel, who makes him chase her around her apartment and makes more noise during sex than Sally did. He thinks of her night and day, wants sex constantly, masturbates when not around her, and thinks he has finally found the perfect sexual partner. Because Benjamin is a romantic, and by now of an age where his mother is pressuring him to produce grandchildren, he conceives of this new relationship as potentially *the* relationship, the one that will last him all his life. He concludes that things are working, and that he is in a relationship that solves the problems he had with Sally. Rachel is the one for him.

Yet ultimately he realizes that though Rachel plays hard to get, she does not give him the feeling (how do we get these feelings?) that she is aroused by him as an individual. It is any penis she wants, Benjamin concludes, and his will do well enough. Benjamin tells himself he is looking for someone who is attracted to him as an individual. He didn't know this about himself. He may even lack the vocabulary to express this feeling, and be unable to say why it is that Rachel fails to give it to him.

Benjamin is thinking: his first relationship didn't end in marriage. Neither did the second. Perhaps this realization allows him to end the second affair much more quickly than he did the first. Perhaps he concludes that no relationship will work, and has to go through a period during which his buddies tease him for being such a Romeo, assuming as he did that an affair is the same as a lifetime commitment. Maybe it takes him a while to come to terms with the fact that he has now had two relationships, neither of which has worked, and that this does not necessarily mean he is a loser (or does it?).

At this point we speed up the film. For a time Benjamin sleeps around indiscriminately, looking for woman who are attracted to him. Finally he realizes that the very structure he is embarked on, no-strings sex with a series of women, militates against his finding a woman interested in him rather than merely in a roll in the hay. What had seemed an infinite launch with a rising curve (life consisting of a series of short-term relationships) turns out to have an apogee and then to fall. He decides the conventional moralists that talk in terms of one woman have to be right after all. But given his problems finding the right match, he wonders if this is really all it's cracked up to be. What if he had signed on for life with one woman without even having had sex with her, as truly conventional moralists would like? What is the probability of her having been the person to satisfy him?

For a time he plays with the idea that if people are satisfied with their partner, it is not because of the partner, but merely because they have decided they are going to be satisfied. He wonders whether arranged marriage, such as he has read about in India, might not have something to recommend it. He accepts the idea for a time.

He then rebels against this, unable to accept being forced to accommodate himself to a woman with whom he may be sexually incompatible. His new theory is that people either are or are not compatible in bed. One drunken night, a fraternity buddy fellates him:

it feels much better than any oral sex he has ever had with a woman. He wonders for a time if he might not be bisexual or gay. He may be too embarrassed to refer to the incident again with his buddy. He continues to think about the way it felt. The thoughts ultimately fade. After a time he decides he isn't gay. Still, there was something he got from this that no woman had given him. He doesn't know what this means.

If Benjamin is lucky, all this wandering only takes a few years, at most a decade. Perhaps he decides he really is more drawn to men than to women. For his mother's sake, let us say he finds a nice girl whom he loves and who more or less gives him what he wants in bed, and settles down. If he is like most men, his job and the kids keep him a bit beaten down, so sex no longer seems the issue it once did. Here Benjamin's film fades to black. It is time to leave the theater, though it is not clear that Benjamin's problems will have been solved. We still have the chapters of his seven-year itch and his mid-life crisis to cover, among what may perhaps be many others.

Each person is like Benjamin, keeping an unwritten diary of what s/he learns about him- or herself sexually in the course of his or her life. No one is born knowing these things about him- or herself. Nor will we necessarily be correct in knowing about ourselves whether these are underlying predilections rather than phases we are passing through. We may think one, and later decide it is the other, only to go back to thinking it was the first. Whole periods of our mental diary may be blank if we are not gifted with figuring things out about ourselves. All we can do is summarize our sexual journey up to the present, making generalizations and prognoses that may turn out to be wrong.

The phenomenon both Freud and I start with is here, as elsewhere, the same: that a person may not know what his/her sexual map is. It is a work in process, something we work on till we die, or lose interest, whichever comes first. Even if, as Freud held, our sexual personalities are formed in childhood, without working out on the bodies of other people, they do not come to be revealed. And what is revealed is the direct result of our experiences. The goose has to lay the golden eggs, be allowed to do what she does, in order to have value: her insides right now, when we delve into them, are bloody, wet, and uninteresting.

These things only achieve formulation as the result of experience. Our sexual personality is developed not just in perception, but in fact, like the baby I consider below in my assessment of the debate regarding abortion. If the person has other experiences, s/he has other material to work with, and so makes other generalizations about his/her sexual nature. It is unhelpful to say that the truths we discover about ourselves are coincidentally always the truths that were there to be discovered.

The status of what we think we know about ourselves sexually is always under revision. The knowledge that we are drawn to "type" X, our most precise sexual generalization with any degree of social circulation (at least among same-sex friends), is merely a generalization from experience, and not a very tight one at that. Perhaps we are attracted to someone totally against type; this revises our knowledge of ourself. Such generalizations come only at the expense of a great deal of sexual experience; while we are slouching towards such knowledge, we are much less precise in the direction we throw our net in. Such generalizations summarize the past, they predict the future only weakly.

Not to mention that a good deal of sexuality is situational: a woman who seems fabulous to us in a bar in Antibes may well seem uninteresting back in Chicago. Typically (say) we are drawn to leggy blondes, but how to explain the fact that this short brunette has us all in a tizz? Of course, if the attraction is too much against type, say to a man rather than a woman, we may try to deny them for as long as we can. But the individual case always trumps the general.

Heterosexuality From the Outside
What is the relation of the individual to sexual categories? Despite the intensely personal nature of sexual self-definition, we still live in a world that insists on categories of heterosexual and homosexual. Or at least, this is so collectively; because conservative ethics expresses its truths in terms of actions, not actors, conservatives typically resist an "other" category on the same level of heterosexuality. Typically, conservatives deny that homosexuality is a category at all: they insist it's a choice, or a lifestyle. Heterosexuality, by contrast, is something solid. To counter those who argue for the inborn nature of homosexuality, conservatives make a distinction between being homosexual (leaving the meaning of this open just in case science should find the "gay gene") and practicing homosexual acts. The first is neutral, because a fact of biology; the second is what's bad. Love the sinner, hate the sin, as the Catholic Church puts it.

"Queer theory" reverses the terms in saying that one category is primary, or substantial and the other insubstantial. Homosexuality is solid, heterosexuality isn't. As Eve Kosovsky Sedgwick summarizes it, queer theory is based on the premises that everybody is somewhat homosexual and homosexuals are completely so.[21]

From the perspective of each side, what one is is the more logical, solid thing. It reminds us of Voltaire's awed realization that the language most suited for expressing things just happened to be . . . French.

Those denying solidity to homosexuality make up a large proportion of conservatives, whereas those denying solidity to heterosexuality is a minority of liberals. The more typical liberal position will be that individuals are free to do what they want. There are more people having sex more of the time with members of the opposite sex than with members of the same sex, so there are many heterosexual liberals. They do not demand that the people in the next house, or apartment, be engaged in the same sexual practices as they, or with the same type of sex partner. Conservatives, by contrast, typically will make such a demand, since conservative ethics does not have room in its structure for individual variations on acts.

The clash between liberals and conservatives on the topic of sexual orientation is almost comical for the mutual misunderstandings it reveals. Liberals think they have responded to conservative objections when they say, if you don't want to have sex with people of the same sex, don't! For conservatives this isn't the point at all; the point is making sure action-rules are respected. They aren't setting out to squash individuals, though that is the effect. Liberals think conservatives do intend this effect. It is secondary for conservative thought that their ethics means that certain individuals will have a harder time of it than others. For this reason conservative thought always expresses deviations from its norms in terms of individual variations, not collective ones. Individual X has failed to achieve or live up to the norm; this doesn't mean the norm fails to be a norm.

For liberals, the fact that that individuals have a hard time adhering to rules of action is precisely the reason for holding these rules to be invalid. Conservatives can be "compassionate" about (say) the plight of a young man being bullied in his small-town high school for wanting sex with boys rather than girls, but are not for this reason impelled to change the parameters for actions. For liberals, this compassion is not enough. Indeed, it misses the point, which for them is that people should be free to be whatever they are.

The single most influential thinker on the topic of sexual definition in the later twentieth century has been Michel Foucault, writing in his *History of Sexuality*.[22] Foucault's fundamental claim is that in the late nineteenth century a classification of what people did (e.g. "sodomy") became a distinction of who people are. Homosexuals and homosexuality were invented. And this means that heterosexuality became an essence too, something a person was, rather than something s/he did. This is fully as essentializing as Freud's notions of individual essences that remained to be wrested from obscurity. The only difference is that the essence is that of a type.

The creation of the concept of homosexuality, such as Foucault identified as having occurred at the end of the nineteenth century, clearly re-draws the map of the world, essentializing the "Other" concept. Foucault's contribution to the argument was to return the compliment, to regard heterosexuality as equally possessing such an essence, an "Other" with respect to the now-essentialized homosexuality. It is difficult not to admire Foucault: turn about is fair play.

"Queer theory" added the final stage of reasoning. It noted that heterosexuality allows of degrees, as well as of slippages between self-identification and identification from the outside. The theory of heterosexuality that this has produced therefore attempts to chip away at the substantiality of heterosexuality, conceived of as an essence. The problem for heterosexuals is, the notion of heterosexuality that is being chipped away at is not one they recognize. The correct conclusion should in fact be that the conception of sexual typing as essences is incorrect. Heterosexuality seen from within is not an essence any more than homosexuality was when it was declared to be in the nineteenth century.

By accepting an external labeling as the nature of something, we have made it impossible for liberals and conservatives ever to reconcile. We have frozen group viewpoints as unchanging. Conservatives have a solution: turn the clock back to before homosexuality was essentialized. But it's too late for that.

In numerical terms, however, the biggest problem created by the general acceptance of Foucauldian theory is that men who want sex with members of the opposite sex lack a description of their reality they can accept. (I limit my consideration here to men.) Straight men reading queer and feminist theories typically feel they are reading descriptions of an alternative universe, as gay men undoubtedly felt essentializing descriptions of their world produced in the late nineteenth century failed to describe their reality.

It may seem to those looking on from the outside that heterosexuality is an essence, one moreover that enjoys the power position whose identification is central to any Foucauldian analysis. But this is not at all what life feels like to the straight man, who spends most of his time trying to deal with the threat of his own inadequacy. From the outside he may as if he is projecting power outward, but to himself he seems to spend his time proving that he is worthy—of his own manhood. Sometimes he succeeds, but then he has to prove it again, and again, and again. And that means, contrary to Foucault's so-influential formulation, it is not merely an essence. Instead, it is a combination of essence and action: like all defining concepts external to the self, it is both something we are and something we attempt to achieve. A straight man's definition as a man, and a heterosexual, is not with respect to something outside himself, but with respect to something inside it. And this means, with respect to other men.

Being a heterosexual involves definition as a kind of man, even if part of this definition is determined by how he acts with women. This is the reason for the strong streak of misogyny in heterosexuality, paradoxical only for those who look on from the outside. At the same time part of heterosexuality is what is sometimes called homoeroticism. This is not foreign to heterosexuality, it is a constituent part.

To those looking at heterosexuality from outside, however, its essence seems to be primarily defined in relations with women. Sedgwick takes Foucault's notion of the switch from action to essence as a given. Once the fundamental premise is accepted, Sedgwick can allege problems with the very concept of male heterosexuality. Sedgwick starts with the claim that this duality of heterosexual and homosexual is defined by object choice. Why use this particular quality? she asks, when we can think of other qualities that can be used to make other definitions of what people are sexually.[23] Why not take as primary the distinction between group and couples sex? Between masturbation and sex with any other person? Between children and adults as objects of desire?

Sedgwick's critique of heterosexuality, understood as an essence and defined as primarily about object choice, looks like this. Joe and Bill desire women, so they are heterosexual. But the categories of Joe and Bill's objects of desire may have no overlap at all. Any two given men may have entirely different "types" they are attracted to. Two men will never come to blows if one of them prefers fat women over 50 and the other prefers, in Vladimir Nabokov's word for his pre-teenaged Lolita, nymphets. So why is it a relevant piece of information if the only sense of being heterosexual is that all heterosexuals desire some form or women? Perhaps Joe desires all women, Bill all blondes. Or Joe wants to have intercourse with only one woman, Bill with any and all. The fact that all their non-overlapping object categories belong to another larger category seems too thin a commonality to use this as the primary definer of their being. If we presuppose that straightness is defined by object choice, it quickly becomes clear we must conclude that straightness is incoherent or flimsy. From a viewpoint outside heterosexuality, taking this quality as so defining does not, in fact, make sense. But if we accept that it is mostly heterosexual men who are concerned with this, because it allows them to assume that other men will have sexual objects that are not themselves, we can begin to see why this distinction has been taken as primary, or at least for whom it is primary. It's primarily straight boys who are obsessed with certifying other men as straight—once the possibility of their proclaiming themselves something else is a real one. The obsession with heterosexuality and homosexuality is in fact one created by very specific circumstances, for specific people. It's not the general dividing line it's usually taken to be.

For Sedgwick, things become even murkier when we reflect that people's understandings of sexuality vary widely. This means that people will self-describe based on radically varying criteria. "To some people, the nimbus of 'the sexual' seems scarcely to extend beyond the boundaries of discrete genital acts; to others it enfolds them loosely or floats virtually free of them." "Sexuality makes up a large share of the self-perceived identify of some people, a small share of others'." [24]

Sedgwick is regarding the particular boundary line between two elements of a duality skeptically. We can regard even the fact of duality itself with the same attitude. Marjorie Garber's survey of *Bisexuality and the Erotics of Everyday Life* is a lesson by doing in how to challenge the dichotomy of heterosexual and homosexual. [25] It is not by chance that Garber never arrives at a clear formulation as to whether bisexuality, the topic of her romp through history and literature, is a category, or the refusal of a category, a label, or merely the absence of a category or label. Under what circumstances is it "correct" for someone to call him- or herself "bisexual"? She refuses to answer, or rather her answer is the whole panoply of answers given to that question. The book is not without a polemical edge, of course: this is it, the refusal to answer. Bisexuality may be a third element, part of a triad, or it may not be. Or should even this tentatively tripartite structure itself be questioned?

If we look at sexual categories from the outside, as if from a Martian standpoint, they don't make sense. But for that matter, no categories make sense when looked at from the outside. Categories are always larger than the individuals of which they are composed, and there will always by definition be potential slippage between the individuals and the general.

No consideration of defining categories will answer the question, Am I X because I act as if I were X, or do I act as if I were X because I am X? Categories, in whatever realm, are social facts; individuals are always negotiating and re-negotiating their relationship to external boundaries such as this one. The same problems attend to any category larger than ourselves. Say, being Good or Ethical. We all understand this as something we must work to achieve. We may be adherents of theories postulating greater or lesser contributions from, respectively, "nature" or "nurture," or believe that we are, either collectively or individually, born intrinsically good or intrinsically bad. But we will never be able to decide one or the other, and the debate will go on forever. This is so not for any theological reasons, but rather for the fact that a category is something outside of us as an individual.

There is no way ever to decide, absolutely, whether the sexual categories are the result of nature or nurture. All categories transcendent of the individual allow of slippage between the individual and the category. The whole range of positions as to whether the category is more individual or more outside the individual is thus written into the undertaking. Liberals and conservatives will always have each other to argue with on the subject of sexual definition. Neither side will ever be able to defeat the other on logical grounds, though one side or the other may gain the upper hand temporarily.

Because of Foucault's influence, and because the first "blow" was struck by heterosexuals essentializing homosexuality, everyone is starting the argument nowadays with an external description of heterosexuality, including heterosexuals. Most of these simply regard it with puzzlement and walk away. But they don't have an alternative way of considering heterosexuality. It is logical that a gay man would have seen things the way Foucault did, and logical that feminist theory would have found this conception congenial. What is missing is a conception of heterosexuality by heterosexuals.

Homosexuals were merely doing unto others as was done to them. Left to themselves, heterosexuals would probably never have articulated heterosexuality as an essence. A world that you are part of yourself never seems an essence. As it is, heterosexuals probably don't think very much about their heterosexuality, which for them is synonymous with sexuality—something they may think a great deal about.

Unfortunately, straight men are not going to be very good at taking on queer theory's characterization of heterosexuality. This is so partly because they don't intrinsically see the need to justify their heterosexuality, and partly because articulation isn't the way they typically interact with the world. The structure of straight male relationships is determined by what cannot be said and what cannot be done. Straight men are conscious of each others' bodies but cannot comment on that fact directly, and this comment only happens at all after they have been physical together, been actors with each other. They acknowledge a hierarchy by their actions, not by words. Straightness is to a large degree about action. Part of the code of straightness is that action trumps talk. No wonder they haven't been able to reject this oddly essentialized notion of heterosexuality.

Sedgwick is ready to point out difficulties with the view that heterosexuality is about object choice. Yet they show us not, as Sedgwick concludes, that heterosexuality does not exist, but rather that this is not the nature of the thing at all. In a similar way we can point out difficulties with the notion of heterosexuality as an essence, which presumably means, something that is 100% pure. But this is merely to describe the nature of heterosexuality as it really is, not to conclude that heterosexuality is incoherent.

For example by pointing out that straight men are aware of, and hence to a degree receptive to, other men's sexuality. Of course they don't admit it, for not admitting it is part of the nature of being straight. (Not: not being receptive.) This doesn't make them less heterosexual, because that isn't an essence at all. It's part of what it means to be heterosexual. At certain points of their lives, they are almost painfully aware of male sexuality. A high school male locker room is a fire-fight of glances. Everyone knows who is the most muscular, the most developed, those who ooze the most testosterone. The studs strut and preen; the physical weaklings cower in the corner. Typically the studs associate with each other, showing their awareness of and attraction to their own type. Adolescent boys talk to each other about girls, but they are at least talking to each other—perhaps really, about each other. Group masturbation is not uncommon. The torrent of words about sex is unceasing.

As a result of the fact that straight men do not typically acknowledge their physical involvement with each other, pointing it out can be used aggressively by those regarding heterosexuality from the outside. They say: You can't be so straight after all if you do X. In fact the logical response would be, X is part of what it means to be straight.

The attack is based on wrongly assuming that heterosexuality is an essence. To make things more complex, it's not just gay men who treat heterosexuality as an absolute essence. Most straight boys also police each other in the same way, looking for others' weaknesses. Others lose points if they reveal them.

Adolescent sexuality is in flux; in youth it doesn't make sense to try to disengage the homosexual from the heterosexual. Adolescents are prone to "experimentation" (as we say), and we are still see things sufficiently like the ancient Greeks to think that much of what goes on prior to adulthood, at least insofar as sex is concerned, comes out in the wash, so long as the boys grow up into men and produce children.

But this is already a decision, a way of bracketing off one period of life and saying, we need not have clear articulation here. Then why do we have to elsewhere in life? What is the difference between youth and adulthood? Is it really just hormone levels? When boys grow up, they find less overtly physical things to compete about: money, women, cars. It may be that this is the result of a coming to terms with the fact that success in the world is frequently the result of less primal qualities than those that once seemed so important. It may mean that more mature men establish their place in the world, and move on. But it may mean only that life makes it almost impossible to keep up appearances: few men over 30 are worth looking at with their clothes off. So they don't compete with respect to this any more.

The more pertinent reason may well be that men know that direct expression of awareness of other men's sexuality, like admission that heterosexuality is shot through with same-sex definition, is a sign of weakness: it acknowledges the power of the other man. So they simply file this awareness under the rubric of things that cannot be talked about. It sounds Freudian to say that the facts are exactly the opposite of what men say. But in order to understand this phenomenon, we don't need a complicated Freudian explanation complete with warring under-layers. We need only see, once again, that articulation is an action, and in this case such an acknowledgement gives ammunition to the other man, given that all men are trying to get points by pretending that they aren't in the least worried about or even aware of their competition. This is something men learn, with time, not to do.

Non-threatening locutions are invented to place male-male sexual encounters in another category entirely from those that support the fundamental category of self-definition. Men may, as we say, even occasionally "mess around" with each other and not have to question the category of themselves as straight. If we are assume that we are category X, individual deviations will for a time be called exceptions. It will take more than an exception or two for us even to think of the possibility that we might in fact be Y, and more than those few exceptions to admit to others that this is so, given the change public articulation of something wreaks, transferring us out of category A and into category B.

Sailors sometimes say "It isn't queer if it's not tied to the pier." The soldiers' equivalent of this is "It isn't gay if you're underway." Another exception of this sort is Latin cultures' combination of open contempt for homosexuality ("maracón" being a standard insult in Spanish, as "queer" is among seventh-grade boys in the U.S.) with apparent societal acceptance of homosexual action, so long as the action is that of the penetrating partner rather than the penetrated. This is a distinction between "tops" and "bottoms" accepted from the Greco-Roman world.

Virtually all men are involved physically with each other. Typically nowadays we use the least threatening term to describe this male-male interaction, "homosocial." Slightly more threatening than this is "homoerotic." "Homosexual" is more threatening still to most men. But how to order what we see among these apparently so clear divisions? Isn't a game of football on a Saturday afternoon, in which bodies end up in piles, sexual and erotic as well as social?

Some sex researchers, such as Kinsey, have as a result of everyday facts like these given up the so-absolute dichotomy between heterosexual and homosexual and substituted for it a more gradated scale.[26] But this is like substituting a checkerboard for what was formerly a black-white divide. It may approximate somewhat more closely to the curves of reality, but is still highly schematic, and entails its own approximations. Researchers have set up scales that take account of all of these factors and are amalgamated into a whole picture (someone may be homosexual in fantasy but heterosexual in action; able to love only members of the opposite sex but lust after those of the same, or as may be more frequent among men, the opposite). Who says these elements have been given the correct relative weighting? Someone caught in the middle may be initially grateful to be able to say, "I'm a Kinsey 3." This is like agreeing to another set of comparables when we have failed to agree to the first. It suggests equidistance between two magnetic poles, which is unlikely to correspond to his reality.

The Foucauldian dichotomy between essence and action implies conflict: the person's essence is separate from his actions, though these may coincide in fact. For someone seeing heterosexuality from the inside, the amount of conflict will vary. For those sensing disparity between themselves and the postulated general (such as a young gay man coming to terms with his gayness), the categories seem very real indeed, extremely essentialized. To a young male athlete who glories in subduing other men on the playing field and women in the bedroom, there is no sense of conflict: heterosexuality is not essentialized in opposition to the individual. It is something he expresses by living. For him, it will be impossible to separate heterosexuality from masculinity, and perhaps equally impossible to separate masculinity from life itself.

Seen from the inside, being straight is both something you do and something you strive for. That means, it's not an essence, but a work-in-progress of grays. Pointing out these shades of gray doesn't mean heterosexuality is a fraud, only that it is what it always was, at least from the point of view of straight men.

Most straight men lack the facts to point out that, if homosexuality is taken to be an essence, it too can be attacked as fractured on the same grounds a similar understanding of heterosexuality is attacked. Many men who self-identify as gay were married and fathered children, or started with women. This switch may be generational, but we don't really know yet (older gay men presumably could not "come out" as adolescents). Yet not all of them now say that they were fooling themselves by sleeping with women, or doing what was expected. Even when they do, can we be sure that this is not the re-writing of history by the present, or succumbing to the pressure of our currently so-binary classifications? Nor is it impossible for men who self-identify as gay to have sexual relations with women. The whole category of "bisexual," as Garber implies, must necessarily remain ill-defined, because it currently plays the role of the "swing space" where insufficiencies of our rubrics are stored.

Only late at night, perhaps after a physically punishing match of a particularly brutal game that required them to pummel each other, lubricated by alcohol, would straight men admit to others that sexuality, straight sexuality, is something they must constantly seek to achieve, and that fear of inadequacy is a prime motivator in their relations both with men and with women. To admit this to other straight men in daylight hours is to give them the advantage they need to best you.

Sartre was clear that all of us, male and female, are running after the unachievable goal of Being. All of us are seeking objectification in the gaze of the Other.[27] Yet continuing past Sartre we may note that in the case of the body, women can be objectified by men; it is not so clear that men can be objectified by women. We may also think of Laura Mulvey's classic analysis of men as the "possessor of the gaze": men looking at women is an expression of sexual power.[28] Mulvey's real focus is on the movie camera as a stand-in for the male gaze, and the way women appear in narrative movies, turned into what she calls, with what may be unintentional humor, "phallic" women, glistening in sheath dresses, quintessentially something to be looked at by the man.

The novelist and critic John Berger makes the distinction too between men, whose job is to do, and women, whose job is to be—be looked at, that is.[29] Women typically don't look back, except when they are trying to assert power themselves. No one is left to objectify the man except other men, which is why other men are such a fundamental part of heterosexuality.

In the Freudian terms of the contemporary social commentator Susan Bordo, men have a penis that they are constantly trying to turn into a phallus.[30] We men, flaccid for most of our time on Earth, are constantly in awe of The Erection, which we only fitfully achieve. And this goes for the more general sense of being a man as well. The answer to the question of whether I am straight because I act in a certain way or whether I act in a certain way because I am straight is, simply: yes. Both are the case, either simultaneously or in alternation. Self-definition need not always jibe with definition by others. There is room for disagreement, between the person's current ascription and his later one, between what he says and what others say. This is true of all abstractions, and is not particular to the nature of sexuality.

To a degree, the category of heterosexual (or homosexual), like every category, determines the world. To a degree it is determined by it. A man may fail to see other men as possible sexual objects because he thinks of himself as heterosexual. Circumstances may alter and suddenly they are not only fair game, but acceptable game. Acknowledgement of possibility does not necessarily imply implementation of actions, perhaps for the same reason. We may acknowledge to ourselves our desire for sixteen-year-old girls without ever propositioning one of them or even changing our tone of voice around them. We may be very aware of the masculinity of a co-worker without treating him any differently than his less testosterone-ridden colleagues. Indeed, the codes of straightness demand that we pretend we are not even aware of this unless we are willing to be subservient to the dominant male.

A straight man, in sum, is not someone pretending to an essence and doing a bad job of it. It is only those regarding heterosexuality from the outside who said being straight was an essence to begin with. Straight men know better; at most achieving the essence is something we occasionally achieve. All straight men know they are frauds, at least insofar as what they are supposed to be is held to be an essence. How can we be in the power position, as feminists and gay men insist we are, when what we are aching to be is so elusive?

The most developed line of defense against queer theory, however, takes form among what are now called the New Natural Law theorists (see John Corvino's *Same Sex* for a good overview).[31] It is based on the assertion that only heterosexual sex is "natural."

"Natural," once challenged, is usually defended as meaning productive or potentially productive of children. As liberals immediately point out, there are many cases of intercourse, or indeed whole relationships, that do not and even cannot lead to children, such as relationships involving at least one infertile person, or with a woman past menopause, or pregnant. And if the issue is unsuccessful sperm rather than individual insemination, what of the fact that by definition millions of sperm perish even in a successful act of impregnation? Why is it so bad if just this many, plus one, perish in a man's fist or on another man's chest?

Defenders of the "natural" acknowledge that a marriage involving a post-menopausal woman cannot produce children, but argue that at least it does honor to the institution of marriage. It somehow shares the nature of a "true" relationship, even if only in a second-order way. One side sees difference, the other side sees degrees of the same thing. Frequently as a last resort, there is the appeal to revelation, the assertion that homosexuality is against God's will. This lures out the contextual analysts and Biblical exegetes who consider everything from (mis)translations to the use of terms to the context of a given argument to both prove and disprove this assertion.

Thus the "justification" for why heterosexual (usually married) sex is the only permissible form of sex turns on accepting precisely that this is so. "Natural" in this case is a concept created to defend married heterosexual intercourse, and so is incapable of providing any justification at all.

Biology will prove as unsuccessful a justification of a homosexual-heterosexual split. Say one day something in the brain is discovered that has a high correlation to objects of sexual activity, divided into the groups of men and women. (Is a pederast who likes little girls more like a "normal" man or like a pederast who likes little boys?) Men who find themselves drawn to women have (let us say) a lump, and men who end up with men have another, or lack the first, or have a lump twice as large.

The presupposition behind our search for such lumps is that having them or not will prove something. But what could this prove? Like all facts, by itself it proves nothing. What matters is not the fact but what we make of it. If it puts sexual orientation in the same "inescapable" bag as other biological traits (long arms, blonde hair), the assumption is that it will be treated like them. But someone who was determined to treat sexual orientation differently would not be stopped—and this determination can stem from many things, including moral conviction, personal experience, or sheer cussedness. In this case the determined one simply says, yes, homosexuality is a biological fact, but it is different from other facts in that it is also some other quality, call it shazam (a more likely candidate is "immoral").

And then it reminds us that we are after all creatures that act. All concepts, as I indicated above, are combinations of nature and nurture: they are both us and not-us. For this reason an over-emphasis on one will always produce the backlash by the other. We may be born with the proclivity or desire to do X, but this does not mean that we are right to do X. (This argument is currently made by the Catholic Church with respect to homosexual desire.) The nature vs. nurture debate is not one that facts will put an end to. Nature and nurture are positions of argument, they are not constellations of facts—though facts can be used in defending them.

Then there is the current compromise position, which is that yes, there may be some correlation between sexual objects and biology, but other factors enter in as well: we are begging the question if we assume that we must do X merely because of a biological correlation. Here again it is clear that the field is clear for both liberal and conservative positions since the relationship of the individual to an abstract concept will always be amenable to argument.

We should have some sympathy for the New Natural Law theorists. Of course "natural" isn't going to produce the effect these theorists want. But no explanatory concept ever does. It isn't surprising that defenders of the concept of heterosexuality (or any other) should have problems coming up with other factors in the world to justify it when attacked that line up exactly with the divisions the attacked concept made so clear. Why should any concept be the same as any other? What we call an explanation is like a new layer of skin under an old one that has been torn off. Its cells won't line up in the same pattern. It's thus not surprising we can't produce an explanation for why people should be heterosexual, if people really don't see why they should. If the old explanation has been torn off, it's gone.

Heterosexuality From the Inside

We need not abandon the use of sexual designations such as "heterosexual" (and "homosexual"). They had a use until now, which may be the same thing as saying, they had a purpose. And who's to say they don't still have such a purpose?

Instead of telling heterosexuals from the outside what they are, we can ask, How does the concept of heterosexuality function among males who identify themselves as heterosexual? This last formulation is meant to acknowledge the circularity of the definition: just because I say I'm straight doesn't mean that "straight" is a defensible concept. But acknowledging that the use of the concept constitutes an act is the first step to describing rather than knuckle-rapping; in this context it might provide an answer to the question at hand.

I express this combination of action and essence that is heterosexuality as a configuration of power relations—which means, both what we express as individuals, and what we uphold. We can make a comparable sketch for homosexuality.

A straight man sees other men as being situated on the same power level as himself, insofar as he is considering them as men, by which he usually means, men like himself. The caveat is important. Usually, straightness or gayness is irrelevant. Being straight or gay isn't a gas that permeates one's whole existence, it's a fact that is only relevant under specific circumstances. It does not matter if all the students in a math class are male, all female, or mixed, straight or gay. Straight man may treat biological men as belonging to another category than himself, say to the category of bosses, or that of people. Insofar as he is acting as a straight man, however, he acknowledges other men as being the same kind of end-in-himself that he sees himself as being. He considers each man as king of his own tiny space, an equal. (This is descriptive, not prescriptive.)

This produces problems: how to integrate so many independent actors in a larger structure? Masculinity for straight men is an expression of freedom, but this freedom means threat at the same time. Men regard other men warily. It is the acceptance of responsibility as well. As an end in myself, the buck stops with me.

The sensation I have as a straight man meeting another man (which is to say, a man assumed to be straight) for the first time is unlike any other. Unconsciously I square my shoulders and jut my chest out, projecting confidence but not aggression, respect for the other man but calm acceptance on the inviolability of my own boundaries. Inwardly I am a little tense. "Hey," I say, my voice dropping to the low part of its register, if an informal acquaintance; my shoulders may be slouched sideways a bit on this one, like a Rodin statue. "Howyadoin?" if one level more formal. "How do you do?" one more notch. (By this one, my shoulders are square.) And then there is "How do you do, sir?" where the respect for an equal is intensified into the respect for a superior. I assume the other man knows what I know, shares certain presuppositions about life, and is going to offer me the same respect.

Straight men register other men as possible rivals, sizing up a situation to see if we should be in a defensive crouch or not. Our default position with other men is tension; only subsequently do we relax. We know that some things are not our responsibility, but if we fail to act on the things that are, we might as well trade in our balls, as we say in a double metaphor ("balls" for testicles, first off; testicles for potency, then standing for masculinity in second order—or is the second a synecdoche? Metonymy?).

For straight men, masculinity is synonymous with straightness. It means: nobody fucks with me, as we say, indicatively conflating sexual intercourse with bodily interference. A man typically seeks to make his own body clearly masculine, cultivating muscles, a deep voice, a non-fluttery demeanor, and posture that puts chest and shoulders in evidence as much as possible. And he gets pleasure, sometimes intense pleasure, from seeing these in other men. What we might call the Marine Corps ethos is about admiration of masculinity by other men. This is related to the male cult of the body.

Men seem to get more pleasure than women do from interacting with a muscular male with a strong jaw and a hearty handshake. They recognize a fellow worshipper at the shrine of testosterone: they themselves are valorized by seeing someone seeing the same goals. For the same reason, they may also be interested in hard penises, though most men appreciative of masculinity draw the line at that: the penis gets hard, rather than being hard, like muscle. Thus it is of interest only to its possessor, not to another male onlooker. Homosexual action is the end of the straight spectrum, not something alien to it. Thus, apparently, the many warnings against it. If it were something truly alien, straight men would not need the constant surveillance by other straight men that is a fact of straightness to make sure they had not strayed over the line.

The other side of the Janus face of the respect owed other ends-in-themselves, which is to say, other men (to the extent that they are being treated as other men), is the fact of power over women, to the extent that women are being treated as women—which means, in a ripple effect outwards from the central situation of sexual intercourse. The same caveat applies here as to relationships with men. We have no idea how far the ripples should be allowed to go. And it is a misunderstanding of this fact that has bedeviled feminist thought. We can damp them down to practically zero, separate the relationships of intercourse from practically all other actions with women in the world. Life for most men nowadays is rigidly compartmentalized: we don't treat the female boss like "a woman"; we may not even treat female co-workers "as women," resolutely refusing to send out or pick up sexual signals.

A man treating a woman "as a woman" means with reference to intercourse. In sex between men and women, the male is in the power position, the female succumbs. This is not her definition, but it is her role. Better still, the woman demands that the man take her. The very phrases associated with male-female sexuality, as has been frequently pointed out, are akin to those of war, the metaphors of conquering and possessing, spoiling and having. Some attempt by the woman to resist is diverting; indeed it feeds the man's perception of himself as the victorious warrior. So too for occasional role switching, however that is understood, with the man's consent: he allows himself, momentarily, to play the role of the weaker partner. But this switch is with his permission, and he can always take that back.

Because sex is about power, our language is pervaded with terms of disdain for the penetrated, which is to say the vanquished: so-and-so was "screwed," we say, to mean, was placed at a disadvantage, or more clearly, "fucked." "Fuck me," we might say in comic exasperation, meaning "what I did was so stupid that as punishment I deserve to be penetrated." "Suck my dick," a man says dismissively or in fun to another, meaning, you are (or I am pretending that you are) low enough to place yourself in a subservient position to me. And of course saying that something "sucks," meaning that it is a negative thing, is now ubiquitous, and has even entered public usage. Most people who use it seem unaware of its genital origins.

Most of these terms are primarily used as terms of disdain for men who allow themselves to be penetrated. Thus the straight distrust of "bottom" gay men. It might not be too much to suggest that though most straight men would be capable of, indeed relish exerting their power over other men to the extent of penetrating them, the Catch-22 is that they would despise a man who would allow them to do so that they would get no satisfaction from the act. The ultimate unattainable would be penetration of another man who didn't want to be penetrated, which is to say rape. For this at least would preserve the honor of the penetrated man, and make him worth penetrating. At least the thwarted male-male rape scene in the movie *Pulp Fiction* suggests as much.

It is normal, it suggests, to want to exert our power over other men by penetrating them; it is equally normal for men to resist being penetrated. All the jokes men have about the DRE, the "digital rectal exam" (where the physician inserts a rubber-glove-clad finger in the anus to feel for possible prostate cancer) attest to this fact. What is at issue is not physical sensations, but what it says about us in the pecking order. We cannot willingly allow our bodies to be penetrated by another being as like ourselves as another man. A cartoon in, of all places, *The New Yorker*, refers to this. The mild-looking man who has just been examined by the equally mild-looking doctor asks, referring to the pecking order of penetrators and penetrated in jails, "Does this make me your bitch?"

To a certain degree, however, the use of these terms for the male "bottom" as insults suggests disdain for the straight woman as well, who must, by nature of her biology, allow herself to be penetrated by the male. (The insistence that she need not has led to lesbian-inflected feminism. Does this school insist that women not be penetrated by women?) The difference between an "insensitive" lover who merely "has his way" with the woman and the one who derives his pleasure from having her consent to his penetration, may not be so large after all. The victory is more delicious if the victim pleads to be sacrificed. Men realize that women have no individual choice in the matter. This low-level (or second-order?) disdain is not individual, but general, metaphysical rather than personal. Many men love women, or even a single woman; some are afraid of women, or a single woman. But heterosexual sex doesn't "work" if the man does not, more often than not, play "the man's role" in sex. And this means, the more powerful one.

We may assume that a man "in control" of his sexual life will act in a certain way toward the woman the rest of the time. But what is this? It is not implied by what happens during intercourse, and remains to be defined. The unintentionally comic side of Hemingway's fiction, such as "The Short Happy Life of Francis Macomber," lies in Heminway's assumption that a man in a satisfying sexual relationship with a woman will act towards her in the other times in certain ways, and she towards him.

The assumption in Hemingway's story is that the ripples radiate infinitely outwards from the sexual act Perhaps this is true to a degree: we have all seen kittenish women and cocky men, but in the world of the workplace today we have learned that only a very small proportion of our lives need be influenced by our sexuality. Or do we laugh at Hemingway because we wished that things were really the way he said they were?

In "The Short Happy Life," the title character is a coward. On safari in Africa with a guide who enunciates the story's moral (and sleeps with his wife), he first runs from a large animal he is supposed to shoot and then stands up to one. Hemingway has the guide summarize the change this effects in Macomber. [32]

> It had taken a strange chance of hunting, a sudden precipitation into action without for worrying beforehand, to bring this about with Macomber, but regardless of how it had happened, it had most certainly happened. Look at the beggar now, Wilson thought. . ...Probably meant the end of cuckoldry too. ...Fear gone like an operation. Something else grew in its place. Main thing a man had. Made him into a man. Women knew it too. No bloody fear.

Because Macomber's errant wife Margot, an over-the-hill beauty, senses that her philandering is over and that Macomber now holds control over her, she shoots him. We assume Hemingway is thinking: just like a woman, trying to escape their natural servitude. It would be easier to root for Margot as a reaction against this if the story were not so resolutely set up as Francis's coming of age. It is clear that Margot did not wish to accept the fate that biology had arranged for her, and that she had hitherto escaped by marrying an unmanly man, a coward.

Someone who does not wish to accept the use of the term "disdain," even much-weakened, for the feeling of straight men for women, would not accept putting this feeling in the same category with the feeling of straight men for the receptive partner in homosexual intercourse. Such a person would invent a new woman-specific term, and try to link it to the group of "tenderness" and "love."

If a man willingly lines up behind a more masculine male, the subordinate partakes of the superior's strength and acknowledges his priority. This may be why structures like the military are so congenial to many males. Men accept their place in a hierarchy without having to give up their masculinity. To a degree, this superiority is created by the fact of hierarchy. Superiors are worthy of adulation because they are the superiors. More stripes on their shoulders make the man more worthy of respect, not because the stripes denote anything, but for their own sake. But it always helps when a superior possesses intrinsic qualities too such as height, stamina, muscles, and sexual prowess with women—not to mention ability to hold liquor, impressive because it suggests that even with this much weakening, they are still not down for the count.

Queer theorists have made much of institutions like the military, which are based on what we call male bonding. (The term "male bonding" is an attempt to separate straight same-sex physicality from other-sex physicality; it too can be questioned.) But male bonding is not the primordial state of male relationships, as is evident from the fact that so much is made of it when it is achieved. What is primordial is suspicion, defensiveness, and a mutual sniffing out between males. No end-in-himself, such as straight men conceive of themselves to be, can take naturally to another end-in-itself. Because the gulf that is to be crossed is so vast, the other shore—that is to say, the bonding—seems the more amazing. Males are essentially binary: either suspicious loners or, in a subsequent quantum-jump alteration that usually presupposes physical intimacy, bonded to other men. Bonding is the acceptance of the unarticulated compact of no articulation, no touch, the agreement that the entities that have bonded treat one another as ends-in-themselves.

This fact is the great weakness of the New Natural Law theorists, who argue that a male-female relationship somehow fulfills the natural dignity of the human being. A male-female relationship may be what both the male and the female want, and may be enormously rewarding, but it is based on the man treating the woman as something other than an end in herself. A man may love a women, respect her, or even worship her, but during the act of sex, he uses her for his own pleasure, and he takes her, thereby giving the woman her pleasure. Both things may happen simultaneously, but the man feels as if he is launching himself into the void. He is the one who must act, the woman is acted upon by the man.

The one relationship that avoids this disparity is male bonding, that bath of Sameness that is so difficult to describe, the delicious disappearance of the sense of separateness that determines all male-male contacts at their beginning. It is the equivalent for men of being in love with a woman, which is also a disappearance of boundaries. But in many ways it is more intense as a result of contrast, because the threat from the other person was initially much greater in the case of another man.

Expression of desire between men means the binary distinction between two groups of people based on easily-recognizable physical characteristics such as that between men and women is made impossible. So what? we might say. Straight men can learn—say in interacting in the workplace with gay men, as they have learned with straight women—to treat gay men as people (as we say) rather than as one alternative of two, where the second alternative is women. The whole world can be treated with courtesy.

What it means is that both of the two stages of male-male interaction would be lost. The first might not be such a loss, the state of threat. For we would treat all males without knowing if they were threats or not, blandly, rather abstractly. More sadly, the other alternative to which male-male relationships sometimes careens, bonding, would be eliminated as well. For bonding presupposes that you have broken down the boundaries of the self into an undifferentiated pool of Sameness.

For straight men, the easiest way to live is knowing that they can put everyone who looks a certain way, namely either male or female, into a certain power slot in their world-view without further inquiry. Because men like the power position of being the lookers rather than the looked-at, being with other men in the bonding mode meant that they did not have to be wary of being the object of someone's gaze. Men don't care whether other men are looking at women. All they want to know is that the other men are not looking at them. The comfort this creates is real. In some ways, it would be a shame if it were to be impossible. But usually it is impossible, and non-straight men fail to be impressed with the magnitude of the sacrifice.

Because so much of straightness is about action rather than speech, straight men have again and again been able to make themselves comfortable by forbidding action. Thoughts become irrelevant. The Catholic Church forbids same-sex sex, not the desire to do it. The U.S. military ostensibly acts according to the "don't ask, don't tell" paradigm. If only other men would act as if they didn't desire other men, things would be (for the straight men) fine.

Straight men are right to say that unarticulated desires are different from articulated desires. A scene in Ibsen's *A Doll's House* makes this clear, where the deathly ill Dr. Rank finally tells Nora, Torvald Helmer's repressed wife, that he has always loved her. Nora had been about to ask Dr. Rank for a monetary loan to pay off her own debt, taken out to save her husband's life. Moreover, in this scene she is flirting with Dr. Rank, who is a family friend, teasing him with the highly suggestive stocking she is darning. [33]

Dr. Rank is lulled into letting his guard down by the intimacy and confesses his secret. Nora draws back instantly, reprimands him, and bemoans the fact that his confession has now made it impossible for her to ask him the favor she had in mind. Things were fine as long as each knew of his love but did not articulate it; she could pretend she didn't know, and he could retain the freedom of intimacy. Now that his true feelings are out, he can no longer be subsumed under the ill-defined rubric of "family friend." And her code of ethics does not allow her to take money from a man whose interest is avowedly more than Platonic. The military, in the same way, demands only that things not be expressed, that is to say, dealt with in the masculine way. (Nora's anger is at least partly that Dr. Rank has betrayed the code of a "gentleman," based on self-denial and taciturnity.)

The demand that all men be a possible pool of either enemies or bonding buddies is a demand based on simplicity. If we can assume that anyone who looks like A is a potential, even if not actual, object of the expression of sexual power, and that anyone who looks like B can be the potential, if not actual, recipient of another power relationship entirely, movement through life is facilitated. If we have to deal with things like blurrings, life is much more difficult for most people. But this is simply the way life is.

We should acknowledge that something will be lost for straight men if other sexualities may express themselves publicly. The error of queer theory and other descriptions of heterosexuality is to express skepticism that anything at all is being given up. Of course something is being given up. Men are simply more comfortable with other men they can assume to be like themselves.

Yet the world conspires to deny us in so many ways the assumption that others are like us. We must rub shoulders with those who fail to share our tastes in reading, our politics, our religions. Why should it be so tragic to live in a world where we cannot assume congruence of sexual desire? The correct response to straight men who want to ensure that all other men are just like them is that of course something would be lost. However what would be lost does not seem enough to justify what is being asked of other people, namely complete repression of expression for their desire.

Queer theory fails to access the straight point of view. But the straight point of view fails to access the queer one. Do straight boys know what it's like to live in a world where desires cannot even be expressed? Unless they have lived repression of another sort—always a possibility—the answer is probably, no.

Conservatives and liberals reach an impasse on this issue, because such "other person's point of view" thinking as this belongs only to the liberal side. The closest conservatives can get to this is "compassion," which is to say, pity, but no change of position. For liberals, the fact that a general rule leads to extreme pain in particular cases is reason enough to abandon it. For conservatives, who in all likelihood are not such particular cases, they mean only that the individuals in question must make an extra effort.

Argument will not resolve this issue. But it is possible for the world to change to the point where it simply goes away. Not all arguments that are possible are made; some are simply rendered irrelevant by the way things are. Yet these may be problems only of our transitional age. If and when "gay" and "straight" have become so neutral as categories that each man immediately shares the information with another which group he belongs to (assuming for the moment the counter-factual situation of just two, with no switching, no boundary blurring), a straight man will be forewarned. The problem is solved, and it turned out merely to be the relatively technical problem of what external signals correlate to what groups. Yet it will not be argument between liberals and conservatives that gets us to this point.

Some Foucauldian writers offer themselves as spokesmen for the "men's movement," articulating the pain such categories as gay and straight, masculine and not so masculine, cause even to men who do not ultimately adopt another classification. Their argument is typically to say that this may be the nature of the way masculinity is lived now, but was not the way it was lived in the past and need not be the way it will be lived in the future. These writers argue that men are in fact prisoners of their current role, and should try to escape by recovering the mythic past, learning to share their emotions, or escaping from the corporate culture of conformity and blunted sensibilities.

Two such writers are worth considering as examples. Andrew Kimbrell's *The Masculine Mystique* views everything I have been describing—the current masculine cult of the body, the strong silent comportment, the competition—as being a historical perversion of "real" masculinity, brought on by the Industrial Revolution.[34] Kimbrell is concerned with things like getting equal custody rights for men (he's a lawyer), male job injuries, and the early violent demise of young black men, and so sees men's position as one to be remedied, not gloried in.

Like Foucault, whom he never mentions (as well as Marx, equally unmentioned), Kimbrell places this wrong turning at the end of the eighteenth century, linking it to the *levée en masse* initiated in France during the Revolution and continued during the Napoleonic wars. Kimbrell contrasts the resulting image of masculinity to that operative for the "whole" pre-Industrial, pre-military man. Indeed, for Kimbrell it seems that pre-Industrial man had no image of himself, in the sense of vision he had to live up to. Like most Romantic/Marxist Utopians, Kimbrell argues that men in the pre-Industrial age simply did what came naturally.

Kimbrell's argument presupposes a sense of being entrapped: for him, the price men pay for their status as ends-in-themselves is too high. History is invoked for the same reason any argument is invoked (he is setting history against the view that men are naturally competitive, rapacious, and sexually promiscuous). For Kimbrell, Napoleon led to factories and robotic behavior. But this is because Kimbrell doesn't think the state of contemporary men is good. We might equally well say that the French Revolution ushered in the Individual in Europe. For Julien Sorel, hero of Stendhal's *Le Rouge et le Noir*, Napoleon was the symbol of individual male self-realization.

The position comes first, then the net is cast for arguments support it. Kimbrell's point of departure is, roughly, that it's awful to be a man. Whether or not the particular arguments offered end up moving us to his position is almost immaterial. If these don't do the trick, others might. To someone who thinks that being a man, despite its undoubted difficulties, a great adventure and an intoxicating trip, the arguments will ring hollow.

George L. Mosse's *The Image of Man: The Creation of Modern Masculinity*[35] is another argument in a Foucaldian vein, namely that the view of masculinity as something to be achieved I have articulated here is itself a historical development. Mosse puts the beginning of this modern view of masculinity at the traditional place for starting the "modern world," namely the mid- to late eighteenth century.

Mosse comes close to saying that without the exclusion of what it is not, masculinity wouldn't have much definition at all. What it excludes is both what he calls the Jewish body and homosexuality. Moss as a result becomes a special pleader for both of these, looking everywhere for an "alternative" to this view of masculinity as something to be achieved in hardness and resolute action that would be more receptive to these two things. (He thinks socialism had a chance, and then again the flower children of the 1960s. Neither really succeeded in dislodging the mainstream view; for him this is a disappointment.) In addition, the image of modern masculinity is for Mosse tainted by its association with militarism: he claims it was developed in the Napoleonic wars, and came to fruition in the Third Reich.

Mosse spends many pages on the revolting caricatures of Jews in the Third Reich. In Nazi Germany it seems clear that a dominant quality was defined by exclusion, or that men were raised to find their purpose in battle. But this is not necessarily true in the United States today. The male beauty ideal is still what Mosse describes (ripped torso, square chin, tall, standing straight with shoulders back), this ideal gets its valorization largely through our commodity culture. Our ads and movies tend to feature such men, but we do not demonize others. They just don't make it to prime time. We don't have to exclude the Other, money does it for us. Why should it matter that people with ideas such as mine have "only" existed for two hundred years? I can say, that's at least two hundred years of correct seeing.

Chapter Four

Abortion

Fetus vs. Unborn Child

Abortion is another subject related to sexual ethics on which liberal and conservative line up on opposing sides, sabers drawn.

If ethics gives rules for the race of life, abortion is a debate where the contestants haven't been determined yet. Who's in the race is precisely what's at issue.

Liberals are prepared to see the developing child as a sort of creature that may not be the same as other creatures. Because conservative ethics expresses itself in terms of actions, its secondary effect is to deny that sub-divisions between kinds of actors can be important. (In the same way, the fact that I am hungry does not, for the conservative, justify my stealing the loaf of bread: I am not in another category from someone who is not hungry with respect to the bread.) Thus conservative ethics asserts that "life begins at conception," which simply means, it is not set up to process anything but rules expressed in terms of actions. Either you are a person or you are not, there is no other alternative.

Abortion not only concerns the result of sexual action, it is about a realm that, structurally speaking, is quite similar to the sexual: something that threatens to escape the ethical realm into the particular. Talking about a developing child is difficult because it has virtually none of the qualities we associate with people. It (as we must say) doesn't have a taste in food because it doesn't eat, doesn't have sexual feelings because it may not have developed genitals yet, doesn't have a favorite baseball team, nor taste in clothes, and so on. One way to insist that this creature is a person like other people is merely to assert belief in something it has (call it a "soul"); another way takes the form of asserting potentiality—some day this blob will have a taste in clothes (or not). The problem is like Milton's in talking about angels: our usual words can be used in talking about these things that aren't their usual referents, but we don't know how metaphorically. Is the light and dark of pre-day/night Heaven "like" day and night that we know? Should we even be speaking of light and dark, or should we use different words?

There is even disagreement between liberals and conservatives on whether or not abortion should be seen as a sub-topic of sexual ethics. Conservatives will say it clearly is so, given their allegiance to the proposition that reproduction is the purpose of sex. Protection of this purpose will therefore follow. Liberals, for whom sexual purpose is expressed in terms of more individual situations, do not see this link, with the result that the whole discussion of abortion in the sexual realm will seem somewhat strange.

Conservatives do not, typically, want to speak of the very individual make-it-up-as-you-go-along relations involved in sexuality at all. Their attention is thus immediately deflected to children, usually their production and rearing. This is why for conservatives the point of intercourse is the production of children, and why abortion is such anathema. The relation of parents with children is enough more social than the sexual relation that conservatives feel comfortable with it. Typically conservatives conceive of child-rearing as a very predictable relation indeed: the adult applies largely invariable rules. Thus the biological fact of a linkage between sex and children is used as the bridge to change all focus on sex to a focus on children.

When liberals and conservatives argue about abortion, however, they do so based on their respective viewpoints not of sexuality in general, but of what liberals call the fetus, and conservatives call, to make their position clear, the unborn child. Liberals see the fetus as the endpoint of a process that begins before conception. What conservatives see, by contrast, is not a fetus but a child that just isn't a child yet, which is to say the first point of a process whose vector arrow points beyond birth.

The two positions may be visualized as time periods each of which is bounded by a bracket at one end. They overlap in the moment of perceiving the fetus/unborn child, where the respective bracketed ends meet. Their divergence comes from the fact that the bracket is at different ends respectively of the two time lines. In fact they are looking at two things entirely Thus the two groups, liberal and conservative, are like two of the blind men who felt up a distinct part of the elephant and proclaimed the elephant to be like that one part it saw:

the man who held the leg compared the elephant to a tree, the man who held the ear to a leaf, and so on.

In both the liberal and conservative positions, there is a time that remains unconceptualized, and hence what from the other perspective looks like a blind spot. For conservatives the blind spot is before; for liberals the blind spot is after. Liberals have no response when conservatives ask, visualizing the child in diapers, or walking across a stage to accept a diploma, Why should this child not be born? Conversely, if liberals ask, visualizing the time before conception, Why should this child be born rather than the other children that could have been or could still be in its place?, conservatives have no response.

Conservatives compare the fetus/unborn child only with its own non-being, and conclude that it is better to have this child than an absence of this child. The liberal comparison is not between the being or not-being of this one fetus, but the fact that this particular fetus has no greater claim to existence than any other fetus, possible or real. For conservatives, liberals who allow abortion are murderers—as of course both sides would agree they are if the only alternative to this fetus is its death. But that, for liberals, is not the only alternative, given that the fetus is being seen as something that has come to be. Conservatives, unlike liberals, do not see the unborn child surrounded by a cloud of possibility from which it emerged, the time before it was.

This divergence of viewpoint between seeing, on one hand, a situation that is one among many alternatives, and, on the other, merely is, is common in the world outside the debate around sexual ethics. Children who have known only one house do not see the family dwelling the way the parents do, as the culmination of many trade-ups, only as what is. Nor do they appreciate "what the parents went through" to achieve the level of financial stability they now enjoy: for them this has always been so. People who move to a new suburb take for granted things as they are that may continue to upset older residents, who remember when this housing development was an open field, this strip mall a stream.

As we reach adulthood we all achieve the ability to see our parents as if surrounded by a sea of possibles. As we sometimes say, we come to see them as people, rather than taking them for granted as the definers of our world. Education can effect the same shift: we suddenly realize that our way of doing things—whether that be dating rituals, food consumption, or schooling—is only one alternative among many, given that other people elsewhere do things differently, or earlier peoples did so before our time. This is the alteration wrought on contemporary sensibility by Foucault, who tried to relativize the way we conceive of (among other things) homosexuality by comparing it to the way this was conceived in earlier times.

The conservative view begins at conception. This primary level produces the apparently identical but actually secondary assertion that "life begins at conception." Life begins at conception for conservatives because their viewpoint doesn't go any further back than that. For if we include the time before conception in our world-view, that time missing from the conservative conception, it becomes impossible for either side to argue that fetus X has an individual justification for being (a "right to life")—compared, that is, with fetuses that never even got that far, fetuses that weren't.

Each person produced implies many thousands (millions?) that were not. For every child produced, a near-infinity of other children, possible results of sperm that failed to reach the egg in time, has failed to be produced. Thus pro-abortion thinkers may say, so what if parents fail to have child A. They may have child B, which would have failed to be if they had in fact had child A. More generally, if failing to have child A is a moral wrong, then these parents would have been guilty of a moral wrong if they had had child C instead of child A.

Each of us, it might be argued, is a vampire/parasite: we take up room in our mother's womb that our unconceived, and hence unborn, brothers and sisters might have had, and use up her body so that they cannot do so. We make it impossible for them to live. Of course, had they lived, they would have made it impossible for us to do so. For does it even make sense to speak of having been born later, or to another mother? Could that person even have been us, given that the sperm and the egg would have been different?

All thought experiments involving alternate worlds such as time travel, or imagining fetuses as the people they may, or may not, some day become, or the consideration of how different our life would have been had we been born another sex, race, class, nationality, or century, end in stuttering. To see this, let us postulate ourselves existing, but (say) living at the time of the Egyptians. But this means, we would *be* an Egyptian, say, or a Hebrew, and not a modern-day American. And *this* means we would think like an Egyptian (not merely walk like one). Egyptians did not know about modern-day America. And so on. It does not take many steps for us to discover that the "I" has disappeared and we have nothing much at all in common with this postulated twin.

The number of children a human female can conceive in her lifetime is limited, perhaps to something in the neighborhood of 20.

Certainly it is not as many as 50. Let us for the sake of argument double this to 100. But even if we say twice this number, 200, it will always by definition be exponentially less than the children who were not conceived. Are they being deprived of life? Let us postulate women with twice as many eggs, or three times that number. Is the world being denied these unconceived children? Is preventing their birth not the same as murder? Should conservatives not be mandating fertility drugs? And even, say, five children at a time are still a mere fraction of those we can imagine. Let us postulate eggs for all the zillions of sperm to impregnate: has the world been denied the presence of all these people? If what we're talking about is what didn't happen, there is no reason to bound ourselves to what is currently biologically possible, or even biologically possible for human beings as we know them. We can always imagine more children who never saw the light of day.

Yet conservatives do not think this way, because the time before does not figure in conservative thought. This structural fact is usually expressed in the second-order assertion about the existence of something that is only a quality of a being that exists, not one that doesn't exist. Usually this is called a soul. This is then used, in circular fashion, to defend not preventing this ensouled creature from existing.

Conservative ethics, expressed in terms of general rules about actions, has to start with the people who actually are, and so is utterly unconcerned with sperm, eggs, or any "what ifs" located before reality. It is not for nothing that conservatives, when compared to liberals, seem the more pragmatic group of thinkers. But what this means is that everything that is is compared not to what could have been, but with this extant thing's not being—and so too for fetuses, which, logically enough, can only be filed under the same rubric as human beings. The only alternative to what is is its negation, not other possibilities entirely.

Second-level positions

Second-level log-jams are the most absolute, because they are created by things unapparent to the jams. Such a second-level log-jam quickly forms between liberals and conservatives on the subject of abortion. It leaves one side calling the other murderers and that side calling its opponents anti-female. The interesting question then becomes, How is the secondary level constructed from the primary one? We can see such a construction of a secondary level of tenets from the principal one in an article by Jeffrey Reiman called "Abortion, Infanticide and the Asymmetric Value of Human Life."[36]

Reiman is a liberal, what is usually called "pro-choice." His article is an attempt to express a primary level of thought structure through the secondary level of positions and arguments, expressed in the technical language of academic philosophy. To justify his second-level assertion that abortion is not the same as killing an adult, he differentiates between what he suggests are two distinct senses of identity, moral and metaphysical. According to Reiman, a fetus (in conservative-speak, an unborn child) is metaphysically the same as an adult, but not morally. Moral identity takes precedence over metaphysical. Hence aborting a fetus is not the same as killing an adult. QED, at least from his liberal point of view.

Yet all this reasoning is nothing but expression of a fundamental level of thinking that is not shared by conservatives, and so must fail to convince the very people Reiman would so like to bring to heel. Reiman also suggests, though is unwilling to go too far in defending, the position that killing a newborn is not the same as killing a child, or an adult. Goethe felt the same way, and his horror over the execution of a young unwed mother for the murder of her baby prompted the Gretchen story in *Faust I*. Reiman's polemical purpose in distinguishing two different senses of identity is that of saddling his opponents with the less interesting sense and demanding that they be satisfied. We can see therefore why he will be unsuccessful. No conservative opponent in his or her right mind would accept such a deal.

Reiman would concede that a fetus might well be the same as, say, the 21 year old college graduate it could some day turn into, at least in this metaphysical (it is difficult to resist adding the word "trivial") sense. As he argues, things that are true of a 21-year-old may not be true of a fetus. For example, that it should have the right to vote, or be able to take on the responsibility (not to mention have the biological possibility) of parenthood. For this, we would have to establish what for Reiman is the stronger "moral" identity.

The claim that we should not kill this fetus must be based on its possessing a property in common with the 21 year old, not merely what Reimann calls mere metaphysical (and so by implication empty) identity. The question thus becomes, does it possess such a property, and if so what is it?

Reiman wants to be able to control what we call this property, because his whole argument is based on its nature. Reiman's candidate for the property by virtue of which it is wrong to kill adults is self-consciousness of one's self as a living organism. He quotes as his epigram a perception of Voltaire that it is worse to die than never to have been born. Reiman takes this as given and sets out to explain why this is so. And while still at the preliminary stage of clearing the space for this property without having told the reader what his candidate is, he comes to the following interim conclusion: "If the pre-property fetus has no moral claim to get the property [we don't know yet what it is] then there is no moral difference between a fetus that stops existing before it gets the property and a fetus that never starts to exist".[37]

Reiman knows he must forestall objections, and does so immediately. His argument, central to my consideration here, must be quoted at some length. In it he introduces his central notion of what he calls "retroactive 'empersonment'."

> ...we tend to read a kind of personal identity backwards into fetuses, and personal identity carries connotations of moral identity beyond mere [above, I suggested "trivial" or "empty" in this spot] metaphysical identity. If we think of the pre-property fetus as a kind of quasi-person "who" loses the chance to have the special property, then we will think of the pre-property fetus as a person-like victim— which is a moral status that a not-yet-existing fetus lacks. Just because it is so natural to us to think this way, I believe that this (retroactive "empersonment") is the single greatest source of confusion in the abortion debate. If we resist it, then that the fetus has already been existing has no bearing on the moral status of its loss of future existence. Consequently, that loss is morally equivalent to the simple failure of that future stretch of fetal life to begin. And, then, it is no worse morally to end the life of a pre-property fetus than to refuse to produce a new one.[38]

"Pro-choice" liberals, it is clear, do not engage in "retroactive 'empersonment'," whereas conservatives do. This is the basis of their first-level divergence, so criticizing it from the beginning merely identifies Reiman as a liberal, and makes clear why he will never be able to mediate between the two positions. Reiman makes mediation more unlikely, not less. He ignores the divergent time periods implicit to the two viewpoints' conceptualizations. The abortion debate always stalemates in this way when we limit our vision to a geometrical point, where the end-brackets of the two conceptions overlap. As Kant would say, the debate presents antinomies. Antinomies in Kant's world are precisely what I am focusing on here, second-order disagreements that calcify because the primary divergences are not being articulated.

The conservative, conceiving in terms of actions rather than actors, asks a general question of the form, Is abortion permissible? Reiman, showing his liberal credentials, makes this a function both of a more particular question and one expressed in terms of actors, May I abort this fetus? For the conservative, it is the action which is forbidden, so the actor, the I, is irrelevant. For the liberal, the actor has to be relevant because that is the terms of liberal ethics. In the same way, for example in the case of theft, the conservative will ask, Is theft permitted?, whereas the liberal will ask, Am I allowed to steal in these circumstances? For the liberal, this is a case of a particular person with particular situational affiliations taking a loaf of bread (which itself implies all sorts of social facts). For the conservative it is merely a case of stealing, with the actor irrelevant and the action the same whether it is a single cent or a million dollars, a loaf or bread or a diamond necklace.

Abortion is somewhat different in that it involves divergent reactions to what we conceive of as a process, something we define as a kind of especially slippery spot on the ice. For both liberals and conservatives, the gestation period is such a "process," something that is bound to go to a certain end if it is not interrupted, like pushing a stone off a cliff. This means time is intrinsically written into it in the way it is not in, say, acts of theft: we can make these as long or short as we like. If Einstein was right, even God has to wait for the sugar to melt. Everyone must wait nine months for the baby—or nowadays, given the possibility of care of pre-term babies, at least seven. We drop the lump of sugar into our tea; if the tea is hot enough, and not already super-saturated, the sugar will melt. However of course we can fish it out of the tea half-melted. We can catch the rock in mid-fall. And we can interrupt the gestation period.

According to liberal thought, we are allowed to intervene in the case of a natural process. Liberal thought, after all, is alive to the presence of actors, so it is comfortable with the notion that actors are necessary to processes, and can be deleterious to them as well. Conservative thought, to a much greater degree, insists that humans should be passive sideliners once a process, conceived of as a kind of vectored slide in the world, has been identified. This is so because of the underlying structural bias of conservative thought towards expression in terms of actions rather than actors. Actions, here actions in the world and apparently by the world, take on substance of their own.

Our conception of what counts as a process in the world changes over time. Geza Vermes notes that for first-century CE Jewish thought, being ill was tantamount to having sinned; forgiveness from sin was synonymous with curing.[39] This meant that for the time period he is dealing with, illness was a process. Now we do not see it as such. Most people today accept the liberal view that health is a good in and of itself, something we start out having and continue to retain in the normal run of things. Illness, like evil in St. Augustine's view, is not a substance, but only a negative. We conceive of doctoring as reversing a negative, re-establishing normalcy. This means that according to nearly everyone, illness is not itself a process, so that conservatives are not even given the opportunity to argue as their thought impels them, namely that intervention in a process is illegitimate.

Reiman implies, in his critique of "retroactive 'empersonment'," that what I call process-thinking is itself illegitimate. Yet all of us postulate a world that is patterned in these slippery slopes which, at least in our own minds, inevitably produce result X. Difficulties arise only when we disagree regarding which things are processes, or what action is legitimate with respect to one. Getting through the day requires making assumptions about how things are going to turn out. To be sure, these may turn out to be wrong: I assume I'll need to eat lunch, and take a sandwich. I bring the materials to teach my classes. I hear it will rain and grab an umbrella on the way out. If "retroactive 'empersonment'" is wrong, then so is a lot of what we do every day.

Further, process-thinking is at the root of fantasy. And we all need fantasy. The adolescent boy with the *Playboy* imagines that the woman pictured there will be receptive to him, find him attractive, and so on. In fact none of these things is likely, but the magazine's popularity is based precisely on the reader believing that they are, or perhaps more to the point, not even considering their necessity. Dreams of big projects are fantasies in this sense: we may learn how to consider many eventualities, but we can never consider them all, and inevitably we put the best spin on how things are going to turn out.

We are constantly changing our minds about what counts as a process. When we regard such processes skeptically, we speak of "counting our chickens." This phrase comes from a parable whose first step is the gestation period of a living being. In the story, the farmwoman on her way home from market with the basket of fertile eggs imagines them already chickens laying their own eggs, from which will spring so many chicks, themselves subsequently egg layers, and concludes that she will be the richest woman around. Lost in her reverie, she fails to notice the stone in her way (in one variant of the story) and trips, smashing all the eggs.

The moral of the story, presumably, is the folly of assuming that in the garden of forking paths that constitutes our world, any specific sequence of paths is inevitable. People inevitably postulate the sequence most advantageous to themselves. We are free to assume the next step in a process will be a certain one. But the world, or fate, always has the last word. The farmwoman had already hooked Step 2 to Step 1, 3 to 2, and so on up to, perhaps, 5 or 6, without acknowledging all the other paths that Step 1 could take: the possibility that Step 2 could be gooey yolks has simply been overlooked.

A Middle-Eastern variant of this parable is one where the seller of clay pots dozes off, and dreams of the money she will make from selling her pots; this will (after several other steps) enable her to keep a maid whom she will wake from sleep to do her bidding by giving her a kick—thus—and in the sleep not of the maid but of the mistress-that-was-to-be, she kicks and shatters her own pots. This example leaves out the biological process implied in hatching chickens, or having a baby, but its moral is the same.

What Reiman calls "retroactive 'empersonment'" is a form of counting chickens. It postulates our being at the end of a long causal string, somewhere where we are not now located. In the case of a pregnant woman, we imagine a blooming 21 year old that will result from her pregnancy, perhaps just having graduated from an Ivy League university, full of hopes and ideals, kind, generous, respectful, not worse morally in terms of sex and drugs than his/her peers, and are ready to weep at the thought that all this will not be if we kill fetus x. In my terms, this is the basis of the conservative viewpoint, with the only two options to choose from being this person existing (conservatives, postulating the person already, would say: living; "existing" is the alternative to the liberal's other option, which is to say, non-existence) or this person not existing (or living).

In counting this particular set of chickens, we presuppose that at each moment we can decide which path the world will take. Indeed, even the conception of forking paths is a limiting one, for each postulated fork has itself an infinite number of sub-forks, things that could have gone differently than they did. This does not conflict with a conception of the world as absolutely determined, by God or by events: all we are talking about is our conception of events, which by no means has to coincide with what actually happens. In our version of things, the child will not (to take an example from the perennial Christmas favorite movie "It's a Wonderful Life") drown in the lake when he is 10. He won't catch a stray bullet meant for someone else in a drive-by shooting when he's 11. He won't choke on a fish bone when he is 12. He won't fall in with the wrong crowd in high school and drop out. He will get into the Ivy League university . . . And so on.

The paths don't exist until we articulate them, and they are infinite. If a child makes it to the age of 11, this means not only that he has failed to drown at 10, but that at 10 and one second he was not crushed by a falling stone, or run over by a car and so on. We soon find ourselves in Zeno's paradox of the arrow that never reaches its mark if we begin to fill in all the unfollowed "paths" that litter the wayside of everyone who manages to stay alive from one second to the next. And that is only to consider life as opposed to death, not things like exemplary school work, friends, general health, and college acceptances.

Even if the conservative fails to postulate the Ivy League student as an inevitable result of a pregnancy, s/he usually does postulate at least a healthy, normal baby. Usually we postulate the healthy adult. We have to postulate something. Only in extreme cases might we be willing to admit that a particularly bad future might justify not having lived at all, as when we fantasize about Adolf Hitler having been killed in the womb, or having succumbed to illness at an early age. Another case that would cause even a fair number of conservatives to accept the possibility of abortion is that of major genetic damage, say Down Syndrome, or a child that was certain to die at an early age before reaching adulthood.

But a truly consistent conservative would insist that the bar of what we assume as the result of gestation running its course is so low as to be unlowerable. The postulate need not even be of productive life, much less an exemplary one—it need merely be a life, of whatever length. A consistent conservative would say: even if the world were full of mongoloid children, these should have been allowed to be born. As a justification, s/he might say that they contain within themselves the spark of life, and extinguishing this spark would have been an affront to the Creator. In the same way, for the Catholic Church, suicide is never justifiable, no matter how wretched the life of the person contemplating it. Conservative thought expresses itself in terms that render individual cases irrelevant.

The conflict between liberal and conservative regarding abortion is neatly expressed in the antagonistic liberal bumper sticker that reads: "Against Abortion? Don't Do It." It is a taunt. The liberal knows perfectly well that what the conservative wants is not that conservatives should have the option of not aborting, but that no one should have this option, that the action itself be ruled impermissible for all. Conservatives want an absolute principle of action upheld; liberals are for re-casting this in terms of actors, making the individual situation relevant.

In a similar way, the 2003 United States Supreme Court ruling on whether the State of Texas could ban consensual homosexual sex produced people kneeling before the Supreme Court Building in Washington, D.C, praying. They were praying (presumably) not that they themselves would escape the trap of homosexual sex, but that the high Court would proclaim this action illegal for all.

The liberal would point out that one of the forking paths that the situation can follow is precisely that the fetus not develop further at all. The fury of the conservative at knowing the liberal is going to abort a fetus is that of someone whose best-laid plans have gone agley, and that as a result of someone s/he is actually talking to. How dare you? is the conservative response. You have prevented X, Y, or Z! Perhaps, the liberal might respond, had I not put an end to things right now.

To listen to conservatives talk, one would suppose that zygotes shaved and drank beer. Instead, the fact is that of a fetus, we can say very little. This is Reimann's point. We lack the vocabulary to express the arrival in the world of a little stranger who nonetheless assumes the most intimate position in our household, and about whom we know absolutely nothing. All we know is that it's going to be a person. We don't know anything else at all about them, which is why liberals and conservatives fight so virulently over the tiny scrap we do know. Why bother to fight over the nature of this little bit, given all the other things we don't know? This is why: because we know so little.

The problem of abortion is a problem of language. The difficulties we have talking about people coming to be, fetuses or unborn children, are similar to the problems we have talking about people after they are dead, or have been transmuted to another state. Are they alive? If they have bodies, can the bodies feel sensations? Do they need food? Do angels eliminate waste material? Do they have sexes? Are they aware of having lived? Do they recognize other angels as having been their soul mates on Earth? Does the soul of a General know he was a General, the Sergeant a Sergeant? Or is all this washed away? Are angels married? What if they had several wives or husbands on Earth, with all of whom they were happy? Do they live together in Heaven? If not, are they lonely?

Scholastic philosophy tried to answer many of these questions with respect to the once-alive. Angels were all 33, the age of Jesus at His death. They had no sex. They did not eliminate, nor eat. Nowadays it seems to us that the answers are arbitrary. The fact is that if we postulate a realm we know nothing about, we can equally postulate a description of it, but we can't prove anything about it. What if one group insists that all angels are not 33, but 66, or 35, or 1? We can give reasons for all of these, but no one group's description is any more justified than any other.

For purposes of abortion, a zygote for a conservative has the same status as a college graduate. Despite this fact, there is an asymmetry of argument between the way gestation is treated by conservatives compared to the way childrearing is treated. The growth of the infant into an adult is, biologically speaking, just as pre-programmed as the development of the zygote to the child's birth. The infant will, in the normal run of things, grow larger, learn to speak, eventually undergo puberty, and so on. The asymmetry is that conservatives insist on the automatic nature of gestation in a way they do not with the process of childrearing. Their position typically changes at the moment of birth: what before was meant to be suddenly becomes the result of parental will. Child-rearing is an enterprise conservatives are devoutly in favor of, insisting at every step on its active nature, the necessity of vigilance. It is liberals, in what seems a paradox, who tend to take a more laissez-faire attitude: they'll grow up somehow. For conservatives a biological process gives way to one that not only allows, but requires, agent intervention.

This apparent contradiction is explicable if we look for primary qualities of thought-patterns rather than secondary ones. Liberal teleologies (if we may call them such) are individual, and take as their point of departure the Rousseauian view that people are intrinsically fine unless knocked off course. Conservative teleology insists that parents must work ceaselessly to inculcate their children with a sense of an absolute standard. In T.E. Hulme's formulation of the "classical" (conservative) viewpoint, "it is only by . . . organization that anything decent can be got out of" people. [40]

During gestation the individual (the baby) is inaccessible to influence. We can't educate up to an external standard because we can't get at the baby, and it isn't yet able to take anything in, at least not anything we would view as moral. Thus the conservative sense of no action at all being appropriate during gestation, and the conservative fury at what they see as intervention in the pregnancy. Usually this is expressed as interfering in the teleological way of things. The fact that this ceases to be an issue at birth shows us that this cannot be the main issue.

In a similar way, conservatives are adamant that prevention of pregnancy in the form of chemical or physical birth control is different from the "rhythm method" which relies on determining when ovulation has taken place. The first, in their view, is intervention; the second is merely taking advantage of a loophole in the natural run of things. But Catholics allow some unnatural chemical medical interventions under other circumstances; for liberals this fact represents a contradiction. The difference is that virtually no one today sees illness as a process.

The primary-level issue for conservatives is not natural vs. unnatural. Instead, it is that intervention is conceived of as being what pushes the individual towards an external set of standards. Doing nothing, for conservatives, is not the same as doing any particular something, whether positive or negative. The issue before we can communicate with the child is merely that no action at all is appropriate. This is why conservative thought is sometimes, in arguments with liberals, expressed as, action X is not appropriate. Scheduling sex on a day when there is no insemination possible is not the same as preventing it. Allowing a pregnancy to proceed is simply doing nothing, not something.

Rights of the mother
Liberals are correct that conservative thought neglects the plight of the mother. For conservatives, no action during pregnancy is appropriate; in arguments with liberals this position is expressed as, undertake no action. Which is to say, abortion may not take place. Liberals confound the conservative blind spot for the mother with lack of concern for her. The mother simply is not the issue for the conservative, save insofar as she too needs to be educated in an ongoing fashion to absolute principles of action. But pregnancy does not increase this imperative, and the fetus, being conceived of as a process, is therefore something that is not to be interfered with. Because liberals are looking for actors, conversely, they tend to focus on the mother and her needs/wants ("pro-choice"), and abortion is frequently cast as a feminist issue. The baby is not so clearly a person. But this is so only at a secondary level, not a primary one.

Judith Jarvis Thompson's article "A Defense of Abortion" is well known in academic circles.[41] It divertingly exemplifies this sort of defense of the mother's point of view. In doing so, it provides a perfect example of the liberal point of view. In Thompson's analogy, pregnancy is like being kidnapped by a society of music lovers and hooked up for nine months as the living dialysis machine to a great violinist, who otherwise will die.

Thompson's essay is so interesting because she conceives an analogy in which the "baby" (here, the violinist, or his protectors, an international league in support of music) is the aggressor, not (as invariably in the conservative view) the aggressed. Of course the analogy is silly as a view of pregnancy for precisely this reason: it remains to be established that the mother is the victim of a kidnapping by adherents of the baby. Who are they supposed to be in reality? We can't just assume that a mother is in any sense kidnapped by her baby.. Still, the analogy turns the tables on the conservative view, which makes an equivalent assumption, seeing the woman as the passive "handmaiden" of the defenseless unborn child–to evoke the title of Margaret Atwood's novel *The Handmaid's Tale*, about a dystopia where women are merely vessels for childbearing.[42]

Thompson tries to forestall conservative objections that the mother gets herself into the position of pregnancy in a way that the unwilling owner of the kidneys used by the violinist does not. In doing this, she offers yet another analogy, even more interesting than that of the violinist with the faulty kidneys. She postulates a world in which spores could come in the windows and grow into great entities by implanting themselves in the carpet. Even if we take the precaution of having our windows covered with screens, she points out, one spore in a million will get through, technology not being perfect. Are we responsible for this?

This analogy is no more satisfying to conservatives than the story of the violinist. We have to breathe but conservatives will insist that we don't have to have sex. No one will fault us for opening the windows, yet they could fault us for having sex—before marriage, say. Besides, it presupposes precisely that what we are doing when we have sex is something other than putting ourselves in line for impregnation. The conservative view, following the traditional notion of teleology whereby the purpose of sex is procreation, would be unable to accept this. The conservative continues to see the action as "the way to get pregnant—though often you don't," Thompson is offering the alternative view of it as "having sex—and occasionally you get pregnant." No set of analogies, however fetchingly expressed, can bridge this divide.

Art and the Unborn

Jeffrey Reiman takes as his epigraph to his discussion of "retroactive 'empersonment'" a quotation from Voltaire that focuses on the strange difference between the way we conceive the time before our Earthly existence and the way we conceive of the time after. Why, Voltaire asks, "has it been imagined that to die is an evil—when it is clear that not to have been, before our birth, was no evil?"[43]

Reiman comments as follows. The question "reminds us that we normally believe the moral wrongness of killing human beings to be something much worse than not creating them (if the latter is bad at all). . . . We normally think that murder is much worse than failure to procreate via contraception or voluntary abstinence."[44] In fact the moral wrongness of murder may be independent of our fear of the afterlife; Reiman should be comparing natural death to non-procreation. His focus is actually on abortion, which he should be comparing to murder to see if they are fundamentally alike or fundamentally different. He has loaded the dice in his favor by comparing murder not with abortion but with non-conception. Unsurprisingly, non-conception will come off well by contrast. Voltaire suggests it comes off well even by comparison with natural death.

Reiman shows his fundamental liberal sympathies by implicitly allying abortion with non-conception in this way. Indeed, he shows his liberal sympathies even by considering non-conception. Only liberals look at the time line before conception, from whose perspective there is no particular reason for this zygote to have come to be rather than any other. For conservatives, abortion is the alternative only to this person living rather than to another person taking his or her place in either this womb or someone else's, so it is filed under the same rubric as murder. Conservative thought, concerned with the "unborn child," classes it in one direction. Liberal thought, concerned with the "fetus," classes it in the other. Reiman is concerned to differentiate non-conception from murder. Once he has allied abortion with non-conception he has "proven" that abortion is not murder.

Reiman's fundamental perception with respect to this issue is that people are not scared by the thought of non-conception. He says we condemn murder more than non-conception; Voltaire says we even think the idea of natural death more "evil" than the idea of non-conception. Because he fails to realize that even conceptualizing non-conception means his argument will fall upon deaf ears with conservatives, he continues as if he can prove something to those who do not agree with him to begin with. His suggestion is that human life is "quite unusual" in possessing what he calls temporal asymmetry. In fact all he has identified is a quality that most things perceived by people have, namely that they possess no value before we know about them, and sometimes great value when we do.

Normally, Reiman says, "if something has x units of value, then destroying it (after it exists) and intentionally not producing it (before it exists) equally deprive the world of x units of value."[45] He then goes on to locate the strange quality of life that makes its value asymmetric in self-consciousness. Because the fetus lacks this quality, it is in the most fundamental sense pre-human or pre-life, and so its abortion is not morally wrong. But if many things possess this asymmetry, there need not be any quality of life itself that produces it in this particular case. Even if it is true that a person is self-conscious and a fetus not so, this does not prove an absolute distinction between two temporal states of the same person (as a conservative would express it).

Trying to show that lives are different from other things in the world, Reiman postulates an oddly artificial notion of value to which human lives are supposed to be the exception. In fact, humans share the qualities he ascribes to them with other things, and so cannot be bracketed off in this manner, waiting for him to tell us what to do with them. The reason we hold murder, or even natural death, to be worse than non-conception cannot be self-consciousness, for all of the other things that exhibit this same asymmetry of value similarly lack self-consciousness.

The most obvious example of other entities besides humans with asymmetrical value may well be that entity we consider in some of the same terms as a human being, in that we think of both as being "created." Namely the work of art. Almost never do we mourn the unmade work, yet we value many of the works that are made. (Existence is a precondition of value, necessary but not sufficient.) Perhaps in the atypical case of a Mozart, who presumably would have gone on cranking out masterpieces had he not died at an early age, we can feel sad the world has been deprived of the unmade works we imagining marking the unlived decades of his life. But this is only because we extrapolate from what is, imagining not merely 42 symphonies but 142, Mozart's version of the other Beaumarchais play, *The Barber of Seville*, in addition to Rossini's later one, five more violin concertos, and so on. And we do not even think of regretting the unmade works of those who lived out something like their "natural" span of threescore years and ten: we do not, for example, imagine unwritten works by Bach. But why not rail against the givens of biological life that deprives us of more? George Bernard Shaw did, in *Back to Methuselah*, but his view of the tyranny of biology over art never caught on.

Yet most artists do not seem to produce works as biological byproducts the way Mozart, or Bach, did, and we feel no impulse to assume further works, even in the case of an artist that died at an age less than the statistical average for his or her time and place. Even in those few cases like that of Mozart, where we do regret unproduced works, it is generalized products we mourn, not specific ones—unsurprisingly, as they don't exist.

In the case of Romantic artists, in fact, rather than the Classical Mozart, we would do well to assume a death of creativity at an early age. Romanticism typically, like mathematics, was the game of the young. If Wordsworth had died at 40, the literary world would not be appreciably impoverished. Lytton Strachey, in his biographical essays, is fond of this game of imagining people dead at mid-career: would our view of them have been different? His point is, typically, no.[46]

As far as that goes, the brevity of life of some artists can be argued to have a precondition for the masterpieces we have. Think of Keats, who would probably not have written the "Odes" had he not had a sense of impending death, or of Kafka. Longer life is not necessarily a good thing for artists, from the point of view of the consumers of their works. Even an author as seemingly self-destructive as, say, Dylan Thomas, may have produced only because, not despite the fact, that he was so drawn to the bottle. And harried graduate students might well be delighted that James Joyce, wrote only the works he did and no more. Another *Finnegans Wake*? A book as far beyond the *Wake* as this is beyond *Ulysees*? For someone trying to pass doctoral comprehensive exams, this is a vision of hell.

We have no one to compare well-known authors to except themselves. They are absolute particulars. An author like Flaubert is the author of the works he wrote, no more, no less. We do not lose sleep, or even a moment's regret, over the fact that he "only" wrote this many books, though we may savor every one he did write. Nor do we castigate him posthumously for having taken seven years to write *Madame Bovary*, saying, somewhat ill-humoredly, if he had done it in three, he'd have had time to write another book. He was who he was, the time he took was the time he took. History does not judge works by the pound.

In no case do we mourn the works that failed to be produced by dint of the fact that others were being produced in their stead. And from this we can begin to see the relevance of this discussion to the time years before our birth: for every one child produced, countless others failed to be produced in its stead. But precisely because they did fail to be produced, we cannot regret them. We cannot speak of works X and Y that could have occupied the space currently occupied by *Madame Bovary*, because it is not clear who would have written them. Certainly not Flaubert, given that Flaubert is for us the writer who in fact wrote *Madame Bovary*. And would two works have had the value of the single one of *Madame Bovary*? Twice the value? Half the value?

As for the artists who have not reached the canonic status of a Flaubert, we do not waste a second wondering what things they have not produced. It is difficult enough to get the world to pay attention to the ones they did. Moviegoers may be cheered or amused by a movie opening nationwide in a multiplex near them, but they do not waste time regretting all those projects which failed to be green-lighted. None of them is playing tonight, so why should we even think of them? We think of the books available in bookstores, not the ones that languish unpublished—unless we are their authors.

Nor are artworks the only entities other than humans that possess what Reiman calls asymmetric value. Many, even perhaps most things only have value to the extent that they exist, or at least exist to the extent they exist for us. (This seems like an important distinction, and I return to it with respect to abortion.) I can't lust after the expensive suit I've just seen and can't afford until I see it. I can't envy the biceps of the man lifting across from me in the gym until I see them; if I don't see him I can't be jealous. If my friends don't all have BMWs, I don't feel I need one. Indeed virtually all advertising works, as Vance Packard pointed out in the 1950s, by the creation of desire. [47] Until it is suggested to us that we need X, Y, or Z, usually we don't.

In the same way the objects of all emotions, perhaps all feelings, have asymmetric value: I can't love someone I don't know. Until I see Y, I can't lust after that person. Of course, I can sense sexual urges, but I can't crystallize them until I postulate or see an object. In the same way we can, perhaps, sense the amorphous desire for love, but until the object it crystallizes around appears, we don't love anyone. One of the peculiarities of love relevant to this argument is that it remains unclear whether we love individuals primarily as carriers of our generalized need to love, or whether we love them primarily as individuals. We are born with the need to love, it sometimes seems, and suddenly someone appears who makes it clear to us what the particular shape of our particular love is, in that this person seems to respond to all of our desires. After the fact, we say, I love X, but until X appeared, we would probably have been unable to describe the person whom we would love. If we can describe too precisely before the fact the person we have never seen, it may well seem that we do not love this individual, but only the missing puzzle piece.

We take a sick person to the hospital and invest time and money in that person; we do not invest this in someone who doesn't exist, and so who isn't sick. We cry when our favorite vase is broken, and may even spend countless hours to fix it. We do not spend those hours fixing a vase that doesn't exist, and so which isn't broken. Think of the Portland Vase in the British Museum, shattered in the nineteenth century into slivers and since then painstakingly restored. Sometimes our life's work, as in the re-building of Warsaw, is to restore to a previous state, something we wouldn't do if the state had never existed. It seems bizarre to me that the economist Daniel Kahneman should have received a Nobel Prize for pointing out these facts with respect to economics. Can economics prior to Kahneman have really been so insulated from the realities of human action?

Many, perhaps even most things, exhibit asymmetrical value. We can miss something that was, but it is difficult to miss something that has never been. All of us know the feeling of looking at a cityscape, and mentally filling in a building that now is not there. In the wake of September 11, 2001, few people in the United States need to have this phenomenon explained. Yet it was equally a shock for those who remembered the city before the World Trade Center was built to look up and see the towers intruding on the landscape. Indeed, when they went up they were initially much derided until people got used to their presence, and no one can pretend that they ever failed to stick out. Had they never existed, their absence would cause no regret, and of course their presence, postulated never to have happened, no shock. Except, that is, perhaps in the head of the imagining architect, the person we call a visionary: the one who imagines the world different than it is, alone among millions. This person is comparable to the writer, and to the mother.

All of us remember the changes wrought upon our surroundings in our own lifetime. The necessity to constantly superimpose what is against what was makes most of us mournful in the long run, which is one of the signs of old age. Pity the poor Cumean Sybil not only for her poor health in concert with her immortality, but also for the mental exhaustion of having to deal with all the changes of so many generations! Yet our children are not mournful: members of the new generation take for granted what they start with. They don't remember, and know only by hearsay or from pictures, that the old buildings used to be so and so, and thus do not have to deal with the sense of change when they look at the urban landscape that simply lacks them.

Asymmetry of value, typical rather than atypical of the things of which our world is composed, is not based on self-consciousness, but on consciousness: on the consciousness, that is, of the person who perceives the thing. I miss John when he is gone or dead; I cannot miss him if I didn't know him. In the same way, I can't miss him before he is born. Indeed, my relationship with him depends on many things, including his age with respect to me. John who was my friend is different from the baby John, with whom I would (assuming my own adult status) have interacted in a very different way. If I weren't Baby John's parent, the harsh reality is that I would miss him less if he died than I miss adult John who was my workout partner and drinking buddy. This is presumably the source of Reiman's intuition that infanticide, even if still wrong, is not wrong for the reasons or to the extent that murder of a grown person is wrong.

It may seem that I am confounding things that I alone am ignorant of such as, on one hand, the existence of person X (whom I will subsequently marry) or the suit I am about to catch sight of, and, on the other, things that nobody at all knows about. Into this latter category fall angels, unborn children, and unmade artworks. Indeed, even within the first category, differentiation may seem desirable. My future wife may be living her life just fine without me. However the suit I have yet to see and buy was made for the sole purpose of being purchased, if not by me, then by someone else my size.

Conservative ethical positions would insist on this distinction, expressing the value of human life in objective, not subjective terms. Human life has value in itself, not merely because I am here to sense it. But this is value ascribed to the general, not the specific—both in the case of the person existing and the one who ascribes value to this. This is so for structural reasons.

Thus for proponents of conservative ethics, say the Catholic Church, it is not John as opposed to some other unliving person who has value (there is no reason why John rather than someone else should be taking up space on Earth), just the living person who happens to be John. Even if John is the last man on Earth, with no one to mourn his death, conservative thought would insist that his life has value. But this is because he is an instantiation of the general. If I do not know John, I cannot miss him when he is gone. He may nonetheless have value, but not because he is John, only because he is a living being, or a person. Thus missing John as an individual when he is dead is not a topic a conservative ethical position is comfortable with, and conservative ethical positions are being consistent when they suggest we rejoice in John's afterlife. Individuals are never the point for conservative ethics, because conservative ethics is based on external rules that individuals must constantly strive to uphold. Immorality for conservative ethics is always the result of divergence of the individual from an external standard.

Sometimes the degree of generality of knowledge of an object I discover is central to its definition. Science, for example, is by definition the discovery of things that nobody knows, not the repetitive proving of the existence of things everybody knows. The third grade is not undertaking a scientific experiment when it feeds one plant household chemicals and another water, because we (that is to say, adults) know how this experiment must come out if it is properly done. Indeed, if they fail to kill the chemical-fed plant, we know someone has been cheating and feeding it nutrients on the sly. All it is doing is re-creating experiments in the manner of science. But this is only so because science talks precisely in terms of an objective world. It isn't science unless it's objective. And that means, it is asserted precisely to transcend value, being merely objective. Once we focus on the phenomenon of asymmetry of value, however, we are talking about cases where a precondition of value is existence. Thus, to return to Jeffrey Reiman, there is nothing anomalous about the value we ascribe to other people's lives: we are after all doing the ascribing.

Sometimes we are on one side of this asymmetrical relationship of value, in being the person who brings the thing to being; sometimes we are on the other. In his short story "Lost in the Funhouse," for example, John Barth has considered how different the world looks for the creator of the artwork, in his metaphor the sensitive adolescent who sees behind the scenes in the funhouse, from the way it looks to the consumer, those who ride on the carriages.[48] Sometimes, as in the case of artists and mothers-to-be, the person on the "producer" side of the relationship is only one individual, with everyone else on the other side. Sometimes there are many producers and a single consumer, as in the case of the suit I crave.

Only things that have been can be missed. Things that are not yet, because they don't exist, don't take up our time. Yet the fact is that existence can be sensed by some people and not by others. Someone feels the need for, say, a certain book, so s/he causes it to be. This is a need that no one else feels but the author. Yet if we ask, what is it that this person feels the lack of? s/he doesn't usually know, because the thing hasn't been "created" yet. That is why the author has to write the book, not merely refer to it. It doesn't exist to be referred to. In the same way the unborn child, by being filed under the rubric of "person in waiting," can be given existence—by someone who thinks of it as existing.

For the person interested in this entity as an individual, the period up to birth cannot merely be taken for granted. In a similar way, limiting our view to the world of "before," we find ourselves in a gray area wondering how we can speak of the fetus as a person when we know so little about the person it may one day become. It is like speaking of the object of a love that has not yet crystallized, or a work of art that an artist is only meditating but has not yet started to make. We don't know what form it is going to take. This means, we don't know who/what it is going to be. Indeed, we don't know even whether it is going to be. Many works have been abandoned; many pregnancies end for whatever reason. This is the liberal point of view.

Reiman's argument solves no problems, it only puts more strongly into relief the basic divergence between liberals and conservatives. Liberals conceive of the fetus in the mother like an unmade work of art, important only for the creator. The mother causes the individual baby to come to be. Conservatives do not think in terms of individual babies, but of babies in the abstract. We can postulate the position of an artistic conservative who is uninterested in the precise nature of the work of art produced, but very interested in a certain number of them being produced, or of everyone designated as an "artist" forced to create, made to brood over something, anything. (We can imagine a dystopian novel after this plan, a sort of *Handmaid's Tale* for artists.)

For liberals, the point of view of the artist is the same as the point of view of the mother. The artist is as essential to the artworks' coming to be as the mother is to the baby. Without the artist/mother, the work/baby does not exist. (The conservative postulates it as existing, and simply waits until it arrives.) Until, more specifically, it is actually born, it does not in any real sense exist. The artist knows the completed work when s/he sees it (that is to say, when s/he makes it); but neither s/he nor anyone else would probably have been able to describe it initially, at least not in the early stages of planning.

In a similar way, the pregnant woman may look forward to the generalized child, but she cannot articulate whom she is looking forward to much more precisely than this. The child has to develop, just as the work has to be made: the process of development in the womb, just like the process of making the work, is necessary for it to come to be. In neither case is the mere passage of time sufficient. Because the new thing represents an alteration of the world, somebody has to be the agent of its coming to existence.

Or at least this is the way most artists nowadays conceive of their plans for an unmade work, and most mothers. Of course, there is the neo-Platonic conception (via the Renaissance thinker Ficino) of, say, a Michelangelo, comparable to the conservative view of gestation. Michelangelo may have conceived of liberating the already-extant statue from the marble block, but the fact is that only he was in a position to be able to feel that way. An outside judge would have been unable to say, certainly at any early stage, whether the strokes of the chisel were well directed or ill-directed, moved toward liberating the foreordained figure from the marble or imprisoning it further. We are only in a position to judge when, say, a human figure emerges from which the sculptor suddenly lops off an arm. We have an idea of what a "complete" human being looks like and think we can assume that the artist saw this as well. That may be speculation on our part, as in fact the limbless sculptures of Rodin show. In their day they were derided for looking like the victims of Turkish atrocities, then recently discovered, with hacked-off limbs. Indeed, debate continues on whether the roughed-out "Slaves" of Michelangelo are finished or not.

For the creator of the object, as we may call the person causing it to come to be, or those who know about it, the object has value before it exists, because that person is in charge of, and necessary for, its coming to be. In the same way, the advertising agency whose picture of a BMW causes me such automotive lust knew about the car before I did, and brought it to our generalized attention, that is, to the readers of the magazine, of whom I happen to be one. The person who designed the suit I want created it, the factory made it, and the shop put it in the window. All these people knew about this suit before I did, but that does not prevent its value for me from having gone abruptly from zero, at the time when I didn't know about it, to very high, when I did.

The liberal way of looking at the fetus postulates that its nature is the way a work of art fails to exist before its creation to anyone but its mother, the artist. The fetus, by and large, is not seen by anyone, and typically is "visible" only as a bulge in the mother. Once the baby emerges into the light of day, it can be perceived by many people, and so in a metaphysical sense "exists" in a way it did not before—just as the book in progress fails to exist for anyone but the author until it sits in piles in the bookstore (assuming it gets that far). At least this is true when it is considered as an individual; as instantiations of a general, as conservatives conceive of the unborn, they can be defined into existence. Yet can alter where we are in this asymmetry of value. We can manually haul a not-yet-extant thing (which to a degree is the same as a private thing) into the light of day, which means that there are gray areas between the meditation of a work and the finished product, and gray areas before full babyhood. The author's partner or amanuensis may hear about the work while it is being made, and, if the author dies before completing it, can tell the world that this and such were the artist's intentions. The survivor may even gather together drafts and cause the work to come to be that would otherwise have remained sheets of paper in the back of someone's closet.

Similarly, we may see or even print and show sonogram pictures of a fetus and make it, in this way, that much more extant for the world: we change its status from private to public, in a sense "publish" rough drafts. What parent has not felt his or her baby more "real" after seeing images of its beating heart? Drawings in a pregnancy book, typically only read by mothers intending on carrying the pregnancies to term, of what a baby looks like at, say, five months, serve the same purpose. For the same reason conservative billboards insist that "Abortion Stops a Beating Heart." This is not merely drawing attention to something that is; conceiving of the fetus as having a beating heart actually changes its ontological status.

Conservatives do not care about unmade works of art, at least not enough to force the issue until they appear. They do seem to care about unborn children, however. They both lionize motherhood, and reserve the right to control it. Which is to say, they are partisans of motherhood, not of mothers. This is consistent with the way conservative ethics are expressed in terms of actions, not actors.

Conservatives oppose abortion not because they believe this woman should be having this baby, but rather that, say, married women of childbearing age ought to be having babies. Conservatives are thus being consistent when they see the non-pregnant woman of child-bearing age as a situation-to-be-altered. (This is not the same as seeing the time before in the individual case.) If, by contrast, in the liberal view a non-pregnant married woman between 20 and 40, or whatever the conservative formulation turns out to be, is presumed to be un-pregnant unless we are told or see otherwise, the fetus always comes as a surprise.

The conservative stance on abortion is "pro-life" in the abstract: babies as opposed to no babies. Not this baby as opposed to another baby, or a baby now as opposed to a baby later, or my baby as opposed to another person's baby. And who can be opposed to babies in the abstract? No wonder they feel such fury at their ideological opponents.

Now we see why it is that, as Voltaire pointed out, the time before birth is not considered scary. It is only liberals who consider this time at all. And by definition everyone who had this time was born. Most of us who try to envision ourselves not having been born at all are overwhelmed by a sense of paradox, as when we contemplate the unheard tree falling in the forest. We try to imagine ourselves not ever having existed. But who is it doing that imagining? For the world-weary man like the German poet Novalis (Friedrich von Hardenburg), this state seems blissful slumber without the pains of life or those of death. But if we didn't know the pains of life, we wouldn't find it blissful, or indeed anything at all.

Under the influence of their second-order tenet (which of course can take on a life of its own—as anything we repeat over and over, any credo, takes on a life of its own) that "life begins at conception," contemporary conservatives mark themselves as living in a different world from Voltaire, for whom the important point was birth, not conception. Contemporary conservatives see birth as almost an incidental occurrence. Instead they plant their flag at a moment that was inaccessible to the eighteenth century, the invasion of the egg by a sperm.

But it is only because the intervening time has allowed us to (so to say) publish this moment that we can talk of it at all. In Voltaire's world, one before sonograms, electron microscopes, and care of premature babies, the only possible "publication" was birth or miscarriage. Knowing that there were predictable occurrences before birth has altered our view of the world. Now conservatives speak knowingly of DNA codes, the better to support their second-order thesis that even the zygote is, in some "scientific" (beat that!) way, human.

Yet from seeing how conservative thought has moved the point they claim rights to nine months backwards in time as medical discoveries allowed us to establish patterns leading to the production of a new individual, we can surmise that, were science to find a patterning even before the moment of conception, say a proclivity of one sperm to be the winner, or even some degree of probability that man X would copulate with woman Y (pheromones, say, clear from individual adult

DNA patterning), it is highly likely that the conservative view would move its flag yet further back in time and claim this was the beginning of life.

Whatever we currently think of as the first access to the teachable individual (and the tenet that the first access is A, B, or C is alterable precisely because this is a second-order thesis), this for the conservative will be where life begins, the point at which their view is capable of being interested. The conservative focus on conception has made it difficult to argue that courtship is part of the production of the baby, but why not? And if courtship, why not the adolescence of the parents, influencing as it did the people they would come in contact with? Their own births? And so on.

Conservatives, therefore, oppose abortion in general, not a series of particular abortions. Yet given the fundamental nature of conservative thought to express itself in abstractions which humans must work to attain, its adherents have no way of fine-tuning their consideration of situations: terminating/killing one fetus for conservatives can lead potentially to terminating/killing all fetuses. If one abortion is allowed, then, for conservatives, all are allowed.

For liberal thought, this is not true, which is why liberals are so infuriated by the implication of the conservative self-description "pro-life" that they themselves are anti-life. Liberal thought can make distinctions between one case and another. This is so, once again, because liberal thought locates its standards within each individual; error arises from divergence from a center innate to us, not inability to reach a common standard outside of us, as it does for conservatives.

Liberal thought is thus consistent in adopting the point of view of the producer. It is only in each individual case that the fetus surges from non-being. (In the general case, which is what the consumer, or conservative viewpoint sees, they merely are.) The state of fetus non-being for the liberal is a private perception, something that is no one's business but the woman's and her immediate circle. Hence the outrage of liberals that conservatives are messing about in personal business that doesn't concern them. Conservatives don't see themselves as invading anyone's personal space, only as asserting the general.

For the same reason, conservatives feel free to say beforehand that, say, no one should be committing homosexual acts. They don't have to pry in bedrooms to say this, since they are actually uninterested in individuals. Yet liberals are bound to perceive them as doing just this.

Chapter Five

Sex in (and out of) Marriage

Very few people today, whether liberal or conservative, openly oppose marriage. We may oppose the reality of the thing, as the 50% of Americans who currently divorce may be said to be opposing the reality. Yet theoretical attacks on marriage are relatively few. Marriage meets with nearly universal approval.

It is approval that almost seems like relief: marriage is the place where sex is "okay." If sex is so difficult to classify, it would clearly be a great load off people's shoulders if they could simply point to a place where people go to deal with this fact, even if they cannot provide any further help once people have gone there. The marriage plays of Strindberg, and Ingmar Bergman's "Scenes from a Marriage" in the same vein, make clear that marriage can easily become a cage in which two animals tear each other apart.[49] Indeed, the identification of sex with marriage is itself suspect. Many couples sense a waning of their sexual interest in a relationship that includes the mundane, not to mention children. Middle-aged men divorcing their wives and marrying their secretaries (only to be divorced by these in turn) are a modern cliché. The need to constantly keep sexual interest alive in a marriage is a staple of women's magazines like *Cosmopolitan*. *Newsweek* magazine, in spring in 2003, devoted its cover story to sexless marriages.[50]

To say that marriage is a response to the problem of sex does not mean that marriage solves this problem. Which is why conservatives hold that the purpose of marriage is to beget and raise children: this renders the particular relationships between the individuals irrelevant. It's the equivalent of saying, the purpose of life is not happiness, it's to do God's will—a quintessentially conservative position, given that the nature of "happiness" must be defined by the individual, and God's will is usually defined for us by institutions.

Marriage takes off the front burner, for most people and for ethics of both the liberal and conservative stripe, many of the problems with sex. Marriage provides a social structure that incorporates the personal and so seems to solve the problem of the in-between nature of sex. The solution is not perfect, even for people who both can and are looking to get married. Yet it as if we had generally agreed that the solution, messy and far from perfect, is all we are going to take the time to produce. It is good enough. Even what disagreement there is regarding other aspects of marriage is muted, as we see below regarding the question of fidelity. For both liberals and conservative ethics, marriage makes people sexually more predictable than they were before. We have a sexual partner; with this person we can do as much or as little as we choose. Ethics is about making the world predictable.

Both sides would probably say: in marriage, we have the feeling— some would say, the illusion—that there is at least one person in the world for whom we have absolute value. Of course, as historians of ideas and sociologists remind us, this is not what we in the West have always been looking for in marriage. For centuries, marriage was understood as an alliance between families, not individuals. Love didn't enter into it. However once having determined that this sensation of love was available, its place was determined to be in the institution of marriage.

We may put this in the terms of Kantian morality, Kant being a thinker whose views of sex and marriage are central to my consideration here. Marriage is the ultimate case of treating someone as an end in him- or herself. In marriage we have the feeling that everything the other person does has absolute significance, and because the other person feels the same about us, so do we.

Of course, there is something illogical about the initial acceptance of a particular other person as someone filling this role to begin with. Surely the Shakespeare who wrote *A Midsummer Night's Dream*, suggesting that passions are the result of chance or the spells of the fairies, would have agreed. The queen of the fairies, Titania, finds herself enamored of Bottom the Weaver with the head of an ass. "Let me kiss thy fair large ears," she tells him, while in the throes of passion. When she is given the antidote, she is appalled at her behavior. All love, Shakespeare seems to be telling us, is intrinsically folly. Why should this one creature have the power to give us value and meaning?

Both parental and divine love give us something like the same sense of absolute value as married love. If we are lucky, we feel we have these merely because of the fact of our birth. Yet certainty and power are in this case in inverse relation to individuality. Both of these kinds of love are undifferentiated. God loves everyone equally, except perhaps those who sin against His commandments. Parental love, we suspect at some point, is similarly undifferentiating: we could have been quite different than we are and our parents would still love us just as much. This is good news in that the love is unqualified. Yet with time we realize our parents love us merely as their child, the way God loves us only because we are human, not for what makes us who we are.

In marriage, conceived of as a relationship with the one person who has chosen us out of all others, adults are loved in a way that supplies the deficiency in parental and Godly love. The valorization, we feel, is of ourselves alone, not as a member of a larger group, or the person who fills a designated role. Perhaps for this reason, marriage in the West has so often been linked with both God and children. God is traditionally asked to approve the union, and it is conceived of as the conduit for children. Marriage gives us a relationship in which we seem to matter absolutely to another person, yet a person whom we have found—not one to whom we were (so to say) issued, as we are to parents, or the Being who created us.

Marriage can be expressed in terms of the Kantian moral imperative, treating the other person as if s/he is an end in him- or herself. In marriage, each treats the other partner as an end-in-him- or herself. Each partner defers to the others. To be treated as an end in ourself means to be treated as self-sufficient. Being treated as an end in ourself is the logical end-state of the rules of what we call common courtesy or more succinctly, respect.

Marriage is the extreme case of respect. Treating another person as an end in him- or herself means deferring to that person; in a marriage each partner defers continually and absolutely to the other. Each is most fundamentally concerned that the wishes and desires of the others be fulfilled, that he or she be realized as a person. What would we like?, the waiter asks us; this is courtesy and respect. Our wants and desires, at least in this specific set of circumstances, have value in themselves. In the same way, but without the social limitations under which we have contact with a waiter, we defer to our marital partner. What would you like, dear?, we ask. We do not seek to guide our spouse, as we do children (if we do there is something wrong with the marriage, most people nowadays would feel), nor do we order that person around. We await his or her desires, and take our pleasure in fulfilling these. We are, or should be, each of us a perfect Jeeves to the other. Yet because each partner is in a sense subservient to the other, both are equal; the relationship is acknowledged as an exception.

Nowhere but in marriage does the world allow us a relationship where we engage in this game of mutual deference that is the essence of treating another, and being treated, as an end in ourselves. In other circumstances we engage in limited relationships, civility for shorter periods. But in all other relationships, we want something from the other person; this is the reason we break in upon his or her self-sufficiency. Marriage, by contrast, is a state: we may want particular things from our spouse, but the relationship itself is not based on want, it merely is.

Marriage is universally thought to be a good thing, a very special thing, worthy of support in principle even when it doesn't work out in fact. Demurrals to the institution of marriage come from extremes of both liberal and conservative. In neither case do they represent mainstream thought. Mainstream ethics, both liberal and conservative, seems unwilling to argue further about sex once a matrix has been found, as in marriage, that combines the two realms of individual and social. The only pitched ethical battles that remain are regarding the (so to say) protruding ends of things that do not enter so easily into marriage, such as homosexuality, sex before marriage, and abortion.

Because the problem of the hybrid status of sex is not solved by marriage, but only acknowledged and accommodated, objections remain possible from some die-hard liberals and equally die-hard conservatives. The genesis of these problems for liberals in the fact that respect always defers to the other person. People are addressed by their titles, in the buffering phrases we call politeness, in ways that indicate our eagerness to hear their point of view. We wait for their reaction, we do not push ours on them. Respect is the basis of liberal morality: it privileges the other as an individual.

Yet in sex, we're undeniably out to satisfy our own needs. As Kant perceived, in sex we use another person not as an end in him- or herself, but as a means to our own ends. This can in part consist of satisfying the other person's needs too. Yet too great respect in sex means sex never happens at all. Kant expresses the fundamentally self-interested and unfair nature of sex as follows:

> Since the sexual impulse is not an inclination that one human has for another, *qua* human, but an inclination for their sex, it is therefore a *principium* of the debasement of humanity, a source for the preference of one sex over the other, and the dishonouring of that sex by satisfying the inclination. The desire of a man for a woman is

not directed to her as a human being; on the contrary, the woman's humanity is of no concern to him, and the only object of his desire is her sex. [51]

Kant is emphasizing the general nature of sex: the desire of a Man for a Woman; he contrasts this to "humanity," which remains to be defined. It makes distinctions between sexes, at least in heterosexual sex. Yet he could equally well have emphasized the extreme particularity of sex. Sex is as oddly individual. I want this person right here, right now, not another person. By "humanity," Kant is evoking the standard liberal need to express rules in terms of actors. This means, without distinguishing between the actors. And it also means rejecting differences between men and women. (Because conservatives express rules in terms of actions, they have no objection to differing roles for the two sexes.)

Kant stands shoulder to shoulder with feminist formulations that insist on the fundamental unfairness to the woman of male-female sex. And this means, in marriage as well as outside of it: the mere fact that a preacher has waved his hands over two people does not, for such rigorous objectors, change the unfairness of things. Kant is echoed, for example, by Andrea Dworkin, who puts things clearly. [52]

To make her version of Kant's point regarding the distinctly slanted playing field in most male-female sex, Dworkin quotes the early twentieth-century Theodore Van De Velde, author of the popular manual *Ideal Marriage.*

> What both man and woman, driven by obscure primitive urges, wish to feel in the sexual act, is the essential force of maleness, which expresses itself in a sort of violent and absolute possession of the woman. And so both of them can and do exult in a certain degree of male aggression and dominance—whether actual or apparent—which proclaims this essential force.

Most men would probably pump the air and yell "Yeah! Bring it on!" The women they live with might lower their eyes modestly but smile in understanding.

Dworkin's commentary, however, is as follows:

> In other words, men possess women when men fuck women because both experience the man being male. In this view . . . maleness is aggressive and violent . . . in being fucked [the woman] is possessed . . . is taken over. [53]

Van De Velde is putting his formulation in a positive light; Dworkin is outraged. Kant may not be outraged, but he is certainly disapproving.

All three writers would presumably agree that the sex act isn't very refined. We want something from the other person, and use brute force to get it. More to the point, the man wants something from the woman, and uses force that is, paradoxically, welcomed by her, since the woman wants him to want her. What could be further from treating our partner as an end in him- or herself, indeed, as the ultimate end in him- or herself?

Practically all of our vocabulary to express one person's humiliating and getting the better of another comes from sexual vocabulary: someone was fucked, screwed, reamed, and so on. Some of the source of this is the taboo on being the passive partner in male-male sex. It is "worse" for a man to be fucked than a woman, since women were, it seems, predestined for this role. It is somehow all right for a woman, who is constructed after all to be fucked. Yet she is still fucked, even if she is fulfilling her role. Many straight men do despise women for the fact that women are the ones who are fucked, screwed, and reamed. Why else the popularity of shots in male porn films showing men ejaculating in women's faces? Feminist writers are quite right: male power in the sexual act is part of a scale that ends in misogyny. Of course this does not mean it always ends there, any more than homoeroticism between straight males necessarily ends with the two men in bed.

It is not logically possible to go from this position to the conclusion Kant reaches, agreeing with Milton and countless other Christian thinkers, that marriage was the only set of circumstances in which people were "entitled to make use of their sexual impulse, without impairing their humanity."[54] Marriage does not solve the problem, and Kant's justification for his position that it does must be nonsense. However it does provide a sort of practical stalemate: marriage, while solving no problems, at least acknowledges them and designates the battlefield where the problems are to be worked out. The solution provided by marriage is practical rather than theoretical.

This is Kant's incoherent justification for marriage:

> The sole condition, under which there is freedom to make use of one's sexual impulse, is based upon the right to dispose over the whole person. . . . But this right that I have, so to dispose, and thus also to employ the organa sexualia to satisfy the sexual impulse—

how do I obtain it? In that I give the other person precisely such a right over *my* whole person, and this happens only in marriage. [55]

He explains further what happens in marriage:

> If I hand over my whole person to the other, and thereby obtain the person of the other in place of it, I get myself back again, and have thereby regained possession of myself . . . The two persons thus constitute a unity of will. [56]

As some disrespectful commentators, such as Alan Sobel, in his article "Masturbation," have pointed out, this makes all marital sex masturbatory for Kant, though Kant never acknowledged this point. [57]

I give myself to the other, the other gives him/herself to me. In what way do I get myself back again? I get the other person, not myself. At most it could be argued that I get the other person, who has me, which means that in getting the other person I get myself as it were wrapped up into the bargain . . . but of course this is silly, not to mention an infinite regress of a chicken and the egg sort. If we trade each other, say so that each meets the other in mid-air as it is flying from me to the other, we get only the other, not the other plus ourselves. If one side gives him/herself first, then when the other gives him/herself back, that can contain the initial self that was given—but of course this only works in one direction. If we perennially give ourselves to each other, so that we are not only ourselves, but ourselves giving ourselves to the other, it is still unclear in what way we get ourselves back.

To be sure, this notion of each partner in a marriage giving him- or herself to the other sounds like my notion above of each being the servant of the other. And indeed Kant may have meant it as such. Yet this is the opposite of a power relation, such as sex. It may be the basis of marriage but it is precisely the reason why sex is incompatible with marriage in theoretical terms, as well as the practical justification for it.

Probably those eager to show that sex actually works out pretty well in marriage would say, When we love another person, we have that person's best interests at heart. We can have sex with him/her, but we only do so when we know it is welcome to the other, as part of a larger relationship that includes (say) listening to details of his or her day, doing his/her laundry, getting his/her morning newspaper. We have sex with some*one*, not merely with a body, presumably someone whom we like, and whose body also attracts us.

All this may be true, and the reason why sex in marriage is held to be so fulfilling. But it misses Kant's point. If any and all sex is intrinsically disrespectful (as I put it; Kant says that it denies the humanity of the other person), it is unacceptable in marriage, when we have so great an investment in the other person. If we spend all our time deferring to the other's wishes, seeing him/her as a person, trying to fulfill his/her desires, how do we move from this to suddenly grappling, sweaty, on the floor? In logical terms, this remains an alien action, one that should be drummed out of marriage rather than even tolerated within it. Perhaps Tolstoy's narrator in "The Kreutzer Sonata" was right after all: celibacy is the only way.

Yet most of us do not go on theory, but live in practice. Most of us do have sex within marriage, and even manage to enjoy it. Most men manage to face themselves in the mirror the next morning (Dworkin implies they shouldn't be able to). Shortly after the man has thrown the woman on the bed and ripped her clothes from her, held her down and penetrated her, he is found helping her on with her coat, or consulting with her about the taxes, or discussing the best way to deal with the neighbor's tree. The woman too somehow manages to be friendly to a creature who has overmastered her and fucked her, in what for Dworkin is apparently a metaphoric as well as literal sense (if "fucking" for sexual intercourse *is* literal). It's going on all the time, in most of the houses down the block, and has been going on for a long time.

Extreme conservatives, for their part, object to sex because of the way it seems to be giving in to transitory pleasure, and are not willing to remove their objections totally for the fact of marriage, though most do end up by giving in grudgingly. Marriage is the second-best solution. Celibacy would be better, but if people aren't capable of that, then, well, go ahead.

This is the influential position of St. Paul, expressed in 1 Corinthians 7:7-10.

> I wish that all men were even as I myself am. However, each man has his own gift from God, one in this manner, and another in that. But I say to the unmarried and the widows that it is good for them if they remain even as I. But if they do not have self control, let them marry; for it is better to marry than to burn. [58]

Burn with lust, that is, in the views of most modern commentators.

This is a greater problem for the more active partner, typically the man. Conservatives will frequently look favorably on any man who, despite marriage, opts for celibacy; they will by contrast look very unfavorably on any wife who does the same. By contrast, Kantian suspicion of sexuality based on the correct perception that it fails to treat people as ends in themselves, focuses on protecting the more passive partner in marriage, usually understood to be the woman. Liberals will have a soft spot for any woman who refuses to be overmastered by her husband and refuses him her favors, but none for a man who refuses his wife sex.

Most mainstream conservatives, following St. Paul, admit themselves trumped by marriage: past this point they cannot go. They focus on the time outside marriage. Thus the current conservative mantra is abstinence until marriage. An opinion piece in the *Washington Post* from May 12, 2002 by Philip D. Harvey, entitled "Adulthood Without Sex," points out that the average age of marriage in the U.S. is 27.[59] It suggests conservatives surely cannot want the average age of marriage lower, and that it is absurd to tell people to abstain from sex until the age of 27, or more.

This is a liberal argument, focusing on the actors, pointing out the disadvantages to these actors of a course of action. For conservatives, the effects of the course of action are irrelevant, as the action is held to have value in itself. This argument will fail to convince conservatives, since it begins with the actors and considers the actions with respect to them. Conservatives begin with each individual, who thus remains unarticulated; each individual aims at the same external rule of action. In no individual case can the (say) 18-year-old know for a fact that s/he will remain unmarried until age 27, even though the statistical evidence suggests that this is will be so. Conservatives are comfortable with asking people to be celibate until an average age of 27, because they can always point out that nothing constrains the individual to be celibate until the age of 27. Usually they do not consider the fact that those doing the asking are not typically themselves even as young as 27, or celibate. The individual would in any case be irrelevant to the principle.

Each individual, the conservative will insist, is free to marry or not marry. The liberal is wielding an ex post facto average as if it were a weapon; because the conservative fails to conceptualize the individual as one of many individuals (the conservative world-view being composed of actions), s/he will deny the power of averages. Only an argument that showed how (say) a law had made it impossible to marry before age 27 would raise sympathetic ire from the conservative. For this would be unwarranted meddling with individual freedom.

This particular op-ed piece concluded that what we should be saying to young adults is that they should be abstinent until adulthood and then responsible until marriage. This is neither a liberal nor a conservative position with respect to sex, or perhaps it is uncomfortably both, and so is likely to satisfy neither. It says is that sex is not an issue requiring an ethical pronouncement: there may be reasons for discouraging sex among minors (say, their inability to handle such an incendiary issue), but these have nothing to do with sex *per se*. Its concern once sexual activity starts is that individuals not hurt themselves or each others. As Harvey puts it, "Sexual relations are an important component of human happiness, and there is no moral purpose served by abstaining from sex if two people are mature and responsible. Why should they be deprived of sex?" Such a view removes sex from the table as the issue: it is normal, its absence is not a good, in fact the reverse. The issue is not sex, but happiness (a liberal conception, not a conservative one). When it is an issue, however, it turns out that neither liberals nor conservatives are going to approve of it as part of their ethics.

But ethics is only one vocabulary for describing the world, couched in terms of generalities. In opposition to all ethics, we have the rest of life, which neither lines up for rules, nor permits generalizations. This is expressed as particulars. Marriage, in particular, may not hang together in ethical terms, at least not so long as sex is included within it. Nonetheless both liberals and conservatives continue to speak well of it. But do they even know what this "marriage" is that they are talking about.

The concept of marriage is theory-poor, and this is why it works in practice. It's an ill-defined notion that works precisely because it is so ill-defined. It's only a practical "solution." Because it's the only solution we have, however, it gets everyone's approval, and is the focus of a good deal of our societal attention.

Because it is so theory-poor, a practical compromise that is bound to be wracked with problems in fact, the notion of what constitutes marriage changes all the time. The concept of marriage has changed in the last century from being a single Earthly union to include what has come to be called "serial monogamy": marriages separated by divorces. As those opposing the "Natural Law" theorists (with their insistence that the purpose of marriage is the production of children) point out, there are already marriages where the couples live apart, where there is no sex between the partners, where each partner has sex with other people, with or without their partner's consent, and of course where the partners are unable to conceive children, being too old or biologically unable. Some of us can accept *ménages à trois* as marriages, or restricted relationships as a kind of marriage (restricted in time, say, or in the things the people are supposed to share). Theoretical consistency isn't necessarily a virtue, and its lack isn't necessarily an indication of failure. Like the novel, which every generation has to re-invent (will it be realistic? Fantasy? Subjective? Objective?), marriage has such strength because it is so ill-defined. Because marriage is a thing whose shape is acquired in the living, it works best when left to take on whatever shape it takes on. Marriage isn't a theoretical solution to the half-and-half nature of sex, which doesn't change. But it does lend a certain degree of predictability to things, assuming most people end up in this state. It's the only solution (or "solution") we have, which is why everyone is going to re-make marriage to include his or her own situation, rather than simply going off and doing something different.

Each expansion of the concept of marriage will meet with resistance, but it is the same kind of resistance as the resistance in the suburbs to more construction, the resisters being those living in houses already constructed. The novel flourishes precisely because it can be so many things; it is a classification of default, not a set of how-to rules. Marriage continues to flourish because it's left alone to change.

For our particular times, this means that the attempt to exclude homosexual marriage is doomed to failure. The clamor demanding that it be included is just too loud, and there just aren't any other viable alternatives. Homosexual unions are just like others we identify as marriages except for a single quality; so too are other relationships distanced only by a single quality from an "ideal" marriage (couple can't have children, live apart, and so on). It's far-fetched to think we're going to be able to keep it from lodging naturally under the rubric of "marriage," even if we want to. What other rubric are we to file such a relationship under except marriage? It's as if we demanded another word for "hug" to describe what two men sometimes do with each other when they meet, saying that "hug" in its only acceptable sense refers to what a man and a woman do.

This is so not for logical reasons, but simply because the demand is being made that we do so. We don't know what marriage will be asked to include at a future time. Those with an investment in gay marriage are well advised to keep up the din and the pressure, for only that will effect the change. That is, the din and the pressure effect the real change that the law only comes subsequently to acknowledge.

Marriage is a practical response to the fact that sex otherwise lacks a "home"—marriage is the home that's been found for it. No other has, hence the necessity to expand, tuck, and fit this one institution.

Not that others have not tried to solve the problem more directly. Indeed, some gay men, those who argue that gay men are intrinsically promiscuous and should not be wanting a homosexual version of what is prototypically a male-female paradigm, propose such a solution. Namely, acknowledging that sex, at least between men, should have its own space, neither of the social realm or of the personal. This position was the most common position for those proposing "gay liberation" during the period that began with the 1969 rebellion against a police raid at the Stonewall bar in New York and ended with the emergence of AIDS in the early 1980s.

A straight version of this notion of a space for sex is sometimes allowed heterosexual men in their rutting period, the time during which young men are allowed to "sow their wild oats." Still, it is gay men who have given the best sense of a shape to this world—a world that existed in its most uninhibited form for only a couple of decades. To judge from the popular cable TV series "Queer as Folk," this world still exists in the new millennium, at least in people's minds and on television.

Apologists for gay liberation are opposed by writers such as Andrew Sullivan , who insists that promiscuity is not liberation, nor is it intrinsic to homosexuality.[60] The homosexual right holds that while the homosexual party atmosphere of the 70s was an understandable backlash phase, it should and will ultimately disappear into something like a gay version of heterosexual marriage.

Still, there seems to be some general feeling, among heterosexuals as well as homosexuals, that men naturally tend to promiscuity, and that it is women who temper this in the heterosexual world. The sex columnist Dan Savage, who is gay, wrote in one of his "Savage Love" columns that it is women who act as the brake on straight male promiscuity. When challenged by a woman who vaunted her sexual interest in her boyfriend, Savage responded by pointing out that many gay couplings are anonymous, initiated with a look, and can involve many partners in the course of a night of cruising. He pointed out to his correspondent that this is virtually unknown in straight sex. His thesis is that men are naturally ejaculators; only the drag of female caution slows things down in the straight world. Savage's point is that gay men are only doing what most straight men would do if they could get away with it; because they are doing it with other men, who see things their way, it works. This would offer an alternative to marriage, at least for gay men.

Such a view of men is close to the bio-evolutionary argument (considered and to an extent debunked by Tim Birkhead in *Promiscuity*[61]) that men are programmed to spread their seed, women to chose their inseminators carefully. Hence men are naturally promiscuous, females naturally interested in tying their partners down, at least metaphorically.

The bio-evolutionary argument is beside the point in all the ways bio-evolutionary arguments are. We focus on the behavior we want to justify, and claim that because it is noted, that means it has been biologically encouraged. In addition, under these particular circumstances, it seems counter-intuitive to accept the conservative link of ejaculation with the production of children. Typically the most promiscuous men are those least interested in producing children. Indeed, men today are generally petrified at the thought of getting a strange woman pregnant. Don Juan saw himself as "conquering" the woman, not as spreading his seed. To which bio-evolution must of course reply that intention has nothing to do with it. Dissemination of sperm is dissemination of sperm, whatever the individual thinks he is doing. This makes clear the circularity of the position: we have decided that promiscuity is dissemination of sperm with the purpose of insemination, not (say) having an orgasm. The evolutionary value of frequent orgasms is not so clear, so we do not claim that this is what is "hard-wired" into us.

Other writers have suggested that the reason women tend to want fewer, and higher quality, partners, culminating in a single partner, may be that the female brain releases oxytosins at orgasm, the same hormones released by nursing, or even just seeing, a baby. Women are condemned to love their sex partners. Writers on the differences between the sexes, such as John Gray have emphasized that men and women want different things from sex.[62] Some have even denied that men do, in any way we can measure, want to be promiscuous to a greater extent than women do. In any case, for most men and women, gay and straight, there does not seem to be much of an alternative to marriage.

Fidelity in Marriage

Limiting sex to marriage for married people at least makes people predictable. Sex outside of marriage makes people once again unpredictable—and unpredictability is the bug-bear of all ethics.

Liberals are interested in supporting a relationship where an individual is the object of attention; conservatives are interested in having people adhere to absolute rules expressed in terms of actions. Thus the interests of both groups converge in a sexual relationship that excludes all other partners.

As a result, ethical challenges to the concept of marital fidelity are weak. Again, this is because of the theoretical poverty of the concept of marriage: shooting at it is like shooting at clouds. The bullets simply pass through it. Most people agree we should be faithful in marriage, but allow the possibility that in fact things might not work out this way, without being able to justify theoretically the relationship between these two things.

There is however no way that we can theoretically justify our acknowledgement of contingency. The attempt to do so leads to problems. Take, for example, the objections of Susan Mendus, a conservative thinker, to the views of Derek Parfit, a liberal, in her article entitled "Marital Faithfulness."[63] Parfit, in his own article quoted by Mendus, entitled "Later Selves and Moral Principles," argues that the identity of the individual from cradle to grave is weaker than sometimes asserted. In particular, he says, it is impossible to promise something to another person over a long period of time, given the likelihood that that other person will have changed over time, replaced by a "later self." Thus, according to Parfit, marriage vows are logically vacuous. We cannot now promise something for a time far in the future.

This is an attempt to give a theoretical basis to the contingency of the factual world. It must fail precisely because the contingent is, after all, contingent. We can gesture towards it, but we cannot justify it or make it predictable. Of course Mendus will be able to deflect this position, but her defense is simply to retreat to the sure ground of what is predictable already. She can't prove that the practical world won't erode this, only that from the perspective of the solid land we can pretend it won't, or say we won't allow it to happen. (It might happen anyway.)

Mendus agrees that we can change, as she must. But she contends that this does not make it impossible for us to promise something now for the future. We can still hold to this promise out of principle. To make the point, she quotes Mrs. Micawber from Dickens's *Great Expectations*: "I will never desert Mr. Micawber." This assertion makes sense, Mendus argues. In Mendus's words, Mrs. Micawber means precisely that she will never desert Mr. Micawber.[64] This current intention for the future is logically non-contradictory.

In arguing for a weak unity of the human being (or perhaps none at all), Parfit is showing his sympathy for Heraclitus's assertion that we can never step in the same river twice. Later commentators, and some wags, have pointed out that the pre-Socratic should have said we can never step in the same river once. Parfit would also presumably side with the empiricist Hume against Cartesian essentialism. Descartes' most famous conclusion was that because he knew he was thinking, he could conclude that he existed: "Cogito, ergo sum." Yet for Empiricists, Descartes is begging the question: who, they ask, is the "I" that thinks, and therefore is? What holds together the sensations of the self? Because of the fact of the mutability of things, people try to fence off greater or smaller parts of life from that mutability. This is what creates institutions, promises, and the like, all of which are an attempt to control the future. Yet the future by definition has the last laugh.

What Mendus gets from her argument with Parfit, however, is slight. Mendus is concerned merely to show that promising something now for the distant future is not impossible. In her words, this means that if

> A is unconditionally committed to B, that is not a prediction that A will never desert B, it is a claim that there is in A a present intention to do something permanently, where that is distinct from A's having a permanent intention. . . . Thus an unconditional commitment to another person today . . . is not incompatible with that commitment being given up at a later date.[65]

Mendus avoids having to make a distinction between promising to remain married to someone (an action within our control) and promising to love him or her forever, something which does not seem within our control. If we intend both now for the future, we can in fact promise both, and there is no distinction between them.

The object of Mendus's intellectual ire is someone who says, "I promise now to love you forevermore, on the following conditions . . ." Yet at the same time she is willing to accept someone being surprised by circumstances beyond his or her control. However issuing a statement of intention with conditions specific to the individuals involved may not end up to be so different from a statement of intention with acknowledgement of the condition-linked nature of relationships in general. Mendus would have to accept someone saying, "I promise now to love you forevermore, and though I cannot now think of altered circumstances that would change the nature of my love for you, I have read the article by Susan Mendus and know that things do change in the world and so, by logical extension, so might things in our situation, even to the point where (though I am not saying this will happen or even that I envision it happening in the precise case) someone like me might cease to love someone like you."

For both Mendus and Parfit, there is a distinction between intending something almost immediately, as when I intend to get up in a few seconds and get my food from the microwave, and. intending something years or even decades from now, such as fidelity to my partner, in the words of the Beatles' song, "when I'm 64." For both Mendus and Parfit, the second is more problematic than the first, given the number of unforeseen events that can intervene to make it difficult to have that intention come to fruition. They agree that the second is qualitatively different from the first.

But even if the number of things that can intervene is greater the longer the period of time involved, the two cases are only different in degree, not type. Indeed, even the difference of degree is based only on something we infer. A long period of time may in fact pass with no substantial changes in the particular area under scrutiny. Conversely, nothing says great changes may not happen in a small period of time: the roof can fall down before I get up to get the food out of the microwave, I can have a heart attack, and so on. It may be less likely that something of this sort will occur in the decades between this point and the day I turn 64, but this is only because there are more opportunities, not because the two cases are of different types. If I can intend to get the food from the microwave, therefore (and both thinkers and most everyone else would agree we can), Mendus is clearly right that I can intend to be faithful to my life-partner.

Mendus agrees with Parfit that long-term intentions are a horse of a different color from short-term intentions. Both agree that the longer the time period involved before we can say we have exhausted the intention, or have kept to it, the more times there will be when we wish to break it. As I have put it above, the future has the last laugh; we don't really know what will happen. And this is what I am calling an acknowledgement of the theoretical weakness of all discussion about marriage. If we promise fidelity now, there will be many times in fifty years when we want to be unfaithful, vs. only a few, or none at all, in a few months. Even if we have the future under control in theory, it may cause us to alter, even if we would be unable to say now that this will be so.

Mendus's response to reflecting that the longer we are married, the more often we may wish to be unfaithful, would presumably be that we have the option in each of these tempting cases of simply saying "no." Nothing obliges us to be unfaithful, for many decades are simply a succession of discreet moments. In each moment we have only to decide, unfailingly, for faithfulness, and we will find ourselves having been faithful, even when we are 64, and beyond. If the issue is G. E. Moore's, also discussed by Mendus, of the impossibility of promising to love somebody—love being a feeling over which (at least to a degree) we have no control—Mendus would still focus on the aspects of a relationship that we can control. We may not be "in" the same kind of love, but we can promise something, which we call love, and this is what (by definition) can last past the age of 64.

Her goal, after all, is to make sense of Mrs. Micawber's assertion that "she will never desert Mr. Micawber." Presumably this can work out even if Mrs. Micawber has ceased to love Mr. Micawber. As far as the assertion by two people getting married that they will love each other forever, Mendus thinks they have to believe this, even if they are aware of what statistics show. Each case can be different; perhaps we will be the ones to beat the odds. Like all conservatives, Mendus regards divergences from the rule-based action as individual variations, and hence under individual control.

What of the practical fact that though it is possible always to decide in favor of principle X, the very necessity of reiterating it over and over may ultimately mean we weary of doing so? The sheer weight of time and the necessity of asserting this principle as the correct decision in every case of "temptation"—that is, every case where we are inclined to decide in favor of another option—finally render it so hollow that we are left with nothing more than the repetition of the principle for the sake of the principle? Indeed, this is the point where rebellions typically take place, when the person who has doggedly followed the now-empty principle for lo these many years finally feels it so hollow it can no longer be defended, and in an instant throws it all over. Some outsiders, having had no inkling this was coming, would be surprised; others, precisely because there had been no sign, would not be. Sometimes the very attempt to be consistent backfires.

Parfit and Mendus are dancing the dance of liberal and conservative, respectively. The conservative position is expressed in terms of an absolute rule that particular circumstances cannot alter; the liberal position considers each particular set of circumstances and then determines what is best for those circumstances. Mendus is expressing a conservative position by saying we can always be faithful out of principle. Her argument is merely that this is a theoretical possibility. This is clearly the case.

Some ethical doctrines are clearer than Mendus is about asserting that we should always do the same thing, such as remain faithful to our partner. The way this is expressed, however, is a bit turned-around, for it names as an action what we may not do. We may not commit adultery, which is to say abandon marital faithfulness. Adultery according to the Church is intrinsically a sin: we must always be faithful, no matter what.

Let us say I argue as follows: I really need/want to commit adultery, but am told by the Church or whomever that I may not. The problem with expressing this commitment to permanence as a prohibition on any more fine-tuned action is that the reason for prohibiting the specific action, here adultery, remains hidden. This is because the prohibition on adultery of conservative thinkers and institutions is a second-order prohibition. We see this from the fact that if the prohibited action, adultery, is not understood as a specific alternative to the general, there seems no reason for the general prohibition on the specific. Is adultery *always* wrong? Can it never be justified? Adultery, always defined in terms of another action, namely sex, is the particular exception to the permanent rule of marital faithfulness. Thus a general prohibition of it cannot further be justified in theoretical terms.

Alan Goldman's article "Plain Sex" makes this point, thus adopting a liberal position, in that it tries to decouple sex from any other thing.[66] It denies that a set of actions regarding sex can, intrinsically, be wrong: we must see the multiplicity of sex acts in their particularity and ask if a particular instance of something is wrong or right. The general form of a sex act cannot, according to Goldman, have moral value. If adultery is wrong, it is not wrong because it is sex, but because of other things. But adultery can only be defined in terms of sex, because any definition of adultery will be in general terms. The problem with adultery from the point of view of those who condemn it is precisely that it takes the form of particular exceptions to general rules, yet its prohibition must in turn be expressed in terms of a general.

A position that is liberal with respect to position B may well become the relative conservative of position C. Yet in any confrontation regarding actions we may say that the liberal position for that confrontation is the one insisting on the relevance of the more precise set of givens, the more particular circumstances. The position that marital faithfulness has moral value of its own is neither more nor less defensible than any other assertion. But like all assertions, it is amenable to being turned into the conservative position in a new challenge by the more specific-oriented liberal.

The liberal might agree that marital faithfulness was a good thing because of other principles, such as that lying (especially to one's spouse) is bad, or that pain caused to another person is bad. These seem like absolute rules too. But they would be rules that, in the context of this argument, would be more linked to circumstances than the one that adultery is always wrong.

Most people are willing to admit in the case of marriage, in the way they are not similarly unanimous in the case of process-thinking, such as the sugar melting or the gestation of an infant, that we must simply wait and see what the future brings. Fidelity may be a goal. But if it is a process at all, it is a very weak one, more analogous to the time after birth than the time before birth. For conservatives the time before birth is a "hard" process, and the time after not a process at all, or a very weak one (the baby grows into a child, but the conservative focus is on the active component of this process on the part of the parents). Almost everyone agrees that we should aim at marital fidelity without being able to say whether or not this will be achieved; somehow we are not bothered by what ought to be a duality but isn't.

Chapter Six

Pornography

In rejecting sex, ethics is only expressing its ineluctable nature. Part of this nature is speaking ill of things it doesn't, so to say, understand. This disapproval of ethics is not to be confused with societal repression in the Freudian sense. Ethical beliefs of individuals can produce a situation where policemen enforce strictures on other people. But these are always a sum of individual cases, and can be eliminated in theory, even if with great difficulty in practice.

The negative response towards sex on the part of all ethics is broad enough to include pornography, the consumption of images or descriptions of sexual acts, or acts involving sexuality. Yet the remarkable thing about pornography is that disapproval of it is stronger than disapproval of other, even more common sexual expressions. Abortion, homosexuality, and pornography are the lightning rods of ethical fulmination. In the case of pornography it is not, as in the case of abortion, expressed in a conflict of liberal vs. conservative, but by the united front of liberal and conservative against pornography.

Perusing a "dirty" magazine (as we say) in the privacy of our own home has both a personal and a social component: personal because there is frequently only one human being in the room, which makes it even more personal than partnered sex; social because the magazine was produced and sold by other people, and it can be waved around as evidence in a courtroom for all to see and disapprove of. Furthermore, we can, and opponents of pornography usually do, ask too what the effect of consuming pornography is on subsequent actions with living people as a means of emphasizing its social aspect.

Yet pornography is equally rooted in the personal. Pornography intrinsically "squints" in two directions and so is not fully either one.

This is more evidently true of pornography than of any other form of sexuality. Nothing can change this situation, and the debate over pornography will go away only when people decide to fall silent. It will never be resolved.

All sexuality has components of the social and of the personal. The component of the personal is larger in the case of pornography than in more standard expressions of sexuality, such as partnered sex. Ethics has to do only with the social, and thus it may seem paradoxical that it is precisely the smallness of the component of the social component in pornography that is so infuriating to ethical thinkers. Pornography is close to slipping off into the personal realm, where ethics has nothing to say—yet it doesn't, anchored by several trailing threads to the social that rankle all the more for that reason. Pornography seems a window into a world otherwise inaccessible to ethics, the world of the individual. It reveals that people are doing all sorts of things that ethics hasn't been able to regularize.

The most personal sexual expression is fantasy, which seems to require no particular catalyst except the everyday contents of the world, and indeed may well engender no action to express it, at least not one we can link up with a specific cause. Few ethical systems attack sexual fantasy directly, though they may contain admonitions about giving in to its power, or feeding it. Pornography contains a proportion of fantasy, and we will never be able to say how much. It varies from person to person, situation to situation.

Slightly more ethical disapproval is trained on masturbation, which at least is an action in the world and so falls to a great extent under the purview of ethics. Unsurprisingly, for ethics to get (so to say) a grip on masturbation it had to focus on the link with things outside itself, which led to the outlandish claims of the nineteenth century regarding the deleterious effects of masturbation. Pornography is usually linked as well to masturbation; like fantasy, all these things are located close to the line of demarcation with the personal.

Liberals accept masturbation to the extent that they subsume it, along with pornography, to the established social concession to sexuality, namely its institutionalization in long-term, usually married partnered sex. The message of men's magazines ranging from *Playboy* to *Men's Health* is, Masturbation is healthy; use it as part of partnered sex (let your partner watch) or as a supplement (girlfriend away, etc), but don't let it get in the way of partnered sex (if you're jerking off so much you have trouble satisfying your woman or getting it up, cut it out or at least back). Similarly, their message is that porn is good; it gives people new ideas; share it with your loved one.

The somewhat surprising coalition that finds pornography most infuriating is that of mostly female liberals and conservatives of both sexes. Feminists who see gender unfairness in standard male-female sex, and the men who find their arguments convincing, apply liberal doctrines demanding fairness between people to oppose pornography.

Conservatives, having (after a fashion) made their peace with sexuality by limiting it to the narrow confines of partnered sex in marriage, re-double their attacks on any dangling threads of sexuality that escape those limits, such as pornography—which they frequently call "smut." This metaphoric use of an image of dirt jibes with all the comparable images of rottenness and ruin associated with women who engaged in pre- or extra-marital sex, and is the opposite of the images associated with "virtuous" women, those of purity.

Since both are representatives of ethical positions, both by definition are reacting to the extent to which these sexual expressions (so to say) slip off the social table. Because they are more in danger than most sexual expressions of slipping away, the attempt to prevent their doing so must be that much more energetic.

The focus of scientific studies of pornography is on its blurry boundary with the social world, what we might call "add-on" actions: what people do as a result of consuming pornography. Because the boundary is so blurry, science must first bring it into focus by asking specific questions under specific circumstances. And this means, science can never really answer the questions it wants to answer most, because it has answered only specific questions for specific circumstances, not the general question of the relation of pornography to the world.

Indeed, if pornography—as is frequently the case—leads to no action, nothing can be quantified at all. This is the aspect of pornography usually called "erotic," which is usually seen as more acceptable. This is the aspect associated with fantasy and masturbation. No wonder, as one important book, *The Question of Pornography*, remarks, that the definition of "pornographic" is still unclear, as is the distinction (if there is one) between pornography and eroticism.[67] What is clear is that this distinction cannot be clear. We do not even have to use "erotic" to indicate the acceptable subset of "pornographic"; another word will do just as well. Because pornography includes some element of the private world, there will always be a proportion that will not be subject to regulation.

The scientific viewpoint, which has only the option of seeking to quantify the relationship of pornography to the social world, can thus define only one of pornography's neighbors. By definition, it cannot ever define the relationship on the other neighbor, the personal world. Scientific study of pornography (by definition) does not have an opinion about pornography itself. This stance is usually argued to be identical with objectivity. In fact it is merely the structural fact that whatever science looks at directly, being in the center (so to say) of its eyeball, is by definition at the weak point of its visual field. It's the thing to be explained, and so not the real subject of study, which is the explanation, that always ends up by replacing the thing thus not only explained, but explained away.

For example: What is water? Science says: It is *really* a concatenation of molecules, two hydrogen for every oxygen. What is liquidity? Science says: It is *really* a certain density of these molecules... and so on. Which does not mean that water somehow changes what it looks like or how it functions when we have these explanations, only that the explanation undergirds the explained phenomenon. A "scientific" explanation is one that undergirds another; in this sense science is relative. For we may later ask for an explanation for the explanation, and the science retreats to the level of the new undergirding. Science is a process, not a list of doctrines, though at any given time this distinction is moot. Or at least this is how it looks from the outside; to scientists, who must find these explanations (not any old one will do), the post-Kuhn, post-Feyerabend insouciance of humanistic academics insisting on the less than absolute nature of scientific truth is infuriating, Monday morning quarterbacking of the worst sort.[68]

Explanations are rarely produced directly. Instead, one discovery allows explanations for others. There was no way for people in the year 1200 who wondered why the sun rose and set to answer this single question by speaking of the Earth spinning on its axis. A whole structure was necessary before we could add that the reason we perceive the sun rising and setting is that the Earth spins on its axis. Humanist critics of scientific objectivity offer little sense of the fact that these structures must be painfully acquired. Their belief, true enough though it may be, that if we wait long enough science will alter, seems ignorant of what science feels like to those doing it.

Both are right. Science is objective, at any given time. Yet when viewed from sufficiently far away in time and sufficiently distanced from the sweat and action, patterns emerge in the movement from explanation to explanation that make any particular one seem transitory. The distinction is one of point of view.

The objections to pornography from both liberals and conservatives are to its imprecise, indefinable nature, not for any add-on actions it engenders. The impossibility of ever "solving the problem" of pornography is made clear when we realize the comparable impossibility of ever nailing down the relation of art to the social world. Indeed, the debate on pornography usually involves some discussion of the artistic content of books and movies, defining pornography as lacking artistic merit. This connection of pornography to art is not primarily through the fact that pornography comes in the same forms that art comes in, movies or books, but instead that there is overlap in their relationship with respect to the social world. Art is precisely that thing produced by people for people that does not link directly to the social world.

Art is not communication. It does not require any response we can identify as such to confirm that a successful transmission has taken place. This does not mean that art is without its social edge. Art straddles the social and personal worlds. Pornography, with which it is structurally congruent, does so as well. The effects of art are different than the effects of pornography, though there may well be an overlap. Art need not arouse us, and pornography need not trouble us in the way art troubles us, though there are works that do both.

We can't ask merely, What are the effects of pornography? any more than we can ask, What are the effects of my eating this ice cream cone? On what? The ice cream industry? My stomach? The child watching me from across the street? Other things entirely? We have to specify what kind of effects we have in mind.

The failure to have an answer to the question of causality is the norm; even more common is the failure to ask it. Most of the world passes by us without us ever asking what its effects are. What are the effects of seeing a wasp on my screen? Maybe, because I failed to stand up and kill it, I say that the effect was that I was later stung. Or maybe not. What is the effect of yesterday's thunderstorm? This question may have an answer: it may have knocked out our power. But we would say so only if the power was knocked out, that is, if we had something we took to be an effect of the earlier event. Or we may have no answer at all.

What are the effects of our tenth birthday party? Perhaps this had a big effect: we failed to get the present we'd asked for and so realized that our parents didn't love us. Or perhaps it was only one in a string of unexceptionable birthdays that make us regret our childhood as a lost paradise. More likely is that the question is not one we can answer. Questions are not answered until they are posed. We frequently make the mistake of being blind to all the unposed questions we are not answering because our attention is so focused on the ones we have posed, and so are answering.

In most cases, we fail to ask what the effect on us of consuming artworks X, Y and Z might be. So too for a great deal of pornography. We consume it, and that's the end of it. When we are moved to set up experiments to determine results, or effects, we are always answering specific questions, not general ones. (Try asking, What is the effect of my hearing the car I just heard? Certainly our response will be, But why am I even asking this?) If we demand that the impact of pornography be measured by actions of one person on another, "mere" arousal will fall into the realm of the personal and so off the screen. Men frequently feel that their erections are more a matter of public record than female arousal. If we wish to quantify (say) male penis action, then by contrast "mere" female glandular secretions may fall into the realm of the personal. If we feel that (say) quickened heartbeat is already a public (social) phenomenon, then we push the social world yet further inwards. If, in a future world, we can hear thoughts, this reaction too may be made social.

In the same way, hearing a baby's heartbeat is a way to "publish" the baby before the point when previous generations were able to do so. We can still decide that this is not the criterion we are applying, that birth after eight to nine months still counts as the standard that must be achieved before we start the intersection of the baby with the world. Alternately, as conservatives have done, we can push the bounds back. The personal space only recedes relative to the social in these cases. We have no information whether or not it diminishes in absolute size. How can we put a size on this personal space at all?

We will never be able to say, except in individual cases and after the fact, what the "effect" of art is. We can in specific cases be moved to say that its effect was X or Y, but we cannot know all effects with all people before the fact. For the same reason, we cannot answer the question of the effect of pornography in a general way for all people. At most we can specify a precise effect and test for this. Still, whatever definition of effect we offer is a choice among others, and we can only answer that question, the one we have asked.

What we are asking about is by definition a general phenomenon, not a specific situation. This is so by definition of the fact that we are speaking in scientific terminology. We may ask, Does reading *Madame Bovary* cause higher incidences of adultery? This doesn't answer whether reading *Madame Bovary* will cause me to commit adultery. In any case people who disapprove of *Madame Bovary*, or of the character of the same name, will be unmoved by a negative answer to this question, even if science is unable to establish a correlation.

Moreover science may show that X is causally related to Y, but it cannot close out the possibility that Z, which it has not thought of and is not testing for, can also produce Y, or that X can also produce an anti-Y, call it B. We can only say what the effect of things will be when we see what the effect has been. The same is true of pornography.

Will pornography make people more likely to do what is pictured in it, or less? It depends on the individual, which is to say, we don't know. And indeed, as *The Question of Pornography* makes clear, results of scientific studies of pornography divide into two categories, those that suggest that pornography points people toward action, and those that suggest it points them toward inaction, which is to say, toward the social and the private realms, respectively. And to the extent that it points out pornography's border with inaction, it must fall silent.

Disapproval of pornography is a position based on the undefined status of pornography, not on what its links to the social world may subsequently be found to be. Thus such disapproval is antecedent to and logically independent of whatever findings science comes up with. Consider, for example, the reaction of then-President Richard Nixon at the 1970 Presidential Commission on Pornography, which in the words of the authors of *The Question of Pornography*, gave pornography a "clean bill of health."[69]

The point of the recommendations of the Panel was to comment on the connection of pornography with the social world. Its conclusion was this: "Research to date provides no substantial basis for the belief that erotic materials constitute a primary or significant cause of the development of character deficits or that they operate as a significant determinative factor in causing crime and delinquency."[70] Even dissent was expressed in terms of connection with the social world: "Chief Justice Burger, a Nixon appointee, cited the minority report issued by dissenting members of the commission (which asserted that there was at least an arguable correlation between pornography and harmful behavior) rather than the commission report itself as partial justification for more strict obscenity laws."[71] Then-President Nixon "immediately rejected" the report saying: "I have evaluated that report and categorically reject its morally bankrupt conclusions and major recommendations".[72] Scientific findings are not the point for someone correctly perceiving the intrinsically edgy nature of pornography.

This is true from the liberal perspective as well. The writer Susan Brownmiller asks, rhetorically: "Does one need scientific methodology in order to conclude that the anti-female propaganda that permeates our nation's cultural output promotes a climate in which acts of sexual hostility directed against women are not only tolerated but ideologically encouraged?"[73] Even if studies cannot be produced to show direct correlation between the consumption of pornography and undesirable actions, this is because even actions which pass for acceptable, such as standard male-female sex, are themselves undesirable. Even if science fails to find any evidence of add-on harm from pornography, any more actions, or worse, than would otherwise be done, those who disapprove of pornography are right that pornography is itself an action, not merely a neutral representation. By portraying actions in such a fashion that many people can share in the portrayal, pornography effects an increased socialization of something that otherwise could be kept relegated to the realm of the personal. Pornography itself is seen as reprehensible because it makes fantasy more social than it otherwise was.

Two-person sex is already more social than mere sexual fantasy. Talking about sexual fantasy is more social than not talking about it, and looking at sexually explicit magazines that may be consumed individually is more social than not consuming them. Convening a commission to consider pornography and publishing its findings is even more public. Discussing pornography is an act of rendering more public, just as publication of the pornography itself is. It is just possible that sleeping dogs might have been let lie, but once they have been awakened, the position that they must be publicly tamed is understandable.

The debate about pornography is like picking a sore that becomes worse through the picking and demands more attention. Liberals who do not disapprove of pornography, usually men, sometimes feel the condemnation of pornography, like the condemnation of abortion, is more an exercise in public self-presentation than in anything else. If people wouldn't make so much of it, the problem would cease to be a problem—and this by definition, since problems grow as more people see them as problems. Talking about pornography gives it more "air time" than relegating it to the realm of the personal. It is to this extent more a part of our lives.

By the same token, the anti-pornography coalition is surely correct in saying that pornography, the representation of sex acts or acts with sexual content, gives those acts more "air time" than they would have had if there had been no pornography. It gives people ideas. The minimum of these ideas is that such practices exist. We do not even have to argue that looking at pornography dulls people to what they see. It is at least true that before seeing (say) this video act X portrayed in it hadn't been so explicitly in our minds, or perhaps hadn't been part of our imaginations at all. Afterwards it has at least taken up room in our heads.

For it is a fact of human life that, once we have conceived of something, we can conceive of it—that is to say, in a way we had not been able to before. Sex is one of those things most of us would not think of until someone showed us or explained it to us. Once we have gotten over our shock, it may look pretty interesting. This may be the end of the line: we may do nothing further with this fact. Still, its effect on us has not, by definition, been zero. Everything we perceive has at least the effect of having taken a certain amount of time on our mental stage. I have argued above that we cannot further say, except in precise instances from a precise angle, what the add-on effects of these things are. But we don't have to be able to do this in order to disapprove of pornography. Those who disapprove of pornography can base this disapproval merely on the fact of these things taking up space in our heads that they had not previously taken up.

Art, in a similar way, takes up room in our heads, and has a similarly unpredictable connection with "add-on" actions. Any information or portrayal changes us. We accept that this is part of the world. We read a novel, say, about a woman who leaves her family and goes to the big city. She turns out badly. For some people, this may serve as a warning, a "what not to do." But at least the possibility of leaving the family is considered openly, whatever its results in the story. If we are stifling under the weight of a family, we may find this liberating: we put into practice the possibility of leaving, denying that we too will come to such a bad end, and leave our family. Even if we do not leave our family as a result of reading this book, we can think about doing so more vividly. Even if we do not return in our minds to this situation, for a time it occupied a place. Oh yes, we say. Women can leave their families and go to the city.

If we read about marital problems and we had never known that such things could happen, we accept that they can happen. In the same way, if someone close to us tells us about these things, we accept that they can happen. When we first think about them they may seem strange, but the mere fact of now being part of our mental furniture means they will ultimately settle in and seem to us ultimately as if they had been there all along. If we have had (say) a sibling die of AIDS, we accept that this truly is a possibility. If we ourselves get a divorce after assuming for years that we of course were never going to divorce, then being divorced changes place from being something unthinkable to being quite thinkable indeed. We get accustomed to the fact that people we know, in fact we ourselves, are divorced.

Changing the mental furniture of people's minds alters them. Such change can be, as we say, for the good. For example, in movies, bigoted white people in the pre-Civil Rights era are forced to befriend black people and come to see that they are just people too. However we can't say in any general way whether people will be inspired to do what they see on the screen, or the opposite, or something else entirely. We certainly cannot assume that monkey will do what it sees. Surely few people would have been able to imagine the horrors of Dachau or Auschwitz before the opening of the camps, but seeing pictures of these things has inspired few people to create their own.

Sometimes we provide information precisely to (so to say) vaccinate other people: telling people about the camps so that it never happens again, for instance, or talking to our children about safe sex, warning them of perils. Before we gave these things "air time" in their heads, they probably didn't devote any time at all to them. We want to get there first, and be able to vaccinate them, control how they see things subsequently.

The reason opponents of pornography have such an ambivalent feeling toward science may well be their deep intuition that science is simply irrelevant to the fact of having a place in our heads. After seeing porn of kinky things we may well say, Oh, paddling. Yes, I've seen pictures of that. Or: a man penetrated by a woman with a strap-on. Yes, I've read about that. And this almost inevitably means, we accept it to at least a certain degree. It exists.

Representation of all sorts is full of things that are not being communicated by one person to us that nonetheless can become part of our mental furniture. Art typically arouses the suspicions of people eager to control what is in our heads—and rightly so. We see things in art, and so can make use of them. That is why it is so liberating to people who want to escape the control of communication. The public prosecution against Flaubert's novel of adultery and death, *Madame Bovary*, was at least half justified, and the successful defense, that the heroine was punished for her betrayal of her husband, only half convincing. The mere fact of having considered adultery gives it air time. The prosecutor was not obliged to argue that the portrayal of adultery was positive, or that the heroine need be someone we identify with, though in fact we do tend to identify with Emma Bovary. Merely raising of the subject alters the way we think about it, usually by making it more credible. Literally, this means believable: we believe that it is a possibility.

Pornography need have no add-on effects to be reprehensible in the eyes of those people who do not want others to have the things it portrays take up mental space. If the fact of knowing that others have seen X or Y is upsetting in itself, pornography will be intrinsically upsetting. For people who think a woman being penetrated by a man is reprehensible, even the most "standard" of erotic material will be reprehensible. For others the threshold may be higher. Wherever our personal threshold is, depicting such things gives them air time. They take up space in our heads and alter our world-view, irrespective of what we subsequently do or do not do.

Gay pornography causes problems for opponents of pornography, and usually ends up being disapproved of because it shows homosexual sex rather than for the reasons straight pornography is disapproved of. In the case of straight pornography, typically it is women who are being (say) bound or ejaculated upon. Viewers rise to their defense: women should not be shown in this ignominious state. In the case of gay pornography, though people may be humiliated and bound, it is not so easy to attach a label to the passive partner. Whom would we defend against humiliation? We can't express it in terms of one sex or the other. We have to be more specific. Would we be defending just those men who want to be so humiliated? This is counter-intuitive.

The argument against comparably humiliating scenes in straight pornography is usually that wanting to be humiliated as an individual is not a good enough justification. The particular woman may be willing to do what she does, but she should not be, as filming this scene and disseminating the image does harm to all women. The agreement of the porn star does not change the fact that these things are unacceptable. Things are even clearer if the porn star feels coerced, perhaps by the monetary pay-off, to do things she in fact disapproves of? (The porn actress Linda Lovelace has made a post-porn career of disapproving of porn.) Even if this actress is being forced to do these things, the portrayal gives credence to the idea that a real woman might like it. We see the image.

Most of us, faced with new information, have no reason to question it. We may not know initially that merely because we have seen a man ejaculate in a woman's face in every porn video we watched back at the frat house in college, this is not something we should try at home. Someone has to tell us. No one says that the transmission is always direct between a portrayal and our own action, but if information is not questioned, it is simply added to the things we know, and increases the likelihood that some version of this will be expressed in the world.

Typically, conservatives subscribe to what seems to be a more simplistic view of cause and effect with respect to pornography than do liberals. Their assumption is frequently that if people see something, they will immediately want to go out and do likewise. If something is in a representation that conservatives do not want to see in the real world, the book is bad. Typically it is conservatives who call for banning of books or representations, even (as with pornography) in the absence of any evidence that there are deleterious effects. To liberals this response seems unsophisticated.

In accusing conservatives of too-literal understanding of representation, however, liberals do them a disservice. At a secondary level, conservatives may be forced into asserting that whatever they find objectionable has negative add-on effects. But this is only because people are used to thinking in scientific terms. The "dulling" of sensibility that many conservatives deplore as a result of representation is not an effect in addition to ingesting the representation, it is precisely that ingesting with no immediate ill effects. We need only disapprove of the representation, we need not lose ourselves in unprovable and irrelevant assertions about subsequent effects.

Once we have given something space in our world, it exists for us. The anti-pornography forces would be well advised to limit their claims to this incontrovertible fact, as it is more than enough to justify their opposition of pornography, and in fact is the real issue. The real issue for the anti-pornography forces is not the form that science has altered their objections into: does viewing (reading, etc) pornography make people do X, Y, and Z, or even look more favorably on X, Y, or Z? They need not wait for a verdict on this; it is enough that X, Y, and Z are made that much more real. But this is viewing this sexual practice as a social one, not a personal one.

Chapter Seven

How Does the World Fit Together?

All ethics treats sex as if it could be expressed in social terms, the terms of ethics. For this reason all ethical considerations of sex are inadequate. Ethical questions are specific sorts of questions that change our views of the things "ethicized." Ethical pronouncements are expressed in terms of generalizations. All such pronouncements are tips of icebergs, tiny islands of regularity in a sea of irregularity. The sexual relationship between two individuals, being neither completely social nor completely individual, threatens to escape the purview of both liberal and conservative ethics with respect to sexuality.

Someone like Philip D. Harvey, the author of the op/ed piece cited above who fails to regard sex as a problem, is refusing to cast this behavior in terms of ethics at all. It is in the almost-cases of ethics, or cases where people refuse certain subjects to the purview of ethical thinking, that we get a hint of the fact that while we are engaged in ethical thinking, we are as a direct result failing to take account of those parts of the world that are not so ethicized. Things for which we have ethical strictures, whether conservative or liberal, are the tiny minority in the world; otherwise we are surrounded by pure particulars.

Particulars do not create conflict. It is only at the nodes of conflict that we have a sense of ordering the world, choosing what will go in this metaphoric space. And it is only at nodes of conflict that ethics become relevant. We have to express a conflict as alternatives that must be decided between. For example, Do I think X or Y, and why? When people answer questions like these, they write books to share their discoveries with the world, asserting that the conflict has been resolved. The result is ethics.

But our sense that we have put the world in order is always illusory, because all it really ever means is that we have resolved a particular conflict. While we have been resolving this one conflict we have by definition failed to resolve an infinity of others that may, some day, seem to require resolution by others. More unsettlingly, we have in the meantime encountered an infinity of particulars that never even vie for the status of things that can conflict. Finally, what was a conflict for us requiring resolution may well not be so for another person.

We lose sight of this because all real questions, the ones that bother us and to which we propose solutions, do involve collisions, which means we have to answer them. Thus we fall into the trap of not realizing that only questions that matter to us are answered. Wittgenstein fell into this trap in the *Tractatus* when he made fun of "metaphysical" questions, such as whether the good was more or less identical than the beautiful. Such questions had no point for Wittgenstein, but this lack of point is not the characterizing quality of metaphysics, or something unique to it. It seems likely Wittgenstein would have found the question, How does an ice cream cone relate to John Stuart Mill? equally frustrating: But all this means is, he would have had as little reason for seeing the question as demanding an answer as he did his metaphysical one. Clearly this question meant something to someone at some point, or it would never have been asked. Pointlessness of question is always only pointlessness for a specific person, and it doesn't characterize a specific undertaking. It's the rule rather than the exception, and all it means is, we don't see the point.

The fact is that most of life poses no problems, and so in the sense I mean it here is not connected. We never ask the question, How do these things fit together? How does going to the bathroom connect with reading Kant? How does feeding the birds connect with fixing breakfast? How does making the bed connect with scraping the burn off the toast? Most of life is simply lived; we do not ask these questions. But if the unexamined life is not worth living, the question arises: What exactly is it that needs to be examined about it? Individual people will tell us at any given time that X, Y, or Z needs to be examined. But the fact is that not everything can be examined. To begin with, we don't have enough time in our life to do so. Furthermore, when we come to the questions that others tell us need to be examined, we frequently find that we do not think they need to be. Questions fade over time—all of the minutiae of scholastic philosophy, for example—or they fail to have any pressing interest for the person in the next cubicle, house, city, or country. Ethics is not an overview for life, it is merely a way of dealing with conflicts, which in fact are the exception rather than the rule.

How is it that some questions need to be answered, and many, most of the others, do not? Is there any intrinsic difference between the questions that need to be answered and those that don't? Given the fact that most questions are unasked, and hence have no power, is there any reason to demand answers for the questions that are asked, except for the fact that they are asked?

The mere fact that something can be asked in question form, therefore, does not mean that it demands an answer. At the same time, the questions that people have seriously demanded answers for do not look any different grammatically or syntactically from the questions that have never (to our knowledge) required much time investment. If the person asking a question doesn't have a reason for asking it, which is to say, a question to be answered, we dismiss the question. "Why" can be asked about anything, as we know from talking with a four-year-old. There has to be a reason for asking this question, something, we would say, at stake. This something is what I am calling a collision. What is the connection between a sigh and the Brooklyn Bridge? If we see the Brooklyn Bridge do we have to figure out anything? If we hear a song do we have to react? Do we have to analyze the food we eat before we eat it?

In all cases, the answer may be "maybe," and in some cases the answer may be "yes," but it cannot always be "yes," and when it is, justification must be provided. We cannot be figuring out more than one connection at a time; if it takes us ten years to figure out a particular connection, that is ten years worth of figuring out of other connections that simply fails to happen. Yet most things in life do not require any reaction from us. We are not required to do anything when we see the Brooklyn Bridge, except cross it, if we are going in one of its two directions. We are not required to do anything when we read a novel except read it. We are not required to judge a daisy.

Is it possible ever to answer questions for anyone but myself of the form, What is the role of sexuality in our lives? How does this action integrate with others in the world? Does it co-exist with them? Does it try to trump them? Does it take a subordinate role? What do I hope or expect the result of this book to be? Is it description? An attempt to alter the world? If I talk about "sexuality," what relationship does this have to any one person's sexuality. Will I end by proposing a change in the way we talk about sex?

These in turn are specific forms of the general battle, expressed with respect to arguments, that was fought in the early twentieth century in linguistic philosophy with respect to reference and meaning. In linguistic philosophy, the question became, how does the word "tree" relate to the world? Does it somehow travel on the air from our mouth and hook to the object before us? How about the word "and," a connective rather than a noun, and hence less clearly related to things in the world? How about the word "angel," a creature we postulate but have never seen? Or the word "honor," a general concept? Maybe the connection of words with the world doesn't happen at the level of words at all, but at the level of "representational systems" or conventions. Or maybe we don't have to answer the question at all.

The question, How does the world fit together? means, Do any problems really need solving for anybody but me? Or is the conviction that I can solve problems for others an individual delusion? For the purposes of this book it also means, How does the social world fit with the personal world, and with the realm of the sexual that lies between them? If I can delineate their relationship, for whom is the delineation valid? Only for people who accept it? What about people who don't accept it? Does certainty pull us closer to the world, or simply further away?

This line of thought is something like that which informs Virginia Woolf's essay/story "The Mark on the Wall."[74] The essay follows Woolf's thoughts as they meander around the subject of an unidentified spot on the wall she sees from her chair. She can, she acknowledges immediately, get up and see what it is. But this would be to take the easy way out, and would do too much honor to the way the world is usually presented and described. For in our usual scale of values, a mark on the world is lowly indeed and certainly not worth worrying about. Yet, she suggests, this hierarchy of values is only a convenience that excludes far more than it includes.

For example, it would demote to meaninglessness the state of not knowing what the spot is. And are such states of ignorance regarding the world not the rule rather than the exception? Getting up to find out what the spot is, and so in some sense re-establishing mastery over it, would be to keep up the notion that we control the world. Is this not another of our fond illusions? Woolf lists objects we lose, then points out our ignorance of the provenance or final end of the things that seem so solid to us. How much more chaos there is in our contact with the world than order, how much more uncertainty than certainty! Far better to acknowledge the sea of ignorance in which hard facts swim.

It takes an act of courage to give in to uncertainty and acknowledge it, as Woolf is doing in this essay, rather than doing the thing she had been told so often by others to do, namely put an end to it, deny it, just get up and see what the spot is. Such acknowledgment of disorder may give a more accurate portrayal of the world. Woolf's illustration of the illusory nature of this order is the "Table of Precedency" from Whittaker's Almanac: who sits next to whom among the ecclesiastic and aristocratic ranks, who precedes whom in a formal procession, who enters the dining room first and who last. By the 1920s, she tells us, people had largely ceased to believe in this Table, and the whole had begun to seem like a ranking of the angels in heaven, and of as much use. No order is permanent; all is imposed. She understands the point of such imposition (what she calls "nature" trying to preserve its creatures), but does not for that reason accept the invariable claims of those who do the constructing, namely that this order is something they found, rather than created.

Woolf shows us that our order and love of hierarchy blind us to everything in the world that doesn't fit into the ordering, namely disorder and slack moments. Every intellectual work that purports to explain the world to us once and for all, including this one, is a version of Whittaker's Table of Precedency, no matter what its content. (The fatiguing nature of deconstructionist arguments popular in the last century lay in the apparent unawareness of those who made them that these were only specific arguments too, demanding the same rituals of obedience as more overtly hierarchical dogmas: control is control, no matter who is holding the whip.) We need things like the Table of Precedency to resolve nodes of conflict, when we ask whether X or Y belongs in a given space. It is at times like this that we ask the question, How does the world fit together?, which is at the basis of ethics.

Predictability

The generalizations of ethics allow some things to be constant. In a sense, we can say that we buy the predictability they allow at the price of the individual situation, which must be bent to this—however the ethical rule is expressed. We need not personify this conflict the way Freud does to see it as a trade-off; the either/or quality of this situation is merely a logical necessity.

Someone may decide that predictability isn't worth it, though it seems counter-intuitive to deny that it is an intrinsic good. Sartre, in *Being and Nothingness,* condemned all attempts to make the future knowable as examples of "bad faith": man, he insisted, is free.[75] Of course this is true, but this is to deny the obvious fact that man apparently doesn't much like the fact that he's free: that's why there was so much "bad faith" to inveigh against. Infuriatingly for Sartre, most people didn't even seem to want the gift of their own freedom— perhaps, we might suggest, because they had internalized this more thoroughly than Sartre wanted them to. Why not a little sympathy for his so-vilified bourgeois who limit themselves to being a waiter, a teacher, or a barber, believing that their actions are limited by their callings? Perhaps they are merely making use of their freedom to "be" a barber rather than yammering on about it. And what harm is done if they are convinced they are a barber in some way that limits their actions? Most of us would say, they are aware of the conventions of etiquette that bind us.

The highest act according to Sartre is the reciting of the credo of absolute freedom. In the same way, the highest point for the adherents of an organized religion is the reciting of the credo of whatever the organized religion says people are to believe in.

Science is the quintessential discourse of predictability. Does it have limits? Charles S. Peirce, in "Man's Glassy Essence," imagined the world becoming more regular as our scientific knowledge of it grew.[76] It is clear how he came to imagine this: each act of "scientizing" something is an act of abandoning particulars for more generals. Peirce's mistake was to think the source of particulars was bounded: as Rumpelstiltzchen transmutes the straw to gold, the straw is used up. What reason have we, who are positioned so as to see the regularity and understand that it is transmuted irregularity, to conclude that the amount of irregularity is fixed, and so must in some sense be exhausted?

The predictability of ethics, when generalized at all levels of a society, is what we call civilization. Without predictability, there is no such thing as long-term plans. We always want the rest of the world to be predictable, tending to reserve the right to be unpredictable for ourselves. Balancing these two desires is the goal of social structures. Trains should run on time, but which train I take should be up to me and the constraints of my own situation.

The order of civilization is always silhouetted against the disorder to which it contrasts. Thus civilizations are best described by relationship to what they are not. Freud imagined an adversarial relationship, as do many conservatives, for whom the forces of disorder are barbarians hammering at the gates. Another relationship is suggested by the literary scholar Paul Fussell as a prelude to considering the way successful poetry usually both respects and plays with the regularity of meter. Fussell proposes that

> Civilization is an impulse toward order; but high civilizations are those which operate from a base of order without at the same time denying the claims of the unpredictable and even the irrational.[77]

Fussell departs refreshingly from Freud—as must anyone who has things of interest to say of literature—in his insistence that high civilizations tolerate "the unpredictable and even the irrational." Fussell expresses this by saying, that civilization does not "deny the claims" of these things. Civilization is not in danger of being overthrown; the alternative to acting as it should is simply that it falls a bit in the rankings, from a "high" civilization to, presumably, a lower one. It does not go out of its way to encourage the forces it tolerates; neither does it have to speak the language of these forces. These forces are not, as they are for Freud, the outside threat that causes the city within to organize itself along militaristic, Spartan lines. Instead they are things that beg to be tolerated in the name, it seems, of greater benefits for all.

Regularity speaks the language of civilization. Yet alternatives exist. For Fussell, absolute metrical regularity degenerates rapidly into ridiculousness, as in the sentimental poetry of Henry Van Dyke ("America For Me"). Great poetry knows the rules and breaks them when appropriate. How to tell when breaking the rules is appropriate? You have to look at the individual poem. Is the spondee (two stressed syllables in a row) in the middle of the line successful? Is the metrical division of the poem into two equal stanzas of four lines each a good idea or a bad one? We start knowing what the rules are and depart from them on a case-by-case basis. How much easier it would be if we could give absolute rules for writing great poetry! But then, if we could, it wouldn't be such an art. In fact, it wouldn't be an art at all, but only a craft.

In the same way, civilization, which is the urge to regularity, is impoverished by an intolerance of departures from that regularity. Sex is such a departure, a constant one. The private world, which is even less of the social world than the sexual one, is an even greater departure, so much so that it almost fails to make sense to speak of it as a departure. The phone book is not a departure from the sonnet form, because it is simply too far removed. The private world exists as an under-surface world that can at any time be heaved up into the realm of public visibility. Because sex is closer to the regularity of the social world than the personal world, the impulse of the social world to "colonize" it is stronger. What this really means is, the social world half-computes what it sees, and expresses that in its own terms.

Fussell devotes a chapter of his book to free verse, poetry written in the twentieth century with no fixed meter or form. He points out that the most successful examples employ some formulae of regularity, though we must look for these in the individual poems, for example, in Whitman's oracular repetitions. Much free verse lacks any correlation of form to function. There is no reason for the lines to end where they do, or for the lines to be grouped in the groupings they are. Which means, to that extent it's bad poetry.

Sex exists in the same relation to the social as free verse does with respect to formal poetry. It has to follow some rules, but what they are we bend and shape to the particular set of circumstances. Sex is a thorn in the side of civilization; this is the feeling I share with Freud. But not because it is the enemy of civilization. The unpredictable is not the antithesis of civilization, it is the stuff of which civilization is constructed.

Fussell, a liberal, suggests that a civilization that tolerates forces that seem to work against it actually ends up being a "higher" civilization than one that tries to rout them out. The dystopia of civilization gone mad is of course the nature of the fascist or Communist state as portrayed by Huxley or Orwell: thought control, the ultimate regularization of the personal, is the ultimate sign of the social grown too fat upon its own steroids. No one can deny that the world of Orwell's *1984* is a civilization, it just isn't a very attractive one.

But what is an attractive one? And how do we justify this conclusion? I have been arguing that there are bound to be conflicts about the ethics of sexuality. These conflicts always take place in the domain of ethics, which is found in the social world, only one of the domains that border on sexuality. The pretense of structures of regularity is that they provide the rules by which irregularity plays, the skeleton necessary to prevent the organism from flowing in an amorphous mass onto the floor. Yet this is only from the perspective of the structures.

All structures of regularity must assume, even if they do not assert, that they somehow establish suzerainty over others, even if the others are not actively acknowledging that suzerainty. This is separable from public suzerainty, in the form of policemen to enforce the tenets of the structure. Civilization too must decide which of its structures it will enforce in the public sphere, and which it will leave to the private. An ethical tenet banning abortion may well be translated into law that affects real people. The suzerainty of this structure is clear. The suzerainty of, say, Kant's notion of how the mental map is made from the *Critique of Pure Reason,* is unlikely to find expression in law, though a professor's interpretation of it can (say) determine the grade we get in a college philosophy course.

Yet even Kant makes claims to being more than just something to fill an idle hour. His version of how things are is meant to be valid not only for him, but for everyone.

All thought is the attempt to control the world, to get us to do something differently (even if what is done is thinking). It tries to render particulars irrelevant. If it is thought about how people interact with each other, which is to say ethical thought, changes must somehow be either at a lower level of the system than the highest or be forbidden. We have said what the allowable changes are, and this list may not itself change. We can sketch out the variation patterns, the particular order of the variations as they unfold can therefore be held to be irrelevant.

Even someone as metaphysical as Kant wants some change in the world, even if this is in the way people talk, or what they believe. In *The Critique of Pure Reason*, Kant wants us to see that science is legitimate, and that this is so because of basic structures of the way human beings perceive. If our ignorance of this demand is as acceptable to Kant as its acceptance, or disagreement as desirable as acquiescence, then it is difficult to see why he should have written at all. Some thought is ultimately anti-thought, such as John Dewey's pragmatism. But this itself is a regularity, and takes up room, and demands allegiance.

The paradox of structures of regularity is that they can hold sway, but only when they are holding sway: only, we might say, when the world is viewed from their perspective. Most structures of regularity are unable to see their own limitations; indeed if they could they probably wouldn't have the regularity they do.

This paradox brings to mind Dr. Seuss's Yertle the Turtle, who climbed on the backs of other turtles and announced that he was ruler of all he could see. Following this principle, he became ruler of a house and a cow by adding a few turtles under him, and then more things, until finally the stack was upset by the bottom turtle, named (for purposes of rhyming with "stack," Zack). The house, of course, was unaffected by his seeing it, as was the mule.

If Kant divides noumenal from phenomenal and no one but him knows he has done so, is it done? Can works of thought "control" worlds that do not acknowledge them? A king demands ceremonies of subjugation from those he rules; otherwise, how to say that he rules them? Surely this was Hegel's point in his famous "master/slave dialectic" chapter from his *Phenomenology of Mind*. We'd probably say that the master is more important than the slave—that's the nature of the hierarchy, after all. But the fact is that without the slave, the master is nothing, which is to say, not a master. Masters require slaves for their self-definition. Since slaves presumably don't want to be slaves, they don't need the master in the same way.

The unregulated, the personal, can trump the regulated, but the regulated is not likely to be able to acknowledge that possibility. I think of the tortuous debate between Mendus and Parfit, considered above: we can assert that we will, come what may, pursue a predictable and regulated course, but at the same time we can know that this rarely happens that way. Most regularities don't even get to the point of acknowledging this possibility in the abstract.

Regularity is self-defeating. The more we have battened down the hatches, the tighter we have closed the gates of the city, the more likely it seems to be that things will happen that we have not planned for, or at least that we will be more aware of them. This is not the same as Freud's "return of the repressed"; I am not talking about repression but about ignorance.

The more absolutely we do whatever it is we do, the more certain that this will become identified with that time, that place, so that when things have moved on, we will come up with something new. The more we feature two-button suits in this year's line the greater the certainty that next year will shun them completely. The harder deconstructionism is pushed down the throats of graduate students, the more certain that in a decade or two it will seem last year's craze. This is so simply because of the passage of time, and the alteration in the human race produced by births and deaths.

The more we try to get our son to be like us, the more certain that he will rebel, simply because he has to do some things himself. Once again, I offer an alternative to Freud: no Oedipal complex, only the fact that other people's solutions never seem such to us, and we must find our own problems, and our own way. The less we tell people about the world outside our borders, the more likely they will be extremely curious about it when inevitably they do hear about it, and go in search of it.

Shelley's poem "Ozymandias" is a meditation on the transience, given enough time, of human power. There is no one left to cower to the statue of the long dead eponymous pharaoh with its "sneer of cold command." It is broken, bereft of a torso altogether, the face "half sunk" in the desert sands, which, "lone and level," in any case, stretch "far away." The same is true of ideas. In a generation or two, we may generalize, it's likely that people are simply going to get tired of mouthing the same pieties. Force can keep them doing it longer, as the Soviets showed, but if force is all that is keeping people doing it, it is unlikely to last forever. Those being forced will be eternally on the lookout for a way to overthrow their captors, and the captors cannot perennially be on the alert.

People are fickle, and in any case they die. It may be parents' fondest wish for their children to be like them in all particulars, but it rarely works out that way, and if one generation gets lucky enough to produce a devoted child who wants to be just like Dad, the following one is unlikely to do so. The children of high achievers rarely achieve as high; the children of self-made millionaires rarely add to the family fortune. People, we sometimes say, have to be "hungry" to do great things. The children of the well-to-do are rarely hungry.

The next generation may simply be unwilling to keep up the cult of the family deities. In other words, they don't have to go so far as to try and disprove the favorite thinkers of their parents, they need only fail to do these homage, and they will ultimately fall into disuse and disrepair. At least this is true in liberal societies, Western democracies. Conservative societies, such as pre-20th century China, ensured the continuance of things by making these the main tenet of their society. Paying homage to the family gods, traditions, values, and older members was the primary responsibility. This was overtly continuance for its own sake. It worked for much longer, and more effectively than Soviet Communism, which appealed to rationality and at the same time forbid the exercise of rationality. What an uncomfortable combination that was.

The error of the social is believing that it somehow is intrinsically more important than the personal, or the subject of this book, the sexual, because it is more regular. But this is only so to the extent that it raises its voice and so is the only one heard. The personal has by definition no public voice. The voice of sexuality has typically been disorganized, lacking confidence.

If the only voice to be heard is that of regularity, it is understandable that it would believe it is unopposed. But it is opposed daily in a more absolute way than by disagreement. Indeed, disagreement is never the most absolute opposition. Liberal and conservative ethics disagree with each other, and are for all that, and for that reason, joined at the hip. All theorists of human endeavors, including human sciences and philosophy, are more like each other—

even when they disagree most violently—than they are like the ends of the spectrum. Liberals and conservatives who argue with one another show their likeness by battling over the same turf. Writers would always rather have a negative review than no review at all, dissent rather than indifference. Married couples who argue need one another. We didn't have to have the plays of Strindberg or Albee's *Who's Afraid of Virginia Woolf?* to learn this.

People who never interact with one another may actually be further apart than those who disagree. Or they may simply be doing something else. In the same way a scientist may be turning his/her back more completely on a specific ethical position than someone who tries to refute it. The refuter-to-be is at least struggling for the same plot of ground; the scientist who refuses to argue isn't even engaging. Or is the scientist simply not arguing rather than refusing to argue? Does his or her intention matter?

Think of all the people in the building in which I am writing this, Sampson Hall of the U.S. Naval Academy, who are completely uninvolved in anything like the problems that concern me here. And this is the English Department, composed of people closer to being like me than anyone else here at the Naval Academy. How much less does what I write here have a connection with what is going on in Bancroft Hall, home to the Brigade of Midshipmen? Does the other person have to be thinking "I am not engaging with Bruce Fleming" to be not engaged? Freud and Marx have showed us how to make structures that do not require the consent of the governed. Perhaps consciousness isn't the issue. But isn't it necessarily the issue if the structure itself is about the fact of different worlds defined by consciousness of them? Surely consciousness of *this* is not irrelevant?

Recently I alternated reading two books, Robert Nozick's *Anarchy, State, and Utopia,* and a novel by E. F. Benson called *Secret Lives.*[78] Nozick's book is a defense of libertarian principles; Benson's a lovable romp about the author of pulp romances beloved by everyone in the London world of the novel. These pulp romances by the character in Benson's novel are, however, written pseudonymously. None of the (largely female) denizens of the closed world of the square which forms the setting for the novel have any idea that the apparently dashing "Rudolf da Vinci" who churns out purple thrillers (the newspaper's gossip columns are full of reports about his goings-on) is in fact the somewhat eccentric middle-aged lady named Miss Susan Leg, recent tenant in a quiet square in London with a gated garden, who blasts music at all hours of the night and day. We later learn this anti-social habit is the result of her early employment in the cacophony of a typewriting agency; the loud noise keeps her muse speaking.

The world of *Secret Lives,* a real book, evokes a world in which a fictional character writes lurid romances (of which Benson "quotes" lengthy excerpts for the reader's delectation), a world now removed from ours by the greater part of a century. Nozick's book contains a jacket photo of a thin, youngish man with too much hair (the book came out in 1974, still the time of too much hair); Nozick himself died in 2002, and his later jacket photographs show a white-haired, somewhat tamed looking man whose eyebrows were darker than his mane.

I alternated these books, the "serious" book during the day, and *Secret Lives* in the evenings. Of the two, I enjoyed *Secret Lives* much more. I could understand Susan Leg's writing frenzy, the way she would be picked up by the scruff of the neck by her current project, the world blocked out by the gramophone blaring in her ear, to emerge from her seclusion a day later, depleted, the story having taken over like a spirit medium that left her spent.

I also understood the writer's block of the antagonist of the book, Mrs. Mantrip, a well-meaning but priggish woman whose favorite author (the book's charming if somewhat overworked central irony) is none other than this very same Rudolf da Vinci—but who, as Susan Leg's neighbor and landlady, despises her tenant as a somewhat "common" newcomer to the square. Mrs. Mantrip is ostensibly engaged in writing a biography of her father, a priggish, censorious preacher who arrived in the square a generation before when it was considerably less genteel, and who harassed the prostitutes then living there until they left. We know that Mrs. Mantrip is good at heart from the fact that she counts the minutes until she can retreat with the latest novel of "Rudolf da Vinci" and immerse herself in its reading almost as fully as Susan Leg immersed herself in its creation. Inside her crusty, dried-out exterior, we see, is a lurid hothouse flower bursting to get out.

Perhaps as a result of this, each time Mrs. Mantrip sits down to write about her father, she gets nowhere. She pens a few desultory phrases about his ailments and his school years and trails off, unwilling and as yet unable to admit to herself that the good minister, her father, was a colossal bore whose vaunted "cleaning out" the Augean stables of the square (as he saw his activity) was motivated by intolerance and financial gain rather than piety.

I alternated between these two books much as Mrs. Mantrip alternated between her day world and the immersion in Rudolf da

Vinci. How a writer can identify with both of these, the vulgar, so flowing passion of Miss Leg and the stopped-up daytime frigidity of Mrs. Mantrip! And I asked myself, How do they connect with one another, save in the biographical fact of my alternating them? How, for that matter, does the daytime life of Mrs. Mantrip connect with her own secret life. Miss Leg's to her secret life? Do we even have to answer these questions? Is it a problem that I alternate these so different works? These are of course questions Benson wants us to ask. This is an example of a conflict.

This sort of feeling of living a tessillated existence was behind my initial assertion that sex doesn't "fit" with the rest of life. Yet the fact is that I am only aware of this when sex moves (so to speak) from the accustomed place we are used to seeing it. Only people who feel something problematic about the way things are write books such as this that question those things, or postulate alternate explanations, or indeed explanations at all. (As I ask below, the question then arises: how do these books fit in the world?) Nothing really "fits," as Virginia Woolf would point out. But this only becomes problematic when we are faced with conflicts. How does looking out the window at the tree "fit" with my writing this paragraph? How does writing a quick e-mail to a friend? How does thinking about going to the pool in a few minutes, or the sweat threatening to break out on my collarbone?

In one way, it seems I am looking for trouble in asking how disparate things fit together. If I let well enough alone, I simply do first one, then the other, much as Mrs. Mantrip went about her business during the day and read Rudolf da Vinci at night. Perhaps I should be asking, How is it possible for people to spend their lives doing different things? If the questions posed by Nozick are ones that should be answered, then what excuse does Miss Susan Leg have spending her life writing lurid romances, rather than trying to answer them? What excuse has Mrs. Mantrip for reading these? Or for that matter, devoting herself to the production of a biography of a man unlamented and long dead? Each has her own life, neither of which is that of Nozick.

By now the reader of this book, the one by Bruce Fleming, is smiling. First of all, s/he explains patiently, these are fictional people and cannot be compared to a real one such a Nozick, though he is now dead. Second of all, their world was created many decades ago, long before Nozick's book (in part a response to John Rawls's *A Theory of Justice*, which appeared in 1971), and it was "lived" even earlier than that. This is as absurd as asking why Socrates did not write *Madame Bovary*.

Let us in that case remove the apparent problems of fictionality and non-contemporaneity. We will find that the problem is identical. Should I feel guilty reading *Secret Lives* when I "should" be reading Nozick? Perhaps *Secret Lives* should be kept for those times when my brainpower is lower. What if reading it threatens to intrude on my "day" life, the way Miss Leg's writing was her day life? Should I prevent that? If not, is there any reason for reading Nozick at all?

How does Nozick's book fit with Benson's? Does Nozick's trump Benson's? Is it the presupposition for any novel reading? But what of the fact that I can simply put down Nozick, just as Mrs. Mantrip put down the biography of her father, and turn to Benson, or Rudolf da Vinci? Each fills a period of my day; my choice is between them. Of course, I can also choose to read neither.

What is the status of a book in which someone else has figured out answers to questions that concerned him or her? Must they also concern us? If they happen to concern us, is this in any way different from the way we may be drawn to particular novels? Are works explaining the world any more than simply descriptions of the world of their authors rather than of The World in general? How do these fit in the world? Does philosophy trump novels? Science trump philosophy? A sword in a strong right arm trump all of these?

Last week in the checkout line of the supermarket, caught behind an old woman fussily arranging and re-arranging her few purchases on the end of the conveyor belt, who was herself stuck behind a large women with a whole cartful of things all but filling the belt, I sought refuge in what for me is the Other world of tabloid newspapers and personality magazines. Breathless stories about movie actors were the norm here, shown going to a gala, relaxing, dancing in a night club.

These were people whose daytimes were spent causing interruptions of light to form images on the chemicals of film; at night they apparently went out and showed off. And this magazine was happy with this fact; clearly this was enough; this is who these people are, this is what they do. Apparently no one but me wondered why these people were not at home reading Nozick, or perhaps I mean, trying to be Nozick, trying to write his book. I mean this last to veer off into absurdity again, but at the same time to hint already at the problem of ethics: ethics is a thing done, and only one person can do it in a given way. Its relevance for others as a thing done may therefore be limited.

Which in turn made me wonder: Why am I trying to figure out the things I am trying to figure out, if I could just as well not and be another person, leading another life—just as acceptable as the one I am in fact leading? Clearly it was just fine for these people merely to make their movies and party; no one was asking them to figure out how the universe fit together, or whether "liberal" and "conservative" were really first-order differentiations of human beings. If they didn't have to, why did I feel obliged to? Was the impetus I felt operative on me merely self-created? Could I, should I, simply lie down until the impulse went away?

Like Mrs. Mantrip, writing (or rather, not writing) the biography of her unlikable father, something she would have privately printed and that only she would read, if even she would do so, these people were engaged on their particular lives. We, the reader of the fan magazine, didn't demand that they do anything differently than they did, any more than we demanded that Miss Leg quit writing as Rudolf da Vinci and— and what? Teach philosophy? Write a work as great as the *Divine Comedy*? We can't even finish the sentence coherently. She was who she was (at least in someone's mind), not another person. Flaubert was the man who wrote *Madame Bovary*, not the man who failed to write "The Waste Land." Asking how (say) a work of philosophy impacts the world is like asking that Socrates be the man who wrote *Madame Bovary*. Yet people do ask how philosophy impacts the world. Maybe it is not so absurd to ask why Socrates did not write *Madame Bovary*.

I am quite sure that these people, caught in the glare of a flashbulb in a club, will never know about my worries about liberals and conservatives. And I, being a fair-weather fan of their goings-on, interesting myself in their lives only when caught in slow-moving and potentially frustrating checkout lines, will never know about the rest of their lives. They spend their time, it seems, doing one thing, I another. Do we have to figure out how they "fit?" Yet all questions are answers to the question, How do these two or more things fit together? Which one goes in this space?

Why are some things conflicts and not others? We cannot tell by looking at the conflicts, certainly not by looking at ethical pronouncements themselves, for all these by definition have differentiated themselves from non-conflict situations, cases where we never even ask for an ethical ruling. When I put down either book I read and listened to works by Brahms, a man long dead. I entered his world. How does the work of Brahms relate to either writer's output? If Nozick really is necessary to explain the world to us, how is it possible that Brahms spent his time doing what he did rather than writing (reading?) *Anarchy, State, and Utopia*? If the questions Nozick poses are important for anyone but himself, why should everyone else in the world not be castigated for not trying to answer them? Or the questions of the relation of sex to the rest of the world? Yet if Nozick's questions do not impact on anyone but himself, how is it that they can worry me? How does my time with my daughter relate to the book I am writing? How does the sound of traffic I hear outside my window relate to this sentence?

We do not even try to relate most things, and are aware of them as failing to be in relation only in examples such as above, where we start with things in relation, and move cautiously outwards into an area of complete formlessness. Ethics focuses only on relations, and so by definition is an inaccurate portrayal of the way the world really is. The reasons we focus on certain connections—that is, the reasons we feel obliged to resolve difficulties—are various. But for every one focused on, there are an infinity of other possible connections I do not focus on.

This brings us back to the limits of ethics. Let us say I am engaged in a process of thought that purports to explain the world in some way. This can be directly, as in science, indirectly, as in a work of literature, or somewhere in the middle, perhaps philosophy. If I am the potential author of a book explaining the world, I can reason as follows: There was a time before this book was. Indeed, it is not yet. Like the child in the womb, it can be born or not born; I have the power either to make this happen or cause it not to happen. The world denied this work explaining things will not regret its absence, because it will have no idea of its ever having been potential. Indeed, I am unlikely to share the defeat of my inability or unwillingness to cause this book to come to be. If I do, it is unlikely that anyone will be very interested. I only share with others a certain small class of things.

If this book really is so necessary, how is that the world has existed so long without it? How is it possible that, should I not be up to the task, change my mind, or simply have my life disrupted, I could fail to write it? Am I only the passive conduit, the way conservatives conceive of the mother? Or does this thing belong to me?

I am limited in the things I can say here, limited to a type of content required to speak to others. We may not speak the language of disconnectedness, unless we somehow connect it to the language of connection. Readers may grant indulgence for a certain limited time, but if they do not have the threads ultimately tied up for them, they will throw down the book in disgust. Among the things we do not share with others are failures, the effort it took to arrive at a conclusion, the contradictions along the way, rough drafts, and errors. And these are most of the world. I publish my much-revised file of this book, not the version that shows all the cross-outs, the re-writes, the changes of positions, the start-overs. That doesn't even have private interest. There is no one in the world, including me, who is interested in this, unless I need to check something while I am writing. So it never gets shared. They are part of the personal world.

Of course, we do publish working versions of some works. Some things can come out of the personal world into the social. Ezra Pound's editing of T. S. Eliot's "The Waste Land" was the sensation of the late twentieth century in Modernist circles. Yet this is possible in just the same way that, having clasped (say) a movie star to our collective bosom, we listen to him/her babble on television, fascinated by the triviality, the start-overs, the very ordinariness of what they have to say. We are only interested in penetrating the clouds of unformed material when we have already decided that the finished product at their center, the thing expressed in public speech, is worthwhile.

Most things we do go unquestioned, and so do not require resolution. Indeed, most people lead lives, if not of quiet desperation as Thoreau suggested they did, then of unquestioning calm. Writers and thinkers, however, typically want people to question. This is so because of the form of writing a substantial work that no one is waiting for: the author must have had the perception that something was missing in the world, had to be fixed. No writer, however, can want others to question everything, only the thing(s) that s/he wants questioned. For if people cannot, by definition, fit all possible questions into their lives, given that these are of finite duration, and while they are considering X, they cannot be considering Y.

All ethical dilemmas come from a context not articulated by the dilemma itself. All solved problems, or at least things presented as solved problems, presuppose a world that is never articulated. We can get a sense of this unarticulated world by reflecting on the fact that we intersect with written works only if we understand what they are questioning, their own connection with the world, what they collide with. If we do not see how they collide with something we know, they merely are, and we shrug our shoulders and go on.

Because works are tips of icebergs, we can react to them in divergent ways depending on what we see their connection with the world to be, how they collide with the rest of the world. Sometimes the work itself contains articulations of this relationship, but the fact is that this articulation itself has a relationship with the world: a work can never position itself, though some of its content can be the attempt to do so. What this means is that all works are finite. No work can ever solve forever the problems it addresses. Indeed, the problems it addresses change as our perception of the work's context changes. No ethical system can ever put a stop to questioning and challenge.

The Limits of Ethics in General

I open John Stuart Mill's *On Liberty*," an essay which galvanized me when I read it in high school at the age of 16. Mill begins by saying that once, political liberty was expressed in terms of limitation of the sovereign's power on the citizens.[79] He suggests that we are past that stage; for his time, 1857, the threat to liberty is posed by other citizens. He is immediately establishing a context. The liberty he is talking about is not, he says, the old-fashioned kind of liberty, but another kind.

At 16, living in a small town and going to a high school where everyone except me worshipped the football team, I felt, predictably, like a fish out of water. No wonder I thought I'd found the Holy Grail when I read Mill's spirited defense of individualism! I thought I saw how this work intersected the world—or with my world, at any rate, the world of public high school obsessed with being "popular" and wearing just the right kind of shirt. Mill couldn't have known about my world, by definition; I provided the context, the thing to which this was an alternative. This is the same way we react to literature, which by and large does not spell out its own context, the question to which it is an answer. We have to provide this from our own experience. Philosophy, certainly ethics, tries to indicate context; some expression forms, such as science, are all about context.

Now, however, when I re-read *On Liberty*, it is clear that the intellectual center of the book is a technical argument, namely the proposition that the state does not have the right to limit individual freedom of thought and action except to protect other individuals. And to this I find I have no reaction. As a teen-ager I focused, instead, on Mill's critique of group-think, his celebration of the uncommon, the individual, even the eccentric. In high school, all I wanted was reinforcements, someone to say what I thought and no one else did, namely that individual qualities are good, and that we should beware the tyranny of the majority. This time through the book, I found myself questioning Mill's optimistic insistence that encouraging individualism is the most efficient way of keeping a society healthy, his eugenic belief in the infinite perfectibility of mankind's notions, if only people are allowed to point out their errors. Really? I think. This is not immediately so obvious to me.

I now see a different world than Mill did: I see a world where we believe first one thing, then another, and where the possibility of changing others' minds by rational argumentation is limited indeed. I now have a position on something Mill has a position on, and therefore can use his position to question and refine my own. Unlike Mill, I do not think someone who disagrees with us can alter our own view; I can only intersect with this opinion to begin with because I am thinking competing thoughts myself. I didn't think these thoughts at 16, indeed I didn't think them as recently as a few years ago. Most people on the Earth aren't thinking them now. These people would be unlikely to see a problem with Mill, and might read him as effortlessly as I once did.

The best way to get a connection with a work we might otherwise swallow whole rather than chewing is to ask, What is the conflict being addressed? What is the work trying to change? Until we have a sense of this, the work is as unrelated to anything else as an ice cream cone is from a zephyr. Works are answers to questions. If you know what the question is, you "get" the work.

For a time, re-reading *On Liberty*, I was stumped for a response to this question of what conflict it was trying to resolve. Like Woolf, tasting the situation of not knowing what the mark on the wall might be and unwilling to take the easy road of answering the question, I was initially unwilling to begin the process of figuring out how this relates to other things in the world. Yet, like Woolf, I felt the pressure to stop shilly-shallying and decide. What I am writing here cannot be a book about ethics, sexual or otherwise, if what it contains is primarily my inability to react to J. S. Mill, or other standard thinkers. Why should anyone read this book if I don't have a position? In the same way, I cannot be a public speaker if, standing before the podium, I hem and haw and tell stories about my children—or more than one, if possible a well-chosen one, to "break the ice." Writing philosophy requires being sure about something, or at least acting as if we are. The state of unsurity simply does not figure on the radar screen.

The assertion of truth is therefore appropriate to a specific social situation: it occurs in a certain way, and under certain circumstances. Uncertainty is an equally real state, but it cannot enter the "prime time" arena of saying the way things are. The social world, to which assertions of truth belong, has its own rules.

All thought has a finite form, and that form means it cannot be an accurate portrayal of the world, only an expression of that finite form. Yet as a resolution to a particular problem holding center stage on someone's mental screen, it can loom large. The works themselves must adopt a posture of certainty. Whatever their content, their form must be concise, their tone one of quiet competence, their attitude one of unquestioning superiority. They must say to us: I have the answers, that is why you should be reading this book rather than another one, or going to the store, or floating in the pool, or taking a walk.

Nozick begins *Anarchy, State, and Utopia* by speaking of how once he sympathized with many of the points he now attacks. He has not, he notes, included this sympathy in the book he is writing, only the attacks. This reference is a way to include them without including them, at least to diffuse objections by saying, implicitly, Once I was where you still are, but have now seen the error of my ways. The way to write successful philosophy is to state your position forcefully, just as the best way to be a public speaker is to be yourself, but forcefully. Do not apologize for not being someone else. Smile for the camera that catches you emerging from the nightclub if you are a movie star: make it clear that you are unapologetic about not having stayed at home to read (write?) *Anarchy, State, and Utopia.* Be the person you are; that's all anybody is. Perhaps a brazen exterior will prevent people from asking why you are not someone else.

We might even point out that people do not typically even *like* other people who seem to be eternally apologizing for not being someone else. Sexual attractiveness, certainly for men and to an extent for women, is precisely the air of self-possession. Men become sexy, so long as they are within the bounds of the physically normal, by exuding certainty about themselves. A perfect face and body is not necessary for a man to be sexy. The air of being very much at home in his own skin, whatever skin that might be, is.

This is my point above that ethical conflicts regarding sexuality, liberal vs. conservative, need not in fact be resolved; they can be merely stepped away from. For the situation they are involved in is a precise one, and we can see them the way the camera sees the conflict between Japanese and British at the heart of the movie *The Bridge on the River Kwai* as it pulls away from what has filled two hours and shows it to be merely a fly speck in the otherwise endless jungle.

What this means too is that even ethical articulations of tenets I might find sympathetic, such as Mill's defense of individualism, become only finite philosophical tenets. No problem is solved once and for all; it is the process of resolving a living clash that gives works of thought their power. The works themselves have no power over whether or not the clash itself will continue to be one that people feel must be resolved. The world cannot be nailed down forever. We must do it again and again.

We might react to the above paragraph by saying that this, precisely this, is Mill's perception, and his solution is to give people the leeway to solve problems in their own way. Of course this is so, which is why it seems so appealing. Yet unless we can access this work as a live response to a real question (which only means, see the same problem Mill did) it will simply seem finite, inert, itself merely a barrier to be gotten over. Nothing can protect Mill against this fate except skillful re-interpreters, usually in the form of professors, who make connections with the world of the students and the work they are reading that the students themselves are not capable of making. And these may be accepted or rejected, depending on the students' willingness to allow such mediators. If the professor has an appealing personality, Mill may filter through to the students. If s/he does not, Mill may get lost by the wayside: both of these are equally possible outcomes, both facts in the world. And it does no good to proclaim that the personality of the people involved in an intellectual exchange doesn't matter. If the person who says even this isn't appealing, this proclamation itself will fail to get through.

The stultifying quality of works that do not, in our view, solve problems that matter to us explains what I call Proust's Problem: the fact that things that matter to others, that we are told must matter to us, only do so infrequently. If we accept others' valuations for things, we will almost inevitably be bitterly disappointed. The Princesse de Guermantes will turn out to be a tiresome old woman. The Venice of song and story will reveal itself in reality to be a tired city with a bad sewage system, and Paris only the stageset of our personal dramas rather than an end in itself.

We read that X has asserted Y, and have no way of reacting. Fine, we say. So X asserts Y. Many students have this reaction to many of the "classics" of world literature. This is why education is such a slipshod, piecemeal enterprise, and why lists of "have to read" books are doomed to failure. Typically we read, and the work fails to affect us. Yet if there is not some external reason impelling us to read works, such as a degree we "have to" finish, we probably won't keep at it, for the experience is far from satisfying. In fact, it usually ends up being a waste of time.

Figuring out how two specific pieces fit together makes us feel, for a moment, that we have reunified the whole world, put all pieces together. Our exultation can be contagious, and other people can believe it with us. This is what leads to movements, cults. People can celebrate for many years, for centuries, even for millennia, the specific resolutions of specific problems; they can spend most of their time so celebrating. Yet these resolutions are nonetheless specific.

What this amounts to is mistaking a particular collision of two things in the world for a global collision, a particular substitution of one thing for another with all things. We thus have the illusion that everything has been connected. But what of the people in the supermarket tabloid who are living their own lives, or of someone a century ago who didn't think like us, or (more troubling for most of us) of the next generation that, in all probability, won't give a fig for what concerns us? They stand as useful reminders that this sense of touching the whole, while real for certain circumstances, dissipates under other circumstances, and for most other people.

I can walk away from *On Liberty* without ever relating Mill's thesis to the rest of the world. At my stage in life, no one is making me pass a class on Mill, and I am my own boss as far as what I do with him is concerned. Still, this is the sign of a lazy mind, and I have long ago learned to overcome biological resistance to the onerous task of "taking on" works I read. I try to articulate to myself my objections to this thesis, read reactions to this kind of thinking, bone up on the secondary literature, and figure out my position. I will feel I have "gone to the bottom" of the issue.

Those works that clearly collide with each other quickly become beloved of professors. We professors teach Locke vs. Kant in philosophy, state of nature theorists vs. utilitarians; we teach Modernism as a reaction against Romanticism, Romanticism as a reaction against Pope. Students may leave institutions of formal education with the feeling that thought is like a game of pool, full of balls constantly knocking into one another, a series of collisions. Indeed, the whole debate of the brief period of postmodern thought regarding science focused on the collision of what we learned, from Thomas Kuhn, to call paradigms. This was not a new departure in thought but only a continuation of the old focus on connections, which is to say collisions. For even if the point of a work is to buttress a view already held, the implicit assumption is that this needs to happen, that the view is in need of buttressing.

Outside of the classroom, we have to wait for two billiard balls to collide; for many people years can go by without their doing so. How does *Secret Lives* relate to Nozick? How do Rudolf da Vinci's potboilers relate to Mrs. Mantrip's life of her father? It's even possible these question, silly or contrived though they seem, have answers. The strength of big theories that organize lots of material, such for example as Marxism, is that they offer answers to questions like these. The problem is, it's always the same answer, such as, potboilers are escapes from the drudgery of reality, as all literature is in some way the emanation of the economic under-structure. Unitary answers of this sort are broad and not very deep, since the structure always looks at the same aspect of the work. And what it says about this aspect never varies.

Escape literature, for example, is for Marxist theory eternally escape literature, and what it's escaping is X, Y, and Z; it can't be anything else. What is being escaped doesn't change either. This is so not merely in what are called "vulgar-Marxist" views. More subtle Marxist analysis simply spends more time on what is individual about the work and less time, proportionately, on what hooks it to the overarching system.

Furthermore, until Marx suggested there was a connection between, say, Mozart and over-eating in eighteenth-century Europe, no one would have said there was. The same is true for Freud; the connections these systems make possible are connections that had to be established.

If Marx and Freud had been, strictly speaking, true, all of Freud's works and all of Marx's could have failed to be written and the world would still be the same as a world that contained them, and that used their language. Clearly this is not so. The premise of most works of thought, that what they claim is true but people don't acknowledge their truth, is contradictory. If acknowledgement of truth has any importance greater than zero, then they are doing more than stating this truth. Truth doesn't have to be acknowledged if it's true.

The least self-contradictory of the overarching structures are those that do not require human interaction, human alteration as a result. Freudianism and Marxism are as workable as they are because they do not require us to be thinking their contents. In fact, they work better when we are not. This solves the zero sum game intrinsic to all thought. If I am thinking X, I cannot be thinking Y or Z. The economic understructure does its thing whatever I am thinking about it; my id is bubbling away despite the thin veneer of my conscious world.

Religion solves this problem considerably less well. Its claims are equally to absolute truth, but it tends to require human interaction in the form of credos, professions of faith and allegiance, and so on. Ethics doesn't solve the zero sum game well either; this is the reason why it is an ongoing problem, or at least involves ongoing problems. It consists precisely of those structures that conflict, because it is involved with human actions, which are strung out in time and space. Further, it focuses on conflicts. Or rather, its value is clear only when conflicts arise. We may learn, say, a list of "thou shalt"s, but until the day comes when we want to do something else other than this, they will seem somewhat beside the point.

Ethics changes the world if in no other way than by bringing its conflicts to our consciousness, making us pay attention to them, hoping to make us enter into its conflicts. Yet we cannot simultaneously consider all conflicts, or indeed more than one at a time. Ethics walks the rocky road of any zero sum game that wants limited resources, in this case our attention. It can make a case for getting our attention, but it does so on the always specious grounds that it should have had our attention to begin with.

Science solves the zero sum game best of all the overarching structures because it requires nothing from us. It is a structure about things that merely are. For this reason, other enterprises have tried to model themselves on science. Science is that enterprise which completely abandons the claim that humans have to acknowledge it for it to be true. This is the power of the structure of science; this way of thinking is something that had to be discovered. A way of thinking that does not require human consent, only human confirmation! No wonder it took mankind centuries to come up with this. And no wonder it has always been opposed by ethics, fighting about what people should and should not do. Science adopts the language it does of an objective world, atoms, molecules, forces, and waves (and so on) precisely because they are terms that do not require humans to sign off on them.

We can see science alternately as the enterprise that considers the substrate of existence, or instead only as the enterprise that uses terms such as "substrate of existence" because we react in a certain way to them. Science after all, is a human undertaking. We are always justified in asking, how does it fit in among other undertakings? We can prove science, but we do not have to acknowledge it. My heart pumps and the planets swirl whether or not I know about them.

Mill considers the phenomenon of decreasing allegiance over time to doctrines that require human acceptance. He thinks doctrines become empty only because conflict keeps doctrines fresh, which is why he is for allowing, even encouraging, questioning. The founders of all creeds, he notes, complain that successive generations lack the conviction of the first. People with a bill of goods to sell have to be "hungry," and the only way they will be hungry is if they fear failure in propagating their ideas.

> Their meaning continues to be felt in undiminished strength, and is perhaps brought out into even fuller consciousness, so long as the struggle lasts to give the doctrine or creed an ascendancy over other creeds. [80]

Mill is putting his finger on the fact that most of the world is unconnected. We can only see the point of an abstract work if we see what it replaces, or what it is an alternative to. A doctrine that is accepted merely is. It is like one of the innumerable works that we read and react to by shrugging our shoulders. Or the way we don't ask what the connection is between doing the laundry and listening to a bird. If (let us say) our parents want us to be enthusiastic about one particular creed, they may be more upset at the fact that we are indifferent to this set of beliefs than they would be at our being indifferent to the thousands of other expressions to which we are similarly indifferent. Yet most coming of age stories are variations on this situation: the parents want the children to see things their way, the children don't. With any luck, the struggle doesn't last much beyond the children's legal majority; occasionally it goes until the death of the parent. But then the roof, typically, falls in. At least the dead parent would have seen it this way. For the suddenly-liberated child, it simply means peace.

Mill was right that beliefs have to collide with other beliefs before we register them. But all beliefs are finite, even Mill's. How does eating an ice cream cone collide with Mill? We can answer the question, if we have to: both an ice cream cone and a book cost money. Both are commodities (what would we do without Marx?). Both are expressed in language (what would we do without Wittgenstein?). Both are expressions of the individual desire (what would we do without Freud?). Both take up time (Proust?). Both can be green, or purple, given proper flavors and bindings. As Foucault points out in *Les mots et les choses* (*The Order of Things*), there are many rubrics under which we can order the world.[81] The point is we usually use none of them. We could, if we had to, come up with some conflict between Mill and ice cream (which one do we want to spend time/money on right now?). Even if we do manage to answer this question, someone will come along for whom it is uninteresting, or repressive, or irrelevant.

Collisions in the world are frequently determined by things beyond our control, what other people want us to deal with. This makes them problems we have to deal with. *The Washington Post* for May 16,

2002, suggests a number of conflicts. The front-page news concerns Palestine-Israeli violence. Two groups of people want to be in the same space. A more local article concerns the attempt by a boy in Frederick, Maryland to have a stone on which the Ten Commandments are carved removed from a public park. The chairman of the local Christian Coalition is quoted as saying that he will fight this attempt "with every fiber of his being." The mayoral race in Newark, NJ is covered: two men, the old-school mayor and the young hopeful, both want the same thing, namely to be mayor.

These seem like, and indeed are, real problems. They happen in our world, right now, and are things others are interested in. They create passionate responses. Because there is a constant stream of things we are supposed to deal with right here, right now, we may be impelled to think that the vast expanses of the problemless world are correlated to a kind of thinking. This is Wittgenstein's mistake. But the problems of newspapers from a decade ago are no less dead, in most cases, than the questions of metaphysics are for most people. It's just that metaphysics stays around longer than newspapers do. Indeed, by contrast, it is perfectly possible for a topic in a decade-old newspaper to be more interesting to us, demanding more strongly of answers, than a book of metaphysics that came out just this year.

The default position of our life is one of lack of collision, not the exceptional one of having to deal with a collision. Thinkers, those people focusing on specific collisions (and demanding that we focus on them too) either forget or obscure this important truth. Consider the following passage from the book by Nozick considered above.

> Soldiers who know their country is waging an aggressive war and who are manning anti-aircraft guns in defense of a military emplacement may *not* in self-defense fire upon the planes of the attacked nation which is acting in self-defense, even though the planes are over their heads and are about to bomb *them*. It is a soldier's responsibility to determine if his side's cause is just; if he finds the issue tangled, unclear, or confusing, he may not shift the responsibility to his leaders, who will certainly tell him their cause is just.[82]

What is so startling about this is, in fact, the same thing that ultimately dogs Nozick's initially appealing libertarian principles in general. Namely, that they fail to take account of the way we actually live our lives. We live in a world from which collisions arise, rather than a world defined by collisions. Not thinking about things is our natural state; we use thought to solve particular problems. Yet Nozick is demanding that soldiers be constantly thinking—about the very thing that, most of us would assume, had been resolved by the very fact of their wearing the uniform. Nozick is demanding that soldiers constantly revisit what military systems would assume to be a dead issue.

In more general terms, Nozick seems unaware that what may be freedom for him is servitude for the next generation forced to follow his tenets. Some tenets look like this: Worship God, and do it this way. Others look like this: Follow liberterian principles, and do it this way. Most people would say, while you are a soldier, you must follow orders. While serving as a soldier, you act like a soldier. What you do as a private citizen may be your responsibility, but wearing the uniform means precisely that you do not have to ask questions such as those he demands soldiers ask. Those holding this position would be ill-advised to add as a caveat, at least this is true of people who have voluntarily signed on, though it is not of those who have been conscripted; the disadvantages of such a concession are obvious. Yet given the importance for the libertarian mind of voluntary informed consent, my suspicion is that Nozick would be less interested in pursuing his argument against voluntary soldiers.

Then again, he might not. Nozick has answers to the "implicit consent" argument. This holds that, by accepting the benefits of the system, young men give their implicit consent to being drafted. If the law changes, they don't have to give this consent, so it is revealed as a circular argument to the effect that whatever the system demands of one, one has given one's consent to. A better argument refuses to play the libertarian "consent" game at all and says that while one is in the military, one has a responsibility to obey orders.

Nozick demands that the life of a soldier be a morally active one. What if we don't want to do this? Must we anyway? No organized religion is so amorphous that it fails to include rituals that must be carried out, credos that must be recited, meetings that must be attended, clothes that must not be worn, food that must not be eaten. Nozick questions (demands thought for, makes a collision of) issues that we would have thought were so basic as to have been accepted. Demanding that soldiers ask such questions bears the same relation to their lives as if someone had suddenly come up to me on the street and told me that I should be ashamed of myself for eating. The case could be made that I should be, but if it is not limited, say to eating a specific food, I am likely to deny it the time it needs to be re-examined. Other things during this period get pushed aside, given that it is something that would take over my whole being, leaving no time for anything else. Practical objections are important. When are soldiers to do the research necessary to coming up with an informed final opinion, especially if they may not ask their leaders? What are they to do before they reach such desired finality (it seems Nozick knows what conclusion they must come to)? May they fire their weapons in the interim?

What would Nozick say to them if they were not reciting the credo of his religion, metaphorically speaking, asking the questions he wants them to ask? Would he call them immoral? Lazy? Not good students of philosophy? Of Nozick? But who says these are bad things? No thought is completely self-interested, not even an individual-centered one like Nozick's.

Is libertarian thought, in my terms, conservative or liberal? It seems at first glance liberal: if Mill is liberal, so is Nozick. This means he should be expressing his absolutes in terms of actors. Is free enterprise a liberal or a conservative mantra? It is conservatives (as we use the word in the current political climate) who tend to want everyone to do the same thing (those people Mill decried): abstain from sex before marriage, avoid homosexual sex, eschew abortion. Libertarian thought, as its label suggests, is in this sense (it seems) liberal, insisting that people be allowed to do as they like as individuals. Yet at the same time libertarian thought is deeply conservative, in that it rejects social programs expressed in terms of what all people should have, insisting on the legitimacy of differences that have arisen from history, and implying a kind of Social Darwinism.

Ayn Rand famously called libertarians "hippies of the right," which suggests some of the apparent difficulty in putting a label on them. Their primary structural level should show whether the principles are expressed in terms of actions or actors. Libertarianism is ethics at the edge of ethics; it flirts with being something else entirely, a case of one rather than a general rule. Yet to the extent it is an ethics, it is actually a structure of $1 + 1 + 1 + 1$. Which is to say, in my terms, a conservative structure, unable to make generalizations about actors, and instead expressing its absolutes in terms of actions. Specifically, libertarianism is most fundamentally a negative. It says what the state is not allowed to do. This is expression in terms of actions.

Being an individual is not the same as espousing a philosophy of being an individual. We can merely be an individual without espousing the philosophy, or at least this can be argued. Indeed, it can be argued that all of us are individuals, willy nilly And if we are not, and are criticized for this by philosophers, what should it matter to us. For us this is not a problem, and the worst they can say about us is that we are lazy and stupid, and do not worship at their church, or mouth the creed of fill-in-the-blank. Let them fail us in their courses; we don't care. All of us at some point grow out of having to take courses, and then we may do as we like.

Indeed, numbers are on our side: there are an infinity more of things to do that are not this one particular thing, whatever it is, than the one particular thing. And so not doing it hardly puts us on the losing side of history, as people believing in a teleology of history like to say, though it may put us at a disadvantage in the short run, where everyone else is worshipping at the church of X, even if that church is the libertarian one, that assures us the state has no right to demand we worship at any church.

Libertarian ethics, we may say, calcifies (makes a religion of, in my metaphor) the world of particulars that stands as an alternative to it. In the libertarian world, each person is autarkic, and makes as many of his own goods as possible. This too is a metaphor: it means, s/he asks fundamental questions from zero. The libertarian world is one in which we are asked to re-invent many wheels. According to the libertarians, the virtue of doing so is that we have re-invented them, from our point of view therefore invented them. Instead of merely paying our taxes and getting on with our lives, for example, we must decide how our money is going to go. It is a very active world, where we are constantly making decisions.

Here as always, the most useful question in understanding something is, What is this an alternative to? What are the libertarians trying to get us to change? Libertarians might say, people are lazy and don't want to have to re-invent all these wheels, they just want to be left alone. We might see it differently: libertarian doctrine, like all doctrine, is a particular use of our limited mental time. It tells us what conflicts we are to devote our attention to. Libertarian thought is a world-view devoted to thought, fraught with conflicts, what we might call a suspicious world-view. No wonder it works best for modern-day equivalents of the crusty New England farmer who spends all his time hugging his rifle and threatening poachers. What of people who don't want to be slaves to this particular collision? Perhaps they just want to eat their ice cream cone, not judge it, or say how it relates to zephyrs.

Libertarian dogma is dogma like every other. Ethics is a machine we must feed. Was I showing my callowness by returning with joy to *Secret Lives* and heaving *Anarchy, State, and Utopia* into the corner?

Or was I making a statement about human freedom? If I throw aside Nozick, it is not because his claims are false, only because they are finite, which means I do not have to pay attention to them. If he is bothered by this (but he can't be bothered by anything, as he's dead, and in any case wouldn't have had a clue what happened this particular spring day in Annapolis, Maryland) let him, we might say, turn to an expression form such as literature, where people who don't see what questions the works are answers to simply put down the works without disagreeing with them, or science, which carries on its impersonal work of proof and disproof aloof from human reactions altogether.

Or is he a closet Marxist or Freudian, edging towards the impersonality of science, holding that whatever I do or say, I am actually proving his point? I would not say I was, given that I would be deep in *Secret Lives*, and in any case unwilling to talk about Nozick. It is not possible to envision a work of thought that was completely, sincerely uninterested in converts. Such a work, it seems, would not be thought at all, but (at one end of the spectrum) literature, which simply makes individualized worlds and shrugs its shoulders if people are not interested in entering them, or (at the other end) science, which truly is uninterested in whether or not people accept its findings, so long as they are provable. The push to get unpopular scientific discoveries past moral mafias may be related to science, but it is not science itself.

The much-mauled question of the nature of truth took a central role in twentieth century philosophy. On one side we had the objectivists, correspondence theory, Kant, and science. On the other we had thinkers like Charles S. Peirce, Richard Rorty, and John Dewey who insisted that there is no such thing as objective truth. But this conflict, like the conflict of liberal and conservative in sexual ethics, is an internecine squabble. The circumstances under which we are required to address this conflict are limited, usually to a university classroom or a professional journal. Usually we don't consider it.

That is an answer to the question, if we are looking for one (we needn't be). Namely, that truth is that thing we try to define when we engage in an argument that is about the nature of truth. When I am lying in a field watching the clouds, I am not trying to define truth. When I am doing interval runs and feel as if my guts are being turned inside out, I am not trying to define truth. Right now, writing this, I am not trying to define truth.

This is not edging towards a Peircean notion of truth as the consensus of the whole, or a Rorty-like insistence that it's something we never get. Of course we can get truth, in the same way we can promise to be faithful to someone else forever, to invoke once more Mendus and Parfit. When we get truth, we have to really think we have gotten it. And that's what truth is, the thing we're looking for at any rate (we may revise our view that we've gotten it).

Those who spend much of their lives, or the part they think important, in this social situation where they seek to define truth will believe that their definitions somehow, like Yertle the Turtle's suzerainty over the world, controls things outside of them. In *Achieving Our Country*, Rorty summarizes this belief, though he is questioning only the particular beliefs he refers to, and I am questioning whether any beliefs really control the circumstances outside of those that produced them.

> We are told over and over again that Lacan has shown human desire to be inherently unsatisfiable, that Derrida has shown meaning to be undecidable, that Lyotard has shown commensuration between oppressed and oppressors to be impossible. [83]

I laughed out loud at this passage, though I think Rorty did not mean me to. I think he meant me to be sad, and somewhat reflective. His point is that we should be trying to make America better as a result of seeing her faults, not merely issuing blanket condemnations unrelated to action. I imagined someone back in Peoria opening his morning newspaper to find the screaming banner headline, HUMAN DESIRE SHOWN TO BE INHERENTLY UNSATISFIABLE: LACAN. Does this mean that John Doe is wrong in thinking that he really enjoyed (say) his dinner last night? Or that, despite what he believes, he will not in fact be glad to get out on the golf links? Or that he will not be a happy man the day he (say) walks his daughter down the aisle, despite what he believes before, during, and after?

It is easy to laugh at the parochial pretensions to power of powerless academics: they may not influence much of anything, but they sure do talk big! But this is to trivialize the problem: it's really too deep for tears. Whatever Lacan says is merely what Lacan says, as whatever Nozick, or Fleming says, is only what Nozick, or Fleming says. Or this is true for social situations outside of those in which these men say what they say, namely classrooms, or scholarly conferences, or publications.

The social situation can change. If epigones shove Lacan down the throat of students everywhere, require their passing tests in his doctrines, and make him a household name, he will have influenced the world, and his power will be great indeed. Lacan becomes the truth to the extent that his doctrines become, or are made, the answer to the specific question, What is the truth?

This is not a question of numbers. Something that only one person, or none, holds to be the truth may nonetheless be the truth; something widely believed may be false. But this too is an alteration that must be made. Nor is there any intrinsic value in having a million people parrot a dogma as opposed to only one; all we do when we propagate a doctrine is propagate it. We don't make it more true. We do, however, make more people say it is true, believe it be true, use it as the answer to the question, What is true? If we say, does this mean it *is* true?, the answer is always specific. Why do we ask?, we should ask. Do you have any reason to think it isn't true? We may acknowledge in the abstract, the way Mendus acknowledges that even the most well-intentioned marriage may fall apart, that we may one day find this out to be false. But it isn't true if we say it's true while knowing now that it's false.

All works of thought, even the most abstruse, are attempts to nail down things in the world, render change a subset to the unchanging, which they have codified. A "Far Side" cartoon by Gary Larson provides a metaphor of the problem endemic to them all: a typically Larsonesque (scruffy) man stands before his house holding a dripping paintbrush and a pot of paint. On all the objects around him he has written names. On his own garments he has written "Shirt," and "Pants"; "The House" is scrawled across the front of his domicile, "Door" on the door, even "The Dog" and "The Cat" on the two disgruntled looking pets at his feet. "There," he says in the caption, "that should clear a few things up."

Kant must have felt the same way after dividing the noumenal from the phenomenal realm. All of us sense that we have cleared a few things up. Perhaps Nozick felt that way when he finished *Anarchy, State, and Utopia.* I may feel the same way writing these words. But what if everybody, the everybody about whom Kant, or Nozick, or even Bruce Fleming is making pronouncements, is off reading *Secret Lives*? Or being photographed exiting from a club at 3 a.m.? Or merely existing? We can say as loudly as we want that their lives too are divided into noumenal and phenomenal realms, or that they are following a less than optimal state system whether or not they know it. They will still be off doing what they are doing.

The thinker who has ordered the world, of course, can take consolation in thinking that whether or not all these silly mortals know it, they are still living in a world where noumenal is divided from phenomenal. If we demanded that everyone actually read our work for it to be true, we'd be lost. Yet what if no one ever reads our work? Is the world still divided into noumenal and phenomenal? Even if someone is reading our works, what of those who are not? Are their worlds not so divided?

Any halfway competent philosopher can answer this apparently freshman-level question: Look, s/he says wearily, the distinction is between subjective and objective. In a subjective sense perhaps these ignorant people's worlds are not so divided; however in an objective sense we can at least argue that they are. But, we say, (playing the infuriating 4-year-old), what if we are ignorant of this distinction? And so on. The general problem is not solved, though of course the particular may be. (My attempt is to confuse the distinction between general and particular. Does this pose a problem?)

The world is composed of particulars that, by and large, we fail to perceive as such, since when we make the attempt to connect them, they are by definition fighting for the same turf, and so end up being connected. Connection in the world is, as I have implied above, intrinsically conflict. We have to decide which of two or more contenders will occupy the space/time/whatever in question. Because we are conscious of conflict as something requiring thought, we do not conceptualize the craziness of the quilt of which our world actually consists.

Modernist writers such as Virginia Woolf were aiming at this point with the development of "stream of consciousness" literature. Who knew what a jumble our minds were until the transcript of the contents of the mind, say Leopold Bloom's, was actually presented to us? We don't seem so disorganized to ourselves because we're the ones passing from topic to topic, which make sense to us. For this reason "stream of consciousness" is not in fact an accurate portrayal of the world, merely an interesting literary device. For the same reason Sartre's insistence that "existence precedes essence" is comprehensible, but equally finite: what is he reacting to? What is the conflict he is trying to resolve? By definition it can only be one particular conflict, and his resolution a resolution of this conflict, not the resolution of conflicts in general.

All of us deal with the world in the form of crisis management. We resolve conflicts that seem to us so. If conflicts are the nodes at which parts of the world connect with other parts, the question arises, What makes something a conflict rather than merely two parallel events that never meet?—such as my alternating reading Nozick with *Secret Lives*, or the secret lives of *Secret Lives*.

Think of the crazy quilt of, say, the newspaper. It ties everything together with the rather thin unity of time. Its premise is that anything happening anywhere in the world since the last edition of the newspaper came out is potentially of interest. Anything that happens, from Borneo to Berlin to Birmingham, from fires to riots to small children being fished up out of streams, can appear in the newspaper. We turn from an article about a new birth control pill to the latest atrocities in fill-in-the-blank, and from that to a review of a movie that has just come out.

All newspaper articles require a "hook," which is to say some current angle. An article about the big bang theory does not belong in a newspaper, but an article about an article about the big bang theory, which has just appeared, does. So accustomed are we to the strangeness of this way of linking things that we no longer find it strange. It is not the here-and-nowness of newspaper conflicts, things requiring solution, that dooms them to a shorter half-life than, say a sociology book. A sociology book may be more dated (as we say) in a decade than today's front-page story.

The chief effect of the premise of a newspaper, to remain in a common world of the here and now, is its objectivity, or at least "objectivity," a fact of style. The constraints of newspaper writing are not merely those of inches; they are of the form itself. Subjective states of stories' subjects are included only in small bits, to give color. Description is kept to a minimum. The style is flat and uninflected. This is so because none of these things is directly relevant to the time-space continuum which holds newspapers in such a stranglehold. In this world, today (or this week) we have people of certain ages, heights, and addresses doing X, Y, and Z. Period.

Literature lacks this unifying assumption, this time/space lock. As a result its stories need not be given hooks to something that has just happened. They can diverge from "just the facts, Jack." We wait to see what the point of literature is; if we do not immediately grasp the point of a newspaper article, we throw it down in disgust—and rightly so.

Thinkers such as John Searle have been puzzled by the way the sentences of literature look the same as the sentences of newspapers.[84] But the sentences of today's newspaper do not change, at least not as black and white squiggles on the page, when read a year from now, or a century. Our reactions to them do. In the same way the assertion that "Joe Smith committed suicide at 12 o'clock" in today's newspaper is different from the same assertion in a novel. We could say that our presuppositions color our reactions here, knowing in advance that we are reading a novel, or the newspaper. But the novel contains no masthead with a date, is not sold daily, and so on. Of course individual sentences can look identical, but the difference between them is not their relation to an outside "reality," just what the unifying structure of the expression form is.

The reason most of us take the conflicts of a newspaper seriously is that the newspaper itself is living proof that others take them seriously as well. And we tend to take seriously what other people take seriously. The premise of shared time-space continuum, in fact, makes this issue central with a newspaper. Newspapers in a sense demand our attention the way other people can demand our attention: their issues become, willy-nilly, our issues, their conflicts our conflicts.

Everything in a newspaper is there because it bears some relationship to events that have just happened (considering 24 hours as a geometrical point). A novel, by contrast, needs another principle of unity. We express this by saying that a novel makes a world of its own. It doesn't, of course; the deeper we sink into such a world (as we might describe the sensation) the greater conflict it has with the world outside. Literature we pay attention to is not escape save in the sense that it is particular, the same way sex is a particular. The more riveting we find a novel, the more clearly we see it in relation to the rest of our lives. For the alternative to this is indifference, when the novel really is a world of its own.

Novels, like all things we pay active attention to, have to collide with something else for us to pay attention to them. This may be primarily in the author's mind, and never articulated: such an author may well wait many decades before a reader sees a connection with the rest of the world. We like to speak of genius being "recognized" after the author's death, but in fact all this phenomenon of posthumous glorification means is that it took longer than usual for a reader or readers to see the author's works as being in conflict with the world.

Early in the development of the novel, the conflict was found in the story: the plot of the novel had itself to contain the connection with the world, conflict between the protagonist and other characters. For most readers and writers, this is still the source of a novel's connection with the world. Novels that are only plot, however, are fairly biodegradable, as their interest is used up when the particular characters overcome their adversaries. More long-lived novels all contain some thematic dragon that is slain.

Novelists before Flaubert understood that the conflict could be with forces, or abstractions, but they had not made these struggles the centerpiece of their works. What we call "modern" novels, which is not to the same as all novels written in the last hundred years, have made the conflict external to the relationships between the characters. Other possibilities exist; conflict is where it's found.

The reason reading a serious novel is more difficult than reading the newspaper is that it exists on a longer leash from the world than newspapers. This is what makes it what it is. We don't always know what the point of a work of art is, what it is conflicting with, why we should pay attention to it. We have to figure it out, in a way we don't have to figure out the point of a newspaper. Escape novels, such as those written by Rudolf da Vinci in Benson's novel, make their implicit contrast clear from the first page: everything that happens here will be unreal. The conflict they address is clear: the dullness of real life.

Much of the bulk of a work of art is, therefore, particular. We don't know what aspects collide with the world until we pay attention to everything. Sometimes we realize that we are being strung along: At some point we may realize that all that's on the page is, say, more of the same bickering that took place in Chapter One, and begin to skip. Virginia Woolf's works sometimes contain long skippable passages; *The Waves* comes to mind, or *The Years*. Iris Murdoch's novels begin to pall when you realize the people, eternally talking, are still going strong twenty chapters after you'd have thought they'd shut up. But in all works we have to distinguish the skeleton from the muscle as we read. For many readers of novels this is the delicious freedom they offer, a kind of vertigo at opening the first page and beginning. By the time we get the point of things, we may no longer be interested.

People who seek the abstract, people of thought, typically find novels too particular to be of any interest, and distracting. One novel doesn't necessarily have any connection to another; they may peacefully coexist without being in conflict. Nor is it even clear that they are alternatives to one another. We might say that literature is biologically female, while structures of thought are biologically male: the business parts of literature are packed away inside, whereas those of thought dangle aggressively out into the world—and so are more vulnerable as well.

We don't need to read novels to have this sensation of visiting different worlds; if we could somehow break the back of the time-space continuum that unites the elements of the daily newspaper we would have enough disparate worlds to last a lifetime. But we can't, and they aren't developed enough to the point where we can see them as independent from one another. Channel surfing, another experience of visiting many worlds in quick succession, is ultimately soporific. Human beings apparently need immersion for a longer period of time in each world.

Literature offers an alternative to the generalized connection to the world of the newspaper (it is this quality that makes us speak of the newspaper as "true"); it insists on individualized connections. It wants you to see its connection with the world is, but it is the connection only of this structure, not all structures. For this reason, Marxist or Freudian interpretation of novels tends to rob them of what is purely literary in their nature and turn them into newspaper reports on economics or childhood traumas. Welleck and Warren, authors of the seminal *Theory of Literature*, were much derided in the backlash against New Criticism for making the distinction between intrinsic (good) and extrinsic (bad) criticism of literature.[85] But the fact is that literature defines its connections with the world one by one, for the life of the particular work alone, and hence is not amenable to generalization. If we can establish a generalization, we have turned the literature into something else. How else is a kind of connection to the world that is used once and then (so to speak) thrown away to identify itself?

How convenient it would be if we could say something other than what Welleck and Warren do say, namely that that is just the way literature is. The people who read literature don't ask to have it justified, only the people trying to turn it into something else—the people, that is, who think it problematic in itself. But this simply means, the people for whom literature itself is not part of a collision in the world. They just don't get the point, aren't any more interested in a novel than the bored reader of a newspaper in Peoria who, pre-Sept 11, would have turned over any news about Afghanistan. Suddenly Afghanistan matters to people in the US, in a more general version of the way that we are suddenly interested in articles about, say, infertility, if we ourselves have trouble conceiving.

Our realization that literature is this sort of precise structure about the world is shown in the way we speak of reading something, say the Bible, "as literature." We might say this means, bracketing out whether or not it is true. Which is to say, holding in abeyance the nature of its connection to the world.

Literature is theoretically infinite. There is no limit to the particular connections to the world that can be exploited, since the supply of people is equally infinite: things change. Thinkers tend to disapprove of literature, to the extent that they try to order it into their world structure, for precisely this reason. It escapes them. In Susan Sontag's famous phrase, criticism is the revenge of the intellectual on art.[86] How could thought not disapprove of something as intrinsically amenable to change as literature?

For the same reason ethicists of both (all) stripes, people who consider human action as amenable to codification in rules, disapprove of sex. Literature is typically compared to masturbation, in that both are performed with only a single person, but it is far closer to partnered sex; in each case there are two elements (reading is not solitude); in each case what happens is a private matter. Ethics typically disapproves of the inhuman world of science too.

Self-limiting and absolute structures
Realizing the intrinsically limited nature of structures is the font of wisdom. Some boundaries can never be crossed: we know from reading Sophocles' *Antigone* that the political realm has its limits. As Creon, the play's tragic hero learns, no one can legislate the realm after death. Problems can be temporarily solved, but their solutions are not guaranteed to last forever. We can educate, but it had better be in the form of "let me show you these things" rather than the form of "you *will* learn this." Our children grow up, leave us, and will ultimately judge us: our best bet is to guide with a firm but yielding hand on the tiller.

All structures, articulations of the predictable, are silhouetted against the realm of things they are not, the personal world. Thus it might seem that structures which acknowledge their own limitation would in some sense be better or truer structures. Such a structure, for example, is the U.S. political system, with its balancing of powers in the government, its separation of church and state, and its explicit statements allowing all personal freedoms not explicitly abrogated by the Constitution. Democracy, it might seem, is better than absolutism, more intellectually solid, because it acknowledges the limited nature of structures. Of course this becomes its own dogma, and must be taught to future generations as a continually vital one, one that is silhouetted against its alternatives, indeed threatened by them. If the proposition that democracy is better than its alternatives seems like a dead issue, people may not be willing to rise to its defense.

There is always the tendency to abandon a structure that not only allows but encourages questioning for one that purports to have all the answers. This is what has happened to American democracy in the early twenty-first century: powerful people who fail to realize the rarity of a system based on self-limitation have substituted for that a system of dogmatisms. This is not democracy, nor freedom: it is simply one more structure that is bound to be overturned because it fails to admit its own contingency.

At the core of American democracy is the distinction between the private and the social realms I have taken as my starting point here. The American system allows any number of private or semi-private absolutisms, so long as they are kept within the realm either of the personal or of the micro-worlds of the minimally social, smaller groups of like-thinking people. These were encouraged by the framers of the Constitution precisely on the theory that their influence would cancel each other out. But the absolutist nature of this limited structure becomes clear when such micro-absolutisms attempt to move from the personal or semi-personal into the most general levels of the social sphere. At this point they threaten to become public absolutisms, and are put down. This sometimes comes as a surprise to people who have failed to register the most fundamental distinction of all in American society, the one between the private and the public. Used to doing or saying anything they like so long as this is kept in the private realm, they find it somehow contradictory that they are not allowed to do the same in the public. The only people who do not suffer this shock are those who, suddenly finding themselves in power, set about with a frenzy imposing their own view of things on others.

Typically, however, private viewpoints cannot be foisted on others. Sometimes this fails to satisfy the young. Young people will not know that structures cannot last forever, that everything sputters out in silence, that the hand that held the whip grows old and finally, falters, that statues can be torn down and streets re-named: all is mutable. Self-limiting structures prevent things that some people want to do, namely re-make the world in their own image.

To such people, structure made up of self-limiting structures seem insufficiently intense, insufficiently forward-looking, almost defeatist. Limited structures, too, will seem to those seeking less "yes, but" kinds of worlds to be feeble, as the West currently seems in theoretical if not military terms to Eastern theocracies. The unwillingness to state one truth for all people, all time, that is written into the American constitution, and the toleration of other religions that is a constant in Western democracies seems weak tea indeed compared to an absolute assertion. The urge to predictability is not the exclusive property of the right, though this is the direction it is currently being expressed from; it is an equally absolute demand of the left.

The only difference between an absolutist assertion limited to the private world and one that flourishes as an absolutism in the social world is, unsurprisingly, the difference between the private and the social world. The structure itself doesn't look any different as a structure. To say that American society is composed of self-limiting structures means that it demands that thought be completed by action, thought placed in the world.

In this distinction may lie the much-remarked-on pragmatism of American society. People may say anything they want, but the power of these words ends in the reality of the public space. Indeed there is something paradoxical about what American society asks us to do. We may believe anything absolutely within certain confines—these are not even limited to the individual, and can be expanded to many others. They must however be conceived of as groups of $1 + 1 + 1 + 1$. They can become large, but they have no greater official sanction than if they were small.

But this is merely America. Not all structures have to be self-limiting, and those that are not are not inferior structures. Suggesting that structures must themselves build in their own limitations is like Sartre's insistence that people recite the credo of their own freedom. Perhaps by freely choosing a more limited existence they are already expressing that freedom, if not reciting its credo. There is nothing theoretically incoherent about a structure that does not admit its own limitations, either those fundamentalist Christians who insist that each of us must accept Jesus Christ as our personal savior or those Islamic fundamentalists who insist that Muslims must live in regions where the shari'a, or Islamic religious law, is being applied by Believers.

In American society, the social structure limits personal structures so that, as structures, they can be unlimited. It is the societal over-structure that provides the limitation, not the structures themselves. There is no reason to be intellectually dismissive of apparently simpler structures that do not, in this fashion, admit their own limitation. They are not logically incoherent because they do not. Indeed, they are for many people much more satisfying. And in any case they are a fact of life. There will always be someone who is dissatisfied with the bloodlessness, the apparent sloth and inactivity of doing nothing rather than something, such as ultimately is the lot of all self-limiting structures.

But American democracy demands that we accept that these can be only personal structures. This is what many of those who do not accept the fundamental distinction between personal and social sense as the constraint of American society, and what the absolutists who have abruptly found themselves in power are setting out to overcome. The constant disillusion of dreamers and thinkers in American society lies in the fact that ultimately their dreams must be abandoned or turned to practical ends, which is to say, enter the social world or be turned away from it.

The advantages of the American system are practical, not theoretical, because they establish a relationship between the theoretical and the practical. Some of its components are in the personal realm, what Jefferson called the pursuit of happiness, and some are in the social: it demands completion in action. Its odd nature means it must constantly be explained, its place in the world made clear—by placing it in the world. We must be educated to its fundamental tenet, and the trade-offs this implies.

The self-limiting structures of American democracy demand both theoretical and practical completion. This is so because a self-limiting structure is a structure; it is no less finite than any other. It takes time for its defense, it occupies space in the world, and can be rejected, ignored, or turned away from, just the way I can put down Nozick and pick up *Secret Lives*. It's a particular kind of horse, but it's still a horse: we have to groom it and muck out its stall. Furthermore, once we've done this, we still have to go off to our real job. The system purposely fails to answer many questions individuals would like to have answered. It insists that the answers be individual. Those who sense the constraints of the American system most fully are looking for answers in the social realm to what the American system insists be individual, personal ones.

The connection with the world of the American system is different from the well-known phenomenon of intellectual relativisms seeking to anchor themselves by asserting their allegiance to seemingly immutable facts of social organization. Think of the extreme right-wing religious, social, and political turn of a T.S. Eliot, and the proto- or not-so-proto Fascist sympathies of a W.B. Yeats or an Ezra Pound. The attraction of pessimistic intellectual relativisms to the illusion of hard reality is clear: it seems to anchor the world. We can only go on being rootless for so long.

A contemporary American version of this is the recent call for a renewed American patriotism from Rorty, a deeply relativist philosopher. From the perspective of liberal ethics, which couches its absolutes in terms of individuals, Rorty is being parochial, communitarian: why limit his interest merely to Americans? From

Rorty's point of view, this must have seemed like the largest possible grouping that still had some evocative power.

The motivation behind communitarianism, the appeal to group values as the end point of value justification (what people do is right if enough of them do it) is clear. It's an attempt to anchor relativism of thought in the "real world," and is what liberals invariably turn to when they get tired of not having answers to conservative questions. For conservatives, actions aren't more justified because a group does them.

If we deny that values can be justified by non-individual criteria (if we reject the pattern of conservative ethics), and are unwilling to anchor them to individuals, then only what people in fact do can serve as a justification. Calling these a "community" is the circular reasoning that accomplishes this, for the "community" or whatever we call it must have qualities that the sum of the individuals that compose it do not, the ability to justify ethics. But since a community (or whatever) must be precisely the thing that does this, one person's "community" will be another's group, mob, or collection. Rorty's patriotism "works" to link a relativistic ethics to the world so long as we do not compare the thing he is patriotic about (in this case, literally the *patrie*, the country) to others. Seen from the inside, the group seems an absolute; from the outside it is only another relativism.

The conflict between communitarians and liberals is as predictable as all clashes between liberals and conservatives. Liberals always seek to transcend any groupings, because their principles are expressed in terms of actors. Let us therefore say that somehow, some day, being a member of the International Community will the same warm fuzzy feelings that being an American sometimes has. We can construct new levels of communities: the European Community may not have gone very far towards this goal, in that being a citizen of the EU does not have the evocative power that being, say, a Frenchman or a Swiss does. But it does have some power, more than zero at any rate; this may some day grow. Liberals will oppose this with a yet larger category, yet to be determined: perhaps all galactic beings. Group definitions do not conflict with conservative ethics, but they do with liberal.

Relativist structures are not the same as self-limiting ones. The late 20th century has been rife with intellectual relativisms, whose inevitable failing was that they could not acknowledge their own relativism. Sometimes the writings of their founders, say a Derrida or a Nietzsche, openly acknowledged the gadfly aspect of what they were about. But this does not allow for institutionalization, and so the epigones set to work to calcify this so-evanescent relativism, a purely intellectual exercise, retro-fitting it for its role as a dogma in the world.

Self-limiting structures take as their content their own placement in the world; the necessity for completing them in action is part of their nature. This is not true for relativist structures, which become perverted when they turn into great solid lumps of doctrine. In the same way religion becomes perverted when it ossifies into doctrine. Democracy must be taught, it is something lived out, a picnic to which each individual brings the food. There are many questions democracy does not answer, a fact that never fails to surprise people who do not understand the distinction between the personal and the social realms.

Notes

[1] Alan Soble, "Antioch's 'Sexual Offense Policy'."

[2] Robert Solomon, "Sexual Paradigms."

[3] John Milton, *Paradise Lost IV*, 312-320.

[4] Ibid.

[5] Ibid, 742-752.

[6] Kathleen Deveny, "We're Not in the Mood."

[7] Sigmund Freud, *Civilization and Its Discontents*

[8] Ibid, 44.

[9] Most trenchant have been the views of Frederick Crews.

[10] Herbert Marcuse, *Eros and Civilization*.

[11] Charles Krauthammer, "No Respect Politics."

[12] Pope Paul VI, "Humanae Vitae."

[13] Michael Levin, "Why Homosexuality Is Abnormal."

[14] Voltaire, *Candide*.

[15] Levin, 98.

[16] T.E. Hulme, "Romanticism and Classicism," 116.

[17] Ibid., 117

[18] David Riesman and Nathan Glazer, *The Lonely Crowd*.

[19] Levin, 109.

[20] Milton X, 898-906.

[21] Eve Kosovsky Sedgwick, *Epistemology of the Closet*.

[22] Michel Foucault, *History of Sexuality*.

[23] Sedgwick, 35.

[24] Sedgwick, 25.

[25] Marjorie Garber, *Bisexuality and the Eroticism of Everyday Life*.

[26] Alfred Kinsey, Wardell B. Pomeroy, Clyde E. Martin, *Sexual Activity in the Human Male*.

[27] Jean-Paul Sartre, *Being and Nothingness*.

[28] Laura Mulvey, "Visual Pleasure and Narrative Cinema."

[29] John Berger, *About Looking*.

[30] Susan Bordo, *The Male Body*.

[31] John Corvino, *Same Sex*.

[32] Ernest Hemingway, "The Short Happy Life of Francis Macomber."

[33] Henrick Ibsen, *A Doll's House*.

[34] Andrew Kimbrell, *The Masculine Mystique*.

[35] George L. Mosse, *The Image of Man*.

[36] Jeffrey Reiman, "Abortion, Infanticide, and the Asymmetric Value of Human Life."

[37] Reiman, 266.

[38] Reiman, 266-267.

[39] Geza Vermes, *Jesus the Jew*.

[40] Hulme, 116.
[41] Judith Jarvis Thompson, "A Defense of Abortion."
[42] Margaret Atwood, *The Handmaid's Tale.*
[43] Reiman, 261
[44] Ibid, 262
[45] Ibid., 263
[46] Lytton Strachey, *Biographical Essays.*
[47] Vance Packard, *The Hidden Persuaders.*
[48] John Barth, "Lost in the Funhouse."
[49] Ingmar Bergman, *Scenes From a Marriage* (*The Marriage Scenarios*).
[50] Deveny, "We're Not in the Mood."
[51] Immanuel Kant, *:Lectures on Ethics* (156/27:385).
[52] Andrea Dworkin, *Intercourse.*
[53] Dworkin, 64.
[54] Kant, Ibid.
[55] Kant, (158/27:388).
[56] Ibid.
[57] Alan Sobel, *"Masturbation."*
[58] St. Paul, I Corinthians.
[59] Philip Harvey, "Adulthood Without Sex."
[60] Andrew Sullivan, *Virtually Normal.*
[61] Tim Birkhead, *Promiscuity.*
[62] John Gray, *Men are From Mars, Women are From Venus.*
[63] Susan Mendus, "Marital Faithfulness."
[64] Ibid, 133.
[65] Ibid, 134.
[66] Alan Goldman, "Plain Sex."
[67] Donnerstein et al., *The Question of Pornography.*
[68] Thomas Kuhn, *The Structure of Scientific Revolutions*; Paul Feyerabend, *Against Method.*
[69] Donnerstein, 33.
[70] Ibid, 34.
[71] Ibid, 35
[72] Ibid.
[73] Quoted in Donnerstein, 51.
[74] Virginia Woolf, "The Mark on the Wall."
[75] Jean-Paul Sartre, *Being and Nothingness.*
[76] Charles S. Peirce, "Man's Glassy Essence."
[77] Paul Fussell, *Poetic Meter and Poetic Form*, 4.
[78] Robert Nozick, *Anarchy, State and Utopia.* E. F. Benson, *Secret Lives.*
[79] John Stuart Mill, "On Liberty."
[80] Mill, 47.
[81] Michel Foucault, *The Order of Things.*
[82] Nozick, 100.
[83] Richard Rorty, *Achieving Our Country*, 36.
[84] John Searle, "The Logical Status of Fictional Discourse."

[85] René Welleck and Austin Warren, *Theory of Literature.*
[86] Susan Sontag, *Against Interpretation.*

Bibliography

Atwood, Margaret. *The Handmaid's Tale.* New York: Anchor, 1998.

Baker, Robert B, Kathleen J. Wininger, and Frederick A. Elliston, eds. *Philosophy and Sex, Third Edition.* Amherst, NY: Prometheus Books, 1998.

Barth, John. *Lost in the Funhouse: Fiction for Print, Tape, and Live Voice.* New York: Anchor Books, 1988.

Benson, E.F. *Secret Lives.* London: Chatto and Windus, 1985.

Berger, John. *About Looking.* New York: Vintage Books, 1992.

Bergman, Ingmar. *The Marriage Scenarios: Scenes from a Marriage/ Face to Face/ Autumn Sonata.* New York: Marion Boyars, 1989.

Birkhead, Tim. *Promiscuity: An Evolutionary History of Sperm Competition.* Cambridge, MA: Harvard University Press, 2000.

Bordo, Susan. *The Male Body: A New Look at Men in Public and in Private.* New York: Farrar, Straus, and Giroux, 2000.

Corvino, John, ed. *Same Sex: Debating the Ethics, Science, and Culture of Homosexuality.* Lanham, MD: Rowman and Littlefield, 1997.

Crews, Frederick, et al. *The Memory Wars.* New York: New York Review Press, 1997.

Deveny, Kathleen. "We're Not in the Mood." *Newsweek* , 30 June 2003, 41-46.

Donnerstein, Edward, Daniel Linz, and Steven Penrod. *The Question of Pornography: Research Findings and Policy Implications.* New York: Free Press, 1987.

Dworkin, Andrea. *Intercourse.* New York: Free Press, 1997.

Feyerabend, Paul. *Against Method.* New York: Verso Press, 1993.

Foucault, Michel. *History of Sexuality, An Introduction.* New York: Vintage Books, 1990.

---. *The Order of Things: An Archaeology of the Human Sciences.* New York: Vintage Books, 1994.

Freud, Sigmund. *Civilization and its Discontents.* Translated and edited by James Strachey. New York: W.W. Norton, 1961.

Fussell, Paul. *Poetic Peter and Poetic Form.* Revised Ed. New York: McGraw-Hill, 1979.

Garber, Marjorie. *Bisexuality and the Erotics of Everyday Life.* New York: Routledge, 2000.

Goldman, Alan. "Plain Sex." *Philosophy and Public Affairs* 6, no. 3 (1977): 267-87.

Gray, John. *Men Are From Mars, Women Are From Venus.* New York: HarperCollins, 1993.

Harvey, Philip D. "Adulthood Without Sex." *Washington Post,* 12 May 2002, 7(B).

Hemingway,Ernest. "The Short Happy Life of Francis Macomber." In *The Complete Short Stories of Ernest Hemingway,* 5-28. New York: Scribner, 1998.

Hulme, T.E. "Romanticism and Classicism." In *Speculations: Essays on Humanism and the Philosophy of Art,* ed. Herbert Read, 111-140. London: Chatto and Windus, 1936.

Ibsen, Henrik. *A Doll's House.* New York: Dover, 1992.

Kant, Immanuel. *Lectures on Ethics.* Edited by Peter Heath, J.B. Schneewind. Cambridge: Cambridge University Press, 2001.

Kimbrell, Andrew. *The Masculine Mystique: The Politics of Masculinity.* New York: Ballantine Books, 1995.

Kinsey, Alfred, Wardell B. Pomeroy, Clyde E. Martin. *Sexual Activity in the Human Male.* Indiana University Press, 1998.

Krauthammer, Charles. "No-Respect Politics." *Washington Post,* 26 July 2002, 33(A).

Kuhn, Thomas S. *The Structure of Scientific Revolutions.* Chicago: University of Chicago Press, 1996.

Levin, Michael. "Why Homosexuality is Abnormal." In *Philosophy and Sex, Third Edition,* ed. Robert B. Baker, Kathleen J. Wininger, and Frederick A. Elliston, 95-128. Amherst, NY: Prometheus Books 1998.

Marcuse, Herbert. *Eros and Civilization: A Philosophical Inquiry into Freud.* Boston: Beacon, 1974.

Mendus, Susan. "Marital Faithfulness." In *Philosophy and Sex,* 3rd ed, ed. Robert B. Baker, Kathleen J. Wininger, and Frederick A. Elliston, 130-138. Amherst, NY: Prometheus Books, 1998.

Mill, John Stuart. *On Liberty and Other Essays.* New York: Macmillan, 1926.

Milton, John. *Paradise Lost.* New York: Odyssey Press, 1935.

Mosse, George L. *The Image of Man: The Creation of Modern Masculinity.* New York: Oxford University Press, 1996.

Mulvey, Laura. "Visual Pleasure and Narrative Cinema." *Screen* 16, no. 3 (1975): 6-18

Nozick, Robert. *Anarchy, State, and Utopia.* New York: Basic Books, 1974.

Packard, Vance. *The Hidden Persuaders.* New York: Pocket Books, 1985.

Paul VI, Pope. *"Humanae Vitae."* In *Philosophy and Sex*, 3ʳᵈ ed., ed. Robert B. Baker, Kathleen J. Wininger, and Frederick A. Elliston, 96-105. Amherst, NY: Prometheus Books, 1998.

Peirce, Charles S. "Man's Glassy Essence." In *The Essential Peirce*, ed. Nathan Houser and Christian Kloesel, 334-351. Bloomington, IN: Indiana University Press, 1993.

Reiman, Jeffrey. "Abortion, Infanticide, and the Asymmetric Value of Human Life." In *Philosophy and Sex*, 3ʳᵈ ed., ed. Robert B. Baker, Kathleen J. Wininger, and Frederick A. Elliston, 261-280. Amherst, NY: Prometheus Books 1998.

Riesman, David and Nathan Glazer. *The Lonely Crowd, Revised Edition: A Study of the Changing American Character*. New Haven: Yale University Press, 2001.

Rorty, Richard. *Achieving our Country: Leftist Thought in Twentieth-Century America*. Cambridge, MA: Harvard University Press, 1998.

Sartre, Jean-Paul. *Being and Nothingness*. New York: Washington Square Press, 1993.

Searle, John. "The Logical Status of Fictional Discourse." In *Expression and Meaning: Studies in the Theory of Speech Acts, by* John Searle, 58-75. Cambridge: Cambridge University Press, 1985.

Sedgwick, Eve Kosovsky. *Epistemology of the Closet*. Berkeley: University of California Press, 1992.

Soble, Alan, "Antioch's 'Sexual Offense Policy': A Philosophical Exploration." *Journal of Social Philosophy* 28, no. 1 (1997): 22-36. Also in *The Philosophy of Sex*, 4ᵗʰ ed, ed. Alan Soble. Lanham, MD: Rowman and Littlefield, 2002.

---. "Masturbation." In *Human Sexuality,* ed. Igor Primoratz, 139-150. Brookfield, VT: Dartmouth 1997.

---. *The Philosophy of Sex: Contemporary Readings*. 4ᵗʰ ed. Lanham, MD. Rowman and Littlefield, 2002.

---. *The Philosophy of Sex: Contemporary Readings*. 3ʳᵈ ed. Lanham, MD. Rowman and Littlefield, 1997.

Solomon, Robert. "Sexual Paradigms." In *The Philosophy of Sex, Contemporary Readings*, 3ʳᵈ ed., ed. Alan Soble, 21-30. Lanham, MD. Rowman and Littlefield, 1997.

Sontag, Susan. *Against Interpretation and Other Essays*. New York: Picador, 2001.

Strachey, Lytton. *Biographical Essays*. New York: Harvest Books, 1969.

Sullivan, Andrew. *Virtually Normal: An Argument About Homosexuality.* New York: Vintage Books, 1996.

Thomson, Judith Jarvis. "A Defense of Abortion," in *Philosophy and Sex,* 3rd ed., ed Robert B Baker, Kathleen J. Wininger, and Frederick A. Elliston, 231-245. Amherst, NY: Prometheus Books, 1998.

Tolstoy, Leo. "The Kreutzer Sonata." In *The Kreutzer Sonata and Other Short Stories*, by Leo Tolstoy, 64-140. New York: Dover, 1993.

Vermes, Geza. *Jesus the Jew: A Historian's Reading of the Gospels.* Fortress Press, 1981.

Voltaire. *Candide, or Optimism.* Translated and edited by Robert M. Adams. New York: W.W. Norton, 1966.

Welleck, René and Austin Warren. *Theory of Literature: New Revised Edition.* New York: Harvest Books, 1984.

Woolf, Virginia. "The Mark the Wall." In *A Haunted House and other short stories,* 37-46. New York: Harvest Books, 1966.

BRUCE FLEMING is a professor of English at the U.S. Naval Academy, Annapolis. He is a graduate of Haverford College, and did his graduate work at the University of Chicago and Vanderbilt University. He was a Fulbright Scholar at the Free University, Berlin, and taught at the University of Freiburg and, as a Fulbright Professor, at the National University of Rwanda. He is the author of a book on aesthetics that won the Book Award in Comparative Studies of the Northeast Modern Language Association, a book on cross-cultural issues, two books on Modernism, and a collection of dance essays. His most recent scholarly book is *Art and Argument: What Words Can't Do, and What They Can.* He is also an O. Henry-prize-winning fiction writer whose first novel, *Twilley*, was compared by critics to works by Proust, Thoreau, Henry James, and David Lynch. He lives near Annapolis with his wife and family.

Index